What
Really
Happened
in the
Garden
of Eden?

What
Really
Happened
in the
Garden
of Eden?

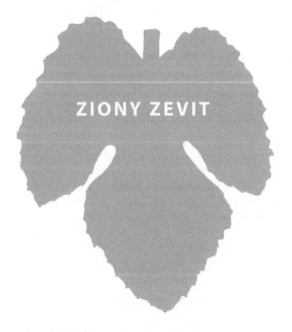

ZIONY ZEVIT

Yale UNIVERSITY PRESS

NEW HAVEN AND LONDON

Yale University Press books may be purchased in quantity for educational, business, or
promotional use. For information, please e-mail sales.press@yale.edu (U.S. office) or
sales@yaleup.co.uk (U.K. office).

Scripture quotations identified as NJPS throughout this book are reprinted from the *Tanakh: The Holy Scriptures* by permission of the University of Nebraska Press. Copyright 1985
The Jewish Publication Society, Philadelphia.

Designed by Mary Valencia.
Set in Minion and Myriad type by Westchester Book Group, Danbury, Connecticut.
Printed in the United States of America.

Library of Congress Cataloging-in-Publication Data

Zevit, Ziony.
 What really happened in the Garden of Eden? / Ziony Zevit.
  pages cm
 Includes bibliographical references and index.
  ISBN 978-0-300-17869-2 (cloth : alk. paper) 1. Eden. 2. Fall of man. 3. Bible.
Genesis II–III—Criticism, interpretation, etc. I. Title.
  BS1237.Z48 2013
  222'.1106—dc23

2013017554

A catalogue record for this book is available from the British Library.

This paper meets the requirements of ANSI/NISO Z39.48–1992 (Permanence of Paper).

10 9 8 7 6 5 4 3 2 1

for
Zehava and Eli, Noam and Ayelet, Yonatan and Reut
whose eyes open anew each day and
who see more than what appears

Contents

A Preface about "Really"

Even people who have never read the Garden story in Genesis know its essential elements and are familiar with its interpretation as the story of "the Fall." God first made Adam out of the dust of the earth and placed him in the idyllic Garden of Eden as a caretaker. Later, he made Eve out of Adam's rib and presented her to Adam as a helpmate. God placed only one restriction on their activities: They were not to eat fruit from a certain tree commonly referred to as the Tree of Knowledge of Good and Evil. The snake, however, tempted Eve into consuming the forbidden fruit. Eve in turn seduced Adam, who ate also. This great sin and its aftermath constitute the drama of the Fall.

Once everything came to light, the three involved in violating God's prohibition were punished harshly. The snake lost its feet, so now every snake crawls on its belly. Eve's punishment was more severe. She and her female descendents were sentenced to suffer pain and anguish in childbearing, to long for their husbands sexually, and to be under their husbands' control. For her descendents to behave otherwise was, by implication, to act unnaturally and to violate God's explicit directives. Adam and his male descendents were sentenced to a life of constant labor, each earning bread by the sweat of his brow. That was not all. Concerned that humans might also eat from the Tree of Life, the couple were driven from the Garden in Eden and left to fend for themselves.

Out of the Garden and in the world the sinful couple had sexual relations and Eve conceived. Eventually, she gave birth to three sons: the first, Cain, became the first murderer; the second, Abel, became the first victim; and the third, Seth, became the one from whom all living humans are somehow descended. Their three children were born tarnished by the sin of their parents, and all living humans are similarly tarnished.

This idea found popular expression in the *New England Primer*, first published in 1690, that was used to teach children the English alphabet for almost two hundred years. To illustrate the letter *A* it presented the following rhyme: "In Adam's Fall / We sinned all." The solution for the fallen state of humanity was spelled out in the rhyme for the letter *B*: "Thy Life to Mend / This Book Attend." Though witty, these two lines from the *Primer* reflect powerful ideas in Western civilization that influenced the writing of my book.

One of the many questions that the story triggers is whether or not what most people say or think the Bible says concerning the Garden story is what the Bible actually says. The difference between these possibilities may be illustrated by juxtaposing the following two questions and querying the rhetorical import of "really" in the second question: (1) What happened in the Garden of Eden? (2) What really happened in the Garden of Eden?

The first "What happened?" is concerned with surface phenomena, with what the eye sees and the ear hears when reading the story through once. In the second formulation—"What really happened?"—the additional word intimates that there may be more to the story but that whatever constitutes the "more" has to be sought; it indicates that the "more" is there when one knows where to look and how to see.

My intention in using the word *really* in the book's title is tied to the brief story of what precipitated my writing of this book. In part, this book originated as a response to complaints against and comments about the story of Adam and Eve as broadly understood by students—mainly women—in classes that I taught on Biblical Literature. Some of these classes were offered in regular university programs, others in informal settings such as continuing education classes and Elder Hostel programs. The women ranged in age from the late teens to the late seventies. Most, not all, were members of churches and synagogues who sometimes identified themselves to me as conservatives or liberals. Usually they had positive views about feminism. Those who paraded their religious affiliation tended to ask questions of a theological nature; others posed historical and sociological questions from the vantage point of informed agnosticism and atheism. People from the second group regularly distinguished themselves from those of the first by prefacing their remarks or questions with expressions such as "I'm an atheist but . . ." or "I don't think that God exists but . . ." or "I don't believe in the Bible but . . ." It took me a while to realize that although they identified themselves theologically vis-à-vis a deity who, according to their individual backgrounds and philosophies, may or may not exist, they were concerned with the first four chapters of Genesis that definitely do exist. They were sufficiently concerned to take a class or to attend a public lecture and to ask questions.

All were troubled by different aspects of the story or its interpretation: Why is it called "the Fall"? What is the Fall? How bad was Eve's sin? Why did God curse humanity? What is "original sin"? Why is the story in the Bible at all? Did it really happen, or is it a myth? All of these questions are comprehensible as negative reactions to, or rejections of, standard responses to the "What happened?" question.

Initially, I referred questioners to some new publication or shared some recent insight from the perspective of feminist criticism. As questioning became more persistent, however, I grew uncomfortable with some of what I was fobbing off as answers. The material to which I directed questioners was too removed from what medieval Jewish exegetes labeled the *peshat* of a text. *Peshat*, a Hebrew word, was coined by medieval scholars to refer to the straightforward or "plain" meaning of a text in its writ and script in the original language in its literary, biblical context as conceived by the particular exegete. As a person living in the twenty-first century, I expanded the definition of *peshat* to encompass the meaning of a text in the intellectual world of the ancient Near East within which the biblical story was originally read.

Reading biblical texts following this contextual approach in order to discover their *peshat* is a concern of some contemporary Catholic and Protestant authorities. It is reflected in the encyclical, a letter to clergy, *Divino Afflante Spiritu*, issued by Pope Pius XII in 1943:

> What is the literal sense of a passage is not always as obvious in the speeches and writings of the ancient authors of the East, as it is in the works of our own time . . . ; the interpreter must go back wholly in

spirit to those remote centuries of the East and with the aid of history, archaeology, ethnology and other sciences, accurately determine what modes of writing the authors of that ancient period would be likely to use, and in fact did use.

For the ancient peoples of the Near East, in order to express their ideas, did not always employ those forms or kinds of speech which we use today; but rather those used by the men of their time and centuries.[1]

Elsewhere in this document Pius XII made clear that the literal sense is not necessarily the most important meaning that a given text can have, but without it, there could be no subsequent Catholic interpretation and application.

A Protestant formulation of the same idea is found in *Old Testament Survey* (1982), written by the conservative Protestant scholars W. S. LaSor, D. A. Hubbard, and F. Wm. Bush:

Yet at the same time, the modern reader must try to see the Old Testament passages on their own terms. The reader must ask: "What was the Old Testament author saying to his own times?" He or she must sit with the hearers in the marketplace, city gate, temple, or synagogue and try to understand his words as they heard them. He or she must see God through their eyes and discern his purposes in their lives.

In other words, one must be sensitive to the original context of an Old Testament passage. Why was it written and when? What problems called it into being? What question was it initially intended to answer? What did it tell the people about God's will and ways or about their responsibilities that they would not otherwise have known? Only when one understands the intent of a passage for the author's own times, can he then catch the full significance of the passage for Christian faith and life. The Old Testament context will not tell all one needs to know about the meaning of the passage. But unless one starts there, it becomes easy to twist the Scriptures to one's own purpose. Rather, the sense of the individual authors must be grasped in order to capture the meaning put there by the overall Author, the Spirit of God, who speaks through all of Scripture and whose speaking gives the whole Bible its authority for his people.[2]

Both formulations maintain the principle enunciated in 2 Timothy 3:16 that "all scripture is inspired by God and is useful for teaching, for reproof, for correction, and for instruction in righteousness." Both recognize honestly that a scripture's usefulness depends on the specific meaning of individual passages in context, meaning that can be established only through the study of original languages and texts, tasks requiring special expertise.

This realization led me to consider the impact of inserting *really* into the "What happened?" question. When I did so, I recognized that for me the word evoked issues of truth, objectivity, and facticity beyond surface appearances. Therefore, I formulated my own question: What was the *peshat* of the Garden story within (1) its literary context in the Israel of the eighth–sixth centuries BCE, (2) the intellectual context of the Iron Age, which ended with the destruction of Solomon's temple and the exile of Jerusalem's elites to Babylonia in 586 BCE, (3) the broader literary contexts of the story in the Hebrew Bible (the "Old Testament"; Tanakh) and the Greek New Testament, and (4) the cultural context of early Judaism and Christianity? This gem of a question immediately generated a host of more focused questions about vocabulary and grammar, as well as about literary, historical, and philosophical matters, only some of which I undertook to answer: Why did God create the man? Was he created sin-free? Exactly why was the woman created? What is a helpmate? Why was the woman created from a rib? What is the Fall? Who is responsible for it? Was the serpent Satan? Was the Garden of Eden paradise? Where was the Garden? Each of these questions was preceded by the words "according to the story."[3]

I thought that answers based on linguistic and literary criteria considered in their historical and cultural contexts, if achievable, might be of interest to people like my former students and would assuage discontentment with the story. Subsequent discussions with colleagues, a chatty fellow in a kosher take-out Chinese restaurant, my barber, as well as with personal friends in business, crafts, and trades revealed to me that interest in such questions is much broader than I had first anticipated. My own intent, however, did not extend formally beyond suggesting a new *peshat*.

*

It is clear on both historical and sociological grounds that "religion" infuses culture and is infused by it. It cannot be contained by a "sacred" label and segregated neatly from the rest of culture, which is then referred to as "secular." Accordingly, to respond to both the questions raised here and others, this book explores many elements of Israelite religious culture: language, law, geography, labor ethics, social hierarchies, notions of divine imminence, and, unsurprisingly, various stories from the Bible as well as stories from other Near Eastern cultures that thrived during the biblical period. This approach works with the broad understanding that religion, in the present as in the past, is lived and comes to expression in the world through what people say, do, write, and create everywhere on every day of the week.

Many questions asked in this book are old, and earlier generations provided themselves with satisfactory answers. But answers that we find acceptable today may differ because they envelop recent discoveries that stimulate new insights. Even when an answer appears the same, it is different because the informational context and intellectual climate of question and answer have changed.

This does not imply that insights produced in the past may be ignored when responding to contemporary questions; rather, it means that their limited adequacy for determining answers to today's questions must be recognized.

Sometimes old commentary is of interest primarily to historians as an artifact reflecting what some or many people once thought, but sometimes it provides important insights and suggests approaches to the Bible that are useful in the contemporary search for understanding and new knowledge. At other times, it is clear that ancient, medieval, and premodern scholars got it right, even by the most demanding of contemporary standards. That is the reason that I consulted their works and cite them often in this book. They contribute measurably to the search for answers to what *really* happened.

The philosophical attitude that I take in writing this book may be called "contentment." I am gratified to work in history because I find examining how people thought in the past an aesthetic pleasure. I find discovering the original meanings of words and texts an enriching experience, and applying proper methodologies to achieve these results a challenging, worthwhile, and even artful undertaking. I assume that many of those whose observations in the past contributed to the formation of my own ideas felt the same way.

As research progressed, answers to the different questions emerged, often surprising me and shocking or delighting friends and colleagues at scholarly meetings, at public lectures, and in private conversations. When the answers to the many disparate questions meshed, they resulted in a text-bonded understanding of the story that was representative of its cultural milieu and far-reaching in its simplicity.

What follows, then, is a cultural reading of the Garden story, informed both by my own stance in the cultures of contemporary Western society and contemporary scholarship and by the ancient culture of those who produced and read the story. Anyone who thinks that discussion of Genesis or Adam and Eve falls exclusively within a narrow part of culture called "religion" and is restricted to it should keep Ira Gershwin's lyric in mind: "It ain't necessarily so."

Acknowledgments

I am grateful to students who, during the 1991–93 academic years, first asked the questions and to colleagues who reacted to papers presented at the annual meetings of the Society for Biblical Literature in 1993 and 1994 in which I tested initial answers. Members of the Biblical Symposium of the Hebrew University and of the Bible Faculty Seminars at Haifa University and at Bar Ilan University, where I presented some tentative, general conclusions in 1995, offered useful suggestions and posed additional questions for me to consider. A second round of thanks is due students who posed new, useful questions during the 1996–97 academic years and to my colleagues in the American Oriental Society who, in 1997, commented on and helped improve some of the answers that appear now in this book.

I express my appreciation to the Rockefeller Foundation for enabling me to update and revise the growing manuscript during my tenure as visiting scholar at the foundation's Bellagio Study and Conference Center at the Villa Serbelloni in February–March 2001. Colleagues there from around the world, representing disparate disciplines in the humanities, social sciences, and physical sciences, taught me where my work required amplification and clarification for people curious about the topic but not specialists in the Bible or Semitic languages. Fellow members of the now defunct, intimate Biblical Colloquium West, the first to hear much of the full analysis presented in this book at our annual retreat in February 2004, and colleagues at the Annual Meeting of the Catholic Biblical Association who attended my extensive Research Report presentation in August 2004 provided much constructive criticism and many productive demurrers that led to additional corrections and additions.

Stephen Hanselman, Julie Hanselman, and Debby Segura read and critiqued some of the early chapters of this book; Zehava Zevit did likewise with Chapters 16–20. Jeanette Friedman read through the entire manuscript and was generous with her comments and suggestions. They provided me with good ideas and inspired two years of additional research and writing. Henry L. Carrigan read, commented on, critiqued, and helped me to improve the final manuscript immensely. Mary Pasti, my editor at Yale University Press, sharpened the manuscript, improving the quality of my writing through her careful, close readings, her flow of queries, comments, and quips, and her insightful suggestions.

Rick Burke, former director of the Ostrow Library at the American Jewish University; Paul Miller, current director; and Patricia Fenton, manager of Judaica and Public Services, conjured up books within days of my requests. Their good-willed support facilitated my research for this and other projects over many years. David Deis of Dreamline Cartography created the maps for this book, and Debby Segura provided an alphabet chart and two line drawings. Ron Petrisca and Yasmin Hubashi of the Technology Department at the American Jewish University helped prepare most of the other figures for publication.

My dear friends Yaela and Yohanan Wosner on many occasions provided an intellectually stimulating haven in Jerusalem, where I wrote and revised many parts of this manuscript a few times over the years.

I am grateful to Stephen Hanselman, my agent, who helped make this book possible, and Jennifer Banks, senior editor at Yale University Press, for accepting it onto the Press's list.

And I thank my wife, Rachel, for her unfailing good sense and humor, her good company, and her encouragement.

To all, thank you.

Introduction:

The Fall Is with Us Always

Christians and Jews have read the narrative about Adam and Eve in the Garden for more than two millennia, or at least they have heard about it. Preachers and scholars regularly address its plot, themes, and theology—none of which are understood to bode well for humanity. Because of constant retelling, the story is so ingrained in popular awareness that it is possible to know it through hearsay and folklore alone.

Many Americans who spent a summer or two at camp may have made their first acquaintance with the story through the hand-clapping spiritual "Them Bones Will Rise Again" in one of its many variations. The following lyrics, with the chorus and the repetitions of the title line omitted, are typical:

> Now the Lord decided to make a man.
> He took some water and he took some sand,
> Took a rib from Adam's side,
> Made Miss Eve for to be his bride,
>
> Well, he made a garden rich and fair,
> Told them to eat what they found there.
> To one tall tree they must not go.
> There, forever the fruit must grow.

Around that tree old Satan slunk,
And at Miss Eve his eye he wunk.
"Eve, those apples look mighty fine.
Just try one—the Lord won't mind!"

First she took a little slice,
Smacked her lips and said, "'Twas nice."
Next she gave a little pull;
Soon she had her apron full.

Soon the Lord came a-walking round,
Spied those peelings on the ground.
"Adam, Adam, where art thou?"
"Here I am, Lord, I'm a-coming now."

"You ate my apples, I believe."
"Wasn't me, Lord, it was Eve."
The Lord rose up in his mighty wrath,
Told them, "Beat it down the path.

"Adam, you must leave this place,
Earn your living by the sweat of your face."
They took a pick, and they took a plow—
That's why we're all working now.

That's all there is, there ain't no more.
Eve got the apple and Adam got the core.
That's the story of the Fall from Grace
Until Jesus saved the human race.

Though humorous and light-hearted, the song closely adheres to the Bible's story. Where it differs, the song reflects widely held beliefs about the story. For example, the song identifies the serpent who speaks with Eve in the Bible as Satan, characterizing him as a folksy, flirtatious conniver. It connects Satan directly to Eve's misbehavior that resulted in sin, exile from the "garden rich and fair," and a sentence of hard labor for all humanity.

The song reflects interpretations of the story that originated in the Middle Ages and earlier. It assumes that apples were the forbidden fruit, which was never identified in the Bible's story. Likewise, unlike the biblical story, in which both Eve and Adam ate the forbidden fruit, the song assigns blame only to Eve, failing to mention that Adam ate also. The last two lines draw the song into the orbit of standard Christian theology, teaching that salvation from the fallen state became available only with the coming of Jesus.

*

Because jokes are usually part of popular oral culture, they are of particular importance in ascertaining how widespread knowledge of the Fall is outside religious settings. Jokesters intend their audiences to comprehend a punch line quickly, without having to stop and think. Examining jokes about Adam and Eve allows us, then, to determine the common knowledge that jokesters assume their audience to possess. Insofar as the following three jokes "work," even on adults and college students who admit to not having read the story, they may be used to guesstimate what many know about the Fall.

Joke 1

One day in the Garden of Eden, Eve called to God, "Lord, I have a problem."

"What's your problem, Eve?"

"I know that you created me and put me in this lovely garden with all the animals. But I'm just not happy any more."

"Why not, Eve? What's gone wrong?"

"Well, Lord, I guess that I'm getting lonely. These animals don't talk. And to tell you the truth, fresh apples just don't do it for me any more."

"Eve, I have a solution. I'll create a man for you."

"What's a man, Lord?"

"Well, he's a bit like you, but flawed. He's tough and not easy to get along with. But he will be bigger and faster than you so he can help out when needed. But he'll be a bit slower than you and you'll have to help him figure out what to do."

Eve thought for a few moments, scratched her head, and asked, "What's the catch, Lord?"

"Well, there will be one condition attached."

Eve smiled wisely and asked, "And what's that, Lord?"

"You'll have to let him think that I made him first."

The humor in this joke lies in the assumption that the audience knows that Adam was created before Eve and that the animals were formed for his benefit as God sought a helper for him. The punch line plays on the image of the so-called dominant male as a somewhat oafish character who can be controlled by a wily woman. This alludes both to the idea that it was Eve who seduced Adam into eating the forbidden fruit and to the divine order that the man would rule over the woman. The punch line works by restoring the backwards world set up by the joke to its ostensible mirror image as known through the biblical story.

Later in this book, I will demonstrate that the idea of Adam's seduction is based on a mistranslation of the biblical text.

Joke 2

One day in the Garden of Eden, Adam called out to God, "Lord, I have a problem."

"What's your problem, Adam?"

"I'm lonely and the animals aren't fun. The food is a bit flat and there's nobody to talk with."

"Well, Adam, I have a solution. I'll create a woman for you."

"What's a woman, Lord?"

"Well, a bit like you, but she'll know how to take care of you. She'll cook good dinners; she'll give you a massage after you shower. She'll fill you in on what happened all day. She'll remind you what you have to do. She'll be your friend."

Adam thought for a few moments, scratched his head, and asked, "How much is this going to cost me, Lord?"

"I was thinking about an arm and a leg."

Adam smiled wisely and asked, "And what could I get for a rib?"

The assumption here is a common awareness that the first woman was formed from Adam's rib to be his helper. The punch line works because it treats literally the figure of speech "costs an arm and a leg," which usually translates as "costs a great deal," while explaining how it is that God decided to make Eve out of Adam's rib.

Below, I will explain how this comprehension of Eve's origin developed from a misunderstanding of the biblical text.

Joke 3

Mr. Yotan wanted to encourage students in the school cafeteria to select healthy desserts from among the items offered, particularly fruit. He leaned a neatly printed sign against a bowl of chocolate-chip cookies: "Take only one! God is watching." About ten minutes later, he noticed that someone had appended a note to his sign: "Take all you want. God is watching the apples."

The allusion to the story of the Fall is more oblique in this joke than in the two preceding ones. The humor is based on the assumption that the forbidden fruit was the apple and plays on the notion that God was concerned with theft from his apple tree. The punch line works because it suggests how to get away with a misdemeanor without getting caught and punished as were Adam and Eve. In fact, the Bible story makes clear that all fruit from the tree was prohibited, not just second helpings.

People whose knowledge of the Fall was gained through the song "Them Bones Will Rise Again" could understand each of these jokes.

To be understood, these jokes all require knowledge about the sequence of events in the Garden, the relationship between Adam and Eve, Eve's intelligence, the couple's sin, and their punishment.

The third joke assumes that everybody in the lunch line knew that they should take only one chocolate-chip cookie for dessert. The punch line is effective because it tolerates low-grade unethical behavior with a wink and a smile. It appeals to the touch of petty larceny that many believe lies in the souls of all people and that accepts questionable acts of self-gratification, particularly when a misappropriation can be justified as victimless.

*

Advertisers, as specialists in manipulating the hearts and souls of people, sometimes expect their target audience to have a sophisticated comprehension of the Garden story. They use the story of Adam and Eve overtly when appealing to the barely suppressed desire for self-indulgence characteristic of potential consumers. They appeal to wealthy clients and play on guilt effectively when selling expensive cars, handbags, or watches— "Don't feel guilty. You deserve it."

Waiters in some restaurants use a similar tactic when plying a calorie-rich dessert: "It is wicked, but you will enjoy it. Would you like to share it?" What the waiter conveys is not only that the cake or mousse or parfait is exceptionally good but that consuming it is not good for you and consequently may be a source of guilty pleasure.

The message of both advertisers and waiters is that to act against better judgment can provide pleasure and self-satisfaction. Their allusions to the Garden story combine consumption, guilt, and pleasure to give an oblique but clear message: "Sin in haste; repent, if you chose to do so, in leisure."

Contemporary awareness of the story among adults raised in some denominations sometimes generates an uneasy sense of guilt when they feel too good about themselves. Some, after achieving fame, success, and wealth, come to fear a fall, a precipitous decline in their fortune. The most common expression of such concern is charitable giving. It is explained variously as "giving back" or "righting the scale" or "helping the less fortunate" or "helping those less blessed than I." One of its purposes is to direct questionably gotten (though not illegal) wealth into paths of righteousness: schools, hospitals, churches, synagogues, and shelters for various categories of unfortunate people. It is a way of diverting God's attention away from extravagant accumulation or consumption to extravagant good.

The examples of jokesters, advertisers, waiters, and even charitable givers address both the story and the idea of the Fall as light elements in popular culture. But the idea of the Fall is simultaneously a major building block in the construction of Christian theologies. In Christian thought, it is the event that necessitated a counterevent for the salvation of humanity: the resurrection of Christ, which, though interpreted variously, is generally understood as a sign of divine grace. Accordingly, the significance of the Fall extends through interpretive instruction and preaching and beyond abstract theology into the lives of many, influencing thought and behavior.[1] It is so deeply interwoven into some aspects of Western culture that it also influences those who do not believe its message but recognize certain attitudes that it engenders as common wisdom based on human experience.

*

Through the polarity between "fallen" and "saved" in Christian theological interpretation, the story of Adam and Eve in the Garden has shaped and continues to influence attitudes toward wealth (as with the charitable givers), family structure, and authority, as well as theories of personality types and deviant behaviors.[2]

In *Damnation and Deviance* (1978), Mordechai Rotenberg, a philosopher of psychotherapeutic modalities, draws attention to the influence of Calvinist theology of the Fall on "people-changing" professions in the West. He argues that this theology, with its well-defined notions of who is predestined for election and who for damnation, generated beliefs about what constitute deviant behaviors and why they are often considered irreversible. He also traces how such beliefs contribute to the problem of social alienation. Rotenberg maintains that after certain assumptions about deviance became embedded in culture, they came to be viewed as axiomatic within various social-science disciplines. Then he points out how they give rise to pernicious outcomes in therapeutic situations when the people-changers—social workers, prison officials, parole officers, family therapists, and psychotherapists—and their clients share the view that the clients are among the unsaved.[3]

*

Adam and Eve had everything before the Fall and then nothing. A lapse in judgment, an impulsive decision, resulted in a sin that precipitated the forfeiture of a blissful life in a state of grace before the presence of God. Outside the Garden they labored to survive and became prey to all types of misfortune that visit those out of God's favor. We, their descendents, labor to improve our lot and the lot of humanity. But, like Adam and Eve, we are always skirting misdeeds and tottering on the brink of a new fall.

Thoughts such as these may have filled the mind of Katherine Lee Bates when she wrote the words to "America the Beautiful" in 1893 as a meditation on the nature of America's soul. She was both awed and inspired by the natural and human scenery that she viewed through her window on a train trip from the East Coast of the United States to Denver one summer. Her poem, which many believe should become the national anthem of the United States, refers to scenes of awe-inspiring natural beauty and marvelous human achievement. Bates discerned human achievement in the transformations that disciplined labor had brought to the land and that freewheeling Protestant capitalism had brought to the cities.

Every stanza begins with a description of something wondrous about the dynamic Eden still being settled and built. She mentions spacious skies, purple mountains, and fruited plains, pilgrim migration routes, liberty, and alabaster cities but concludes each stanza with a prayer on behalf of

America. Four examples represent her major themes: "America, America, God shed his grace on thee, and crown thy good with brotherhood from sea to shining sea"; "God mend thy every flaw, confirm thy soul in self-control, thy liberty in law"; "May God thy gold refine till all success be nobleness and every gain divine"; and "God shed his grace on thee till selfish gain no longer stain the banner of the free."

The prayers address moral faults that she perceived: lack of brotherhood and self-control, illicit and selfish gain, and liberty unbridled by law. Bates recognized the faults as arising out of the exuberance of American freedom, but presupposed that the forces driving America, however virtuous, must be subordinate to antecedent values taught by God. Her prayers express her belief that until people learn to control themselves and act properly, they require God's grace to manage. Those requiring God's grace are the fallen. They are the focus of her prayers. The historical origin of the conception that some or all people require such grace is one of the many concerns of this book.

The actual biblical text that may have inspired Bates is Jeremiah 9:3–11. In these verses, God condemns Israelites for cheating and lying, for deceiving their brothers and neighbors; he denounces them for ambushing one another instead of behaving as friends. Consequently, Jeremiah announces that God will melt them and test them and bring retribution on the nation that will affect the mountains and the habitations in the wilderness, that he will drive away animals and so change nature that it will be abandoned. He will then destroy the city of Jerusalem and make other cities desolate.

Jeremiah's verses refer to nature and to the human inventions that Bates praised—paths in the wilderness, cities—as well as to the faults she saw. At the level of the individual, however, the list of faults alludes obliquely to Adam and Eve in the Garden. They disobeyed a divine law: they lacked self-control and took what was not theirs. Their backbiting and counteraccusations before the divine judge were hardly a demonstration of amity. Because of their acquisitive selfishness they lost everything.

In Bates's view, America required God's grace because what happened to Adam and Eve in Eden could happen to the people she viewed through the window of her train. For her, sensitivity to the Fall and its consequences could inspire Americans to act in ways that would make them worthy of God's grace and of his forgiveness when they did wrong.

*

In Part I of this book, I describe when, where, and why these ideas developed and raise the following question: Why is the Old Testament / Hebrew Bible unaware of the idea of the Fall? In Part II, I question the notion that the "sin" was due to a lapse in judgment and examine whether or not the Garden story indicates that Adam and Eve experienced any sense of guilt over what they had done. In Part III, I illustrate how the Garden story is addressed and evaluated in the Old Testament / Hebrew Bible in books other than Genesis.

This book explores the origin of understandings of the Fall in both the high and low cultural traditions of the West reflected in the examples presented above. It illustrates that much of what is considered obvious and self-apparent in the biblical story is neither obvious nor self-apparent when the story is read closely and examined carefully. Moreover, it argues that much, not all, of what people believe about the story is based on misconstruals of the story's language and incorrect interpretations of the sequence and meaning of events.

PART ONE

Now and Then

We know that the whole creation has been groaning in travail together until now.

—Paul, *Epistle to the Romans* 8:22 (ca. 50–60)

"and he closed, *wayyisgor*, the flesh beneath it"—From the beginning of the book until this passage, the letter *samech* is not written. Because she was created, the *s*atan was created with her.

—*Bereshith Rabbah* 17:6 (fourth century)

The deliberate sin of the first man is the cause of original sin.

—Augustine of Hippo, *On Marriage and Concupiscence*, II, xxvi, 43 (419/420)

[The] members of the race should not have died, had not the first two merited this by their disobedience; for by them so great a sin was committed that by it the human nature was altered for the worse, and was transmitted also to their posterity, liable to sin and subject to death.

—Augustine of Hippo, *City of God*, XIV: I (426)

Whoever has lived long enough to find out what life is, knows how deep a debt of gratitude we owe to Adam. He brought death into the world.

—Mark Twain, *Pudd'nhead Wilson* (1894)

1 THE FALL IN INTERPRETATION

In popular perception, the Garden story in Genesis teaches about humanity's forfeiture of an ideal relationship with God and about the origins of sexuality and lust in acts of disobedience and rebellion against him. It explains the derivation of some human woes in divine curses: the struggle for livelihood and the pain of childbirth. It instructs wives to submit to the rule of their husbands. It informs us about the curse on *Reptilia squamata serpentes* (*Ophidia*) that brought about its novel form of locomotion. Finally, the story explains, at least as some interpret it, why, after a life of struggle, all humans die.

Adam and Hawwa (Eve, by her Hebrew name) were banished from the paradisiacal Garden into the world that we, all of us, their descendents, now occupy.[1] Like them after they left the Garden, we look back to the past wistfully, knowing that what we have will never be as good as what we could have had, because something is inherently wrong with us. We are fallen creatures.

And lest somebody argue that perhaps after banishment the original relationship between people and God could have been restored, the Bible provides further evidence attesting to the fall of humanity. The firstborn of the primal couple, named Qayin (Cain), was jealous of his younger brother, Hebel (Abel), and killed him (Gen 4:8); Lamech, a descendent of Qayin, was violent, arrogant, and boastful: "I have slain a man for wounding me, and a child for bruising me" (Gen 4:23–24). Indeed, one scholar suggests that it is possible to view all Israelite history after the killing of innocent Hebel as connected chains of violent events lubricated by an ever-flowing stream of blood.[2] Hardly an auspicious beginning for humankind! For more than two millennia this understanding has provided an interpretive lens through which the Bible has been read and explained.

This most important and certainly not farfetched interpretation presents a gloomy understanding of humanity that conceives of people as, at best, incompetent, wrongdoing muddlers in an inhospitable and often dangerous world. At worst, it may have contributed a sense of justifiable normality to the sanguineous history of the West, where noble warriors fought sword in hand with Bible exegesis in heart and mind.

A JAUNDICED READING

The understanding of the Garden story as the story of a Fall sets a brooding tone that carries over into the other narratives in Genesis. We have only to think about the description of lascivious divine beings selecting wives from among the beautiful daughters of humankind (Gen 6:1–4), of God's declarations that people think "nothing but evil all the day" (Gen 6:5) and that the "desire of the human mind is evil from its youth" (Gen 8:21), of the drunkenness of Noah and the subsequent prurient voyeurism of his son Ham (Gen 9:20–29), and even of certain ethically questionable behavior on the part of Israel's patriarchs and matriarchs, people living under the protective cloaks of divine care, favor, and guidance.

Fearing that men in Egypt and in the Philistine city of Gerar would kill him so that they could take his beautiful wife, Abraham asked Sarah to pass herself off as his unmarried sister. She acquiesced and was taken into the harem of the unsuspecting local kings, triggering dire consequences for their innocent loyal subjects. God afflicted Egyptians and Gerarites with plagues. In the end, Sarah remained untouched and unharmed, while Abraham increased his personal wealth (Gen 12:10–20; 20:1–18).

Sarah mistreated her pregnant servant, Hagar (Gen 16:1–6), and later sent both Hagar and her son, Ishmael, off into the wilderness to die (Gen 21:9–13). Isaac, like his father before him, had his wife misrepresent herself as his sister when he, too, journeyed to Gerar (Gen 26:6–11).

Jacob, the consummate deceiver, exploited his brother Esau's hunger to obtain the status of firstborn (Gen 25:28–34). Later, at the instigation, and with the complicity, of his mother, Rebecca, Jacob took advantage of his father's blindness, deceiving him so that he, Jacob, would receive the blessing that Isaac had intended for Esau (Gen 27:1–30). Fleeing his brother's wrath, Jacob moved to Mesopotamia, where he joined the household of his uncle Laban, Rebecca's brother. There, he met poetic justice.

His duplicitous uncle Laban agreed to marry his daughter Rachel to Jacob. At the last moment, Laban substituted his older, possibly nearsighted daughter, Leah, for the younger Rachel, a fact that Jacob discovered only in the morning light, after the marriage had been consummated.

Jacob later tricked his father-in-law through his ability to breed flock animals selectively and thus increase his share of the profits (Gen 30:37–43). Jacob's escapades were such that a prophet preaching around 539 BCE could declare about him: "Your first father sinned" (Isa 43:1, 22, 27).

In the next generation, Joseph, favorite son of Jacob, tattled on his brothers (Gen 37:2). Motivated by jealousy, anger, and a desire for revenge, they sold him into slavery and allowed their father, Jacob, to believe that he was dead (Gen 37:25–36).

Descendents of Jacob's sons, the Israelites, continued to behave improperly. After Moses led them out from slavery in Egypt, they rebelled against God in the wilderness by constructing and worshipping a golden calf (Exod 32:1–4), complaining about *manna*, a special food provided to them, while longing for their Egyptian diet of meat and vegetables (Num 11:4–5) and refusing to conquer the Promised Land (Num 13:30–14:10). God condemned that generation to die in the wilderness.

Forty years after the exodus from Egypt, after the death of those who refused to enter the land promised to the descendents of Abraham, Isaac, and Jacob, a new generation came along under the leadership of Joshua (Josh 1–24). After his death, their children engaged in idolatry: "The children of Israel did evil in the eyes of the Lord and worshipped the Baalim" (Judg 2:11).

The book of Judges describes the period after the settlement of the Promised Land as characterized by seven cycles of idolatry, which led God to abandon Israel. Abandonment was followed by punishment at the hands of local enemies, which stimulated repentance. Repentance created a space during which a warrior leader saved the Israelites from their enemies and restored peace to the land. As memories of the distant past faded, however, tranquillity gave way to backsliding, and again "they did what was evil in the eyes of the Lord" (Judg 3:12; 4:1; 6:1, etc.).

The book of Samuel tells about the rise and establishment of a monarchy at the request of the people. The book of Kings goes on to describe the centuries from the reign of Solomon until the capture of Jerusalem and the first exile from Israel in 597 BCE, followed by the destruction of Jerusalem and Solomon's temple and the second exile in 586 BCE, as four hundred years of continuous disobedience to divine commands (2 Kings 21:10–15; 22:16–17).[3]

WHY BAD THINGS HAPPEN TO PEOPLE

Around 445 BCE, almost 140 years after the destruction of Solomon's temple, Nehemiah, a Jewish official representing the interests of the Persian court, came to Jerusalem. Assuming a direct connection between the depressed circumstances of Jews in the city and what he considered their impious behavior, he undertook to improve their lot in both the material and the religious spheres. To set things right with God, he encouraged public fasting, acts of contrition and confession, tithing, and observance of the Sabbath (Neh 9:1–5; 13:1–27).

Nehemiah composed a great negative confession that drew on Israel's historical tradition to describe his people's past as a long series of misdeeds and rebellions (Neh 9:16–31). The point of his public confession was to acknowledge that all misfortunes that had befallen Israel were of their own making: "You are in the right concerning all that comes upon us, because you acted faithfully and we did evil" (Neh 9:33). Nehemiah's list of misdeeds is of interest for two reasons.

First, Nehemiah indicted his contemporaries. In an era of "it's not my fault" thinking by down-and-out Israelites, he accused them of bearing collective responsibility for their own misfortune. Just as their ancestors had suffered for the sins of their own generations, the current generation's tribulations were the consequence of their own misdeeds. In making this argument, Nehemiah redefined the scope of individual culpability that Jeremiah and Ezekiel had developed 140 years earlier (Jer 31:29; Ezek 18:2).

These two prophets confronted people claiming that the calamities befalling them just before the destruction of Jerusalem in 586 BCE were unjustified, since only their ancestors had done wrong: "The fathers have eaten sour grapes but the children's teeth are set on edge." The idea behind the aphorism is found in the Decalogue: "I, the Lord, am a jealous god accounting the guilt of the parents upon the children, on the third and on the fourth generations of those who reject me" (Exod 20:5; 34:7, with slightly different wording).

In context, the Exodus passages refer to the postponement of punishment for a particular offense: serving other gods. In any event, both Jeremiah and Ezekiel rebutted the proverb with its underlying idea arguing instead that only the teeth of those who eat sour grapes are set on edge. They denied that individuals are punished for the wrongdoing of their ancestors. This idea of Jeremiah and Ezekiel is an expansive generalization based on a legal principle found in Deuteronomy 24:16: "Parents shall not be put to death for children, or children put to death for parents. A person shall be put to death for his own crime."

Nehemiah expanded the concept of individual retribution, treating the people of his day as a corporate body. Every generation that is punished is punished for its own wrongdoing.

Second, although Nehemiah read through the past with fault-finding eyes, the oldest relevant wrongful act that Nehemiah discerned in history was Israel's collective refusal to conquer the land in the days of Moses and the subsequent sin of worshipping the golden calf (Neh 9:15–18).[4] He made no mention of any prior wrongdoings.

WHY PEOPLE DO BAD THINGS

Two hundred years after Nehemiah, some individuals found fault with his explanation of collective responsibility, as well as with the idea of individual responsibility that Jeremiah and Ezekiel had espoused. They changed the question from "What did we do wrong?" to "Why, despite awareness of what we ought to do, do we do wrong and incur guilt?"

To answer their new question, they accepted Nehemiah's historical approach—that a search of the past could provide a relevant answer for their contemporary question. Simultaneously, they expanded his list of misdeeds by moving into the more distant past. They sleuthed after the etiology of humankind's proclivity for the perverse, seeking, like medical researchers, the source of the sickness, as it were. Backtracking on the dark, thorny trail of misdeeds described in their scriptures led them further back than the exodus. They examined the lives of Jacob and his family, and of Isaac, and then of Abraham and Sarah as these were known to them. They continued, going back ten generations to Noah, from whose children all peoples in the world are descended. From Noah, the path led back another ten generations to the first couple in the Garden, and to the series of events that came to be described by Christian theologians as "the Fall."[5]

EARLY ATTEMPTS AT ANALYSIS

In an address to women, the church father Tertullian (160–220 CE) laid out the implications of the events in the Garden, allocating culpability in a form still quite recognizable in the twenty-first century:

> I think . . . that you would have dressed in mourning garments and even neglected your exterior, acting the part of mourning and repentant Eve in order to expiate more fully by all sorts of penitential garb that which woman derives from Eve—the ignomy, I mean, of original sin and the odium of being the cause of the fall of the human race.
>
> In sorrow and anxiety, you will bring forth, O woman, and you are subject to your husband, and he is your master. Do you not believe that you are [each] an Eve?
>
> The sentence of God on this sex of yours lives on even in our times and so it is necessary that the guilt should live on, also. You are the one who opened the door to the Devil . . . you are the one who persuaded he whom the Devil was not strong enough to attack. All too easily you destroyed the image of God, man.[6]

While Tertullian's analysis of the Garden story with its salty singling out of women shaped much in Christian thought for many centuries, his analysis was not uniquely Christian. It can be traced back to pre-Christian Jewish teachers who first faulted Adam as liable in the biblical story. Some spread the blame to include Hawwa, whereas others shifted it entirely to her. Tertullian reflects the latter position.

The reassignment of liability was due in part to Hellenistic attitudes toward women and in part to an evolving perception that some element of the punishment for the sin was transmitted biologically, like the spots on Jacob's goats. Additionally, the science of the time accepted that heredity played an important role in establishing the character and nature of an individual, but was uncertain about which parent transmitted which traits to offspring. Consequently, once the Fall became associated with human character, science insisted that the imprint of fallenness had to be passed on from parents to offspring. Differing scientific views about which parent transmitted which characteristic to offspring explain the different assignations of liability, now to Adam and now to Hawwa.

A Jewish composition of the late first century CE, 2 Esdras, a book in the Apocrypha (= 4 Esdras in Catholic Bibles), expressed the already well-developed notion that Adam's sin in Eden affected all his descendents: "O Adam, what have you done? For though it was you who sinned, the fall was not yours alone, but ours also who are your descendents" (2 Esd 7:118). The author of 2 Esdras explained that although Adam was judged only for the deed, the human proclivity to sinfulness was innate: "the first Adam, burdened with an evil heart, transgressed and was overcome, as were all who were descended from him. Thus the disease became permanent" (2 Esd 3:21–22); and "a grain of evil seed was sown in Adam's heart from the beginning, and how much ungodliness it has produced until now, and will produce until the time of threshing comes" (2 Esd 4:30). According to this understanding, Adam did evil because the inclination to do so was part of how he had been created in the beginning. Adam's tendency was owing to a primal birth defect transmitted to all his descendents. Support for this could be found by reading Genesis 8:21 as a diagnostic statement: "the inclination of man's heart is evil from his youth."

The author of 2 Baruch, a Jewish composition of the early second century CE, proposed a slightly different explanation that spread blame: "O Adam, what did you do to all who were born from you? And what will be said of the first Eve who obeyed the serpent, so that this whole multitude is going to corruption?" (2 Bar 48:42–43). The explanation that the first sin led to a mutation affecting human progeny for all generations may be imagined—allowing for anachronism—as a pernicious application of the discredited genetic theories proposed much later by Jean-Baptiste Lamarck (1744–1829).

The French biologist explained that changes in the environment influence changes in creatures that are subsequently passed on to their young.

His most famous example was the giraffe's long neck that stretched and improved as giraffes reached up to consume the higher-growing leaves on trees. Like Lamarck, the author of 2 Baruch thought that the single misuse of ethical choice in the Garden resulted in the implantation of a horrendous negative trait in human germplasm. "Fallenness," for him, was not an individual's propensity or a developed taste for ethical misbehavior but an acquired trait or state of being become permanent.[7]

The earliest attestation of the "Eve is to blame" explanation in a Jewish source is in the pre-Christian apocryphal book known both as Ecclesiasticus and as the Wisdom of Jesus Ben Sirah. It is the only apocryphal book identified by the name of its actual author. Ben Sirah, a sage active in Jerusalem at the end of the third and the beginning of the second century BCE, belonged to the elite of establishment families whose worldview was increasingly informed by and open to many types of Hellenistic insights, values, and attitudes. He earned his living and reputation instructing sons of these families in the ways of Jewish piety and summarized many of his teachings in a Hebrew book around 180 BCE. Although large portions of his book are known from medieval Hebrew manuscripts discovered around 1900, we know the complete work only through the Greek translation made by his grandson around 130 BCE.[8]

Ben Sirah's teachings were popular and circulated widely in both Hebrew and Greek for almost four centuries. Rabbis of the first and second centuries CE knew his work, alluded to his teachings, and quoted them—a significant fact when considering their attitudes toward women. In an elaborate comparison of virtuous and evil women, Ben Sirah taught the following:

> From a woman sin had its beginning, and because of her we all die. Allow no outlet to water and no boldness of speech in an evil wife. If she does not go as you direct, separate her from yourself. (Ben Sirah 25:24–26)[9]

One other work pertinent to this discussion was written originally in Hebrew or Aramaic during the second century BCE but is preserved completely only in Greek and Armenian translations: the Testaments of the Twelve Patriarchs. Contemporaneous with Ben Sirah's book and popular through the first century CE, it differs from the works cited above in that it reveals unambiguously the pessimistic attitude of some Jewish thinkers toward humanity in general and women in particular, though without direct reference to the Garden story.

The first part of this composition, "The Testament of Reuben," presents the deathbed advice of Reuben, Jacob's oldest son, to his own sons. Repentant of the sin that he had committed by defiling the bed of his father—a reference to Genesis 35:22, "and Reuben went and lay with Bilhah, his father's concubine"—for which he was chastised by Jacob in Genesis 49:4, Reuben sought to justify himself. He explained that what he had done with Bilhah was due in part to the various natural spirits established against humankind that give rise to the deeds of youth. These spirits are life, "with which man is created as a composite being"; seeing, "with which comes desire"; hearing; smell; speech; and taste. The seventh spirit is the spirit of "procreation and intercourse, with which come sins through fondness for pleasure. For this reason, it was the last in the creation and the first in youth, because it is filled with ignorance; it leads the young person like a blind man into a ditch and like an animal over a cliff." In his rambling exposition, Reuben warned that "women are evil," and "lacking authority or power over man, they scheme treacherously how they might entice him to themselves."[10]

In view of both Ben Sirah and "The Testament of Reuben" that circulated in the Jewish-Hellenistic cultural and ethical milieu, Paul of Tarsus's analysis of the state of humanity in the book of Romans is clearly not innovative. He shared some of his culture's attitudes toward women, as well as some Jewish interpretations of scripture in support of those attitudes. He accepted the views of 2 Esdras and 2 Baruch regarding who was culpable in the Garden. He differed, however, from most other Jews of his generation in his particular understanding of sin's proper remediation:

> [S]in entered the world through one man, and death came through sin, and so death spread to all because all men sinned. . . . Death held sway from Adam to Moses, even over those who had not sinned in the same manner as Adam who was like the one who was to come. . . . For if the many died through that one man's sin, many more surely have the grace of God and the gift that came in the grace of that one man, Jesus Christ. (Rom 5:12–15)[11]

Paul and the authors of 2 Esdras and 2 Baruch concur. What transpired in Eden resulted in a state of estrangement marked by a hereditarily transmitted, ineradicable blot on human souls. Paul explained that what the one man caused could be corrected or palliated only through the unique and spiritually heroic measures of another, Jesus, the messiah. That first blot—whether innate or acquired—determined or altered permanently the nature of Adam, progenitor of all humanity, and came to expression through his singular sin. Subsequently, Adam transmitted this imperfection of soul to all his descendents.

In the early centuries of the Common Era, 30–300, there were women and men who comprehended the general condition of humanity as irreparably distanced from the one true God. Humanity, in their view, was thus incapable of achieving its own moral potential. As a consequence, they experienced anxiety about the implications of this situation for the destiny of individual humans after death. These women and men gravitated toward like-minded people, forming communities with those who shared their analyses, empathized and commiserated with their personal concerns, and provided them with comforting intellectual and spiritual solutions. Among these were the Jewish and gentile founders of early churches and their first converts. People born into these communities were educated to perceive the world through teachings now become traditional, to be concerned about the nature of their humanness and the plight of their souls, to experience anxiety about sin, sexuality, and death, and to seek justification before God.[12] Their philosophies informed their insights into the important stories of the Bible and determined which other books and letters they would copy and study for instruction.

Although Paul's understanding of the Garden story as one of original sin and fall expanded early Jewish ideas, such interpretations faded from Jewish writings after the first century CE even as they were fostered in those of some church fathers. Under the influence of emerging rabbinic Judaism, books such as 2 Esdras, 2 Baruch, the Testaments of the Twelve Patriarchs, and even the Wisdom of Ben Sirah were ignored and then forgotten by Jews. Early churches, however, kept them in their libraries of esteemed texts along with many other books, such as the books of Judith, Tobit, and the Maccabees, with different churches esteeming and preserving different books. Many of these are found in Catholic and Eastern Orthodox Bibles, and some are collected into a separate section called the Apocrypha in Protestant Bibles. Today, most Jews are unaware of their existence.

Despite denials that such interpretations, though part of the Jewish milieu in the first centuries of the Common Era, did not penetrate rabbinic Judaism, they did—with a twist. Some rabbis addressed the challenging underlying problems highlighted in these books but proposed different solutions.

The Babylonian Talmud, compiled around the end of the fifth century, preserves a tradition that the two major rabbinical schools of the first century debated about the perverseness of humanity:

> For two and a half years, scholars of the House of Shammai and those of the House of Hillel debated. The former asserted that it would have been better for man not to have been created. The latter maintained that it was better for man to have been created than not to have been created. Finally, they voted and concluded that it would have been better for man not to have been created than to have been created. "Now, however, that he has been created, let him search his [past] deeds, or as others say, let him examine his [future] actions." (*b. Erubin* 13b)[13]

The scholars reported in this text all acknowledged that humans are imperfect beings, but they viewed this imperfection not as a hereditary flaw but as a disadvantage. People could overcome it by consciously thinking about the consequences of their actions and learning from their misdeeds. Scholars of both the House of Shammai and the House of Hillel held humans to account for their behavior. Although their debate addressed the negative consequences of human perversity and suggested how to restrict and minimize them, it did not account for the origin of human perversity. Rabbinic views on this topic are presented in a fourth-century collection of earlier rabbinic homilies.

> Antonius [Caesar] asked our teacher [Rabbi Judah, the Prince]: From what moment is the evil inclination placed in a person? After he leaves his mother's womb or before he leaves his mother's womb?
>
> He said to him: Before he leaves his mother's womb.
>
> He [Antonius] said to him: No. Were it placed in him while in his mother's womb, he would dig through her womb and emerge.
>
> Rabbi [Judah] agreed with him because his view was like the scripture "the inclination of a man's heart is evil from his youth" (Gen 8:21).
>
> Rabbi Yudan says, "It [that is, the word that you understand as referring to youth] is written *m-n-'-r-y-w* [that is, without a letter *waw* that would have been expected after the *'ayyin* had the word meant "youth"] and means, from the time that he bestirs himself [an explanation based

on the verbal root *n-ʿ-r*, in the Piel "to move out from X"] from his mother's womb. (*Midrash Rabbah* 34:10)

This discussion entertains three points of view and eliminates only one. Rabbi Judah thought at first that it was possible that the germ for wrongdoing was implanted in utero. Antonius dissuaded him by arguing on "logical" grounds that it could happen only after birth. If not, the tendency to harm would manifest itself in the behavior of the mature embryo. Judah accepted Antonius's view that implantation was a postpartum event because the view was reasonable and supported by a biblical verse. Yudan accepted Judah's conclusion, but not his idea that the inclination is implanted in infancy. He read the consonants of the word understood as "youth" to mean "his bestirring," that is, at the time when a person is first able to act on his own.

The discussion completely rejects the explanation coinciding most closely with the idea of a primal birth defect. It accepts as a given, however, the idea that an evil inclination exists in humans. Left unsettled is whether the inclination first manifests in infancy or in childhood.

Of the two other explanations propounded in late antiquity under the influence of Hellenism and the interactions between emerging Christian churches, Jewish sects, and rabbinic Judaism, the primal birth defect explanation triumphed over the moral mutation explanation. The defect was considered to have actualized itself in the Garden and to have expressed itself in sin. And because the defect has remained in humans since the Garden, sin is always present.

Thanks to the powerfully persuasive and uncomplicated logic of Paul, the defect explanation prevailed in Christianity, and Christianity molded the religious culture of Europe and parts of the Middle East that gave rise to what we recognize as Western civilization.[14]

THE FALL IN THE WEST

Western civilization is a religious civilization, the product of Christianity's working itself out in the world. Conceived of as Christian, Western civilization is comparable to Islamic civilization, Hindu civilization, and Buddhist civilization, each of which influences large parts of humanity in distinct geographical regions. Like the others, Christian civilization has a worldview that incorporates in itself an understanding of the function of the cosmos, the place of humans in this cosmos, and the nature of human beings. Individuals socialized within one of these civilizations recognize commonalities with people from another civilization, but they also comprehend the many gaps between their own and others in values, ethics, morals, and what it means to be a human being within society. The different ways that these elements are valued, combined, and expressed determine what makes each civilization unique.

Even though Christian civilization is composed of many divisions that often oppose, compete, or conflict with each other, most people living within it share attitudes and a view of humanity influenced by the notion of the Fall. Jews, too, and more recently Muslims, socialized within the intellectual norms of Western culture, especially those pertaining to the nature and control of desires and impulses, share some of these attitudes.[15] In countries where the ethos is determined by Islam, awareness of the Fall is absent; this particular concept is not part of Islam's intellectual heritage. Likewise, it is absent from the worldviews of the Hindu and Buddhist civilizations.

According to one Jewish comprehension of the Fall, influenced by Talmudic and by various Gnostic and esoteric Christian traditions, a catastrophic disruption of the divine plan introduced impurity into the cosmos. Using ideas evolved by Jewish kabbalists in Palestine during the sixteenth century, mystics also generated ideas about corrective thinking and about activities, along with special rituals, that could counter the polluting and demonic forces released in Eden. Their teachings spread from Safed in Galilee through the Jewish world and currently influence intuitive speculations about the nature of God and the soul in all but the most philosophical corners of Judaism.[16] Consequently, one need not be a confessing member of any church or Christian denomination to accept as appropriate some attitudes toward human nature engendered by concepts of the Fall. They are ubiquitous throughout Western civilization.

Uncomfortable with this hegemonic understanding, Tryggve N. D. Mettinger, a Swedish scholar, suggests that the biblical story is about the consequences of a failed test. Mettinger proposes that God's command prohibiting Adam from eating of the Tree of Knowledge is comparable to his testing of Abraham by commanding him to sacrifice his son, Isaac, and to his testing of Job by ruining his life. He argues that Adam's failure, no matter how extenuating and complicated the circumstances, cost him an opportunity to achieve immortality. By eating from the forbidden tree, Adam and his spouse forfeited an opportunity to eat from the other important tree in the Garden, the Tree of Life, about which they had not been informed.

In Mettinger's understanding, the intent of the story is not to teach a negative lesson about the Fall of humanity but to impart a slightly more positive one that might be of use to Israelite readers of the story: obedience to divine commandments leads to life. His interpretation is a soft version of the traditional one. It may be characterized as an attempt to cushion the Fall.[17]

Even Secular Humanism, which defines itself in opposition to Christianity and Judaism and which rejects the authority of Christian and Jewish teachings on most matters remotely connected to what might be called human nature, maps disputed ideological territory in terms defined by Christianity. Jacques Berlinerblau, author of *The Secular Bible*, puts it this way:

> The Good Book no longer needs to be the exclusive or central text of the Occident to exert its impact. After thousands of years of imaginative exegesis . . . its diverse messages and contradictory readings have become lodged in the muscle memory of civilization. It influences us via channels that are obscure and difficult to discern. Conceptions of morality, sexual ethics, beauty, and so on, derived by Biblical interpreters are not so much knowingly thought about and rationally assessed as they are enacted on a daily basis in a reflex-like manner. . . . The nonbeliever who is about to engage in an evening of Bacchanalia . . . will experience feelings of guilt or euphoria that have much to do with trespassing on Biblical ideas of female chastity.[18]

Berlinerblau's point is that many of what are deemed "secular humanistic values" consist of values developed in Christian settings presented without the language of the church.

Abolitionism, unionism, the social welfare movement, the civil rights movement, and political feminism—all potent political movements in the West during the nineteenth and twentieth centuries—found their initial ideological expression in Christianity's particular understanding of humanity and sense of anthropology. (This helps explain the general absence of such movements in modern countries largely untouched or uninfluenced by Christianity.) These movements, initially promoted by the spiritually saved and intellectually enlightened, sought to raise people from a perceived fallen state, or at least to make life in such a state more tolerable. A constituent element of ideologies underlying such move-ments was a sense of what the Fall meant for humanity and for individual human beings.

2   THE FALL IN THE HEBREW BIBLE

The Garden story exemplifies a type of very distinguished story. Stories of this type exercise such power and influence on the consciousness and awareness of those believing in their complete or essential truthfulness that they act on them. This type of story is what scholars of religion and many contemporary theologians label "myth." So long as any story maintains its power (1) to define the correct relationship between people and God and how it is to be maintained and (2) to influence conceptions of the cosmos, rules for the organization of societies, and individual conduct, it is considered living myth. When its authority wanes and individuals and societies no longer believe it, it is dead myth. For example, Canaanite myths about their gods Baal, Anat, and Asherah, known to us from the Ugaritic texts written about thirty-four hundred years ago and discovered by archaeologists in the twentieth century, are dead myths. So are the pre-Christian myths of Europe about Thor, Balder, and Eastre.

The first use of "myth" to refer to an event as not true or as an event or happening not to be believed is traced to a few passages in the New Testament: 1 Timothy 1:4, "instruct certain people . . . not to busy themselves with myths"; 2 Timothy 4:4, "people . . . will turn away from listening to the truth and wander away to myths"; Titus 1:14, "rebuke them sharply so that they may become sound in the faith, not paying attention to Jewish myths or to the comments of those who reject truth"; and 2 Peter 1:16, "we did not depend on cleverly devised myths when we made known to you the power and coming of our lord Jesus Christ." After Bible-based religion successfully challenged indigenous religions in many parts of the world, the aboriginal myths that people still knew were considered false. Now, in contemporary English, the word *myth* is often used to describe an untrue story about the gods or any debunked story once thought to be factual.

When *myth* is used in this book, however, it is with its positive descriptive meaning. The English language lacks a synonym that encapsulates the complex ideas evoked by this particular word. With this meaning in mind, *myth* is an appropriate descriptor for the Gospel accounts of Jesus's birth and Passion, the Garden story (in contemporary Christianity but not in Judaism), and the Giving of the Torah (the first five books of the Bible) at Mount Sinai (in contemporary Judaism but not necessarily in Christianity).

A MYTH OR JUST A STORY?

Was the Garden story or that part of it identified as the Fall a myth in ancient Israel?

What is odd about the Garden story—comprehended as a literary expression of views about human-divine interactions and as a message informing belief and behavior—is that it, or the attitudes that it engenders, still dominate Western consciousness, even though it lacked any such influence in Israelite culture of the Iron Age (1150–586 BCE).[1] Indeed, it is difficult to argue that the author of the story considered events in the Garden paradigmatic for humankind's subsequent behavior. Similarly, it is difficult to maintain that this story betrays the author's generally negative assessment of humanity or the physical world outside the Garden, the world that he, his family, and his audience inhabited.

Certainly prophets, especially those fond of condemning incorrigible Israel for all its perceived wrongdoings, could have alluded to the story or to a character in it. For example, in condemning the citizens of Jerusalem who disobeyed divine commands, Isaiah, who preached for almost four decades around 742–701 BCE, could have said, "You don't understand, you don't listen, just like Adam—indeed, like Hawwa." But he did not. Instead he said: "An ox knows its owner and an ass the feeding trough of its master; Israel didn't know; my people didn't understand" (Isa 1:3).

Amos (active ca. 760–750 BCE), a particularly mean-spirited prophet who lived a generation before Isaiah, condemned the sleek, wealthy women of Samaria as "Cows of Bashan . . . who exploit the poor, rob the needy, and who say to their husbands 'bring and let us drink'" (Amos 4:1–2). He could have said, "Cows of Bashan, like Hawwa you entice your husbands to act improperly and unnaturally." But he did not. When Amos condemned Amaziah, the priest who ordered him out of the temple at Bethel, Amos could have said, "Like Adam driven from the Garden, you and your wife shall die in an unclean land." But he did not. Instead he said: "Your wife shall whore in the town, your sons and daughters will fall by the sword and you yourself shall die on unclean soil" (Amos 7:17).

Hosea (active ca. 750–725 BCE), a younger contemporary of Amos's who condemned willfully faithless Israel for following other deities and portrayed Israel as an adulterous wife, could have proclaimed: "Like Hawwa following the advice of the serpent, like Adam imitating Hawwa and eating that which the Lord prohibited, you say, 'I will go after my lovers.'" But he did not include any reference to the Garden story in his speech: "Their mother whored, she who birthed them acted shamelessly; she said, 'I will go after my lovers who give my bread and my water, my wool and my linen, my oil and my drink'" (Hosea 2:7).

Ezekiel (active ca. 593–571 BCE), who employed crass misogynistic metaphors in his description of Jerusalem as a nymphomaniac, could have alluded negatively to the events in the Garden—"Children of those who sinned in Eden, born of their lust, confident in your beauty and fame, you played the harlot"—but he did not (Ezek 16:15–50). In fact, no Israelite prophet did.

Prophetic literature, which originated in public harangues, is an important indicator of shared, common pre-knowledge. Even casual readers perusing the prophets' speeches in the Bible can infer what these prophets assumed about their audience's fund of general information. It is strange, then, that the common twenty-first-century understanding of the Garden story as the Fall, which would have been rhetorically powerful when Solomon's temple stood, is not reflected at all in prophetic texts.

Neither Adam nor Hawwa is ever singled out in the prophetic literature as a source for Israel's misfortunes or for the miscreant actions of any other people. Even Ecclesiastes, a composition of the Late Persian–Early Hellenistic period (ca. 350–250 BCE), reserves its misogyny for a certain type of woman: "I find more bitter than death the woman who is all traps, her mind snares, her hands fetters. He who is acceptable to God escapes from her; he who is displeasing is caught by her" (Eccles 7:26). Despite his sour attitude, the crotchety author of this verse does not consider the wiles and deceit of the type that he condemns due to inherited nature.

All this contrasts sharply with Paul's chiding allusions to the Garden story in his letters (ca. 50–60 CE). To the congregation in Corinth he wrote: "But I am afraid that as the serpent deceived Eve by his cunning, your thoughts will be led astray" (2 Cor 11:3). To the congregation in Rome he wrote: "[S]in entered the world through one man and through sin death, and so death spread to all people" (Rom 5:12). For Paul and the churches in Corinth and Rome, the Garden story was recognizably a myth with theological authority, but it did not have mythological standing for authors of the prophetic books in the Hebrew Bible.

In First Temple psalmody of the Iron Age, as in the prophetic corpus, no allusions to the Fall understanding of the Garden story occur. No psalmist complained that she or he suffered because of events in Eden. No negative confession of wrongdoings alludes to some inherent guilt or flaw in human nature connected to antediluvian ancestors.

Even in the negative confessions in Nehemiah 9:16–31 (discussed in Chapter 1) and in Psalm 78, no association with the Garden story is found. Psalm 78 lists sins and rebellions from the time of the exodus through the period of the Judges until the establishment of the Temple during Solomon's reign, around 960 BCE. Nehemiah's list, composed in the fifth century BCE, also starts with the exodus, but concludes with Israel's defiant refusal to pay attention to prophetic admonishments and an allusion to the punishment that ensued, the Babylonian exile of 586 BCE.

Both mea culpa lists are anchored firmly in what the Iron Age psalmist and the later Persian official perceived as historical time. Every sin that they listed was a unique act committed at a particular time and place. Each was unrelated to, and not symptomatic of, any underlying human pathology. The composite lists reflected bad decisions by rational people. Both lists overtly indicate that the people of Israel suffered collectively only because of wrongs they perpetrated willfully and not because of some flaw inherent in their humanness as descendents of Adam and Hawwa. It is as if this primal story about what transpired in the

Garden had no implications for ancient Israelites and no application to their situation.[2]

The deduction articulated in the preceding paragraphs is admittedly based on an argument from silences. But, as the ratiocinative Sherlock Holmes demonstrated in *The Hound of the Baskervilles*, sometimes silence rings louder than words.

The deduction may be validated by suggesting an understanding of the story in concert with philology—the close study of written texts and their language—and with what is known about Israelite religious thought and culture in the Iron Age. The interpretation must clarify the absence of negative allusions to the Garden story while explaining the presence of positive ones in the Hebrew Bible. Until these tasks are completed in Part II of this book, the arguments presented up to this point will support only a tentative negative response to the question of whether the Garden story was considered a myth in Iron Age Israel.

THREE FEMINIST INTERPRETATIONS

By the last quarter of the twentieth century, sensitivity to an emerging feminist consciousness led scholars and non-traditional religious laity to complain about what generations of clerics over almost two millennia had maintained, namely, that the Bible's story of Adam and Hawwa proclaims the inferiority of women vis-à-vis men as the will of God. The complaints precipitated some responses that can be described as apologetic reinterpretations and other responses that are justifications for the Bible's characterization of women on theoretical, historical, or theological grounds.

Phyllis Trible provides a partial listing of reasons used to support a comprehension of the text as misogynous:

(1) A male God creates man (Gen 2:7) before woman (Gen 2:22). First means superior.

(2) Woman is created for the sake of man as a cure for his loneliness (Gen 2:18–23).

(3) Contrary to nature, woman comes out of man. She is his rib, dependent upon him for life. She thus has a derivative, not an autonomous, existence (Gen 2:21–23).

(4) Man names woman and thus has power over her (Gen 2:23).

(5) Woman tempts man to disobey and is responsible for sin in the world (Gen 3:6). She is untrustworthy, gullible, and simpleminded for having been fooled by the serpent.

(6) Woman is cursed by pain in childbirth, a more severe struggle than man's with the soil. This signifies that her sin is graver than man's.

(7) Woman's desire for man is God's way of keeping her faithful and submissive to her husband, who has the right to rule over her (Gen 3:16).[3]

Trible then rereads the text, scrutinizing it as if it had never been studied before, and draws a series of startling counter-conclusions. Her innovative interpretations, some of which have influenced my own, conclude at the same point as this witticism: After creating Adam, God stepped back, looked at his handiwork, shook his head, and said, "I can do better than that." (See also joke 1 in the introduction to this book.) Her main counter-conclusions are the following:

(1) That the woman was born of Adam's rib does not imply inferiority but rather equality. She is made of the same stuff as the man.

(2) The woman's conversation with the serpent reveals her to be intelligent and perceptive.

(3) God's speeches emphasize obedience, but the woman herself is not cursed specifically. This suggests that the point of the story is not the status of woman vis-à-vis man but the equal obligation of both to obey divine commands.

(4) Adam, addressed as the prime culprit in Genesis 3:8–13, receives the harsher penalty in Genesis 3:17–19 (painful toil all his life until he returns to the ground: "dust to dust"). This indicates that he was primarily responsible for all that befell the couple.[4]

The genius underlying Trible's interpretation of Hawwa is her insight that Hawwa's action was prompted by curiosity, not cupidity. Trible's rereading provides an antidote to, if not a serum against, ideologically motivated misogynistic eisegesis—interpretation based on reading one's own ideas and biases into a text. It returns us to the problem of obedience and to the question of the story as a paradigm in a historical context. Her astute reading, although it furnishes an alternative to standard interpretations, fails to clarify why the primal myth as she understands it was not paradigmatic in Israelite thought: why it was a most unmythic myth.

Unlike Trible, Gale A. Yee is unperturbed by misogynistic interpretations of the story. She maintains that they do not misrepresent the intentions of the story vis-à-vis women or the attitude of the culture in which it was first told. She finds Trible's egalitarian exegesis outdated, reflecting, as it does, feminist ideologies of the 1970s, and dismisses it as incorrect.

Writing in the first decade of the twenty-first century, Yee sets out unapologetically to explain the circumstances under which Israelite culture generated myths and stories portraying women negatively. Applying social-scientific methodologies and ideological criticism rooted in materialistic philosophy to the Garden story, she concludes that Israelite society could produce such a story only because it was hierarchically structured, androcentric, and controlled by royal ideologies focused on male rulers. Consequently, the Garden story must be understood as symbolic of theological, political, familial, and gender relationships within such a system. These relationships, Yee maintains, are predictable on the basis of social-scientific theory and can be exposed through an intrinsic analysis of the story, through a close reading in search of what theory predicts is to be found.[5]

Accordingly, the period when Adam tends the Garden symbolizes a "primordial time when there was no rift between the king and his people." The prohibition on eating certain fruit reflects a control device, similar to royal privileges that are greater than the rights of peasants. The woman, introduced as a means of controlling the man through sexuality, represents the state's attempt to control Israel through a centralized administration. Unfortunately, she spoiled the primordial order through an act symbolic of political disobedience. (See joke 3 in the introduction.) This resulted in the sentencing of both the male and the female to cursed labor; they are relegated to menial labor while royalty enjoyed leisure. The gulf this created between the man and the woman, who is given into the man's control after the Fall, is reflective of the relationship between Israelite men and women, the king and his people, and God and humanity.[6]

For Yee, the Garden story was a true myth in ancient Israel. She proposes that throughout the Bible women are regularly symbolized as the "incarnation of moral evil, sin, devastation, and death" and that this reflects common attitudes during the time of its production.[7] If correct, her interpretation justifies viewing sin-Fall interpretations from 2 Esdras through Paul and from Tertullian to rabbinic midrash as conveyers of the obvious and original meaning of the Garden story.

Even allowing for overstatement in Yee's characterization of Israel's attitude toward women, there is no denying that the women portrayed as symbolic of Israel sinning against God in Hosea 2–3 and Ezekiel 23 approximate Yee's characterization. However, there is also no denying that no word for evil is used to characterize Gomer, Hosea's adulterous wife, or the twin whores Oholah, a symbol for Samaria, and Oholibah, a symbol for Jerusalem, in Ezekiel's speech.

"Moral evil," "sin," and other vinegary words in Yee's characterization of the Bible's presentation of women emerge from the thought-world of Greco-Roman civilization and Hellenistic biblical interpretation. They are not in the text of the Hebrew Bible itself and are found only in post-biblical exegesis. Moreover, in the books of Hosea and Ezekiel, which provide her most potent examples, it is not the women who are condemned for being women; condemned, rather, are the acts of the people who are violating their covenantal obligation to be loyal to God.

Yee's contribution to this discussion is her repeated insistence that any historical interpretation of biblical texts must address the social-historical context out of which a particular story or prophecy emerged.[8] Her specific interpretation of the Garden story as supporting misogynistic readings, however, does not address the text, philology, or, for that matter, history directly. It is controlled by a priori social-economic theories about, rather than by, relevant descriptions of historical events and social institutions.

Athalaya Brenner's interpretation of the story responds to the same concerns that stimulated Trible's work, but is more controlled by philological constraints and informed by historical-critical methodology. Brenner is less inclined to read the text as a contemporary composition or as an ancient text in need of redemption by contemporary hermeneuticists because of its misogynistic attitudes and statements. Brenner differs from Yee, who wrote almost twenty years after her, in that she avoids using social-science theorizing to bulk up the imperfectly known social world of ancient Israel and the role of women within it, preferring to work with what is known from written sources.

Analyzing the story at the end of a monograph on the social role of women in ancient Israel and their projection as literary types, Brenner concludes with the story's moral:

[W]omen—every woman, every Eve—deserve to be managed by their men. They are resilient, obstinate, energetic . . . but also misguided, easily seduced, and morally inferior to their mates. The hardship they suffer in giving birth is their own Ancestress's—and by implication, their own—fault. They are mothers, initiators, and the ultimate preservers of human culture. . . . Indeed, woman is the primal source of trouble and pain for the entire human race—but she is the source of human learning, consciousness, and civilization as well.[9]

Brenner's conclusions are more balanced than Trible's, which are based on a reinterpretation of the text, but they are also more inconsistent, less well rounded, and in greater tension with each other. They lack the clear profile and demanding authority of Yee's conclusions, which are controlled by well-articulated, disciplined, theoretical considerations. Brenner's conclusions could even be read as echoing Tertullian's statement about women's having inherited from Eve the "odium of being the cause of the fall of the human race." To do so, however, would be an injustice to Brenner. Her conclusions are congruent with the results of her judicious analysis of the status of women and their roles in ancient Israel, which, not surprisingly, dovetail with much of what is known about these topics from the contemporaneous ancient Near East. Brenner recognizes that it is historically irresponsible to claim as a historical exegesis a reading that the culture producing the story would not have recognized.[10]

Denise L. Carmody recognizes the tensions between interpretations such as Trible's, Yee's, and Brenner's, on the one hand, and the concerns of feminism as a secular, social ideology and as a movement within religions, on the other:

If we now step back to take stock of how this text rings in a feminist age, we realize, perhaps fully for the first time, that the Bible is one of feminists' great problems. . . .

Insofar as present-day culture allows feminists to start from an assumption that men and women are radically equal in their humanity, it places feminists in a dialectical relationship with the Biblical text.[11]

Trible, Yee, and Brenner stand at the fulcrum of this dialectical relationship and ask the same questions. Trible and Yee, despite the gulf between them, come down on one side because of their commitment to contemporary sensibilities, theology, and particular ideologies; Brenner comes down on the other because she is more committed to the measure of objectivity that the historical-philological method provides, despite her recognition of its limitations.[12]

Trible's analysis leaves us asking about the significance of the theme of disobedience; Brenner's leaves us asking if her characterization of Hawwa is based on the story or if it is an overly rhetorical projection of conclusions from other parts of her study. These matters are of interest and concern to curious adult readers of the Bible, to audiences who attend to the story when it is read in liturgical contexts, as well as to biblical scholars, theologians, and historians of ideas.

Each of these questions assumes some variation of the standard interpretation of the Garden story as the story of the Fall while reacting mainly to its perceived misogyny. This perception, unsupported by details in the story itself, is affirmed only on the basis of reading into the text ideas whose origin can be traced back no earlier than the second century BCE. It is backreading that infuses the ancient story with the mythic authority that so concerns these authors.

The story, however, was written no less than six or seven centuries prior to its Hellenistic interpretation, so its original, primal meaning is to be sought in the time and culture of its author and his audience. If so, it is necessary to have some idea about when the story was composed and who wrote it. Unfortunately, the task of determining these facts is fraught with difficulties and surrounded by controversy.[13]

3 WHO WROTE THE GARDEN STORY AND WHEN?

Although responses to the questions Who wrote the Garden story? and When? may be stated plainly, the answers are complex. My discussion focuses primarily on the who question and addresses the when question secondarily.

We do not know who wrote the Garden story in the sense that we know that Samuel Langhorne Clemens, under the pen name Mark Twain, wrote *Huckleberry Finn*. He has a generally known life story, publishers, and a bibliography. Nor do we know who wrote the Garden story even in the sense that we know William Shakespeare wrote *Hamlet*. Shakespeare, too, has a name, a poorly known life story, and a bibliography, although items are disputed at times.

Tradition holds that Moses wrote the Garden story sometime during the last half of the second millennium BCE. Historical biblical studies suggest that an anonymous author wrote it during the first quarter of the first millennium BCE.

Despite the vagueness surrounding the "Moses" and the "anonymous author" proposals, we are somewhat better off than those who wish to know who wrote the Mesopotamian tale about a historical figure, Gilgamesh, king of the city-state Uruk in what is now southern Iraq, around 2600 BCE. Differing versions of this epic in two languages, Sumerian and Akkadian, were widely circulated and recited for about twenty-five hundred years in territories now composing Iraq, Syria, and northern Israel. Similarly, we understand the authorship of the Garden story better than those who wish to know about the author of *Beowulf*, an epic written twelve hundred or so years ago in southern England about a Scandinavian hero.

Scholars specializing in ancient mythologies can tell us much about the authors of the *Gilgamesh Epic* and *Beowulf*—about their culture and some general details about their lives and thought—but hardly their life stories. To obtain even modest information about these authors, researchers study other texts from the same culture in the same language, historical and archaeological information from and about the relevant periods and places, and any other scraps of data that help answer whatever questions they decide to pose. In trying to learn about ancient authors, modern scholars are alert to historical and geographical allusions in texts as well as to language, compositional styles, and literary devices used, since some texts and their attributes can be dated. All of this knowledge is objective. It is observable and available to whomever is interested, and all statements based on it are subject to rebuttal and debate by competent individuals wishing to engage in such discussions.

Even after specialists finish their research, they often disagree. As a rule, they tend to disagree not over broad issues but over local ones and fine points. That they disagree over issues within defined parameters does not necessarily mean that one of the parties is absolutely incorrect; it may mean only that some items are disputed because they are not clear or because the data necessary for resolving the dispute are not available. Disagreements of this type—extended conversations intended to resolve difficulties—are usually framed within a broad context of specialized knowledge about which all disputants agree before the conversation commences and develops. Such disagreements are crucial for a discipline. While some scholars are disputing an issue, others are studying the dispute itself and proposing innovative ways to reach a resolution and advance knowledge.

The tools that specialists use in their analysis allow all to agree unequivocally that the *Gilgamesh Epic* was not written in Greek but in Sumerian and in various datable dialects of Akkadian and that *Beowulf* was not written in Middle English or set in Scotland or Wales. Specialized knowledge (1) helps restrict the range of possibly correct answers and (2) clarifies why many interpretations and explanations are incorrect.

In addressing the question of who wrote the Garden story, I exploit these conclusions about specialized knowledge to explore two approaches: the first, a literary-theological approach taught primarily in seminaries that advances the notion of Mosaic authorship; the second, a literary-historical approach taught in many seminaries and in most colleges and universities.[1] The first approach tends to regard the Pentateuch—Genesis, Exodus, Leviticus, Numbers, and Deuteronomy—as a complex but essentially unified and well-integrated composition, whereas the second tends to regard it as having been formed through the imperfect combination of four documents or streams of literary tradition.

THE "MOSAIC AUTHORSHIP" APPROACH

The Garden story's presence in Genesis, the first of the Pentateuch's five parts, is significant. Many who follow the inner-biblical reckoning of Bishop Ussher, a seventeenth-century cleric, date the completed Pentateuch to the fifteenth century BCE. Others accept more recent dating based on extra-biblical inscriptional and archaeological data as well as inner-biblical criteria and assign the complete composition to the thirteenth or twelfth century BCE. But to say that Moses wrote the Pentateuch is not the same as saying that God revealed the whole of the Pentateuch to Moses, who then wrote it down. I proceed now to examine this distinction without addressing the matter of dating.

Two of the five books, Genesis and Deuteronomy, contain no statement that their specific contents were revealed by God to Moses. All the material recorded from the creation account beginning in Genesis 1:1 through the death of Joseph in Genesis 50:26 functions as background for the story about the founding of the relationship between the Israelite people and God at Mount Sinai. It clarifies many questions for readers: How did the Israelites come to be in Egypt? How did it happen that they were promised a homeland in part of the Egyptian province of Canaan? How, when, and why did God establish a special relationship with Abraham and his descendents? Who exactly was this Abraham and what were his special ties with other parts of the ancient world? How did the people of Israel fit into the family of humanity? Nothing in Genesis or elsewhere in biblical narratives clarifies how Moses could have known all this.

The narrative of Genesis is not dry description. It presents a view of the cosmos, the deity who controls it, his connection with humanity, and his unique relationship with the descendents of Abraham through Isaac and Jacob. Individual stories tell about God's revelation of himself in many ways and guises to various people, including Adam, Hawwa, and even Qayin; to Noah, Abraham, Lot, Abimelech, Hagar, Isaac, and Jacob. Genesis is all about what happened long before the birth of Moses, an event narrated in the first chapter of the Pentateuch's second section, Exodus.

There is no difficulty in assuming that Moses knew through family tales what happened in his own lifetime and in that of his immediate ancestors. After all, during his early youth he was raised in proximity to the household of Amram, his father, and was in constant contact with his people from the time his brother Aaron met him on his return to Egypt (Exod 4:27) until his death some forty years later. During the year that the people of Israel camped at the foot of Mount Sinai and during the almost thirty-eight years that they spent near Kadesh Barnea in the Sinai Peninsula, he could have caught up on family history and lore. But what were his sources for information bearing on the generations from Adam to Abraham? Noah and his immediate family are crucial because after the flood, they and only they could have passed down an oral history of pre-deluge humanity.

A consideration of the life spans provided in the "begats" of Genesis 5, 10, and 11 indicates that a chain of transmission could have existed before the flood. Ignoring the extremely long life spans that are not relevant to this argument, we can use the begats to calculate a reasonable answer to the question of Moses' sources. Most individuals listed lived to see great-grandchildren and great-great-grandchildren. In each generation, even those of Noah and his sons before the flood, long-lived people of earlier generations could transmit stories that they had learned about events that occurred before they were born: Noah himself could have known Seth, Adam's third son, along with Enosh, Adam's grandson, as well as other early ancestors. But, perhaps Noah received the information around the family table in the house of his father, Lamech, who may have been responsible for Qayin's death (Gen 4:23). Noah's long-lived grandfather Methuselah could have been a channel for old stories. In turn, Noah, Mrs. Noah, and their children must have been the conduits through which the earliest stories reached those born after the flood.

According to the lists in these chapters, Abraham, son of Terah, could have known Noah and his son Shem and all of Shem's main descendents:

Eber, Peleg, Reu, Serug, Nahor, and certainly his own father, Terah, as an adult (Gen 10:25–30; 11:31–32). From Abraham on, certainly from the days of Jacob and his sons, anecdotes and stories from the Mesopotamian "old country" could have been preserved as part of family and eventually tribal lore until the time of Moses himself. With all the oral lore in mind, Moses could have written no more than what he recalled, and from what he recalled, he most likely would have written only what he thought important or interesting.

Adam Clarke, a popular nineteenth-century Methodist theologian, suggested a more compressed process to explain "how these curious and interesting facts were preserved; and how, by tradition, writing, and divine revelation they were brought down to the time of Moses." He determined that, minimally, Methuselah would have sufficed to serve as a bridge between Adam and Noah; Shem could have transmitted material from Noah to Abraham; Isaac, from Abraham to Joseph; and Amram, from Joseph to Moses. In other words, the earliest traditions could have reached Moses through only four tradents, people who hand down traditions accurately. By minimizing the number of tradents and assuming their reliability, Clarke implied that only a minimal amount of static and noise, that is, incomplete information and misinformation, would have entered the oral tradition. Clarke, however, added a theological comment for those who might be uncomfortable with his first response: "Yet, to preclude all possibility of mistake, the unerring Spirit of God directed Moses in the selection of facts, and the ascertaining of his dates."[2]

Long before Clarke, Jews in Late Antiquity asked how Moses knew about what had happened long before his time. An ancient author provided an explanation quite different from the naturalistic ones based on awareness of folklore and oral transmission. The *Book of Jubilees*, written during the first half of the second century BCE, explained that when Moses was on Mount Sinai, God instructed an angel: "Write for Moses from the beginning of creation till my sanctuary has been built among them for all eternity" (*Jubilees* 1:27). The angelic figure is described as telling Moses about Adam and Hawwa in the Garden as if he were an eyewitness participant: "[W]e brought to Adam all the beasts . . . and Adam named all of them. . . . And the Lord said unto us, 'It is not good that the man should be alone'" (*Jubilees* 3:1–4). That being the case, according to the author of *Jubilees*, Moses paraphrased and edited the angel's report when he recorded the information for posterity in Genesis.

The advantage of the explanation in *Jubilees* is that it accounts for Moses' knowledge of matters about which no human could have had definitive information, such as creation, what God said at the end of each day, and what God thought when conversing with the first humans. It also guarantees the authenticity of Genesis by virtue of the authority of the angel doing God's bidding.

The case of Deuteronomy is quite different from that of Genesis. Aside from chapter 34, twelve verses recording the death of Moses, giving an evaluation of his life, and mentioning what happened *after* his death—sentences added perhaps by Joshua, according to one commonsensical rabbinic tradition—Deuteronomy records farewell speeches delivered by Moses to Israelites born during the thirty-eight-year sojourn in the wilderness. They were the children of those who had undergone the exodus and been present at Sinai but who, succumbing to fear, refused to enter the Promised Land. As a consequence of their timidity and lack of faith, they were sentenced to die in the wilderness before their children would be allowed to cross into the land (Num 14:28–30 and Deut 1:29–44). Their punishment lay in having to live with the consequences of their freely made decision not to enter the land, or, to put it differently, it lay in getting what they wanted.

For almost all of Moses' audience in Deuteronomy, the exodus and various events at Mount Sinai were the adventurous stuff of their childhood stories. Less than two months before his own demise in the fortieth year of the exodus, Moses delivered exhortations to obey, reminiscences about the past, object lessons based on past experiences, and instructions to the generation that he had watched come of age in the wilderness. Deuteronomy 1:1–5 introduces Moses' orations: "These are the words that Moses spoke to all of Israel in Transjordan . . . in the fortieth year in the eleventh month on the first of the month, Moses spoke to them . . . according to all that the Lord had commanded him." He gave a personal review and interpretation of selected exodus stories, as well as of statutes, judgments, and norms—mostly nonritual—that children of the new generation were to follow in the land they would enter soon after he, Moses, died.

Deuteronomy refers to old revelations and introduces new material, employing the pronoun "I" and presenting everything as the words of Moses. Throughout, Moses emphasizes that he talks about past times when God presented Israel with instruction through him. For example, he introduces the Ten Commandments (Deut 5:4–18) with "I stood be-tween the Lord and you at that time to convey the Lord's words to you" (5:5; and see 6:1; 8:11). Elsewhere he reminds his audience with a certain sense of urgency that the rules he imparts are to be obeyed because "this day the Lord your god commands you to observe these laws and rules" (26:16). The statement, however, is inaccurate. Only Moses is speaking on the day that he designates as "this day."

The third person narrative style found only in the introductory verses, Deuteronomy 1:1–5, and in chapters 31 and 34, does not detract from the conclusion that Deuteronomy is not a book about Moses but a book in which Moses insists to his audience that what was revealed before, dur-ing, and after Sinai is of immediate and permanent relevance to them and their descendents.[3] Claims of divine authorship or even divine re-sponsibility for its contents or its formulation of basic ideas are absent from Deuteronomy, just as they are from Genesis.

Accordingly, it may be concluded that just as the Pentateuch includes in Deuteronomy Moses' personal speeches to Israel, it includes in Genesis Moses' personal presentation of traditions about the origins of the cos-mos, of humanity, and of Israel. In the Pentateuch, neither Genesis nor Deuteronomy is presented as part of the revelation at Sinai or part of anything that followed. Their inclusion in the Pentateuch, however, may be taken as an indication that both compositions were approved and authorized.

This traditional approach requires some tweaking on the basis of observations about writing and language.

ALPHABET CHANGE

Whether Moses wrote the first biblical text around 1491–1451 BCE, according to Bishop Ussher's dating system, or between 1270 and 1170 BCE, according to some contemporary scholars, research into the history of the alphabet indicates that what Moses wrote differed in appearance con-siderably from what is printed today in Hebrew Bibles and from what is written by trained Jewish scribes on the specially prepared parchment scrolls used in synagogues.

What is now commonly called the "Hebrew" alphabet is actually an Aramaic alphabet developed by people centered on ancient Damascus who spoke a language related to Hebrew. All biblical texts written in what scholars call the "old Hebrew" or "Palaeo-Hebrew" alphabet were transcribed into the Aramaic alphabet between the fifth and the second centuries BCE after the Persian ruler Cyrus the Great conquered the ancient Near East and allowed Jews to return from the Babylonian exile to areas around Jerusalem in 539 BCE. The Persian empire had adopted Aramaic, along with its alphabet, as its official language in the territories that it controlled from southern Egypt to northern India. By 350 BCE, Bible texts were being recopied using the new alphabet, and the old one was increasingly forgotten. Medieval Jewish tradition preserved in the Babylonian Talmud took the historical change in alphabets into account and offered an explanation: Ezra made the change officially with divine approval when he returned from the Babylonian exile to Jerusalem (*b. Sanhedrin* 21b–22a).

Only Samaritans, an ancient community with historical roots in the biblical period whose members viewed themselves as the authentic possessors and guardians of ancient Israelite traditions, resisted the changeover (2 Kings 17:24–32).[4] To this day, they copy Pentateuch scrolls in an evolved form of the Palaeo-Hebrew alphabet and use it in their liturgical books as well as for public bulletins and a community newspaper published in Israel.[5]

In addition to having been written in some early form of the Palaeo-Hebrew alphabet that emerged in the tenth century BCE, Moses' text may not have shown one word separated from the next. The words may have been written as a continuous string of letters, or a dot or short vertical line or a space may have separated one word from another. The text would not have had any punctuation equivalent to periods and commas to indicate boundaries between sentences and pauses within them. Furthermore, it would have been written without any indication of which vowels should be pronounced after consonants. A similar phenomenon in English would result in the following: "smlr phnmnn n nlgsh wld rslt n th fllwng" or even "smlrphnmnnnnlgshwldrsltnthfllwng" (both are repetitions of the previous English sentence).

Graphic signs signaling readers to pause between phrases, to stop between sentences, usually by lowering the voice, and informing them exactly which vowels to pronounce with each consonant were invented for Hebrew only after the sixth century CE, around the same time that

Hebrew Alphabets

This figure illustrates, right to left, how the personal names Adam and Hawwa, the Hebrew word for serpent, *nāḥāš*, and the toponym Eden would have appeared in a fourteenth–thirteenth-century BCE pre-Hebrew alphabet (top line), a ninth-century BCE Hebrew alphabet (second line), a seventh–sixth-century BCE Hebrew alphabet (third line), and a modern Hebrew alphabet evolved from a fifth–fourth-century BCE Aramaic alphabet (bottom line). Each word is written from right to left with signs indicating consonants only: *ʾdm, ḥwh, nḥš,* and *ʿdn*. Every letter in the top line bears a strong resemblance to the Egyptian hieroglyph from which it was originally derived. (Drawing by Debby Segura.)

Beowulf stories were being formulated orally. Until the invention of these signs—combinations of dots and marks over and under the Hebrew letters—much of the information on how to read and pronounce the text was transmitted as part of a complicated oral tradition memorized by specialists. (See the Appendix to this book.)

LANGUAGE CHANGE AND HEBREW

All natural languages—languages spoken by people in the course of their daily lives—change. New words enter, and old words drop out of use, often then being known only to scholars. For example, we use "truth," not "sooth," except in the rare word "soothsayer." Few of us use the words "thou, thee, thine," which once marked singulars in contrast to the plurals "you, you, your." Words change meanings and can be used metaphorically. For example, in contemporary American English, "cool" can refer to clothing and "hot" to music. In these contexts, neither refers to a temperature gradient.

Contemporary speakers of English who wish to read *Beowulf* in the original must study Old English, sometimes called Anglo-Saxon, from about 1,300 years ago. They learn that Old English *idel, giedd, wynn* translate into Modern English as *worthless, word, bliss.* If they select Chaucer's *Canterbury Tales*, they have to master the Middle English of about 625 years ago and learn to translate Middle English *port, holt, jape* with Modern English *demeanor, grove, joke.* Even Shakespeare's Elizabethan English, a mere 425 years old, which was quite comprehensible to his largely illiterate and uneducated audience in the pit of London's Globe Theatre, has to be learned with some effort and investment of time by contemporary English speakers. Most students of English read Shakespeare from glossed texts and learn to translate Elizabethan *fond, brave, roundly* by Modern English *foolish, splendid, plainly.*

Grammar changes, not only vocabulary. Nowadays, English tolerates lack of agreement in number between a noun and the pronoun that stands in for it or between a subject and its verb in conversation. For example, someone may say, "Everyone looks out for their own interests" or "There's a couple of mistakes." Educated speakers of American English from both the East and West coasts increasingly fail to distinguish between "me" and "I" when the pronoun marks an indirect object: "The company sent presents to Bob Smith, Mark Jones, and I." Although a phenomenon of casual speech, this confusion of pronouns can be heard in banter and interviews on both radio and television. It is en route to becoming an accepted feature of formal speech and may eventually penetrate the written language.

Hebrew changed because it was a natural language. What scholars now call biblical Hebrew was written in formal registers of a language that was constantly evolving over more than a millennium. On the basis of the study of Hebrew vocabulary, grammar, and syntax in the Bible itself in comparison to the poetry and prose of other, related ancient Semitic languages such as Akkadian, Aramaic, Phoenician, and Ugaritic (an ancient Canaanite language discovered by French archaeologists in 1928 and deciphered by 1931), contemporary scholars distinguish between Archaic Hebrew, Standard or Classical Iron Age Hebrew, in which most of the Hebrew Bible is written, and Post-Exilic Hebrew.

Archaic Hebrew was in use until around 1000 BCE, before David established Jerusalem as his capital. Standard Iron Age Hebrew was employed from 1000 until 586 BCE—the year Nebuchadnezzar's army captured Jerusalem, destroyed Solomon's temple, and exiled leading families from Judah to Babylon. It continued in use around Jerusalem until around 520 BCE. Then, under the impact of large groups of returnees from Babylon in the fifth century BCE, people whose Hebrew had been affected by the pronunciation habits, vocabulary, and syntax of their spoken

Aramaic and Akkadian dialects, Standard Iron Age Hebrew changed. Around 450 BCE, distinctive forms of Post-Exilic Hebrew emerged that can be found in the biblical books of Ezra, Nehemiah, Ecclesiastes, Esther, and the books of Chronicles. Over the next two hundred years, this Post-Exilic Hebrew evolved into what scholars characterize as Rabbinic, Tannaitic, or Mishnaic Hebrew, also referred to as the Hebrew of Late Antiquity (ca. 200 BCE–300 CE).

This last stage, with its own subdivisions by time period and regional dialect, was the language of Jesus Ben Sirah (ca. 180 BCE). It was the language of Hillel and his students and of the authors of the Dead Sea Scrolls. Jesus of Nazareth and his early disciples spoke it in the first century CE, albeit with an accent influenced by their second spoken language, Galilean Aramaic. Rabbis cited in the Mishnah, compiled at the end of the second century CE, spoke it also.[6] In this Hebrew of Late Antiquity, hundreds of biblical words dropped out of use, replaced by new ones borrowed from Aramaic. Old nouns and verbs lost certain nuances and developed new meanings, and loan words from Greek and Latin were adopted. The whole verbal system changed, becoming simpler and less sophisticated than that of the classical language in which the Garden story had been written. People speaking this language in the second century CE were no longer able to comprehend biblical Hebrew with ease.[7] Shakespeare's English is for us as the Hebrew in the Garden story was for them.

As this compact history of early Hebrew shows, if Moses wrote originally in Archaic Hebrew, his composition has been revised linguistically. This is because the bulk of the Pentateuch, including the Garden story, is known only in Standard Iron Age Hebrew of the type in use between 1000 and 586 BCE. The ancient revisers retained archaic Hebrew only in some tightly wrought poetry, such as the Song of Lamech (Gen 4:23–24), Blessings of Jacob (Gen 49), Song of Heshbon (Num 21:26–30), Songs of Balaam (Num 23–24), and the Blessings of Moses (Deut 33:1–29). The language of these ancient poems did not lend itself to updating without destroying their literary quality, and so they were left more or less alone. Where they occur in historical narratives within the Pentateuch, these poems provided a touch of textured, linguistic authenticity, reminding the audience that the characters in the story did not actually speak "modern" Iron Age Hebrew but an archaic form of the language.[8] As a consequence of these changes and despite the best efforts of modern scholars employing the latest linguistic insights and discoveries, important elements in the vocabulary and grammar of many biblical texts remain unclear; translation is uncertain, and interpretation tentative. I encountered a number of such cases while working on this book.

The ancient updating of prose from an archaic form into a standardized, more comprehensible Iron Age Hebrew may have been encouraged sometime after the dedication of Solomon's Temple and the emergence of Jerusalem as a major religious and administrative center (ca. 940–930 BCE). Encouraged by the royal court and by priests, the project could have been deemed necessary so that all Israel would be able to comprehend and learn from the ancient tales when they were read aloud. There is no way for contemporary researchers to know objectively what was affected by the revision and certainly no way to reconstruct the original forms of these texts.

Under the best of circumstances, then, what is available in the twenty-first century of the Common Era are the contents of the text of the Pentateuch as curated by pious scribes after the tenth-century BCE linguistic "updating" in Jerusalem. This text, however, is known only in a form of the alphabet handed down by scribes who changed the alphabet after the fifth century BCE. Allowing for these developmental changes and assuming that everything was preserved carefully over the centuries, Moses' own approved compositions, along with his records of revelation in what Jewish tradition came to call the Torah, we may treat the Garden story as the work of Moses. It must, however, be read, translated, and interpreted by those who are aware that its language is layered historically and who are capable of working through its nuances to make the story comprehensible.[9]

THE LITERARY-HISTORICAL APPROACH

The literary-historical approach to the question of who wrote the Garden story—also known as the philological-historical or the historical-critical approach—recognizes the special status of Deuteronomy, where Moses wrote in the first person, and likewise recognizes that narratives in Genesis are not characterized as revealed information. It points out, however, that the omniscient narrator whose voice begins in Genesis 1 and who presents God as an actor in its stories continues to narrate in the stories of Exodus, Leviticus, and Numbers. This narrator introduces only the legal sections found from Exodus 12:1 through Numbers 36:13, using formulas such as "And the Lord said to Moses," "These are the laws and statutes which the Lord commanded the children of Israel by way of Moses," and the like. Nowhere, aside from these introductions to laws, does the narrating voice directly or indirectly attribute stories or other types of information to a divine author.[10]

In addition, the literary-historical approach observes that almost all legislation concerned with purity, sacrifice, rituals, and formal observances related to the Tabernacle have their own unique vocabulary and phraseology. Consequently, after synthesizing these observations and collections of data, this approach distinguishes three gross literary blocks in the Pentateuch: (1) Deuteronomy, labeled "D" for the Deuteronomy (or Deuteronomic) source (with the exception of Deuteronomy 34:1–9), (2) some narratives and almost all ritual and cultic legislation in Exodus, Leviticus, and Numbers, labeled "P" for the Priestly source, and (3) most narratives from Genesis through Numbers. This last block has a complicated history and is subdivided into constituent units.

Biblicists applying the literary-historical approach observe that in some narratives the deity is named Lord (= Hebrew *Yahweh*, Gen 11:1–9; 12:1–20), and in others, God (= Hebrew *Elohim*, Gen 1:1–31; 9:1–17). They also observe that sometimes stories are repeated with slight variations in time, plot, and characters (Gen 12:10–20; 20:1–18; 26:6–22) or even with contradictory variations (Gen 32:28–29; 35:9). Then, to explain the origin of these differences, scholars hypothesize that they arose when oral traditors introduced "static and noise" into the original tales, generating different versions of them. These were eventually set down in writing. On the basis of these and other relevant criteria, scholars divide the literature of the third literary block in the Pentateuch into three main sources of unequal size. Two are conventionally labeled by the divine name that they use in narratives until Exodus 3: "J" for the Yahwist source (Yahwist is an English form of the original German *Jahwist*, pronounced /Yahwist/, because in German, *J* is sounded as /Y/), and *E* for the Elohist. The third source in this block is narrative material from P. Miscellaneous items such as small poems and genealogical lists are treated differently by different researchers and are not relevant to this brief description.[11]

The Pentateuch as a whole, then, is held to have originated through the studied editing of these disparate sources, each with its own literary history, into a single composition by one or more redactors. Although the process described sounds somewhat beyond imagination, compositions from Late Antiquity and the ancient Near East illustrate it clearly.[12] Three examples clarify the process.

The *Diatessaron*, a second-century CE harmonization of the Gospels by Tatian, deemed heretical by the early church, shows that the description of how the Pentateuch came into existence is not far-fetched. Tatian undertook to write a single, composite gospel using verses from the traditional four, Matthew, Mark, Luke, and John. His objective was to eliminate all disagreements between them while preserving all or most of the unique details in each, such as the different accounts of the baptism and temptation of Jesus in all four and the birth narratives in Matthew and Luke.[13] His *Diatessaron* was used in Syrian churches until the fifth century.

The Samaritan Pentateuch contains a story of the revelation at Sinai that conflates Exodus 20:18–26 with Deuteronomy 5:22–30. It uses Deuteronomy to supplement the Exodus version. The resultant text is composed of the following snippets connected by six joins: Exodus 20:18–19a + Deuteronomy 5:24–27 + Exodus 20:19b–22 + Deuteronomy 5:28b–29 + Deuteronomy 18:18–22a + Deuteronomy 5:30 + Exodus 20:22b–26. Samaritans have read this version of the story in their Torah for almost two thousand years.[14]

The *Gilgamesh Epic* in its Babylonian form was discovered in the library of the seventh-century BCE Assyrian king Ashurbanipal. On the basis of historiographic documents dated to circa 2200–2100 BCE, Gilgamesh is known to have lived in southern Mesopotamia a few centuries earlier, circa 2700–2500 BCE. Stories featuring him were recorded in Sumerian, a non-Semitic language used in what is now southeast Iraq, as early as 2100 BCE. Five texts exist. These were copied, edited, and translated into Akkadian, a Semitic language, around 1600 BCE. Subsequently, names of some characters were changed, stories were combined, and poems were interpolated, resulting in the late versions from Ashurbanipal's library. Inconsistencies in the story line often reflect "seams" where originally distinct stories were joined when formulating the new composition. The latest known versions of the story are found in texts written during the second century BCE.[15]

The important question for individuals open to this approach, then, is not whether this type of composition was practiced, since the preceding examples illustrate that it was, but whether it played a role in the formation of the Pentateuch.[16]

Each of the identified Pentateuchal sources is generally recognized as being in Iron Age Hebrew. Those sections in archaic Hebrew are usually assigned to a miscellaneous category of traditional lore known to the authors of J and E, who, like the redactors of *Gilgamesh,* selected poems and inserted them selectively into their compositions. The sources themselves, however, are assigned to different centuries within the Iron Age. According to most scholars working with this approach, J and E, which provide most of the narrative in Genesis, Exodus, and Numbers, are dated between 900 and 700 BCE. D is usually dated 700–600 BCE, and P falls between 600 and 500 BCE.[17] All four sources maintained that Moses recorded instructions and laws revealed for Israel, but not that all recorded material was revealed.

Most contemporary scholars who work with the literary-historical approach admit that historical, linguistic, and literary criteria permit them to determine only the final date by which each source came into existence as a document. By 500 BCE, at the latest, early in the Persian period, they were edited into a single composition that, owing to its length, had to be written on five scrolls of papyrus or parchment. Its modern names, the Pentateuch or the Five Books of Moses, that seem to be no earlier than the second century BCE, reflect the idea that it is a single composition divided into five parts.

Much, if not most, of the material recorded in the Yahwist, Elohist, and Priestly sources originated and was first preserved in the oral lore of tribes and by the personnel overseeing major religious centers. Later, these traditions were reduced to writing. Consequently, we understand that the preserved oral traditions are older than the final date of the written sources.

After all the theorizing and close analysis that almost four centuries of scholarship have produced, the Garden story considered below, regularly assigned to the J source, is considered the distillation of a literary tradition whose oral antecedents took shape around two centuries earlier, around 1100 BCE, close to some of the dates proposed by the Mosaic-authorship approach.

PRECURSORS TO THE LITERARY-HISTORICAL APPROACH

Although the type of historical thinking underlying the literary-historical approach is modern—it began to develop in western Europe only

during the seventeenth century and came to fruition during the nineteenth and early twentieth centuries—some thinkers reached similar conclusions more than eighteen hundred years ago but did not express them
systematically. What is possibly the earliest datable reference to a multiplicity of sources in the Pentateuch is from the second century CE.

Ptolemy, a Christian theologian associated with the Valentinian tradition of Gnosticism (deemed heretical in the orthodox Christian tradition),
addressed a letter to a woman named Flora around 150 CE in which he
presents as something well known in certain circles the idea that so-called
Mosaic laws actually had multiple authors:

> Now, first you must learn that, as a whole, the law contained in the
> Pentateuch of Moses was not established by a single author, I mean not
> by god alone: rather, there are certain of its commandments that were
> established by human beings as well. Indeed, our savior's words teach
> us that the Pentateuch divides into three parts. For one division belongs
> to God himself and his legislations; while (another division) belongs to
> Moses—indeed, Moses ordained certain of the commandments not as
> god himself ordained through him, rather based in his own thoughts
> about the matter; and yet a third division belongs to the elders of the
> people, (who) likewise in the beginning must have inserted certain of
> their own commandments. You will now learn how this can be demon-
> strated from the savior's words.[18]

In this crucial paragraph of his letter, Ptolemy does not present the idea
of multiple authorship as something new in general, only something new
to Flora. Assuming its correctness, however, Ptolemy's point is that the
claim can be supported literarily and theologically through citations
from the New Testament, and it is this demonstration that fills the pages
of his letter.

During the same period that Ptolemy is writing to Flora, different rabbis in the Land of Israel are making statements to similar effect. Despite
not being part of the main Jewish tradition of understanding the revelation of the Torah, their views are cited, noticed, and preserved in
various rabbinic compilations. For example, the Talmud refers to Sages,
mentioning the prominent compiler of the Mishnah, Rabbi Judah (end
of second century CE), who said that Joshua wrote the last eight verses of
Deuteronomy 34, which refer to the death of Moses (*b. Bava Batra* 14b,
15a). Others thought that Moses did not write any of the twelve verses of

chapter 34. These opinions are based on the logical unlikeliness of Moses' describing his own death or boasting about his own uniqueness among the prophets before there were other prophets among the Israelites.

Rabbi Ishmael (middle of second century CE) suggested that the Book of the Covenant, roughly Exodus 21:1–24:8, was given by Moses to Israel before the revelation at Sinai (*Mechilta de-Rabbi Ishmael, Bahodesh* 3). His opinion may rest on verses such as Exodus 15:24, about events at Marah, a place traversed before the Israelites arrived at Sinai, "and there he gave him a set rule," and Exodus 18:13–27, which describe the organization of a hierarchically organized judiciary adjudicating disputes on the basis of a known body of law before the Sinai revelation.

Commenting on Deuteronomy 1:2, Abraham Ibn Ezra, a twelfth-century commentator, points to a number of anachronistic passages in the Pentateuch: Genesis 12:6 ("and the Canaanites were then in the land"), Genesis 22:14 ("in the mountain where the Lord is seen"), Deuteronomy 3:11 ("behold his bedstead was a bedstead of iron"), and Deuteronomy 34:1–12 (reporting his death). He notes that Moses could not have written them.[19] His comment on these verses is, "If you understand the secret of [these verses] . . . you will recognize the truth." In his comment to Genesis 12:6 he writes: "It is likely that the Canaanites had just conquered the land from someone else [in the time of Abraham; otherwise why would Moses have had to mention it?], but if that is not the case [that is, if the verse was written at a time when there were no longer Canaanites in the land because they had been killed off in the days of Joshua and the author felt that he had to draw his readers' attention to the existence of Canaanites in the land in the days of Abraham], there is a secret here and the one who understands it will remain silent." Ibn Ezra's views, unlike those of Ptolemy, actually influenced the development of contemporary ways of studying the Pentateuch that form the literary-historical approach.

CONTEMPORARY CONSERVATIVE VARIATIONS

Both the Mosaic-authorship and the literary-historical approaches focus on the literature of the Pentateuch. The first emphasizes continuities and prefers to avoid complexities that historical considerations introduce to a consideration of the text. The second emphasizes literary discontinuities and posits complex historical considerations to explain them. In this section, I present views by two contemporary conservative scholars, one Christian and one Jewish. The first introduces history into the first approach, and the second removes it from the second. Each does what he does in order to tweak and improve an approach that he believes is essentially insightful, useful, and not in opposition to faith.

Kenneth A. Kitchen, a world-class Egyptologist and scholar of ancient Near Eastern civilizations, argues that the Pentateuch was written by Moses in a thirteenth-century BCE dialect of Hebrew in 1220–1180 BCE using an archaic alphabet. As Hebrew changed into the form known from the Pentateuch and after Israelites developed the Old Hebrew alphabet in the tenth century BCE, the Pentateuch text was updated, in the days of David and Solomon. Although scribes transcribing it into the newer alphabet and making copies of it may have changed certain points, Kitchen insists that the underlying text is Mosaic, not a mosaic of sources. He buttresses his position with comprehensive argumentation from archaeological data and a flood of references to ancient Israel's sophisticated cultural milieu. In that cultural context, many adjacent peoples employed writing to preserve sacred texts and to record ritual and sacrificial instructions. Additionally, they used writing to maintain records of events, to carry out commercial transactions, and to conduct personal correspondence. Kitchen observes that in particularly long-lived civilizations, such as those of Egypt and Mesopotamia, writing systems were modified and texts were recopied over centuries, with relatively little loss of essential content. Israel, he argues, did likewise.[20]

Mordechai Breuer (1921–2007), a prominent Orthodox rabbi and author of many scholarly works on the history of the Bible reading traditions and exegesis, asserts that the division of the Pentateuch into four sources cannot be refuted. He argues that acknowledging the sources is perfectly compatible with the notion of a divine revelation to Moses. According to Breuer, the objectively identified differences in vocabulary, style, and theology, along with the internal contradictions and repeated stories, must be acknowledged as part and parcel of the revelation to Moses. Moses recorded all as a prophet.[21] Consequently, Breuer argues that they are there to challenge readers, to be studied and to be explained, not to be explained away apologetically. By recognizing the presence of four literary strands in the Pentateuch while categorically rejecting their description as documents originating in different historical periods, Breuer combines aspects of both the Mosaic-authorship and the literary-historical approaches.

Breuer himself believes on dogmatic grounds that at Sinai, Moses was simply a recording secretary. That makes the complex text of the Pentateuch what was revealed. The task of exegetes is to clarify it and explain its implicit lessons for contemporary readers. Breuer is acutely aware, however, that many cannot or do not accept his dogmatic assertion about the role of Moses. Commenting on the question of whether Moses wrote all of the Pentateuch, Breuer states that the answer to the question is of no major theological consequence in Judaism. He observes that nowhere in classical Jewish sources is it claimed that those who deny Moses' composition of the Torah lose their share in the world to come. Only those who deny the absolute divinity of the Torah are so condemned (*b. Sanhedrin* 90a).[22]

Breuer's approach is very heavy on the "literary" and absolutely unresponsive and hostile to historical considerations. His uncompromising views allow little space for conversation. Kitchen's approach, in contrast, is heavy on the "historical" and generally, but not absolutely, unresponsive to the literary analysis of critical scholars. He does allow, though, for slight changes in the text that may have crept in over the centuries during which scribes copied and recopied the text.

SOME CONCLUSIONS

According to both the Mosaic-authorship and the literary-historical approaches, the Garden story was available to Israelites during the Iron Age in the form that it is encountered today. It is not that the approaches represent two ways of saying the same thing, but with regard to this important conclusion, they are almost congruent.[23]

In following chapters, I refer to "the author" or to "the narrator." This form of reference indicates my particular stand regarding the two approaches. I picture "the author" as a ninth-century BCE man who worked with traditional lore in fashioning the story. For readers more comfortable with the Mosaic-authorship approach, my author is the pious, perhaps inspired scribe who updated the language of the earlier version of the story and spruced it up to make it comprehensible to readers and hearers of his age. This occurred after the Hebrew of Jerusalem had emerged as the literary dialect of the southern kingdom of Judah.

After preparing his ink, our scribe sat down at his writing table, stylus in hand, a clean sheet of papyrus or parchment before him, and the traditions of his people in mind. At that moment, like most authors, he had only vague sense of what he wanted to communicate through the story that he was about to record. As he dipped his stylus in ink, he had to decide on the details that he would present and those that he would omit. He considered the speeches that he would spell out and those that he would leave out. He had to decide on a timeline. Then he had to determine who would be present in any given scene and who would be absent, who would be foregrounded and who backgrounded. He had to conceive of how the entire story would work itself out and how he wanted it to affect his audience. Since there could be no effect if nobody listened, it was essential that his audience be drawn into the narrative, that they find the story intriguing and convincing. Our scribe's story had to follow his readers' storytelling conventions and make sense within their culture, which was also his own.

The challenge for a contemporary reader is how to access this culture and hear the story the way those for whom it was written did, insofar as this is possible. Contemporary literary theory provides a way.

4   WHAT IS A READER-RESPONSE APPROACH
TO INTERPRETING THE GARDEN STORY?

To approach the Garden story free of its Hellenistic-bred, centuries-old interpretation as the story of the Fall, I employ loosely a method labeled "reader-response criticism." Following this method, I examine the relationship between author and original audience by considering what they knew and what was new in what the author was presenting. None of this can occur without studying the major objective element available for critical analysis: the text. Considering the text a communication intended to inform and educate its readers and hearers makes it possible to suggest, using controlled imagination, what effect it may have had on them.[1]

THE READERS

The imagined readers of the ninth-century BCE author (introduced at the end of Chapter 3) were Israelites from the tribal kingdom of Judah. Mainly they were from among the social elites associated with the Jerusalem palace and temple. They were aware of other languages and cultures, of distant peoples and places. Their cultural memory linked them both to Mesopotamia, from where they believed Abraham had come and where Jacob had lived for more than two decades, and to Egypt, where many of their ancestors had been enslaved. Yet their awareness of these centers was based on more than oral traditions and historical memories. These Israelites had occasional living contact with people from these centers through trade, war, and diplomacy and through more intimate contact with foreigners who resided among them temporarily or permanently as "alien residents" and as slaves (Exod 12:48; 20:10; Deut 14:21). Through these contacts, Israelites knew something of their stories, myths, and folkways.

By 850 BCE, the lives and times of David and Solomon and their kingdom of united tribes were historical memories. Many of these memories were passed down orally; others were official and authorized, preserved in royal chronicles.

By 850 BCE, the dialect of Jerusalem Hebrew flourished as a significant literary and administrative language used for writing chronicles, prophecy, psalmody, wisdom literature—all genres found in the Bible—as well as tax receipts, military instructions, and inscriptions such as those found in archaeological excavations. All Israelites were aware of writing as a technology for recording speech in one place so that it could be respoken somewhere else. In fact, the Hebrew word usually translated "to read" is *qārā'*, which means "to call out." Reading, that is, calling out a text, was a type of performance art based on reciting.

Most Israelites of the ninth century BCE, and throughout the period identified by archaeologists as the Iron Age (1150–586 BCE), were probably illiterate. Most could not read or write freely, because these skills were not necessary for them in their quotidian activities. When they required that something be written or read, they had access to trained scribes. The author of the Garden story knew all this when he imagined his audience of readers and listeners.[2]

THE RESPONSE

In the context of this book, "response" refers to how those imagined readers perceived the Garden story as a story, as verbal art, and as a message. It implies that readers know the linguistic and aesthetic conventions of their own culture, with its social, legal, and institutional norms, as well as with its habits of thought and implicit anthropology. The idea behind reader-response criticism is what makes books like this possible. Readers and authors share a language, a culture, and many types of knowledge about the times in which they live and about the past.

My objective in using this approach is to propose an understanding of the Garden story that would have been comprehensible to imagined Jerusalemite-Judahite readers in their social-historical and cultural setting. Under the best of circumstances, this approach, which involves getting into the heads of ancient people, can aspire only to a high degree of probability, not to scientific exactitude. Although it might seem at first glance that this type of undertaking is purely subjective, such is not the case.

KEEPING THE ANALYSIS HONEST

To be plausible and probable, my analysis must conform to the worldview of the Judahites and base itself only on those types of factual knowledge available to them. It may employ only the modes of reasoning they practiced. These facts and modes of reasoning are known imperfectly to contemporary scholarship through linguistic, historical, and archaeological research into the cultures of ancient Israel and adjacent ancient Near Eastern peoples. This research illuminates the cultural climate within which the Garden story was told, retold, written, read aloud, interpreted, and transmitted.

The objective is achievable only by engaging the story in the original language of its composition. Accordingly, the following analysis involves restudying the vocabulary and grammar of this oft-studied tale in the Jerusalem dialect of Hebrew. This undertaking is necessary because most discussions and analyses of the story presuppose a conventional understanding of its language as reflected in standard translations into European languages. Unfortunately, these translations are simultaneously and inevitably both standard and standardizing interpretations. When authorized by clerical organizations, these translations are guaranteed to reflect an "official" understanding based on particular interpretations. Such translations are not necessarily incorrect, but they are often inexact. Consequently, interpretations based on them alone are suspect and almost invite readers sensitive to the problem of "translation as betrayal" to raise both linguistic and historical questions. It is legitimate to inquire why a particular word or phrase or sentence is translated as A and not B, especially when recent research suggests that B is more accurate.

Consider, for example, most standard translations of Genesis 1:1, the first verse of the Bible, which consists of seven Hebrew words. All offer some form of the following: "In the beginning God created the heaven and the earth." On the basis of this well-known rendering, it can be argued that the ancient Israelites believed in *creatio ex nihilo*, that is, creation out of nothing. This happens not to be the case. The famous rendering of this verse actually reflects an interpretation imposed on the Hebrew by Greek-speaking translator-interpreters of the Hellenistic period in the second century BCE. The ancient Jewish translators, perhaps influenced by Aristotle's notion of First Cause and Unmoved Mover, melded popular versions of Aristotelian ideas into their Hellenistic comprehension of God, producing an understanding of creation that became normative in Judaism by the first century BCE and then normative in Christianity from its onset in the first century CE, 150 years later.

A stricter, non-interpretive translation of the same verse is "In the beginning of God's creating the heavens and the earth," which indicates that this verse is not a sentence but a circumstantial clause in a long, complicated sentence spread over three biblical verses. It describes the state of matter in the cosmos before God set about ordering the chaotic mix of darkness, earth, wind, and water to create the heavens and the earth. That single sentence ends "and there was light." A more accurate translation of Genesis 1:1–3, one reflecting the worldview of its author and his original audience, is the following:

> In the beginning of God's creating the heavens and the earth—and the earth was unformed and void and darkness over the face of the deep and a wind of God [or "a powerful wind"] hovering over the face of the waters—and God said, "Let there be light," and there was light.

Most Bible readers are not sensitive to such a worldview because both Christianity and Judaism came to understand creation in Aristotelian terms and because the verse resonates for New Testament readers with the first verse in the Gospel of John: "In the beginning was the Word and the Word was with God and the Word was God." In translations of Genesis 1:1–3, theology trumped linguistic accuracy. In other words, the functional role of this verse in the life and thought of the religious community gave rise to the ex nihilo interpretation/translation. People knew, whether they read the verse or not, what it had to mean. The Greek translation, as a consequence, failed to reflect the meaning of the verse in its original literary, intellectual, and historical contexts, but succeeded in making the unfamiliar familiar, both in language and in conception, to its Greek-speaking, Hellenized audiences. By not replicating the original, it created a text accessible to people no longer part of the cultural world conjured up by the term "ancient Near East."

In the original ancient Near Eastern context, before Aristotle, when the words of Genesis 1:1–3 were written in Hebrew, it was common knowledge that before the extant cosmos was created, deities coexisted with unformed matter. For example, the nine-hundred-line Babylonian creation story, *Enumma Elish*, begins:

> When on high the heavens had not been named,
> and below, the earth had not been called by name,
> when Apsu primeval, their begetter,
> and creatrix Tiamat, who bore them all,
> mingled their waters together,
> and when no reeds sprouted and no marsh land appeared,
> when no gods had been made to exist,
> and had not been called by name,
> and their destinies had not been decreed,
> then gods were formed within them.

The biblical account and the roughly contemporaneous *Enumma Elish* reflect the same idea and express it using similar longish sentences containing many clauses to describe circumstances at the time of creation. After the opening line, however, each story develops differently. The Babylonian epic is about creation and the rise of Marduk to the head of the pantheon. The Genesis 1 account is about the deliberate, benign creation of the world as a place for humanity and about the importance of the Sabbath day. Every phase of creative pronouncements or acts measured out in days is evaluated as "good" or "very good." Because each narrative sprang from unique circumstances in different places, each addressed the concerns of its own culture and exploited the riches and the possibilities inherent in its own language.

Historically oriented reader-response criticism helps eliminate certain approaches to the Garden story as unjustified and without foundation. Accordingly, the analysis of the story in the rest of this book does not address it as a tale of men and gods in which characters are interpreted as embodiments of ideas such as truth, virtue, or cupidity. The story is not interpreted as a veiled account of a historical event or process—such as the ascent of a particular ancient tribe, say, the Adamites, to power. Nor does it regard the story as a typological tale in which Adam and Hawwa foreshadow particular types of later people, such as royal elites and Israelite peasants. It does not consider the Garden story as one that provides hints or insights into secret lore or mystical doctrines. All of these interpretive strategies have already been used to explain the story, or to explain it away, or to make it make sense so that the Bible could be taken seriously, or to clarify it for theological reasons. None of these reasons for reading, or objectives for analyzing, the story interests me.

As read and understood in ancient Israel, the Garden story was a tale about real people, the primeval progenitors, who had lived very long ago and very far away. The reader-response approach enables us to ask what it meant to those who read it in ancient Israel, not how may it be interpreted in a manner pleasing to the sensibilities of people in the twenty-first century.

5   READING, PRESENTING, AND EVALUATING

THE GARDEN STORY

This chapter describes briefly how the middle part of this book is structured and why.

In this middle part, Part II, beginning with Chapter 6, I divide the Garden story into units of narrative, each of which I discuss in a separate chapter using a method called *explication de texte:* the explication, explanation, exposition, exegesis, and interpretation of the text. Users of this method take little for granted about the meaning of each unit, attempting, rather, to study the text as a lover might pore over a love letter or as a litigant might scrutinize a document sent by opposing counsel. Generally, I examine words, then phrases, then sentences. Following that examination, I comment on the unit as a whole, connecting its details to the life and culture of ancient Israel. Generally, but not always.

Since each unit elicits its own questions, discussions in each chapter differ. In some I focus on the plot and its protagonists; in others on ideas about family or about justice; and in still others on human anatomy, clothing, or geography. In a number of chapters I focus on how the author manipulated his language to create literary effects or to present information conveying particular ideas. My reason for adopting the methodology of *explication de texte* is that it is flexible and that it helped me produce a holistic comprehension of the Garden story.

AN INCOMPLETE TRANSLATION

Each unit discussed in Chapters 6–22 of Part II is presented by an incomplete translation, one that leaves in transliterated Hebrew the words and phrases to be discussed. These untranslated words and phrases are what I believe require elucidation and clarification. This incomplete translation, unlike standard ones, reflects Hebrew word order and stylistics as closely as possible with one significant exception. English, unlike narrative prose in biblical Hebrew, regularly places subjects before predicates. In this matter, I decided to bow to English convention for the sake of comprehension.

My decision concerning the order of subjects and predicates in the translation involves both a net gain and a net loss. The gain is a sense of familiarity and comfort with the text for English readers. The loss is that sense of tingling foreignness experienced when arriving for the first time at a place where people speak an incomprehensible language and appear to behave unusually. Unfamiliarity sharpens the sense of a linguistic and cultural gap, especially between contemporary English, written from left to right, and Classical Hebrew, written from right to left. It heightens anticipation about encountering new ways of viewing the world, acting within it, and thinking about it. For some, however, the experience can be disconcerting, uncomfortably disorienting, and off-putting.

THE ORDER OF WORDS IN THE TRANSLATION

English sentences usually have the following word order: Subject + Verb + modifying elements. Examples: Christopher + read + the book + yesterday. God + created + the heavens and the earth. The Lord + spoke + to Noah.

Biblical Hebrew narrative prose, however, regularly begins sentences with a conjunction, *and,* connected to a verb followed by the subject, which in turn is followed by modifying elements. This can be expressed in shorthand as follows: and + Verb + Subject + modifying elements. Were the first example from the preceding paragraph expressed in this order, it would come out dizzyingly as "And read Christopher the book yesterday."

Because the common order in Hebrew is Verb + Subject while that of English is Subject + Verb, strict translations adhering to the practice of the original are difficult to comprehend in English. A strict translation following the Hebrew word order of Genesis 7:1 could appear as follows: "And he-said YHWH [i.e., the Lord] to-Noah: 'Come you and all your-house to the-ark because you I-saw righteous before-me in-the-generation the-this.'" Words connected by a hyphen in this English translation represent a single word in the Hebrew original. In standard English the same verse reads: "And the Lord said to Noah, 'Come, you and your house into the ark because I saw you righteous before me in this generation.'"

To avoid strangeness, my translations from the Hebrew follow English convention without comment with two exceptions: Genesis 3:1 and 4:1. The text of these passages deviates from the Hebrew Verb + Subject order and deploys a Subject + Verb ordering of constituents. In both verses, the irregular and relatively uncommon Subject + Verb order affects the meaning of each verse profoundly and that of the story as a whole.

TRANSLITERATED HEBREW

Tourists who do not know the language of a country that they are visiting are familiar with phrasebooks listing expressions that they may need to get around or get along: words that translate into English as "Hello." "Where is X?" "How much?" "Please." Excuse me." The foreign equivalents are usually provided in Latin letters following English pronunciation patterns—or French or German, depending on the intended audience—saving travelers the trouble of having to learn an unfamiliar pronunciation system or even an unfamiliar writing system, such as those used to record Korean, Hindi, or Arabic. Working with familiar sounds and letters eliminates some of the foreignness of the unknown language. In the following chapters, transliteration helps slide readers past the barrier of the Hebrew alphabet while the meanings of Hebrew words are being reevaluated. The system adopted for this book is described in the Appendix.

WRITING THE DIVINE NAME

This book represents the divine name, sometimes written "Jehovah," as "YHWH." This spelling reflects the name's consonantal skeleton in Hebrew without the accompanying vowels. Jewish practice of at least the past twelve hundred years, ever since vowel notations were invented, marks the name with the vowels of the Hebrew word meaning "Lord";

the vowels direct readers to pronounce the name as if the Hebrew word for "Lord," *'adōnāy*, were actually written in the text. This is akin to seeing "etc." in a sentence but reading "and so on" rather than, as in Latin, "et cetera." The practice of not pronouncing the name is actually much older than twelve hundred years.

In the Greek translation of the Pentateuch, circa 250 BCE, the divine name was regularly translated with the Greek word *kyrios*, "Lord," indicating that although the translators saw the consonants *YHWH* in their Hebrew text, they read the Hebrew word *'adōnāy* and translated the word, not the name. Of greater significance, the Greek translation indicates that the Jewish scholars called Masoretes, who invented the system of recording vowels circa 600–700 CE, preserved an authentic reading tradition that can be dated to at least 250 BCE, more than eight centuries before their time.

The transliteration *Jehovah* originated when someone erroneously applied the vowels of *'adōnāy* to the consonants *YHWH. Jehovah* is an artificial concoction, its spelling with a *J* and *v* easily explained. In early English as in contemporary German, the letter *J* was pronounced /y/; Germanic languages spoken in countries where Jews settled during the Middle Ages did not have a /w/ consonant. Over time, Jews in these lands changed the pronunciation of the Hebrew consonantal *waw* from /w/ to /v/, and this change is reflected in the English spelling.

Though a proper name, YHWH is usually rendered as "Lord," as in the translation of Genesis 7:1 presented above. In some academic settings, and in academic journals and books, many scholars prefer to write the name out with vowels and to pronounce it "Yahweh," basing their vocalization, on the authority of Exodus 3:14–15, on a hypothesized form of the Hebrew verb meaning "to be."

In the following chapters, I regularly refer to the deity not by name but by *God*, a capitalized form of an old Germanic term meaning "deity." *God* is not God's personal name. This convention is of long standing and the reference is clear.

STANDARD TRANSLATION-INTERPRETATIONS

The reason for presenting the Garden story in small narrative units with an unconventional word order and with untranslated words is to establish grounds for a translation and an interpretation unlike standard

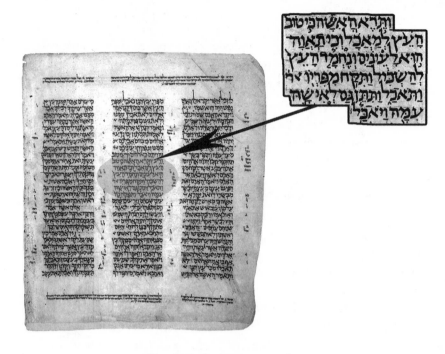

Genesis 3:6 in a Masoretic Codex

The Leningrad Codex, the oldest-known complete manuscript of the Hebrew Bible, was written in Cairo in 1010 by a scribe named Samuel ben Yaakov. Its letter shapes are similar to those of the Aramaic alphabet adopted for writing Hebrew much earlier, between 450 and 350 BCE. The dots, lines, and curves above, below, and sometimes within letters were invented and developed by Jewish scholars called Masoretes after the beginning of the sixth century CE. Their purpose was to indicate the vowels and pauses of different duration between groups of words, phrases, and sentences; the inset shows them in detail. Until their invention, all of this information was transmitted orally from readers of one generation to the next. (After a photograph by Bruce and Kenneth Zuckerman, West Semitic Research, with the collaboration of the Ancient Biblical Manuscript Center. Courtesy of the Russian National Museum [Saltykov-Shchedrin].)

ones in significant ways. It is therefore both useful and ethically proper to begin by considering four standard translation-interpretations of the Garden story that are highly regarded and widely used in churches, seminaries, colleges, and universities: the King James Version, the New Revised Standard Version, the New American Bible translation, and the New Jewish Publication Society translation. These are the translations through which most English readers encounter the Garden story in a prayer service, a study session, or a literature class.

The King James or Authorized Version (KJV) was first published in 1611. Translated from the original Hebrew by particularly gifted and accomplished Christian Hebraists, it remains the most popular and widely used translation of the Hebrew Bible into English. The American literary critic John Livingston Lowes (1867–1945) referred to it as "the noblest monument of English prose," a fitting description for reasons that he adumbrated in a 1936 essay.[1] Although many clergy, scholars, and teachers of English literature share his estimation of the literary excellence of this translation, they also consider it somewhat outdated as a translation for valid reasons. Changes in the English language since 1611 render parts of it difficult and even incomprehensible to contemporary readers, while many advances in the understanding of ancient Hebrew grammar and vocabulary over the past four centuries reveal that is incorrect in places. Nevertheless, the KJV, much beloved by those familiar with its elegantly cadenced prose, remains in wide use. It is publicly identified as a Protestant translation. One bonus of the KJV translation is that it uses italics to indicate those words added for clarity that are not in the original Hebrew text.

The New Revised Standard Version (NRSV) is a fourth-generation revision of the King James Version that takes into account changes in English and new knowledge about Hebrew. The changes that it introduces are based on accuracy, clarity, euphony, and current English usage. First published in 1989, the NRSV is authorized for use by major Christian churches: Protestant, Anglican, Roman Catholic, and Eastern Orthodox.[2]

Scholars of the Catholic Biblical Association of America translated the text of the New American Bible (NAB), first published in 1970, from the original languages. Their objective was to provide Catholics with a sense of the original biblical text in as correct a form as possible. Because the project was undertaken mainly to provide an accurate translation, not a paraphrase, translators did not necessarily tidy up the text by eliminating multiplied adjectives or simplifying figures of speech. As a consequence of its stilted English, the NAB is often less eloquent than the NRSV; but readers should appreciate that the NAB usually represents the original language faithfully. Occasional inelegancies in this translation signal to sensitive readers that the underlying Hebrew is not perfectly clear, grammatically correct, or unambiguous.[3]

The New Jewish Publication Society translation (NJPS), or Tanakh, as it is officially known, was published in 1985. Containing only the Hebrew Bible, unlike the others, which also contain the New Testament, it was intended to replace the Jewish Publication Society translation of 1917, which was, in many respects, a Jewish revision of the King James Version. The NJPS represents the work of Jewish scholars whose agenda was similar to that of the scholars who worked on the NRSV and the NAB except that in evaluating various possibilities when translating difficult passages, the NJPS translators also considered opinions propounded by Jewish grammarians, lexicographers, and exegetes from Late Antiquity through the seventeenth century, as well as the most recent advances in Hebrew and biblical studies by scholars of all faiths.[4]

I have chosen to present these four versions of the Garden story in Genesis synoptically, in parallel columns, which makes it easy to compare translations. In most cases where these parallel translations agree, the underlying Hebrew text offers few problems. Sometimes, however, agreement between the three modern translations simply reflects a conventional understanding about interpretation popular when the newer translations were published in the 1970s and 1980s. These types of agreement will be discussed in the following chapters. Throughout the following synoptic translations, I have normalized the typography of the word "Lord," not using all capital letters or a different font to distinguish it from other words. This follows the Hebrew convention of using standard letter shapes when writing the name of God.

Where translations disagree beyond preferences for different synonyms or alternative ways of expressing the same idea, disagreement signals that the meaning of the Hebrew and its interpretation have not been settled. The major reason for including these translations is to furnish readers with multiple benchmarks against which the translations, analyses, and comments in the chapters of Part II may be compared, contrasted, and evaluated.

King James Version (KJV)	New Revised Standard Version (NRSV)	New American Bible (NAB)	New Jewish Publication Society translation (NJPS)
Genesis 2	Genesis 2	Genesis 2	Genesis 2
see Chapter 6			
4. These *are* the generations of the heavens and of the earth when they were created, in the day that the Lord God made the earth and the heavens,	4. These are the generations of the heavens and the earth when they were created. In the day that the Lord God made the earth and the heavens,	4. Such is the story of heaven and earth at their creation. At the time when the Lord God made the earth and the heavens—	4. Such is the story of heaven and earth when they were created. When the Lord God made earth and heaven—
5. And every plant of the field before it was in the earth, and every herb of the field before it grew: for the Lord God had not caused it to rain upon the earth, and *there was* not a man to till the ground.	5. when no plant of the field was yet in the earth and no herb of the field had yet sprung up—for the Lord God had not caused it to rain upon the earth, and there was no one to till the ground;	5. while as yet there was no field shrub on earth and no grass of the field had sprouted, for the Lord God had sent no rain upon the earth and there was no man to till the soil,	5. when no shrub of the field was yet on earth and no grasses of the field had yet sprouted, because the Lord God had not sent rain upon the earth and there was no man to till the soil,
6. But there went up a mist from the earth, and watered the whole face of the ground.	6. but a stream would rise from the earth, and water the whole face of the ground—	6. but a stream was welling up out of the earth and was watering all the surface of the ground—	6. but a flow would well up from the ground and water the whole surface of the earth—
7. and the Lord God formed man *of* the dust of the ground and breathed into his nostrils the breath of life; and man became a living soul.	7. then the Lord God formed man from the dust of the ground, and breathed into his nostrils the breath of life; and the man became a living being.	7. the Lord God formed man out of the clay of the ground and blew into his nostrils the breath of life, and so man became a living being.	7. the Lord God formed man from the dust of the earth. He blew into his nostrils the breath of life, and man became a living being.

KJV	NRSV	NAB	NJPS
Genesis 2	Genesis 2	Genesis 2	Genesis 2

see Chapters 7–8

KJV	NRSV	NAB	NJPS
8. And the Lord God planted a garden eastward in Eden; and there he put the man whom he had formed.	8. And the Lord God planted a garden in Eden, in the east; and there he put the man whom he had formed.	8. Then the Lord God planted a garden in Eden, in the east, and he placed there the man whom he had formed.	8. The Lord God planted a garden in Eden, in the east, and placed there the man whom He had formed.
9. And out of the ground made the Lord God to grow every tree that is pleasant to the sight, and good for food; the tree of life also in the midst of the garden, and the tree of knowledge of good and evil.	9. Out of the ground the Lord God made to grow every tree that is pleasant to the sight and good for food, the tree of life also in the midst of the garden, and the tree of the knowledge of good and evil.	9. Out of the ground the Lord God made various trees grow that were delightful to look at and good for food, with the tree of life in the middle of the garden and the tree of the knowledge of good and bad.	9. And from the ground the Lord God caused to grow every tree that was pleasing to the sight and good for food, with the tree of life in the middle of the garden, and the tree of knowledge of good and bad.
10. And a river went out of Eden to water the garden; and from thence it was parted, and became into four heads.	10. A river flows out of Eden to water the garden, and from there it divides and becomes four branches.	10. A river rises in Eden to water the garden; beyond there it divides and becomes four branches.	10. A river issues from Eden to water the garden, and it then divides and becomes four branches.

see Chapter 8

KJV	NRSV	NAB	NJPS
11. The name of the first *is* Pison: that *is* it which compasseth the whole land of Havilah, where *there is* gold;	11. The name of the first is Pishon; it is the one that flows around the whole land of Havilah, where there is gold;	11. The name of the first is the Pishon; it is the one that winds through the whole land of Havilah, where there is gold.	11. The name of the first is Pishon, the one that winds through the whole land of Havilah, where the gold is.

KJV	NRSV	NAB	NJPS
Genesis 2	Genesis 2	Genesis 2	Genesis 2

see Chapter 8

12. And the gold of that land *is* good: there *is* bdellium and the onyx stone.	12. and the gold of that land is good; bdellium and onyx stone are there.	12. The gold of that land is excellent; bdellium and lapis lazuli are also there.	12. (The gold of that land is good; bdellium is there, and lapis lazuli.)
13. And the name of the second river *is* Gihon: the same *is* it that compasseth the whole land of Ethiopia.	13. The name of the second river is Gihon; it is the one that flows around the whole land of Cush.	13. The name of the second river is the Gihon; it is the one that winds all through the land of Cush.	13. The name of the second river is Gihon, the one that winds through the whole land of Cush.
14. And the name of the third river *is* Hiddekel: that *is* it which goeth toward the east of Assyria. And the fourth river *is* Euphrates.	14. The name of the third river is Tigris, which flows east of Assyria. And the fourth river is the Euphrates.	14. The name of the third river is the Tigris; it is the one that flows east of Asshur. The fourth river is the Euphrates.	14. The name of the third river is Tigris, the one that flows east of Asshur. And the fourth river is the Euphrates.

see Chapter 9

15. And the Lord God took the man, and put him into the garden of Eden to dress it and to keep it.	15. The Lord God took the man and put him in the garden of Eden to till it and keep it.	15. The Lord God then took the man and settled him in the garden of Eden, to cultivate and care for it.	15. The Lord God took the man and placed him in the garden of Eden to till it and tend it.

see Chapter 10

16. And the Lord God commanded the man, saying, Of every tree of the garden thou mayest freely eat:	16. And the Lord God commanded the man, "You may freely eat of every tree of the garden;	16. The Lord God gave man this order: "You are free to eat from any of the trees of the garden	16. And the Lord God commanded the man, saying, "Of every tree of the garden you are free to eat;

KJV	NRSV	NAB	NJPS
Genesis 2	Genesis 2	Genesis 2	Genesis 2

see Chapter 10

KJV	NRSV	NAB	NJPS
17. But of the tree of the knowledge of good and evil, thou shalt not eat of it: for in the day that thou eatest thereof thou shalt surely die.	17. but of the tree of the knowledge of good and evil you shall not eat, for in the day that you eat of it you shall die."	17. except the tree of the knowledge of good and bad. From that tree you shall not eat; the moment you eat from it you are surely doomed to die."	17. but as for the tree of knowledge of good and bad, you must not eat of it; for as soon as you eat of it, you shall die."

see Chapter 11

KJV	NRSV	NAB	NJPS
18. And the Lord God said, *It is* not good that the man should be alone; I will make him an help meet for him.	18. Then the Lord God said, "It is not good that the man should be alone; I will make him a helper as his partner."	18. The Lord God said: "It is not good for the man to be alone. I will make a suitable partner for him."	18. The Lord God said, "It is not good for man to be alone; I will make a fitting helper for him."
19. And out of the ground the Lord God formed every beast of the field, and every fowl of the air; and brought *them* unto Adam to see what he would call them: and whatsoever Adam called every living creature, that *was* the name thereof.	19. So out of the ground the Lord God formed every animal of the field and every bird of the air, and brought them to the man to see what he would call them; and whatever the man called every living creature, that was its name.	19. So the Lord God formed out of the ground various wild animals and various birds of the air, and he brought them to the man to see what he would call them; whatever the man called each of them would be its name.	19. And the Lord God formed out of the earth all the wild beasts and all the birds of the sky, and brought them to the man to see what he would call them; and whatever the man called each living creature, that would be its name.
20. And Adam gave names to all cattle, and to the fowl of the air, and to every beast of the field; but for Adam there was not found an help meet for him.	20. The man gave names to all cattle, and to the birds of the air, and to every animal of the field; but for the man there was not found a helper as his partner.	20. The man gave names to all the cattle, all the birds of the air, and all the wild animals; but none proved to be the suitable partner for the man.	20. And the man gave names to all the cattle and to the birds of the sky and to all the wild beasts; but for Adam no fitting helper was found.

KJV	NRSV	NAB	NJPS
Genesis 2	Genesis 2	Genesis 2	Genesis 2

see Chapter 12

KJV	NRSV	NAB	NJPS
21. And the Lord God caused a deep sleep to fall upon Adam, and he slept: and he took one of his ribs, and closed up the flesh instead thereof.	21. So the Lord God caused a deep sleep to fall upon the man, and he slept; then he took one of his ribs and closed up its place with flesh.	21. So the Lord God cast a deep sleep on the man, and while he was asleep, he took out one of his ribs and closed up its place with flesh.	21. So the Lord God cast a deep sleep upon the man; and, while he slept, He took one of his ribs and closed up the flesh at that spot.
22. And the rib, which the Lord God had taken from man, made he a woman, and brought her unto the man.	22. And the rib that the Lord God had taken from the man he made into a woman and brought her to the man.	22. The Lord God then built up into a woman the rib that he had taken from the man. When he brought her to the man,	22. And the Lord God fashioned the rib that He had taken from the man into a woman; and He brought her to the man.
23. And Adam said, This *is* now bone of my bones, and flesh of my flesh: she shall be called Woman, because she was taken out of Man.	23. Then the man said, "This at last is bone of my bones / and flesh of my flesh; / this one shall be called Woman, / for out of Man this one was taken."	23. the man said: "This one, at last, is bone of my bones / and flesh of my flesh / This one shall be called 'woman,' / for out of 'her man' this one has been taken."	23. Then the man said, "This one at last / Is bone of my bones / And flesh of my flesh. / This one shall be called Woman, / For from man was she taken."

see Chapter 13

KJV	NRSV	NAB	NJPS
24. Therefore shall a man leave his father and his mother, and shall cleave unto his wife: and they shall be one flesh.	24. Therefore a man leaves his father and his mother and clings to his wife, and they become one flesh.	24. That is why a man leaves his father and mother and clings to his wife, and the two of them become one body.	24. Hence a man leaves his father and mother and clings to his wife, so that they become one flesh.

KJV	NRSV	NAB	NJPS
Genesis 2	Genesis 2	Genesis 2	Genesis 2

see Chapter 14

KJV	NRSV	NAB	NJPS
25. And they were both naked, the man and his wife, and were not ashamed.	25. And the man and his wife were both naked, and were not ashamed.	25. The man and his wife were both naked, yet they felt no shame.	25. The two of them were naked, the man and his wife, yet they felt no shame.
Genesis 3	Genesis 3	Genesis 3	Genesis 3

see Chapter 15

KJV	NRSV	NAB	NJPS
1. Now the serpent was more subtil than any beast of the field which the Lord God had made. And he said unto the woman, Yea, hath God said, Ye shall not eat of every tree of the garden?	1. Now the serpent was more crafty than any other wild animal that the Lord God had made. He said to the woman, "Did God say, 'You shall not eat from any tree in the garden'?"	1. Now the serpent was the most cunning of all the animals that the Lord God had made. The serpent asked the woman, "Did God really tell you not to eat from any of the trees in the garden?"	1. Now the serpent was the shrewdest of all the wild beasts that the Lord God had made. He said to the woman, "Did God really say: You shall not eat of any tree of the garden?"
2. And the woman said unto the serpent, We may eat of the fruit of the trees of the garden:	2. The woman said to the serpent, "We may eat of the fruit of the trees in the garden;	2. The woman answered the serpent: "We may eat of the fruit of the trees in the garden;	2. The woman replied to the serpent, "We may eat of the fruit of the other trees of the garden.
3. But of the fruit of the tree which *is* in the midst of the garden, God hath said, Ye shall not eat of it, neither shall ye touch it, lest ye die.	3. but God said, 'You shall not eat of the fruit of the tree that is in the middle of the garden, nor shall you touch it or you shall die.'"	3. it is only about the fruit of the tree in the middle of the garden that God said, 'You shall not eat it or even touch it, lest you die.'"	3. It is only about the fruit of the tree in the middle of the garden that God said: 'You shall not eat of it or touch it, lest you die.'"
4. And the serpent said unto the woman, Ye shall not surely die:	4. But the serpent said to the woman, "You will not die;	4. But the serpent said to the woman: "You certainly will not die!	4. And the serpent said to the woman, "You are not going to die,

KJV	NRSV	NAB	NJPS
Genesis 3	Genesis 3	Genesis 3	Genesis 3

see Chapter 15

KJV	NRSV	NAB	NJPS
5. For God doth know that in the day ye eat thereof, then your eyes shall be opened, and ye shall be as gods, knowing good and evil.	5. for God knows that when you eat of it your eyes will be opened, and you will be like God, knowing good and evil."	5. No, God knows well that the moment you eat of it you will be like gods who know what is good and what is bad."	5. but God knows that as soon as you eat of it your eyes will be opened and you will be like divine beings who know good and bad."
6. And when the woman saw that the tree *was* good for food, and that it *was* pleasant to the eyes, and a tree to be desired to make *one* wise, she took of the fruit thereof, and did eat, and gave also unto her husband with her; and he did eat.	6. So when the woman saw that the tree was good for food, and that it was a delight to the eyes, and that the tree was to be desired to make one wise, she took of its fruit and ate; and she also gave some to her husband, who was with her, and he ate.	6. The woman saw that the tree was good for food, pleasing to the eyes, and desirable for gaining wisdom. So she took some of its fruit and ate it; and she also gave some to her husband, who was with her, and he ate it.	6. When the woman saw that the tree was good for eating and a delight to the eyes, and that the tree was desirable as a source of wisdom, she took of its fruit and ate. She also gave some to her husband, and he ate.

see Chapters 16–17

KJV	NRSV	NAB	NJPS
7. And the eyes of them both were opened, and they knew that they *were* naked; and they sewed fig leaves together, and made themselves aprons.	7. Then the eyes of both were opened, and they knew that they were naked; and they sewed fig leaves together and made loincloths for themselves.	7. Then the eyes of both of them were opened, and they realized that they were naked; so they sewed fig leaves together and made loincloths for themselves.	7. Then the eyes of both of them were opened and they perceived that they were naked; and they sewed together fig leaves and made themselves loincloths.

KJV	NRSV	NAB	NJPS
Genesis 3	Genesis 3	Genesis 3	Genesis 3

see Chapters 16–17

KJV	NRSV	NAB	NJPS
8. And they heard the voice of the Lord God walking in the garden in the cool of the day: and Adam and his wife hid themselves from the presence of the Lord God amongst the trees of the garden.	8. They heard the sound of the Lord God walking in the garden at the time of the evening breeze, and the man and his wife hid themselves from the presence of the Lord God among the trees of the garden.	8. When they heard the sound of the Lord God moving about in the garden at the breezy time of the day, the man and his wife hid themselves from the Lord God among the trees of the garden.	8. They heard the sound of the Lord God moving about in the garden at the breezy time of day; and the man and his wife hid from the Lord God among the trees of the garden.
9. And the Lord God called unto Adam, and said unto him, Where *art* thou?	9. But the Lord God called to the man, and said to him, "Where are you?'	9. The Lord god then called to the man and asked him, "Where are you?"	9. The Lord God called out to the man and said to him, "Where are you?"
10. And he said, I heard thy voice in the garden, and I was afraid, because I *was* naked; and I hid myself.	10. He said, "I heard the sound of you in the garden, and I was afraid, because I was naked; and I hid myself."	10. He answered, "I heard you in the garden; but I was afraid, because I was naked, so I hid myself."	10. He replied, "I heard the sound of You in the garden, and I was afraid because I was naked, so I hid."
11. And he said, Who told thee that thou *wast* naked? Hast thou eaten of the tree, whereof I com-manded thee that thou shouldest not eat?	11. He said, "Who told you that you were naked? Have you eaten from the tree of which I commanded you not to eat?"	11. Then he asked, "Who told you that you were naked? You have eaten, then, from the tree of which I had forbidden you to eat!"	11. Then He asked, "Who told you that you were naked? Did you eat of the tree from which I had forbidden you to eat?"

KJV	NRSV	NAB	NJPS
Genesis 3	Genesis 3	Genesis 3	Genesis 3

see Chapter 17

KJV	NRSV	NAB	NJPS
12. And the man said, The woman whom thou gavest *to be* with me, she gave me of the tree, and I did eat.	12. The man said, "The woman whom you gave to be with me, she gave me fruit from the tree, and I ate."	12. The man replied, "The woman whom you put here with me—she gave me fruit from the tree, and so I ate it."	12. The man said, "The woman You put at my side— she gave me of the tree, and I ate."
13. And the Lord God said unto the woman, What *is* this *that* thou hast done? And the woman said, The serpent beguiled me, and I did eat.	13. Then the Lord God said to the woman, "What is this that you have done?" The woman said, "The serpent tricked me, and I ate."	13. The Lord God then asked the woman, "Why did you do such a thing?" The woman answered, "The serpent tricked me into it, so I ate it."	13. And the Lord God said to the woman, "What is this you have done!" The woman replied, "The serpent duped me, and I ate."

see Chapters 18–19

KJV	NRSV	NAB	NJPS
14. And the Lord God said unto the serpent, Because thou hast done this, thou *art* cursed above all cattle, and above every beast of the field; upon thy belly shalt thou go, and dust shalt thou eat all the days of thy life:	14. The Lord God said to the serpent, "Because you have done this/cursed are you among all animals/and among all wild creatures;/upon your belly you shall go,/and dust you shall eat/all the days of your life.	14. Then the Lord God said to the serpent: "Because you have done this, you shall be banned/from all the animals/and from all the wild creatures;/On your belly shall you crawl,/and dirt shall you eat/all the days of your life./	14. The Lord God said to the serpent, "Because you did this,/More cursed shall you be/than all cattle/And all the wild beasts:/ On your belly shall you crawl/And dirt shall you eat/All the days of your life./
15. And I will put enmity between thee and the woman, and between thy seed and her seed; and it shall bruise thy head, and thou shalt bruise his heel.	15. I will put enmity between you and the woman,/and between your offspring and hers;/he will strike your head,/and you will strike his heel."	15. I will put enmity between you and the woman,/and between your offspring and hers;/He will strike at your head,/while you strike at his heel."	15. I will put enmity/ Between you and the woman,/And between your offspring and hers;/They shall strike at your head,/and you shall strike at their heel."

KJV	NRSV	NAB	NJPS
Genesis 3	Genesis 3	Genesis 3	Genesis 3

see Chapters 18, 20

KJV	NRSV	NAB	NJPS
16. Unto the woman he said, I will greatly multiply thy sorrow and thy conception; in sorrow thou shalt bring forth children; and thy desire *shall be* to thy husband, and he shall rule over thee.	16. To the woman he said, "I will greatly increase your pangs in childbearing; / in pain you shall bring forth children, / yet your desire shall be for your husband, / and he shall rule over you."	16. To the woman he said: "I will intensify the pangs of your childbearing; / in pain shall you bring forth children. / Yet your urge shall be for your husband, / and he shall be your master."	16. And to the woman He said, "I will make most severe / Your pangs in childbearing; / In pain shall you bear children. / Yet your urge shall be for your husband, / And he shall rule over you."

see Chapters 18, 21

KJV	NRSV	NAB	NJPS
17. And unto Adam he said, Because thou hast hearkened unto the voice of thy wife, and hast eaten of the tree, of which I commanded thee, saying, Thou shalt not eat of it: cursed *is* the ground for thy sake; in sorrow shalt thou eat *of* it all the days of thy life;	17. And to the man he said, "Because you have listened to the voice of your wife, / and have eaten of the tree about which I commanded you, / 'You shall not eat of it,' / cursed is the ground because of you; / in toil you shall eat of it all the days of your life;	17. To the man he said: "Because you listened to your wife and ate from the tree of which I had forbidden you to eat, "Cursed be the ground because of you! / In toil shall you eat its yield / all the days of your life. /	17. To Adam He said, "Because you did as your wife said and ate of the tree about which I commanded you, 'You shall not eat of it,' Cursed be the ground because of you; / By toil shall you eat of it / All the days of your life: /
18. Thorns also and thistles shall it bring forth to thee; and thou shalt eat the herb of the field;	18. thorns and thistles it shall bring forth for you; / and you shall eat the plants of the field. /	18. Thorns and thistles shall it bring forth to you, / as you eat of the plants of the field. /	18. Thorns and thistles shall it sprout for you. / But your food shall be the grasses of the field;

KJV	NRSV	NAB	NJPS
Genesis 3	Genesis 3	Genesis 3	Genesis 3

see Chapters 18, 21

KJV	NRSV	NAB	NJPS
19. In the sweat of thy face shalt thou eat bread, till thou return unto the ground; for out of it wast thou taken: for dust thou *art,* and unto dust shalt thou return.	19. By the sweat of your face / you shall eat bread / until you return to the ground, / for out of it you were taken; / you are dust, / and to dust you shall return."	19. By the sweat of your face / shall you get bread to eat, / Until you return to the ground, / from which you were taken; / For you are dirt, / and to dirt you shall return."	19. By the sweat of your brow / Shall you get bread to eat, / Until you return to the ground— / For from it you were taken. / For dust you are, / And to dust you shall return."

see Chapter 22

KJV	NRSV	NAB	NJPS
20. And Adam called his wife's name Eve; because she was the mother of all living.	20. The man named his wife Eve, because she was the mother of all living.	20. The man called his wife Eve, because she became the mother of all the living.	20. The man named his wife Eve, because she was the mother of all the living.
21. Unto Adam also and to his wife did the Lord God make coats of skins, and clothed them.	21. And the Lord God made garments of skins for the man and for his wife, and clothed them.	21. For the man and his wife the Lord God made leather garments with which he clothed them.	21. And the Lord God made garments of skins for Adam and his wife, and clothed them.
22. And the Lord God said, Behold, the man is become as one of us, to know good and evil: and now, lest he put forth his hand, and take also of the tree of life, and eat, and live for ever:	22. Then the Lord God said, "See, the man has become like one of us, knowing good and evil; and now, he might reach out his hand and take also from the tree of life, and eat, and live forever"—	22. Then the Lord God said, "See! The man has become like one of us, knowing what is good and what is bad! Therefore, he must not be allowed to put out his hand to take fruit from the tree of life also, and thus eat of it and live forever."	22. And the Lord God said, "Now that the man has become like one of us, knowing good and bad, what if he should stretch out his hand and take also from the tree of life and eat, and live forever!"

KJV	NRSV	NAB	NJPS
Genesis 3	Genesis 3	Genesis 3	Genesis 3

see Chapter 22

KJV	NRSV	NAB	NJPS
23. Therefore the Lord God sent him forth from the garden of Eden, to till the ground from whence he was taken.	23. therefore the Lord God sent him forth from the garden of Eden, to till the ground from which he was taken.	23. The Lord God therefore banished him from the garden of Eden, to till the ground from which he had been taken.	23. So the Lord God banished him from the garden of Eden, to till the soil from which he was taken.
24. So he drove out the man; and he placed at the east of the garden of Eden Cherubims, and a flaming sword which turned every way, to keep the way of the tree of life.	24. He drove out the man; and at the east of the garden of Eden he placed the cherubim, and a sword flaming and turning to guard the way to the tree of life.	24. When he expelled the man, he settled him east of the garden of Eden; and he stationed the cherubim and the fiery revolving sword, to guard the way to the tree of life.	24. He drove the man out, and stationed east of the garden of Eden the cherubim and the fiery ever-turning sword, to guard the way to the tree of life.

Genesis 4	Genesis 4	Genesis 4	Genesis 4

see Chapter 18

KJV	NRSV	NAB	NJPS
1. And Adam knew Eve his wife; and she conceived, and bare Cain, and said, I have gotten a man from the Lord.	1. Now the man knew his wife Eve, and she conceived and bore Cain, saying, "I have produced a man with the help of the Lord."	1. The man had relations with his wife Eve, and she conceived and bore Cain, saying, "I have produced a man with the help of the Lord."	1. Now the man knew his wife Eve, and she conceived and bore Cain, saying, "I have gained a male child with the help of the Lord."
2. And she again bare his brother Abel. And Abel was a keeper of sheep, but Cain was a tiller of the ground.	2. Next she bore his brother Abel. Now Abel was a keeper of sheep, and Cain a tiller of the ground.	2. Next she bore his brother Abel. Abel became a keeper of flocks, and Cain a tiller of the soil.	2. She then bore his brother Abel. Abel became a keeper of sheep, and Cain became a tiller of the soil.

PART TWO

Before Then

The real voyage of discovery consists not in seeking new landscapes, but in having new eyes.

—Marcel Proust

They asked Wisdom, "What is the punishment of sinners?"
She answered them, "Evil will pursue them."
They asked Prophecy, "What is the punishment of sinners?"
She answered them, "The soul that sins will die."
They asked the Holy One Blessed Is He, "What is the punishment of sinners?"
He answered them, "They will repent and it will be forgiven."

—*j. Makkoth* 2:6

6 A DOWN-TO-EARTH STORY

(Gen 2:4–7)

Genesis 2

4a These are the generations of the heavens and the earth
in their being created.
4b On the day of YHWH god's making earth and heavens
5 and every *śīyaḥ* of the field was not yet in the earth
and every *'ēśeb* of the field had not yet sprouted
because YHWH god had not made it rain on the earth
and no *'ādām* existed for working the *'adāmāh*
6 but an *'ēd* ascending from the earth
and it watered all the face of the *'adāmāh*
7 and (then) YHWH god formed the *'ādām*,
'āpār from the *'adāmāh*,
and he blew into his nostrils the breath of life,
and (so) the *'ādām* became a living *nepeš*.

The familiar story of the six days of creation is told in chapter 1 of
Genesis. The Garden story itself begins in chapter 2, verse 4. Its beginning immediately raises three questions.

(1) Why doesn't the story start at the beginning of a new chapter?
(2) Why is it introduced by a sentence that refers back to the cosmic
creation that begins the book of Genesis in chapter 1?

(3) Why does the first verse of the actual story, verse 4b, repeat the introduction of verse 4a?

The answer to the first question is that the chapter division may reflect a Christian polemic. Originally, the Hebrew Bible did not have chapter divisions. It was written as a continuous text with breaks approximating paragraph divisions where narrative scenes or topics under discussion changed. Chapter divisions and verse numbers were first inserted into biblical texts during the Middle Ages by Christian scholars as a way of dividing the text for ease of reference. Jewish scholars began to adopt them only in the thirteenth century so that they could understand to what Christians referred when citing a scripture by chapter and verse.

Genesis chapter 1 ends at verse 31, which refers to the end of the sixth day of creation: "And God saw all that he had made and behold, it was very good. And there was evening and there was morning, the sixth day." The chapter break after this verse unnaturally severs the narrative about the seventh day in Genesis 2:1–3 from the story of the first six days of creation in Genesis 1:1–31. Why did the chapter division lop off the end of the story, about the Sabbath day of rest and its sanctification as holy time?

The (mis)division benefited those celebrating the Lord's Day, sometimes called the Christian Sabbath, on Sunday, the first day of the week. Thus severed for Christian reading, Sabbath on Saturday became associated with the Garden story and the Fall. When read liturgically in the synagogue, the creation story from Genesis 1:1 through Genesis 2:3 is read straight through as a single unit. In the Jewish tradition, the Sabbath, from Friday sundown through Saturday sunset, is considered the culmination of creation.

One consequence of this medieval misdivision has been uncertainty as to where the seven-day creation story ends and the Garden story begins. Although many scholars consider Genesis 2:3 to be the end of the Cosmic Creation story, others propose that it ends with the summarizing statement of Genesis 2:4a. If so, then the Garden story proper begins only at Genesis 2:4b.

Arguments in support of the second position follow a twofold line of reasoning. On the one hand, verse 4a seems an appropriate summary of the creation narrative; on the other, if verse 4a were the first line of the

Garden story, verse 4b would be unnecessary because it repeats the same information.

Against this line of reasoning stands the observation that the Cosmic Creation story is not only about the heavens and the earth but also about the inhabited world, the creation of humans who inhabit it, the establishment of the seventh day as a Sabbath, a day when no creating occurred, and about the sanctification of time. In addition, Genesis 2:1–2 summarizes the first six days adequately—"And the heavens and the earth were finished and all their host"—before introducing the concluding Sabbath theme: "and God finished, on the seventh day, the work that he had done, and he ceased, on the seventh day, from all the work that he had done." The reference to "heavens and earth" in Genesis 2:1 echoes the introductory sentence of the creation story in Genesis 1:1–3: "In the beginning of God's creating the heavens and the earth—and the earth was unformed and void and darkness over the face of the deep and a wind of God hovering over the face of the water—and God said, 'Let there be light,' and there was light." Accordingly, Genesis 2:4a cannot be viewed as a summarizing statement. It must have some other function.

This conclusion, however, fails to clarify why, if verse 4a introduces the Garden story, verse 4b repeats the same information.

Close reading reveals some interesting facts about verse 4b. It is not at all about "the heavens and the earth in their being created." The verse directs readers away from the grand cosmos to "earth and heavens," to plants of the field (earth), to rain (heavens), and to the formation of a human (earth). Moreover, verse 4b is not an independent sentence but an adverbial phrase of time that begins an extremely long sentence that extends to the end of verse 7.

What does all this imply for verse 4a?

The first words of verse 4a constitute a formula repeated ten times in Genesis, "these are the generations of X" (Gen 2:4; 6:9; 10:1; 11:10, 27; 25:12, 19; 36:1, 9; 37:2). Wherever this formula occurs, it draws attention back to a previously mentioned event or set of circumstances or to a person, as if to say, "Remember X, and now listen to this." For example, in Genesis 6:9 "these are the generations of Noah" bridges the previous mention of Noah's birth and the upcoming flood story, but in Genesis 10:1 "and these are the generations of the sons of Noah" bridges the previous mention of what happened to Noah's sons after they left the ark (reported in Gen

9:18–29) and Noah's genealogy, which accounts for nations all over the Near East. In Genesis 11:27, the formula bridges the previous mention of Terah (Gen 11:24–26) and stories about his better-known son, Abraham. In Genesis 37:2, it bridges stories in which Jacob is the main character (Gen 28:10–37:1) and those about his son Joseph.

But what role does the formula play in the Garden story?

In all of the aforementioned examples, the formula occurs at junctures where there appears to be an abrupt break in the subject of the narrative or a change of genre, from a narrative to a genealogical list—in places where the flow between what came before and what comes after can be described as rough.[1] The transition from the Cosmic Creation story of Genesis 1, culminating with the blessing and sanctification of the seventh day in Genesis 2:3, to the earthier Garden story, which introduces a different sequence of creation, was apparently perceived as sudden by the final editor.

The Garden story introduces a different sequence of creation, is oblivious to the Sabbath day, and employs YHWH as the divine name rather than Elohim. In Genesis 2:4a, the formula bridges the first and second story in Genesis as if to say: "This story about the creation of heavens and earth was quite something, wasn't it? But there is more to the story. It is not about the cosmos; it is about people. And this is how the story unfolds." When we view this formula along with all other examples of its occurrence, we discover that it is an editorial join, easing readers over points of discontinuity.

Verses 4b–7 make up a single grammatical sentence, most of which is taken up by clauses describing conditions at the time when YHWH god formed the first human. The structure of this sentence is similar to that of the opening lines of the Babylonian creation story *Enumma Elish* and of Genesis 1:1–3, discussed above in Chapter 4. Just as it is recognizable as a conventional introductory feature in those two contexts, so, too, it signals that what follows here is a foundation story.

Since only verses 6–7 deal with the actual formation of the first human, I discuss them here, postponing my analysis of Genesis 2:5 to the next chapter. The point of verses 6–7 is to introduce the first human to people reading, reciting, and hearing the story, to describe his unimaginable origin to his later descendents. It is a dramatic response to a form of the innocent question "Where do I come from?" Its answer is "scientific" in that it starts with an explanation of the origin of the raw material that God used.

THE FIRST MOVEMENT

The Bible story provides few details about the making of "earth and heavens." After verse 5 portrays a bleak, desiccated landscape to explain what has not yet happened, verse 6 focuses on movement. Something referred to as an *'ēd* was ascending and watering the surface of the soil before God began to form the first person. The Hebrew word translated as "watered," *hišqāh*, is used elsewhere to describe the provision of water in quantities that suffice to slake the thirst of a flock of sheep (Exod 2:16) or people and their animals (Num 20:8). It refers to large amounts of water and is translated according to context by "to irrigate, water, give drink." Accordingly, the verb indicates that the soil was deeply watered, soaked, and the verb calls on readers to imagine waters flowing every which way.

Had the narrator wished to indicate that the soil was merely moistened or dampened, he could have used a verb from the root *r-ṭ-b* to indicate a slight degree of wetness (Job 8:16; 24:8).

Had the author wished to refer to mist, he had available vocabulary to do so. Biblical Hebrew has two expressions that refer to mist, to foglike aggregations of minute water droplets, almost a vapor, near the ground. One is *'anan bōqer*, "a morning cloud," and the other is *ṭal maškīym wehōlēk*, "early rising, moving dew," both of which occur in Hosea 13:3. The second phrase used by Hosea to describe mist contrasts with the image of dew perceived as drops (Job 38:28) that drip or flow together earthward from the heavens (Deut 32:2; 33:28).

Hebrew *'ēd* recurs one additional time in the Bible, in Job 36:27–28, in a difficult sentence in a linguistically difficult book. There it is described as being formed by a large accumulation of water that God gathers to form a mighty rainstorm:

> He draws together drops of water distilled into rain for his *'ēd*
> That the high clouds will flow and pour down mightily on people.

The Hebrew word may be understood by considering its fairly common cognate in Akkadian, the main Semitic language of ancient Mesopotamia during the second and most of the first millennia BCE. Akkadian *edu* is used in texts referring to exceptionally powerful, broad surges of water as with waves during a high tide or an unusually large flooding of rivers during the annual high waters of spring.[2] Based on this usage, Hebrew *'ēd* in Job refers to an exceptional concentrated volume of rain, but in Genesis 2:6, it refers to an extraordinary surge of water welling up from beneath the surface of the ground and soaking the topsoil thoroughly. After the action of the water on the dry ground, raw material was available for the creation of the human. Furthermore, having ascended beyond the surface, the concentrated waters were now also in the heavens, available to become the rain that had not yet fallen.

WHAT ARE LITTLE BOYS MADE OF?

The human was fashioned from *'āpār*, a clod of soil. God, like a brick maker, worked soil rendered malleable by the upsurge. Unfortunately, *'āpār* is often mistranslated as "dust." Examination of how this word is used in biblical Hebrew indicates clearly that *'āpār* refers to compacted lumps or clumps of earth, or to coagulated and concentrated burnt animal remains or vegetable matter and the like (Lev 14:41–42, 45; 17:13; Num 5:17; 2 Sam 24:3; 1 Kings 18:31; 2 Kings 23:6, 13; Job 7:5). It refers to something people can handle, wrap their fingers around, squeeze, and shape, like a mud ball.

Martin Luther anticipated this explanation: "The word *'āpār* properly denotes earth that has just been dug up, or a clod, while our translation has 'dust' to suggest the idea of loose earth. Now Adam was made out of a clod into a living human being."[3]

As with "mist," the biblical author had words to choose among for a precise meaning. If he had wished to indicate that the human was made from dust, particles light enough to be carried by the wind, he could have used *'ābāq* (see Isa 5:24; 29:5; Nah 1:3), but it does not occur here. A second word referring to fine, barely perceptible dust that appears permanently suspended in the air is *šaḥaq* (Deut 33:26; Isa 40:15; Job 37:18, 21).

A third word that some consider homophonic with the word for "clod," *'āpār*, spelled with an initial *'ayyin*, is Hebrew *'ēper*, with an initial *'aleph*. The *'aleph* is a distinctively different letter that represents an unmistakably different sound as its first consonant. Even though the two words appear to be similar, distinguished by a single consonant and a different pattern of vowels, their meanings are distinct. The proper translation of *'ēper* is "ash." It is what remains after something is burned up completely (Num 19:5, 9–10).

The first human was formed from a clod or clump of soil, not from dust and not from ash. Nor was he formed from clay, *ḥōmer* or *ḥēmār*, that bakes in the sun or in a kiln and assumes a permanent form as it dries (Gen 11:3; Exod 1:14; 2:3; Isa 45:9; Jer 18:4–6; Job 4:19; 10:9). The wetted soil from which the human was made would eventually dry out after death.

Living humans are lubricated with complicated hydrokinetic systems. We drink liquids to maintain life; we sweat, we urinate, we expectorate, and we exhale damp air. In old age, when these systems do not function properly, our skin wrinkles as we dry up. In death our bodies decompose, losing their recognizably human shape as they revert to a damp, clodlike state. Then, after desiccation, they decompose further, reverting to an inchoate, soil-like state. The poignant notice in Deuteronomy 34:7 about Moses when he died at 120 years of age supports this understanding: even in hoary old age "his moisture had not disappeared/departed." Often understood as meaning that he had not lost his natural vigor—despite Moses' statement in Deuteronomy 31:2, "I am unable to go out [from the camp to war] and enter [the camp after war]," indicating that he had become weak—it apparently refers to the lubricity and freshness of his skin. Despite advanced years and physical weakness, Moses' skin remained unwrinkled.[4]

The "clod" tradition has its roots in a cultural practice known from northern Mesopotamia. Eighteenth-century BCE texts from Mari, a site on the upper Euphrates, indicate that half a clod of earth was the minimal unit required by an absentee diviner to perform magic that would affect the place or the people residing where it had been collected. One letter to the king of Mari from an unknown sender contains the following: "Moreover, a clod of Tuttul was brought to me. Half of it I have withheld before me to have divination performed and half I am sending herewith to my lord."[5]

A second Mesopotamian reference is the expression "to break a clod (of earth)" that appears in thirteen legal texts dated circa 1550–1500 BCE from Nuzi in northeastern Iraq. As part of a ritual disinheriting an adopted son or daughter, an actual clod was perhaps squished between the fingers and cast to the ground. It was held to represent the personality of the person, his or her essence, and was, therefore, identifiable with the person. This interpretation is verifiable from a magical text prescribing a remedy for nightmares: "He addresses a clod of earth thusly: 'O clod. In your substance my substance has been mingled, in my substance your substance has been mingled.' Then he tells all the (bad) dreams which he dreamt to the clod (and says): 'Just as I throw you, clod, into the water (and you dissolve) so may the evil consequences of my dreams.'"[6]

A similar mix of dry and wet is attested in the Mesopotamian myth of Atrahasis. There, the goddess Mami created humans out of clay (not clods of earth) mixed with the flesh and blood of a god slaughtered for that purpose. In Atrahasis, however, the divine elements of the mix gave rise to the intellect of the creature as well as to his beating heart, the animating element.

A similar notion about the creation of animated humans through the infusion of something that moves and stirs—breath, a beating heart, flowing blood—into an inert, shaped figure is expressed in Psalm 104:29: "Hide your face, they are confused; gather their breath, they perish and to their clod they return."

In combination, these data from Mesopotamia and from Psalms indicate that Israelites also thought that a clod provided the necessary critical mass of inert substance into which "personality" could be infused. Genesis 2:7 reflects this. God molded a wetted clod, a malleable clump of soil, into the shape that he desired and animated it by infusing his breath.

In the Garden story, the breathing creature is not named Adam but is described as the 'ādām, "human" or "person," a common noun in Hebrew that occurs also in legal and ritual parts of the Bible (cf. Exod 4:11; 9:10; Lev 1:2; 18:5). This word is significant because it shows that humans were very unlike the other creatures formed later in the story. In some biblical contexts 'ādām contrasts with words indicating animals (Gen 6:7; 7:23; 9:5; Exod 8:13–14; Lev 27:28; Jer 32:43; 33:10; Ezek 14:13, 17). In Israelite conception, no matter that humans and animals had some biological processes in common, animals were not considered human, and no human beings—even Israel's most intractable enemies—were considered animals. The word 'ādām is also used in some contexts as a collective noun referring to a totality, "people, humanity, mankind" (for example, in Gen 1:26; 9:5–6; Num 5:6).

The word 'ādām itself is connected etymologically to the Hebrew color term 'ādōm and to words in Arabic, Aramaic, Akkadian, and Ugaritic that describe a range of colors from tan and brown to red and scarlet. It is related as well to the common Hebrew words for blood, dām, and soil, 'adāmāh. Because of the obvious assonance between these related words, it is likely that any Israelite hearing the name 'ādām associated it automatically with these other words. As part of this word cluster, 'ādām evoked thoughts not only about origin but about skin color as well: humans, derived from rich soil, were tan, brown, or ruddy.[7]

Much of the thin layer of clayey arable soil in the central mountains of Israel, as in other Mediterranean countries, originated through the weathering of limestone. Its tan-red-brown colorations are caused by the oxidation of iron released from minerals in the limestone subsurface as the iron breaks down, hence the soil's common name, *terra rossa*, "red earth." The largest continuous stretch of terra rossa in the territory that comprised ancient Israel extends along the central mountains and their western slopes from slightly south of Shechem/Nablus down to Hebron.[8]

Completed in total breathing physicality, the dark-skinned person created from a clod is described as having become a *nepeš ḥayyāh*, "a living soul." *Nepeš*, rendered "soul" in this phrase, for lack of a better English equivalent, should not be understood as indicating that a light, ethereal spirit had become embedded within his body. In biblical Hebrew, the word refers to something mobile brushed with physicality.

Israelites thought that *nepeš* was the animating force in creatures, as indicated in verse 7 as well as Genesis 1:24 (domestic and wild animals as well as creeping things) and Leviticus 24:17–18 (humans and animals). From the observation that the word occurs in varied contexts where it refers to self-conscious, autonomous individuals (Gen 46:22–26; Exod 12:16; Lev 4:2, 27), it is clear that Israelites believed that the *nepeš* contained within itself components of what we identify as personality, mind, and consciousness (Exod 23:9; Deut 24:6). To be more specific about *nepeš* in the thought-world of ancient Israel is to venture beyond the evidence available in the Hebrew Bible and other relevant ancient Near Eastern sources.

Whatever the specific nature of the *nepeš*, Israelite lore taught that it was present only in living animals and humans, infused somehow in their blood. Legal passages concerned with the blood of hunted animals (Lev 17:13–14) and focused on the blood of animals slaughtered for food (Deut 12:23–24) identify the *nepeš* with blood. This idea had consequences for their diet. For example, God's instruction to Noah after the flood in Genesis 9:3 permits humans to eat "every living creature that moves," but Genesis 9:4 imposes a restriction: "However, the flesh with its *nepeš*, its blood, you will not eat."[9]

These passages indicate that the word *nepeš* was part of the vocabulary used in Iron Age Hebrew to describe a biological feature identified as common to both animals and humans. Contemporary understandings of *nepeš* as an absolutely immaterial soul, something eternal and purely spiritual, did not begin to evolve in early Jewish thought until the Hellenistic period.[10]

The dark-skinned person became a living soul, a living *nepeš*, when the breath blown into him infused *nepeš* into his blood.

The description of God's hands-on forming of the human is a homely motif repeated elsewhere in the story. The American poet James Weldon Johnson treated it poetically in "The Creation" (1927).[11] In his interpretation, he imagined a large interval of time between the creation of the world and the formation of the first human. These are the final lines of his poem:

> Then God sat down
> On the side of a hill where he could think;
> By a deep, wide river he sat down;
> With his head in his hands,
> God thought and thought,
> Till he thought; I'll make me a man!
>
> Up from the bed of the river
> God scooped the clay;
> And by the bank of the river
> He kneeled him down;
> And there the great God Almighty
> Who lit the sun and fixed it in the sky,
> Who flung the stars to the most far corner of the night,
> Who rounded the earth in the middle of his hand;
> This Great God,
> Like a mammy bending over her baby,
> Kneeled down in the dust
> Toiling over a lump of clay
> Till he shaped it in his own image;
> Then into it he blew the breath of life,
> And man became a living soul.
> Amen. Amen.

Johnson's poem captures the sense of an important motif in the Garden story: God cares. How this motif works itself out in the story is addressed in the following chapters.

7 WHY EDEN? WHY A GARDEN? WHERE WERE THE TREES?

(Gen 2:5, 8–10)

Genesis 2

5   and every *śīyaḥ* of the field was not yet in the earth
    and every *ʿēśeb* of the field had not yet sprouted
        because YHWH god had not made it rain on the earth
        and no human existed for working the soil

              ·   ·   ·

8   And YHWH god planted a *gan* in *ʿēden*, at the east,
    and placed there the human that he had formed.
9   And YHWH god *wayyaṣmaḥ* from the soil every tree
        desirable for seeing and good for eating
        and the Tree of Life *betōwk* the *gan*
        and the Tree of Knowing *ṭōwb wārāʿ*.
10   And a river goes out from *ʿēden* to water the *gan*.
    And from there it divides and becomes four head(water)s.

First, God himself planted the Garden. He did not cause a garden to be planted or call it into existence with words such as "Let there be a garden." The Hebrew verb translated as *planted* in verse 8 refers to a broad range of activities necessary before plants take root. Isaiah describes some of these: breaking ground, clearing away stones, planting (which involves digging holes and irrigation trenches and filling in earth around saplings), putting in a protective hedge, building a wall, pruning and hoeing (Isa 5:2–6). God did it all, personally. And when that work was completed, he brought the human from somewhere else in the world to the Garden (Gen 2:15; see 3:23).

Once everything was prepared, God caused the plants to grow naturally. Nothing suggests that a fully mature garden appeared overnight—there is no refrain "there was evening and there was morning," as in Genesis 1. Saplings and vines grew over a few years, and during those years, the human tended them. The plain meaning of the narrative is that the human was designated agriculturalist-in-residence even before the Garden grew, but not the landscaper who planned and planted it. The human worked.

Much of what is usually imagined in art, humor, and homiletics to be the Bible's comprehension of life in the Garden, often described as *Edenic* or *Paradisiacal*, is a projection from Greek mythology into the Bible. Unlike Greek myths that told about a "Golden Age" at the beginning of human history, Israel's story begins with a toiling man. Greeks imagined the Golden Age as an idyllic, pastoral period of eternal spring, a time of innocence and simplicity and of sustenance provided without human labor. In the following Silver Age, people had to learn to farm and shelter themselves and provide their own clothing. This was followed by a Bronze Age, during which social classes evolved and societies competed against each other, often motivated by greed and jealousy.

In contrast, the Bible's story of humanity begins with a version of what Greek and Roman storytellers might have viewed as a mix of the Bronze and Silver Ages, a period during which one man labored in a garden belonging to somebody of higher station.

Given the availability of famous garden spots in the ancient Near East—the Nile Valley, Mount Lebanon, Damascus, Babylon—and such small, breathtakingly beautiful garden areas as the Artas Valley near Bethlehem, the decision of the author to have God plant his garden in Eden is surprising, but only until the name of the place is scrutinized.

WHAT DOES *EDEN* MEAN?

In the late 1880s, scholars deciphering a recently excavated text in Akkadian came across a new word, *edinu*. For them, it was transparent that the Akkadian word should be connected with the Hebrew *'ēden*, but that did not clarify the meaning of the Akkadian word. They proposed that Akkadian *edinu* was a Semiticized form of the Sumerian (non-Semitic) word *e-di-in*, meaning "steppe." Related examples in English are *Jerusalem*, an Anglicized form of Aramaic *yerūwšlēm* (not of Hebrew *yerušālayim*) and *camel*, an Anglicized form of Hebrew *gāmāl*.

On the basis of their conclusion that the text equated the Akkadian and the Sumerian words, the scholars assumed that *edinu* had become a Semitic word, so its appearance in Hebrew should not be surprising. Accordingly, the Hebrew word in Genesis was understood by informed students of the Bible to indicate that the Garden had been planted in some vast treeless steppe or plain, maybe at the eastern edge of Mesopotamia. This explanation, repeated in commentaries for more than a century, is unlikely for two reasons.

First, aside from one source dated to approximately 1000 BCE and referred to by specialists as Syllabary b, Akkadian regularly translates Sumerian *e-di-in* with a well-known word for "steppe," *ṣēru*. What is found in Syllabary b, then, is not the translation of the Sumerian word but probably an Akkadian scribe's rendering in his writing system of the sound of the word.

Second, thanks to the archaeological discovery of a large inscribed statue in 1979, *ʿēden* is now considered cognate to an Aramaic verb *mʿdn* (whose exact pronunciation is unknown, since vowels are not indicated in its writing system). The Tell Fekheryah statue with the Akkadian-Aramaic bilingual inscription dates to the ninth century BCE.[1] It represents the local governor Hadad-yishi and was excavated in a sacred precinct of Gozan, a site in northeast Syria on the upper Habur River between the Tigris and the Euphrates. The Aramaic verb *mʿdn*, written in the Old Aramaic alphabet on the back of the statue, corresponds to a well-known Akkadian word, *muṭaḥḥidu*, meaning "to enrich, to make abundant," written on the statue's front in cuneiform.[2]

A different word from the root *ʿ-d-n*—the word *ʾa-di-na*, meaning "a fruit"—entered Egyptian from a Northwest Semitic language in the language family of which Hebrew and Aramaic are members.[3] In Genesis 18:12, Abraham's elderly, childless wife, Sarah, laughs to herself when she hears a stranger announce to her husband that within a year she will give birth: "After I have become worn out, will there be bounty, for me?" The Hebrew word that I translate as "bounty" is *ʿednāh*, from the same consonantal root, *ʿ-d-n*. This is the word that gives rise to the English feminine name Edna, usually explained as meaning "pleasure," as well as to the

The Tell Fekheryah Statue and the Key to Understanding the Meaning of *Eden*
The word *m'dn* in the Aramaic inscription on the rear of the skirt of the statue provided the key enabling scholars to determine what the name Eden, Hebrew *'ēden*, means. It corresponds to a well-known word in the Akkadian inscription on the front of the skirt that refers to abundance. At this early stage of development, the Old Aramaic letters (except for the *mem*) are similar to those of the ninth-century BCE Hebrew alphabet (see Chapter 3). (After a photograph courtesy of West Semitic Research.)

names of two of David's warriors: Adino and Adina (2 Sam 23:8; 1 Chron 11:42).

In the Fekheryah inscription, the fertility deity Adad is described as "regulator of water in heaven and earth who rains down wealth, provides pastures and watering places for all people . . . ; regulator of all rivers who causes the whole world to produce abundance." The Aramaic word that I translate as "abundance" is *m'dn*.

Since the name Eden itself evoked the image of an agriculturally productive area, it is not surprising that the word appears in the name of another locale. The prophet Amos refers to a kingdom called Beth Eden, *bēyt 'ēden*, part of a coalition of Aramaic-speaking groups centered on Damascus (Amos 1:5; see also 2 Kings 19:12 = Isa 37:12). This place is identified with Bit Adini, a kingdom located on both sides of the

Euphrates where the Balikh River flows into it from the north. Its name translates as "House of Bounty." The Garden was planted in a place called "Bountiful."

The major wonder of this particular garden on the eastern side of Eden/Bountiful may have been its landlord, who could guarantee rain. The river flowing through it made watering in dry seasons a simple matter of digging and maintaining systems of sluice gates and small channels to bring water to the plant plots and tree groves (Gen 2:5, 10). In this natural setting, the Garden offered the best of Egypt, with its regular supply of irrigation water from the Nile, and the best of the land within which the tribes of Israel lived, with its fairly predictable pattern of generous rainfall: "from the rain of the heavens it drinks water" (Deut 11:11).[4]

The Garden is mentioned elsewhere in biblical literature as a particularly well-endowed site of agriculture, "all of it [the Jordan Plain] richly endowed with water like the garden of YHWH, like Egypt" (Gen 13:10); "he will make its desert like Eden, her steppe like the garden of YHWH" (Isa 51:3); "like the garden of Eden is the land before him, but after him a desert, desolate" (Joel 2:3). These descriptions, directed to people living in Israel, assume that the audience possesses information about fabled Eden and knows it to be more richly endowed with water and capable of producing greater abundance than their own well-endowed land (see Deut 8:7–9; 33:13–14; Joel 2:21–24).

WHY A GARDEN?

In biblical Hebrew, *gan*, "garden," refers to a plantation of trees, fruit-bearing, aromatic, decorative, or in some aesthetic mix (Isa 1:30; Ezek 31:4–9; Song of Songs 4:16; 5:1; 6:2), as well as to a green garden for raising vegetables (1 Kings 21:2). The Hebrew word is related to the verbal root *g-n-n* used to generate verbs referring to protecting and sheltering. It is distinguished from *śādeh*, "open field," where cereals were raised, and *kerem*, "orchard," where grape vines and olive trees were cultivated. Elements of an orchard might have been imagined in a garden, but not fields. Cultivated fields could only have been imagined as situated beyond the confines of a garden.

God's Garden, like that of every Israelite who had one, was not conceived as wondrously self-maintaining in the way that Greek stories imagined the world during the Golden Age. Gardens are civilized artifacts. Manufactured and controlled, they are usually created for some mix of utilitarian and aesthetic purposes.

The story presents the Garden as a project that God undertook in Eden for his own purpose. Since God was understood to have no needs that a garden might satisfy, its sole purpose may have been to provide aesthetic pleasure (Gen 2:9). Such a conception was understood to be beyond the grasp of the about-to-be-formed human, an uncivilized being. But, like all gardens, God's also required hydration and cultivation, tasks within the human's competence (Gen 2:5, 8–9). So, as God planned and planted his garden, he also planned ahead for its upkeep by a human caretaker. Thinking ahead, he anticipated the human's nutritional requirements.

WHAT'S TO EAT?

For nourishment, the caretaker had fruit from trees requiring minimal care (Gen 2:9, 16). But these could not have been considered the human's main victuals by Israelites listening to the story. They would have understood that although the trees provided olive oil along with nuts and fruits, such a diet lacked other elements of what they and all other Mediterranean peoples considered a decent meal. Cereals—wheat was the first choice; barley the second—were central to Israelite diets and to those of most people in the ancient Near East. Where were they to be found in Eden?

Cereals are mentioned in the Garden story as part of the first person's basic diet, but their presence has been concealed under a bushel basket of archaic English and mistranslations. They are referred to in Genesis 2:5, which indicates that the first human had access to produce from plants of the field, the *'ēśeb* that had to be cultivated. These started to sprout once the rain cycle began, about the same time that the human was formed from a clod, although the story does not account for this.

Rendering *'ēśeb* with terms such as *herb* (KJV, NRSV) and *grass* (NAB, NJPS) misses or at least fails to emphasize this point. Nowadays, English *herb* usually refers to seasonal plants, only parts of which are exploited for medicinal purposes or as flavoring agents. But in the seventeenth century, when the King James Version was prepared, *herb* could refer generally to vegetative growth. English *grass*, derived from words meaning "green growth," refers to plants consumed by grazing animals but excludes cereal grains. The semantic situation in biblical Hebrew is somewhat different, and it is the Hebrew that ultimately counts.

The parallelism in Genesis 2:5 between *kol śîyaḥ haśśādeh*, "every plant of the field," and *kol 'ēseb haśśādeh*, "every 'ēseb of the field," along with other attestations of *śîyaḥ* in Genesis 21:15 and Job 30:4, 7, as well as its etymology, suggest that *śîyaḥ* is a general term whereas 'ēseb designates a defined subcategory.

In biblical Hebrew, herbage whose stalks, leaves, or seeds were consumable by either beast or human was lumped under the term 'ēseb. In Genesis 1:29 people consume it as food. In Genesis 9:3, *yereq 'ēseb*, "green" 'ēseb, or "green edible plants," is specified as food for Noah and his descendents, while in Zechariah 10:1, *'ēseb baśśādeh*, "'ēseb in the field," refers to unharvested edible plants in the field. Psalm 104:14 distinguishes between *ḥāṣiyr labbehēmāh*, "fodder for animals," and *'ēseb la'abōdat hā'ādām*, "edible plants for the work of a human that he may bring forth food from the earth."[5]

This analysis is confirmed by the narrative about the seventh plague in Egypt: hail (Exod 9:13–35). The hail destroyed all 'ēseb in the field (Exod 9:22–25). But, if so, the story has to explain on what the Israelites and Egyptians subsisted—and it does. It explains that the flax and barley were ruined, but not the wheat and emmer (an ancient wheat), which ripen late (Exod 9:32). Flax, barley, wheat, and emmer, all human foodstuffs, are subsumed under 'ēseb.

In view of this analysis, it is likely that Genesis 2:5 indicated to Israelite readers that the edible field plants and cereals were intended as foodstuffs for the human after his formation and placement in the Garden.[6] The plants were most likely imagined growing in suitable fields somewhere near but outside the Garden, as in Israelite farmsteads. However, this surmise cannot be proven from anything in the biblical narrative.[7]

Another way of approaching the question of how Iron Age readers and listeners imagined the diet of the first couple is to consider what constituted the normal Israelite diet over the course of a calendar year. This may be accomplished with the help of data recovered from archaeological excavations and from casual references to food in the Bible.

On the basis of excavated remains and paleobotanical studies, archaeologists have learned that a subsistence economy in the Israel of the Iron Age would have included wheat and barley; lentils, peas, chickpeas, bitter vetch, and possibly other legumes; olives, grapes, dates, figs, pomegranates,

The Gezer Calendar and the Agricultural Year

Written on a small limestone tablet, possibly as a student exercise, the calendar was discovered at the site of the biblical Gezer in 1908. Written in a tenth- to early ninth-century BCE Hebrew alphabet, the calendar records the annual agricultural cycle: months of gathering, months of sowing, months of greens, a month of cutting flax, a month of harvesting barley, a month of harvesting and measuring, months of pruning, a month of summer fruit. (Adapted from R. P. H. Vincent, "Un calendrier agricole israélite," *Revue Biblique,* N.S., 6 [1909]: 243.)

wild pears, and peaches; almonds, pistachios, walnuts, and acorns; garlic and onions; and other edible plants that grow wild seasonally. Milk products such as cheeses and whey, and meat would have been available primarily from flocks of sheep and goats and from small herds of cattle raised mainly to pull plows and carts (see Gen 18:8; Judg 4:19; 5:25; Isa 7:15, 22; Gen 18:7; 27:9; 1 Sam 28:24).[8]

In addition to what may be discerned from the archaeological record, the Gezer calendar of the tenth century BCE, perhaps the earliest known archaic Hebrew inscription, refers to greens (*lqš*), flax (*pšt*), barley (*šʿrm*), and summer fruit (*qṣ*).[9] The inscription is important because it comes from Gezer, a city on the western border of Judahite influence during the Iron Age, and because it describes the agricultural cycle in a region suitable for field crops.

In combination, paleobotany, archaeology, biblical references, and the Gezer calendar attest to a diversified pattern of agriculture involving cultivated grains, fruits, and other plants in vegetable plots, fields, and orchards as well as uncultivated plants whose edible parts were gathered. Botanical data from poems in the Song of Songs may be added to the list. These short lyrical compositions provide a highly idealized portrait of a well-watered garden in the territory of a northern Israelite tribe. In it odiferous fruits and aromatic spices are grown: pomegranates, nuts, henna, nard, saffron, and myrrh (Song of Songs 4:12–16; 5:1; 6:1).

All these resources enable us to imagine the rich diversity of plants that Israelites may have thought present in the Garden and growing slightly beyond, but they do not suggest where in this Garden the Tree of Knowing may have been located.

WHERE WERE THE SPECIAL TREES?

Verse 9 provides no information about the location of the Tree of Knowing other than a fuzzy hint in the way that it strings words together in a method that linguists describe as "forward gapping."

Forward gapping in Hebrew is easier to follow after seeing how it works in English: "Bill harvested corn and green beans and peas." The sense of the verb "harvested" is understood to apply forward to corn, beans, and peas, and the adjective "green" describes not only beans but also peas. The gaps in such compound sentences are created by "delete" rules operating when a compound sentence is formed from a number of simple ones: Bill harvested corn. Bill harvested green beans. Bill harvested green peas. With forward gapping, redundant information is deleted.

Consideration of the Hebrew verse's syntax indicates that the verb *wayyaṣmaḥ*, "and he caused to sprout," has three distinct direct objects connected by the conjunction *waw*, "and": every tree, the Tree of Life, and the Tree of Knowing. The description of every tree as desirable for seeing and good for eating carries forward to the two special trees—a conclusion verified by Genesis 3:6—while the preposition *betōwk*, "in/at the within (part)," written before "the Tree of Life," carries forward also to "the Tree of Knowing," a conclusion supported by the woman's use of the same preposition in Genesis 3:2, where she quotes the narrator, not God.[10]

This analysis indicates that the verse locates the Tree of Life ambiguously within the confines delimited by the Garden. It was not necessarily near its center, which could have been specified either by *beqereb*, "in/at the inner part," or *belēb*, "in/at the heart," prepositions whose physiological associations might have hinted at an area near its geographic center. It was not by the Garden's outer perimeter, for which *biqeṣēh*, "in/at the edge/end," or *bigebūl*, "in/at the border," might have been used. It was just there, somewhere away from the edge but not near the middle, maybe about halfway in. And because the force of the preposition carries forward, so, too, was the Tree of Knowing thereabouts. No information in Genesis 2:9 warranted the assumption that the two trees were even proximate to each other or that they were physically distinguished in any manner from other trees in the Garden.

Moreover, the syntactic imbalance of verse 9, with its dangling final tree, has parallels in biblical prose: "And God made the two great lights, the large light for ruling the day and the small light for ruling the night, and (also) the stars" (Gen 1:16); "and to take us for slaves and (also) our donkeys" (Gen 43:18b); "I made with you a covenant and (also) with Israel" (Exod 34:27b); "there will not be among you a sterile male and a sterile female and (also) among your livestock" (Deut 7:14b); "because they and their herds came up, and (also) their tents" (Judg 6:5a). Consequently, nothing in the syntax of verse 9 might have suggested to ancient readers that the trees were proximate.[11]

This syntactic analysis implies that the author intended to refer to two unique trees, a conclusion verified by the narrative snippet in Genesis 3:22–24 that I discuss in Chapter 22. It disallows interpreting the *waw* at the beginning of the phrase *we'ēṣ hadda'at,* the Tree of Knowing, as signaling that what follows explicates or clarifies that which comes before; the *waw*, in other words, is not what Hebrew grammarians sometimes label the *waw explicativum*, rendered into English as "i.e." or "that is" or "that is to say." Were this a *waw explicativum*, the verse would have to be translated: "the Tree of Life, that is, the Tree of Knowing." According to this interpretation, a single unique tree was to be found in the Garden, and it bore either two types of fruit, each with a different nature, or one fruit with two aftereffects.[12]

Although the one-tree interpretation is precluded by the story involving the Tree of Life in Genesis 3:22–24, the syntactic explanation does not rid the larger narrative—extending from Genesis 2:4b to 3:21—of the tension caused by Genesis 2:16–17 and 3:1–6. In these verses, characters refer to the Tree of Knowing as if it alone was unique in the Garden. Silence about the Tree of Life in these passages is owing, perhaps, to the focus of the extant narrative on only the Tree of Knowing. The tension most likely originates in the imperfect editing of this story at either an oral stage of its transmission or, as seems more likely to me, a written stage.[13]

Even though the actual layout of the Garden remains vague in the story, sophisticated ancient Israelite readers could have imagined what it looked like. They would have had a much more difficult problem, however, in determining the location of the Garden in the world as they knew it. Had citizens of Jerusalem been taken outdoors and asked to indicate the direction of the Garden, to which point on the compass would they have extended a finger?

8 WHERE IN THE WORLD WAS EDEN?

(Gen 2:10–14)

Genesis 2

10a   And a river *yōṣē' mē* Eden to water the garden.

10b   And from there it divides and becomes four head(water)s.

11   The name of the first, Pishon.

> It (is the one) that *sōwbēb 'ēt* all the land of
> Havilah where there is gold,

12   and the gold of that land is good.
> Bdellium is there and onyx stone.

13   And the name of the second river, Gihon.

> It (is the one) that *sōwbēb 'ēt* all the land of Kush.

14   And the name of the third river, Hidekel [Tigris].

> It (is the one) that flows east of Ashur.

And the fourth river, it is Perat [Euphrates].

In "Lectures on Genesis," delivered in June or July 1535, Martin Luther suggested that it was time to give up on fruitless searches for Eden. After perusing writings by scriptural exegetes and geographers of his own and earlier periods, Luther metaphorically shrugged his shoulders. The pursuit of Paradise, he wrote, was an exercise in futility: "At this point people discuss where Paradise is located. The interpreters torture themselves in amazing ways. Some favor the idea that it is located within the two tropics under the equinoctial point. Others think that a more temperate climate was necessary, since the place was so fertile. Why waste words? The opinions are numberless. My opinion is briefly this: It is an idle question about something no longer in existence. Moses is writing the history of the time before sin and the Deluge, but we are compelled to speak of conditions as they are after sin and after the Deluge."[1]

In the first century CE, Josephus identified the Pishon and Gihon Rivers mentioned in verses 11 and 13 with the Ganges and the Nile, respectively. Luther, following church tradition, accepted these identifications, but he could not fathom how the Ganges, flowing from north to south, and the Nile, flowing from south to north, could possibly be used to determine the location of Eden, where, according to Genesis, they began their course. Additionally, both were distant from the Tigris and the Euphrates. After much pondering he concluded that "we must not suppose that the appearance of the world is the same today as it was before sin."[2] For Luther, the flood in the days of Noah had so changed the face of the planet that "Paradise is now lost. Nothing more remains of it except these four corrupted and, as it were, leprous rivers, made so first by the sin of man and then by the Flood."[3]

Luther did not attend to a problem that his conclusion—reasonable given his beliefs and the basis of knowledge available to him—precipitated. His determination that the word-map of the story described a fantastic geography that had ceased to exist after the deluge implied that Moses had written a story containing information that could not have made sense to him or to his audience.[4]

Reader-response criticism rejects this mode of interpretation. It suggests not only that the word-map made at least some sense to both the author and his audience but also that it was significant for his communication. More than four centuries of geographical and philological research, unavailable to Luther, is available now.

STREAMING RIVERS

The Hebrew expression in verse 10 translated "goes out + from," *yōṣē' + mē* (or *min*), elsewhere in the Bible refers to water issuing from a source. Thus, in Exodus 17:6 and Numbers 20:8, 10, it refers to water issuing from the rock that Moses struck; in Judges 15:19, to waters flowing out of a cleft made by God in a canyon so that Samson could drink; in Ezekiel

47:1, 8, 12, to water flowing out from the Temple Mount. A noun related to this verb, *mōṣā'*, "place of exit," identifies a spring or source of water in 2 Kings 2:21 and Isaiah 58:11.

According to verse 10, an unnamed river, originating outside the Garden, somewhere in the territory designated Eden/Bountiful, flowed through the Garden. The author appears to indicate, if we extrapolate from the verse, that after exiting the Garden, the unnamed river split into freshets and undefined rivulets, some of which recombined, forming the upper courses of new rivers flowing in different directions.

Mention of the four rivers that emerged from Eden's river contributes nothing to the development of the plot. So what is the role of the information provided in the story, and why was it included?

Although mention of the rivers appears to be a narrative aside—notice how Genesis 2:15–16 recapitulates and then resumes the narrative from 2:8—details in Genesis 2:10b–14 contribute to the story in two ways: they provide an image of powerful, moving waters and plenitude, both of which teasingly bequeath an impression of palpable reality to the unfolding narrative. They also anchor the story in an apparent geographic reality.

The plenitude evoked by the description of the rivers is not of wealth—the gold is not in the Garden and not in Eden, but elsewhere, in Havilah, along with bdellium and onyx. Rather, the plenitude is of arable land.[5] The image of the single stream giving rise to four recalls a conventional evocation of fecundity in central and northern Mesopotamian art. There, abundantly watered plenty was represented by a deity pouring out two or four streams from a single jar.[6] This image was the ancient Mesopotamian equivalent of the Greek cornucopia, the horn of plenty.

Mention of the Tigris and the Euphrates, easily located, situated the Garden in earthly geography. People of Iron Age Judah and Israel knew about these rivers and the direction of their flow, the latter better than the former. During the reigns of David and Solomon (tenth century BCE) and again during the peaceful four-decades-long reigns of Azaryahu (also known as Uzziah) in Judah and Jeroboam II in Israel during the first half of the eighth century BCE, Israelite political influence extended north up to the Orontes River in contemporary Lebanon and northeast across the desert to the banks of the Euphrates in Syria.[7] The Euphrates was so well known that it is referred to in Exodus 23:31 simply as "the river." In the course of these centuries, many generations of Israelite

Four Rivers Flowing from a Sacred Mountain

The mountain-man with rivers meeting at his chest comes from Assyria and dates to around 1500 BCE. (Reprinted by permission from Othmar Keel, *The Symbolism of the Biblical World: Ancient Near Eastern Iconography and the Book of Psalms,* Winona Lake, IN: Eisenbrauns, 1997, p. 118 [fig. 153a]. Drawing by H. Keel-Leu.)

Four Rivers Flowing from a Goddess's Vase

This vase from Assur (Ashur) dates to the eighth–seventh centuries BCE. (Reprinted by permission from Keel, *Symbolism of the Biblical World*, p. 140 [fig. 185]. Drawing by H. Keel-Leu.)

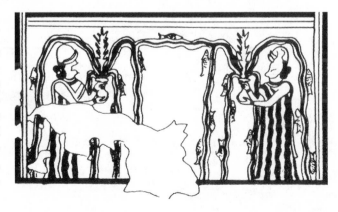

Ea, God of the Deep

Four rivers flow from of Ea, Mesopotamian god of fresh water, in the clay impression of a cylinder seal that dates to around 2000 BCE. (Composite figure drawn by Debby Segura after W. H. Ward, *The Seal Cylinders of Western Asia*, Washington, DC: Carnegie Institution of Washington, 1910, p. 374 [figs. d, e].)

Two Goddesses and Eight Rivers

Four rivers flow from each vase held by a goddess, as in the image of Ea. This depiction comes from Mari, on the upper Euphrates River, and dates to around 1700 BCE. (Reprinted by permission from Keel, *Symbolism of the Biblical World*, p. 143 [fig. 191]. Drawing by H. Keel-Leu.)

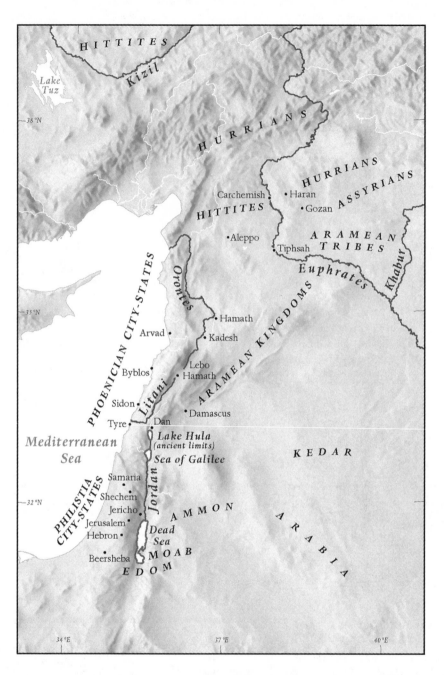

Israel in Its Ancient Near Eastern Setting
(Map by David Deis, Dreamline Cartography.)

traders, soldiers, and diplomats had seen and been ferried across it into the Mesopotamian heartland. Southern Mesopotamia was not completely terra incognita to people from Judah and Israel.

The situation with the Tigris was different. In the ninth century BCE, it would most likely have been known only as the river whose course roughly paralleled that of the Euphrates, the one that people encountered north of the great Mesopotamian plain. By the end of the eighth century BCE, however, many Israelites would have known the Tigris personally, particularly those who had lived in the capital city of Samaria and the surrounding villages. Deported by Assyrians from their homeland after the destruction of Samaria in 722/721 BCE, many were compelled to settle in towns and territories north of the lower Tigris, in parts of contemporary Iraq and Iran (2 Kings 15:29; 1 Chron 5:26; 2 Kings 17:6; 18:11).

Since both the Tigris and the Euphrates flow from northwest to southeast into the Persian Gulf, it appears that Eden should be located somewhere near their headwaters, northwest of the Fertile Crescent. The problem with this obvious solution is that scholars have been unable to locate the two other rivers.

Their failure led E. A. Speiser to propose that Genesis 2:10 refers to the convergence of four rivers. Accordingly, he translated it to read "A river rises in Eden to water the garden; outside, it forms four separate branch streams." The point of Speiser's translation is to present four rivers in Eden conjoining into a single stream to form the Persian Gulf. His conclusion perforce locates Eden and the Garden somewhere in or adjacent to the Persian Gulf.[8]

A SOUTHERN EDEN

Following Speiser, whose Genesis commentary was a popular best-seller, many scholars identified Eden with the paradisiacal Dilmun of Mesopotamian lore and located it on what is now the oil-rich island kingdom of Bahrain, in the Persian Gulf. In one form or another, Speiser's explanation remains popular because it appears to be reinforced by a Sumerian myth describing Dilmun in idyllic terms reminiscent of Isaiah's description of an age when the "wolf shall lie down with the lamb, the leopard with the kid . . . the cow and the bear shall graze and their young shall lie down together, and the lion, like the ox, shall eat straw" (Isa 11:6–9). Dilmun is described much the same way in the myth:

The land Dilmun is pure, the land Dilmun is clean.
The land Dilmun is clean, the land Dilmun is most bright.

In Dilmun the raven utters no cries.
The Ittidu-bird utters not the cry of the Ittidu-bird
The lion kills not;
The wolf snatches not the lamb;
Unknown is the kid-devouring wild dog.[9]

But both the section from Isaiah and the Sumerian myth are irrelevant to this discussion. They were imported into the discourse, first, by associating Eden of the Garden story with a vague notion of Paradise drawn ultimately from the Golden Age of Greek mythology and, second, by implying a biblical connection through the thematic similarity of the myth and the Isaiah verses.

As I pointed out in Chapter 7, the concept of a Golden Age is foreign to Israelite thought. The image of Eden as untroubled and serene is medieval, fashioned from non-Israelite ideas about a place identified as paradise before the Fall. Isaiah was describing a time when the hostile behavior of many animals would be changed, not a place where it would happen. Nothing in Isaiah encourages linking his vision to Eden, and nothing in descriptions of the Garden in the story or elsewhere in the Bible suggests that it was a place where natural beings acted unnaturally. Consequently, the description of Dilmun has no place in the discourse about Eden's location because it is unconnected to anything in the Garden story.

Speiser's comprehension of Genesis 2:10 is probably wrong because the "in" of his translation presupposes that the verse contains a Hebrew preposition *be*, meaning "in." Actually, a quite different preposition, *m/min*, "from," is found. Furthermore, although Speiser's rendering of the participle *yōṣē'* by English "rises" is fair, it is misleading. His selection of this translation obfuscates all senses of "welling up and out, exiting, issuing forth" that this Hebrew verb, and all derived nouns, possess when associated with water.

Hebrew expresses the notion of waters flowing *to* a place with *bā'ūw* + *'el X*, "they [the waters] came + to X" (Ezek 47:8; Ezra 8:15). The absence of this expression and the linguistic inexactitudes of Speiser's translation render any search for Eden in the region of the Persian Gulf problematic. The place where a river's flow terminates, where its waters are discharged, is identified in Hebrew as its *qeṣēh*, its end. This term is used to describe the end of the Jordan River at the north end of the Dead Sea (Josh 15:5; 18:19).

In English, the place where a river flows into a large body of water or discharges its waters into a delta has been referred to metaphorically since the twelfth century as the "mouth of the river." The metaphor may have originated in the first encounters of explorers with rivers in new territories; where the rivers flowed into a lake or ocean is where the explorers entered, hence "mouth." Speiser may have assumed that Hebrew *head(water)* functioned similarly to English *mouth* (of a river).

Undaunted by the inherent problems of Speiser's suggestion, two researchers propose identifications of the unknown rivers that, if correct, lend support to the hypothesis of a southern Eden. One, J. A. Sauer, draws attention to the discovery of an ancient river, 650 miles long, that once traversed the Arabian Peninsula, crossed through present-day Kuwait, and emptied into the Persian Gulf near its northern edge. Tracing its route takes account of long dry riverbeds, or wadis. It originated in the Wadi Ar-Rimah, east of Medina, Saudi Arabia, followed a geological fault, and terminated in the broad Wadi Al Batin, which forms a natural border between Kuwait and Iraq. This river dried up sometime between 3500 and 2000 BCE, when the northern edge of the Persian Gulf was much farther inland. Its middle section was eventually buried under dunes. Knowledge of its existence more than a millennium later, in the Iron Age, if it persisted at all, could have been no more than a vague memory. Near its original headwaters, about 125 miles southeast of present-day Medina, ancient gold mining was carried out.

Sauer identifies this ancient river with the Pishon because of the connection between Havilah and gold.[10] If correct, the northeastern corner of what is now Saudi Arabia would have been ancient Havilah.

Sauer's identification of the Pishon is complemented by a suggestion by Z. Sitchin that the fourth river, the Gihon, is the Karun River, which flows down from Iran into the northern end of the Persian Gulf.[11] If correct, the notation by the author of the Garden story that the Gihon curves by the land of Kush may be taken as a reference to the Kassites, the *kaššu* of Akkadian texts, a non-Semitic people living north of the foothills of the Zagros Mountains, on the western slope of the Iranian Plateau. Some Kassite tribes, whose language is not yet known, penetrated into southern

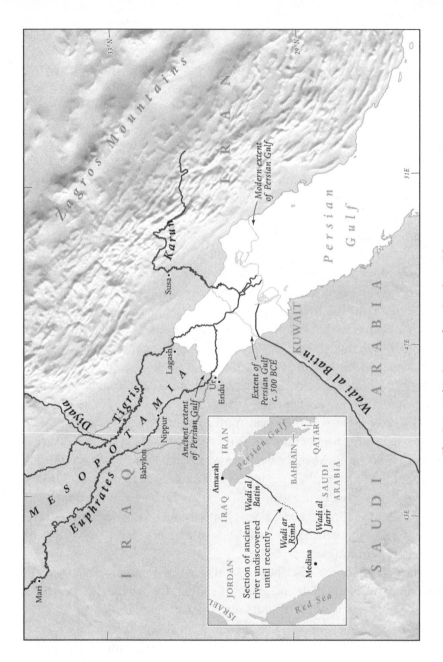

The Geographic Context for a Southern Eden
(Map by David Deis, Dreamline Cartography.)

Mesopotamia from the foothills around 1725 BCE and eventually established kingdoms there. Their original homeland was elsewhere.[12]

CLARIFYING THE LANGUAGE

Unfortunately, these identifications founder on the shoals of grammar and Hebrew usage. Sauer's and Sitchin's proposals require the whole of the Persian Gulf itself, within its ancient limits, to be taken as the *nāhār*, "river," that went out from Eden/Bountiful to water the Garden. This identification is highly unlikely. On account of its size, the Persian Gulf, if known to Israelite writers at all, would have been labeled *'agam*, "lake" (cf. Isa 41:18, Ps 107:35), or, most likely, *yām*, "sea."

A word indicating river would not be appropriate. The waters of the Persian Gulf do not flow or stream, and these movements alone qualify bodies of water for the Hebrew label *nāhār*, "river." The root *n-h-r* underlying the noun is used to form verbs describing the rapid continuous movement of people and even of light (Isa 2:2; Jer 51:44; Mic 4:1; Ps 34:6).

Additionally, if correct, the Garden in Eden would then have to be identified with all the lands around the shoreline of the ancient gulf, and Eden itself would have to be associated either with all the catchment areas whose waters ended up in the gulf or with the extensive ancient marshes at its northwestern edge. Paradoxically, in this ancient geographical setting, Eden would have been watered by more than four rivers, coming from three different directions, that would have drained into the gulf, but not through any single channel.

By telling *from where* the rivers began to stream and revealing something about two of the four rivers, the Garden story indicates clearly that Eden was in the north. Unfortunately, although many proposals to identify the Gihon and Pishon Rivers have been made, their locations remain unknown.[13]

The rhyming of their names is sometimes interpreted as an indication that the names are made up, but a better explanation is available. They rhyme because both terminate with a suffix often used in toponyms—in the names of cities: Ashkelon, Dibon, Gibeon, Hannaton, Hebron; of mountains: Hermon, Lebanon, Zion; and of rivers: Arnon and Kishon. Thus, their rhyming does not constitute an argument for treating the names as fictional. Since geographical names reflecting this suffix do not appear to cluster in any particular region of the ancient Near East, the suffixes do not assist in determining the location, real or fictional, of the rivers.

Once the toponymic suffix is identified, it is possible to study the names of these two rivers minus their suffixes in the hope that the underlying base provides a clue to the original language of each name and hence a hint to where each river was thought to be located. The names may only appear to be Hebrew because of the familiar suffix, or they may be translations from some non-Semitic language into a Semitic language related to Hebrew.

The name Pishon could be derived from the Indo-European Hittite language once used in vast areas of what is now Turkey: Hittite *pešš* means "to rub or scrub with soap."[14] However, the name might also reflect a rarely attested Hebrew root *p-w-š*, which may mean "to move about quickly, gambol" or "to spread out" or, when referring to penned calves, "to paw the ground." The name Gihon could be derived from an Akkadian word *gaḫḫu* or *guḫḫu* meaning "fit of coughing, coughing up."[15] But it might be derived from a related Hebrew root, *g-w-ḥ* or *g-y-ḥ*, meaning "to burst forth." This root aptly clarifies the name of Gihon Spring at the foot of the City of David in Jerusalem that gushes on an irregular schedule many times a day, an unpredictable Old Faithful.

Rivers with these names are not mentioned in known ancient Near Eastern documents. Because they are never mentioned again in the Bible, perhaps because they lay far beyond Israel's geographic concerns and consciousness, it may be that even their general location was unknown to most people. The author of these verses knew this and appended additional information about the unknown rivers, more about the first than the second.

Verses 11–13 provide one significant additional piece of geographical information. Both the Gihon and the Pishon are described by a regularly misinterpreted Hebrew expression, *sōwbēb* + *'et* + Geographical Name, which means "passing or curving or skirting by (outside) the border of Geographical Name." This is quite obvious from the way it is employed in Judges 11:17–18, where the expression describes the Israelites going around, rather than crossing, certain territories en route to the Promised Land: "And Israel sent messengers to the king of Edom saying: 'Please, I will pass through your land.' But the king of Edom did not listen. And he [Israel] sent also to the king of Moab and he did not allow it; so Israel stayed at Kadesh. And (then) he went in the wilderness and *passed/curved/skirted by* the land of Edom and the land of Moab, and came from the east to the land of Moab and camped across the Arnon, and did not enter the border of Moab because the Arnon is the border of Moab."

Similarly, the rivers in Genesis neither "encircled" the lands, as the Hebrew expression is sometimes translated, in which case the lands would have been islands, nor did they flow through them.[16] The expression in verses 11 and 13 indicates that each river bordered a different land: Pishon, the land of Havilah; and Gihon, the land of Kush. With this information it should be possible to identify each river by locating the land by which each flowed. The task, however, is not simple.

The Havilah mentioned in Genesis 10:7 and 29 might be in southern Arabia or Ethiopia, or these passages might refer to two different places bearing the same name. Most people are aware of London and Berlin in Europe, but places with the same names are found also in the United States. The Kush of Genesis 10:8, Isaiah 11:11, and Esther 1:1 might be somewhere in Mesopotamia; the Kush of Isaiah 11:11; Ezekiel 30:4, 9; and Nahum 3:9 might be located south of Egypt along the Red Sea coast. Which of these might have been the Havilah and Kush of Genesis 2:11–13?

An additional complicating factor is the very real possibility that the Havilah and Kush mentioned in the Garden story are not mentioned elsewhere in the Bible. The name Havilah may be associated with Semitic nouns that refer to sand or mud, or to verbs that refer to encircling, whirling, and dancing; or it might translate a non-Semitic name referring to these activities.

I am unaware of a definitive explanation for the meaning of Kush. The Akkadian verb *kašašu*, meaning "to be powerful, hold sway, master," and the related noun *kuššu*, referring to Kassites or to a powerful official in Anatolia, provide only some general direction.[17]

Despite these difficulties and the bewildering range of options that they imply, the evidence presented for locating Eden north of Israel, rather than to its southeast on the far side of Arabia, indicates that most of the suggestions given so far are false leads.[18] They all work from toponyms— from names of places—to geography. Better results are obtainable by working from geography to toponyms.

A NORTHERN EDEN

In 1862, L. Coleman proposed that the ancient Halys River, the modern Kizil Irmak in northern Turkey, be identified as the Pishon. Its headwaters lie slightly northwest of those giving rise to the Euphrates in the Mountains of Ararat, and after a circuitous seven-hundred-mile (1,127-kilometer) route, west, southwest, northwest, then northeast, it empties into the southern Black Sea at Samsun. Coleman connected the reference to Havilah's fabled wealth with ancient Colchis, a region known in classical mythology for its gold, hides, linen, timber, and agricultural produce, for being the destination of Jason and the Argonauts in their search for the Golden Fleece, and for serving as the home of the fabled Medusa with her serpentine locks of hair. Coleman thought that ancient Colchis lay close to Samsun.[19] He erred.

Scholars now identify Colchis with the valley of the Phasis River, the modern Rion/Riuni, on the east side of the Black Sea, hundreds of miles northeast of the Halys. Coleman's identification of the Pishon with the Halys should nonetheless be maintained.

Coleman did not know when he wrote that the Halys, in its southwestern corner, borders the heartland of ancient Hatti, land of the Hittites, a powerful people of the ancient Near East. At the crook of its great bend, the Halys flows by ancient Hattusha, modern Boghazköy, fabled capital of the pre-Israelite Hittite empire. In addition, that city is identified in Akkadian by words that translate as "Silver City," suggesting that among its neighbors it was thought to have been a center of wealth, though not of the gold mentioned in verse 11.[20] Furthermore, as I indicated earlier in this chapter, the name Pishon, for all its Hebrew sound, can be derived from a Hittite word. Finally, west of the ancient Hittite capital and of the Halys River, and southwest of modern Ankara, lay the city-state of Gordium, modern Yassihoyuk, an ancient center for the metal trade throughout Asia Minor and city of the fabled Midas, he with the "golden touch."

Neither the modern nor the classical names of the Halys River prove helpful in identifying it with the Pishon. The Turkish name for the Halys, which means "salt" in Greek, is Kizil Irmak, "red river." The Greek name perhaps reflects the flowing of the river around a huge, barren steppe area that, owing to poor drainage, contains many saline lakes. The Turkish name refers to some aspects of its color at various times of the year. The original Hittite name, Marassantiya, was once also thought to mean "red river," but Hittitologists have discredited that interpretation.[21]

The statement of verse 11 that gold is found in Havilah is augmented by an evaluative judgment that the gold is "good." The unexpected adjective distinguishes between Havilian gold and gold from other places that did

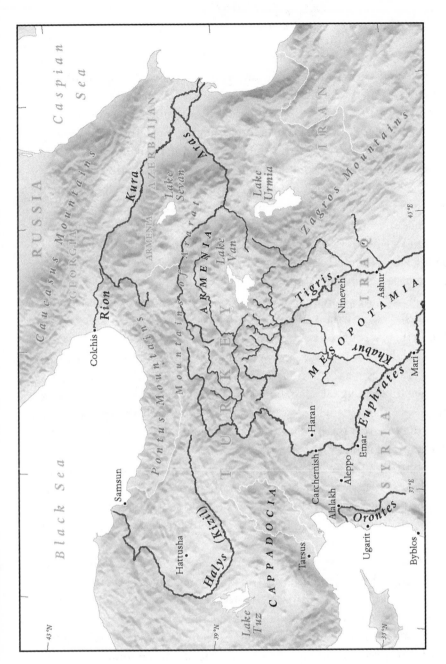

The Geographic Context for a Northern Eden
(Map by David Deis, Dreamline Cartography.)

not merit the label. Perhaps the adjective refers to the unalloyed purity of the gold and/or to the fact that it was easily obtainable. Nowadays in Turkey, gold is found with silver, but in much lower concentrations than with lead, copper, and other minerals. In eastern Asia Minor, however, in early periods, placer gold was recovered by sluicing auriferous gravels over sheepskins in running rivers, a detail underlying the story of Jason and his search for the Golden Fleece along the eastern edges of the Black Sea.[22]

Placer gold is no longer found in Turkey, but geologists have identified fifty-one sites that produce gold and other minerals and seventy-one that produce silver. Of these, gold is reported in the huge area embraced by the Halys River only near its eastern headwaters, where the river flows parallel to but south of the Pontus Mountains. Three gold and silver sites are reported along an imaginary line drawn south of the modern Black Sea town of Ünye, and three gold and three silver sites are on a line south of Giresun.[23] The extant sites suggest that in Early Antiquity, circa 1500–800 BCE, placer gold was available downstream.

Havilah is connected not only with gold but with bdellium, an aromatic gum resin akin to myrrh, and with onyx. This information does not help in locating Havilah, but neither does it disqualify the preceding proposal either. The referent of the Hebrew noun *bedōlaḥ*, "bdellium," is certain because it is cognate with Akkadian *budulḫu* in cuneiform texts that mention it along with other aromatic resins. In the Genesis context, where bdellium is linked with a gemstone, it may refer to a gem whose color is like that of a dark brown resin. In any event, the word for bdellium, *bedōlaḥ*, which is based on four, not three, root consonants, is a loanword in both Hebrew and Akkadian from an as-yet-unidentified non-Semitic language.

Hebrew *'eben haššōwham*, "shoham stone," mentioned in verse 12, is identified with onyx, a gemstone with alternating bands of brown, yellow, and white used often in cameos. The Hebrew noun is a possible cognate of Akkadian *sāmtu*, a noun that refers to a red carnelian. Ancient translations of the Hebrew render the word in many ways that all point in the same direction: *sardius*, an orange-red type of quartz; *sardonyx*, a red-brown type; and *beryllium*, a gemstone that occurs in blue-green, yellow, and red colors. Gems matching this range of possible interpretations are found in territories within the great bend of the Halys.[24] In Early Antiquity, gemstones would have been most easily found in the same stream-beds as the placer gold.

The distinguishing characteristics of Havilah listed by the author do not suffice for a precise identification. Perhaps he translated a name referring generally to the sandy steppe of central Anatolia that included adjacent areas endowed with valued resources. Adjacency to the Halys may have been all that counted. Perhaps the name was used to refer vaguely to an area north of the Halys but south of the Pontus Mountains, an area with no well-defined western boundary.

Coleman also proposed that the extremely long Arax River, the modern Aras River, which originates within a few miles of the Euphrates' headwaters, be identified with the Gihon. The Arax/Aras River flows east, southeast, then northeast across Armenia, emptying into the Caspian Sea south of Baku.[25] The mention in verse 13 that it passed by the "land of Kush" may indicate that the south border of the original homeland of the Kassites lay north of the Aras River and that the modern Lake Sevan was in the center of their territory.[26]

According to these identifications, the ordering of the four rivers in the Garden story is roughly from north to south, from the most distant to the one closest to Israelite territory. The more distant three rivers are characterized as marking southern borders of far-off lands. The fourth river, Euphrates, a one-time northern border marking the extent of Israelite military influence but also a southern border of the Mesopotamian heartland, needed no such characterization. Furthermore, headwaters of all four rivers lie within the territory of Urartu, an ancient kingdom whose territory spread west, northwest, and southwest of modern Lake Van.

If correct, these identifications suggest that the territory thought of as Eden was imagined as lying somewhere in the western part of Urartu but east of the Halys. The Garden was somewhere on Eden's eastern side. It may have been imagined as a landscaped artifact in a high mountain valley near the western edge of the Ararat mountain range, where rivulets streaming down different sides of the mountains contributed to the headwaters of four great rivers.[27] Today, as in Early Antiquity, this area is considered remote, isolated, and difficult to reach. Ancient east-west trade routes during the second and first millennia BCE followed paths north and south of this region but not through it.[28]

Eden with its Garden was to be found in areas nominally controlled by an ancient, non-Semitic people, the Hurrians, partially known from cuneiform sources written in the second millennium BCE as well as from the Bible.[29] For modern students, this information provides clues about the origin of some motifs in the Garden story.

THE HURRIAN CONNECTION

Hurrians were concentrated to the south of the general Mountains of Ararat–Lake Van region. After 1550 BCE, some Hurrian tribes spread eastward into Asia Minor, others moved southeast into northern Mesopotamia, and some migrated south into the Egyptian province of Canaan, settling primarily in what today is northern Syria and Lebanon; a few groups moved on into southern Canaan. The Amarna Letters (ca. 1402–1334 BCE), Akkadian documents from Canaanite rulers found in Egypt at Tell el-Amarna in 1887, attest to a Hurrian presence and influence in Jerusalem before Israelites rose to dominance in the region between the twelfth and tenth centuries BCE.

In the fourteenth century BCE, complaints were addressed to the Egyptian court about the military aggressions of Abdiḫepa, king of Jerusalem. His name indicates that his parents considered him to be a servant of the Hurrian goddess Ḫepa. During the thirteenth century, the century of the exodus, Egyptians could refer to their province of Canaan as the land of the Hurrians because of their perception that Hurrians either comprised a majority of the population that they controlled or controlled the region militarily, even if they were a minority.

According to Israelite traditions preserved in the Bible, Hurrians were thought to be one of the original peoples of Canaan. They are mentioned in the Bible as ḥōrīy, usually rendered in English by "Horites," but "Horians" or "Hurrians" could serve in English translations just as well. Israelites knew of them as settlers in southern Transjordan—the area east of the Jordan River—and across the central and southern Negev into Sinai (Gen 14:6; 36:21–30). According to Deuteronomy 2:12, 22, those in southern Transjordan were destroyed by the Edomite descendents of Esau, Jacob's son, who resettled the territory early in the Iron Age.

Attestations of a significant Hurrian component of the population of Transjordan support the possibility of either their direct or their indirect influence on early Israelite conceptions about the archaic origins of humanity.[30] Although they are the most likely candidates for introducing versions of Mesopotamian traditions into Canaan, Hittites or other peoples from Asia Minor, such as the Jebusites of Jerusalem (Josh 18:28; 2 Sam 5:6) may have served as cultural conduits.[31]

Four elements in Genesis 1–11, the primeval history of humanity, may betray Hurrian influence: (1) the motif of the four rivers, (2) the location of Eden/Bountiful, (3) the resting place of Noah's ark somewhere in the Mountains of Ararat (= Urartu; see Gen 8:41), east of Eden but still in Hurrian territory, and (4) the listing of Noah's northernmost descendents first in the "Table of Nations" in the tenth chapter of Genesis. Those listed as the sons of Japheth in Genesis 10:2–4—Gomer, Magog, Madai, Yavan, Tubal, and so on—are identified as inhabitants of Asia Minor, where Hurrians originally established their own kingdoms, spread their language and culture, and wielded influence, if not actual hegemony, over other ethnic groups during the second millennium BCE.

None of Japheth's descendents mentioned in Genesis were located north of an imaginary east-west line formed by the Pontus Mountains. His firstborn, Gomer, is identified with the Gimmiraya—the Cimmerians of some classical authors—mentioned in ninth-century BCE Assyrian texts. These people lived south of the Pontus Mountains but northeast of Lake Van in the ninth–eighth centuries BCE before expanding west into Asia Minor, east into Assyrian-controlled territory, and south into Armenia during the eighth and seventh centuries BCE. At the time that the list of nations in Genesis 10 was composed, the Gimmiraya were thought to be a people living only at the very northern edge of the world. The world map imagined by Israelites did not include the Black Sea, the Caspian Sea, or the lands, mountains, and peoples in between or beyond them.

For Israelites living in Jerusalem after the eighth century BCE, mention of the Pishon and Gihon Rivers, perhaps the stuff of quasi-legends, along with the Tigris and Euphrates, only contributed to the misty sense that Eden/Bountiful was real but distant and veiled. It was not a utopia but a place at the most removed fringe of the known inhabited world, the ancient equivalent of Tierra del Fuego, at the southern tip of Patagonia.[32]

Eden was somewhere far to the north of ancient Israel, beyond its northern neighbors, who lived along the coast and in the Lebanese mountains, beyond its northern trading partners, who were strung along the southern coast of Asia Minor. But according to Genesis, no matter where it was located, it contained a unique garden that had once been inhabited by the ancestors of all humanity.

9   THE GARDENER AND HIS TASKS

(Gen 2:15)

Genesis 2

15   And YHWH god took the human and placed him in the
garden of Eden to work it and to guard it.

The function of the garden determined how it would be tended.

Biblical references indicate that individual Israelites had fenced gardens and that their kings established gardens within cities or just beyond their walls (1 Kings 21:2; 2 Kings 21:18, 26; 25:4; Song of Songs 4:12–5:1; 6:1–3; Neh 3:15). Israelites probably understood, then, what was involved in maintaining a garden, and they could easily have imagined the work routines of the first human.[1]

THE GARDEN'S LAYOUT

Their gardens could have vegetables, fruit trees, open areas sufficient for a few tethered grazing animals, and beds of spices. Nothing in the Bible indicates the layout of such a garden. It is likely, however, that the most elaborate of them followed conventional designs of Mesopotamian and Egyptian gardens as represented in tomb paintings and reliefs that archaeologists have discovered. If so, Israelites would have imagined the Garden as a very large and splendid example of the types of gardens with which they were familiar or about which they had heard.

An Assyrian Garden

The drawing from eighth-century BCE Nineveh shows a garden fed by an aqueduct in what appears to be a mountainous region. The path leading to a posed image and to the altar suggests that it may have been a temple garden. (From S. Dalley, "Ancient Mesopotamian Gardens and the Identification of the Hanging Gardens," *Garden History* 21 [1993]: 10 [fig. 2]. Reprinted courtesy of Stephanie Dalley.)

In 876 BCE, Ashurnasirpal II, king of Assyria, established a royal garden in his royal city, Kalhu, the biblical Calah (Gen 10:11–12), that featured trees and plants collected during his travels: cedar, cypress, box, myrtle, almond, date palm, ebony, sissoo, olive, tarwind, oak, terebinth, *dukdu*-nut, pistachio, myrrh, fir, oak, willow, pomegranate, plum, pear, quince, fig, grapevine, and more. Ashurnasirpal's garden was watered not only by rain but also by a specially constructed aqueduct connecting sources in the mountains behind the city to the garden itself. Other royal gardens in Mesopotamia also featured vegetable plots. Alongside such botanical gardens, there were sometimes game parks that functioned both as zoos and as private hunting reserves.[2]

In Egypt, a garden typically had a pool that functioned as a reservoir from which water was released through sluice gates into channels for watering. A rectangular vineyard filled its center, with the grapes trained on latticework over a pergola creating a cool area beneath. Trees of various

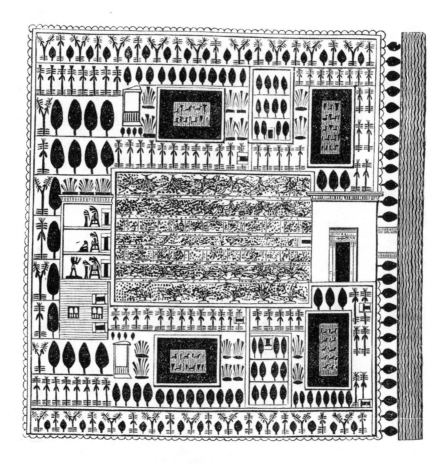

An Egyptian Garden

In this elaborate fifteenth-century BCE Theban garden dedicated to arboriculture, four ponds and small irrigation canals are supplied by a river or large canal flowing just outside the garden walls. (Reprinted from H. Rosellini, *Monomenti dell' Egitto e della Nubia*, vol. 2: *Monomenti Civili,* Pisa: Presso N. Capurro, 1834, p. 69.)

species were planted in symmetrical patterns from the outer walls toward the center. Sometimes stands of trees were planted to delineate smaller plots given over to plantings of flowers and herbs within the garden. Products of these gardens were harvested and used for domestic consumption or to provide wood and offerings in cultic ceremonies.

One Egyptian painting of a funerary garden represents the owner as a bird receiving fruit and water from a divine sycamore fig tree so that he can leave his tomb and live free as a soul bird. To make the point clear, some branches of the tree are painted as the image of a goddess.[3] Although the painting is a thin branch on which to hang a weak hypothesis, it stimu-

Ipuy, an Egyptian Gardener

The gardener represented here is drawing water from a pond to irrigate nearby trees, Thebes, thirteenth century BCE. (Reprinted from J. G. Wilkinson, A *Popular Account of the Ancient Egyptians,* New York: Harper and Brothers, 1854, p. 90.)

Watering the Egyptian Garden

After using two leather buckets to draw water from a pool, this fifteenth-century BCE gardener carries them on a wooden yoke to nearby trees with irrigation pans at their base. (Reprinted from Wilkinson, *Popular Account of the Ancient Egyptians,* p. 34.)

lates speculation that the Tree of Life was a sycomore, a very common tree in the Shephelah, the region between the Hill Country and the Coastal Plain, and in flat regions of Judah, raised both for its fruit and its wood. Egyptian wall drawings of gardens often feature representations of this tree (see also 1 Kings 10:27; 1 Chr 27:28; Isa 9:9; and Amos 7:14).[4]

On the bases of these data bearing on gardens in Israel, Mesopotamia, and Egypt, it is likely that Israelites would have imagined the Garden as having been designed in either a square or rectangular shape, with a river bisecting it. However individual beds and groves were arranged, there would have been some sense of kempt balance to it, with pathways and channels providing a clear frame.

The well-planned, adequately watered, and functioning garden illustrates control over nature even where the distribution of plants may appear chaotic. As political statements, the royal gardens of Assyrian kings signified the "ecumenic sovereignty of the ruler."[5] Israelites would have understood the Garden in Eden, which ultimately combined features of both a botanical garden and an animal park, as a microcosmic reflection of the universal sovereignty of its creator and owner. The fact that the human was placed in the Garden to work it indicates that it was his responsibility to do everything necessary to keep it up, keep it clean, and keep it presentable as a fitting extension of its owner's status.[6] Considered as a package, garden and gardener reflect God's desire to set up an efficient, controlled project.

The narrator indicates that the human was set to work the garden and to guard it. The second part of his task raises the questions From whom? and From what? Who or what might endanger or encroach upon the garden planted by God? At this point in the narrative, animals are not yet formed. What else was there?

OTHER PEOPLE

The story here implies the existence of other people, people formed before the 'ādām or at the same time but in a different place for a different reason. Adam's guarding function was to protect the Garden from them. The existence of these other people is also presupposed elsewhere in the primeval history.

Qayin, sentenced to be a wanderer after killing his brother, complains that "anyone who finds me will kill me" (Gen 4:14). God acknowledges the validity of Qayin's observation and comforts him by threatening vengeance on anybody who kills him: "whoever kills Qayin, he will be avenged sevenfold"; that is, if you kill Qayin, seven of your family will die. Moreover, God provides Qayin with a sign, a conventional indicator recognizable by these other people, warning them to leave him alone (Gen 4:15). Had the author and his audience not understood that other people lived in the inhabitable world outside Eden, the narrative elements of Qayin's fear, God's warning, and the use of a sign would have made no sense. Extrapolating from these minor assumptions, it appears that the author understood that Qayin later settled among some of these other people in the land of Nod, where he found a woman to be his wife (Gen 4:16–17).[7]

The extant biblical narrative, however, is uninterested in these other people because it traces the genealogical descent of all humans known to Israel back to Noah and his family, and from them back both through Qayin (Gen 4:16–23; 5:28) and through Seth, third son of Adam and Hawwa (Gen 4:25–5:31), and thence back to Adam and Hawwa. Other people, whatever their story—a fragment of which is embedded in Genesis 6:1–4—were among those wiped out in the flood along with most of Adam's descendents (Gen 6:5–7, 13).

Genesis 6:1–4, which narrates the story about the interspecies mating of divine males with human females, whose progeny were a race of heroes before the flood, suggests that ancient Israel possessed a store of traditions about these other people. Their story was not included in this composition, perhaps because the author thought it irrelevant.[8]

10   THE SECOND COMMANDMENT

(Gen 2:16–17)

Genesis 2

16   And YHWH god—*wayṣaw* . . . *'al*—the human saying:
                 From every tree of the garden, *'ākōl tō'kēl*
17a   but from the Tree of Knowing *ṭōwb wāra'*—
17b   you will not eat from it because on the day of your
                 eating from it *mōwt tāmūwt.*

A few years ago, I asked a class of undergraduates the following question: According to the Bible, what are the first two commandments that God directed to humanity, not just to Israelites? Some students started thumbing through their Bibles, but others answered without cracking the book. They offered three different answers, all based on Exodus 20:1–3. Here are the verses:

1 And the Lord spoke all these words saying:
2 I am the Lord your God who brought you out from the land of
Egypt from the house of bondage.
3 You shall not have other gods before me. You shall not make for
yourself any graven image or any likeness of anything in the
heavens above or in the earth below or in the waters under the earth.

Catholic students claimed that verses 2–3 together constitute the first commandment. Protestant students were divided. Some agreed with the

Catholic division while others argued that verse 3 contained the first and second commandments. Jewish students claimed that verse 2 was the first commandment and that verse 3 contained the second commandment. Protestants countered the Catholic and the Jewish students, arguing that the first verse was no more than a general introduction and could not be considered a commandment. I pointed out that any count that included verse 2 could not possibly be a response to my question since I had conscientiously phrased it to include all humanity, not just Israelites.

After a little more back and forth, a consensus began to develop that perhaps the Protestant position was the most reasonable. But then two Jewish students offered a rebuttal, arguing that what people call the "Ten Commandments" are not labeled commandments in the Bible itself; in verse 1 they are called "statements" or "words." The first statement is that of verse 2, even though it is not a commandment. This, in fact, indicated that Exodus 20 was irrelevant to my question and that they had to seek other passages.

Silence ensued, and then one student asked, "So, where do we find the answer to the question? What were the first two commandments to humanity?" We had only five minutes left until class was over, so I asked them to turn to Genesis 1:28, where they read: "Be fruitful, and multiply, and fill the land, and master it."

Revelation of the second command enhanced their delight: Genesis 2:16 contains the command to eat. As the period ended and students packed up to leave, one undergraduate uttered his approval of the Bible's priorities: sex and food. After they left the room, a disturbing question crossed my mind: Did Genesis 2:16 actually *command* eating?

WHAT WERE GOD'S INTENTIONS IN ADDRESSING THE HUMAN?

A close look at the text of the Garden story reveals that although readers are informed that God uttered a command, *wayṣaw*, "and he commanded"—from the root ṣ-w-h, "to command"—that could have been neither clear nor obvious to Adam within the frame of the story. Additionally, the narrator appended the preposition ʿal, "on/over/against," after the verb "commanded," spelling out for readers exactly what God's intentions were in uttering the following words.

In biblical Hebrew, the verb *wayṣaw*, "he commanded," and other forms of verbs from the same root are followed by the direct object marker, *'et*, in biblical Hebrew, about 430 times. This marker designates what follows as the object of the verb, indicating only who or what is commanded. Since it has no semantic meaning of its own, translations do not, and often cannot, indicate the presence of 'et in the Hebrew text. Any other information about the relationship between the person issuing the command and the one receiving it or about the nature of the command must be discerned from context. When, however, authors wished to provide a tad more information, they could drop the direct object marker and replace it with one of three prepositions.

The verb is followed by the preposition 'el, "to," in six passages, indicating *to whom the command was directed.*[1] Exodus 16:33b–34a illustrates this: "place it there before YHWH god . . . as YHWH god commanded to Moses." The command to Moses was about something that Aaron had been delegated to do. This usage is straightforward, but the distinction between it and the verb followed by 'et is often unclear.

In thirteen passages in the Bible the verb is followed by the preposition *le* indicating *who or what is affected by the command.*[2] For example, Exodus 1:22, "Pharaoh commanded concerning all his people"; Numbers 32:28, "Moses commanded Elazar . . . concerning them [the Gadites]"; and Isaiah 13:3, "I commanded concerning my sanctified ones."

In seventeen passages, including our verse in the Garden story, the verb is coordinated with the preposition 'al.[3] Many translations ignore the preposition or read these passages as if they contained the direct object marker 'et or the preposition 'el, "to." The verses as rendered approximate this construction: "he commanded the person [to do X]." Prepositions, however, have to be observed closely.

Following the word for command, 'al indicates that the command includes a restrictive or coercive element or that it constrains movement, controls behavior, or involves some other element of an adversative nature. In Genesis 12:20, men are commanded to take action over/against Abraham, called Abram in this story, "and they sent him away"; in 2 Samuel 14:8, David promises to command some people to refrain from killing a widow's son, actions permitted by law and tradition; in 1 Kings 11:11, "you did not observe my covenant and rules that I commanded over you [restraining you from going after other gods]" (see 1 Kings 11:10) ; in Jeremiah 35:6, "our father commanded [and constrained] us saying, 'You will not drink wine, you and your children for ever'"; in Esther 2:10,

"Esther did not reveal her people or her kin because Mordecai had commanded over her [compelling her] not to tell."[4]

Accordingly, Genesis 2:16 should be translated: "And YHWH god commanded and constrained the human, saying: 'From every tree of the garden, eating you will eat, but from the Tree of Knowing *ṭōwb wāraʿ*—you will not eat from it.'" God intended for the human to eat from each and every tree, leaving no option to skip one. The human would have fruit salad mixed with nuts whether he liked it or not. God, however, also intended that the human not eat from one particular tree, but he did not express it clearly. God's first expression could be understood as either trumping the second or not.

WAS THERE A COMMAND?

Ambiguity could have been eliminated had the author composed his verses to read something like the following: "From the Tree of Knowing that is in the Garden I command you, do not eat. From every other tree in the Garden except the Tree of Knowing eat."

Adam, knowing nothing of God's intention, could comprehend only what he heard. God's first utterance could be construed only as a permissive instruction directing that Adam do something: "From every tree in the garden, eating you will eat." Likewise, in verse 17, he was told "you will not eat." The latter expression is a restrictive instruction.

Although approaching the level of a command, the positive instruction of verse 16, "eating you will eat," is not expressed formally in Hebrew with a grammatically specific imperative verbal form. Its grammar lacks the command mode. Likewise, the restrictive qualification of verse 17 is not expressed with the negating word *ʾal* before the future tense verb; with an *ʾal* the sentence could not have been understood as anything other than an absolute prohibition according to conventional Hebrew grammar—but the *ʾal* is not there.

A formal imperative would have been expressed as *ʾekōl*, "Eat!" (as in 1 Sam 9:24; 1 Kings 18:41; 19:5) or *ʾal tōʾkal*, "Do not eat!" or, more literally, "No you will eat!" (Judg 13:4, 7). What the human heard in verse 16 was a directive permitting him to consume fruit from *all* of the trees.[5] What he heard in verse 17 was an oblique instruction to not eat from a particular tree. Indirectly, he learned that *all* trees in this particular garden produced fruit suitable for human consumption. (I defer the discussion of "the Tree of Knowing *ṭōwb wāra*'" to Chapter 16, where the narrative clarifies the nature of this knowledge.) God's words constituted no more than two emphatic instructions. Nothing in the utterance indicated to Adam that he was listening to formal commands. The apparent death threat in verse 17 could have offered the human a clue to God's intention, but even that threat was unclear.[6]

DEATH AND (ITS) EXECUTION

God stated what would happen if the person indulged his appetite and ate from the tree: "On the day of your eating from it, *mōwt tāmūwt*," where the literal Hebrew reads "dying you will die" (Gen 2:17b). The statement uses the same grammatical construction with the infinitive absolute as in verse 16—"X-ing you will X"—but with a different function. In verse 17b, the construction emphasizes the idea of the following finite verb. God did not say, *mōwt tūwmat*, "dying you will be put to death." Both expressions involving death are well known from biblical law and narrative prose. However, they are not synonymous.

The expression *mōwt tūwmat* would have indicated almost unambiguously that the human could expect to be put to death almost immediately (Gen 26:11; Exod 19:22). The author did not use it, opting instead for *mōwt tāmūwt*, which could be interpreted in more than one way.[7] In most contexts where the *mōwt tāmūwt* occurs, it refers to death by natural causes at some undetermined point in the future (Gen 20:7; 1 Sam 14:44; 2 Kings 1:4, 6, 16; Ezek 3:18; 33:8, 14). Such a death was understood to be a divine curtailing of what might have been a longer life span. In no way could it be taken as referring to a summary execution.

This point, no longer comprehensible in the Hellenistic period, raised the problem of truthfulness in the declared penalty for eating from the tree. It forced the author of the *Book of Jubilees*, written around 125 BCE, to interpret "day," in the expression "the day of your eating," as an indefinite period of time that could extend up to a millennium on the basis of Psalm 90:4: "a thousand years in your eyes are like yesterday." Adam died at the ripe age of 930 (Gen 5:5). Consequently, *Jubilees* could explain that Adam did expire on the (one-thousand-year-long) day of his eating, except that the "day" existed only in the eyes of God; it was not determined by the rising and the setting of the sun (*Jubilees* 4:20–30).

This fanciful type of interpretation would not have been necessary for Israelites listening to a story composed in the literary register of their daily language. They would have known that had the linguistically competent author intended that God's words preclude any possibility of a death sentence being commuted, he could have added the unambiguous phrase *lō' tiḥyeh*, "you shall not live," to the decree. The phrase "he/you shall not live" would have eliminated an option for leniency. For example, in Exodus 19:12–13a, touching the sacred mountain of revelation for whatever reason invited execution: "whoever touches the mountain, dying will be caused to die . . . he will not live." In Zechariah 13:3, the phrase addresses false prophecy (see Deut 17:6–7; 18:20); in Exodus 22:17, it is applied to witches (see Deut 18:10–11). In 2 Kings 10:19 it occurs in Jehu's summons to all worshippers of Baal, ordering them to attend a prayer meeting and threatening that anyone not accounted for will not live.[8]

The juridic language of Genesis 2:17, then, indicates that despite the tone, God reserved some latitude for himself to decide whether a penalty would be exacted in the event that his words were disregarded, and if it were to be exacted, how it might be executed.[9] Similar language occurs in Solomon's warning to Shimei, enemy of his dead father: "on the day of your going out [from Jerusalem] and you cross Wadi Qidron, dying you will die" (1 Kings 2:37). Shimei took a chance on how Solomon might interpret the language of the implied penalty and left the city to reclaim runaway slaves. When Solomon learned that Shimei had ignored the warning, he tried Shimei and had him executed (1 Kings 2:39–46).[10]

Nothing in God's statement suggests that at any time was the human imagined to be an eternal being with guaranteed security of employment. Nothing indicated that the punishment for violating the only restriction would result in the termination of eternal life and continual labor by death. In fact, God's concern, evident later on in the story that man might obtain eternal life—Genesis 3:22, "lest he extend his hand and take also from the Tree of Life and eat and live for ever"—militates against this. Man was formed a mortal creature.[11]

Christian readers of the Bible were perplexed by a mortal man being threatened with death and thus developed a metaphysical response to what is essentially a linguistic and literary question. Catholics and Protestants accept the answer in one interpretation or another. The Geneva Reformer, John Calvin (1509–64) expressed it as follows:

But it is asked, what kind of death God means in this place? . . . His earthly life truly would have been temporal; yet he would have passed into heaven without death, and without injury. Death, therefore, is now a terror to us; first, because there is a kind of annihilation, as it respects the body; then, because the soul feels the curse of God. . . . Wherefore the question is superfluous, how it was that God threatened death to Adam on the day in which he should touch the fruit, when he long deferred the punishment? For then was Adam consigned to death, and death began its reign in him, until supervening grace should bring a remedy.[12]

THE PROBLEM OF ELAPSED TIME

The Bible's narrative does not indicate how much time elapsed from the moment that Adam was placed in the Garden and set to work (Gen 2:8–9, 15) until God decided to charge him to eat from every tree except one. God's "command" indicates that he was (at least somewhat) concerned about the human creature toiling in his Garden, but this concern may have emerged only after many days or years of observation. By having God append a veiled threat to his restriction in verse 17, the author subtly indicates that God understood the awakening needs of the human creature and had some insight into its hungers. Adam may have kept on looking at the fruit-bearing trees and caring for them, not understanding that the fruits were edible, but curious all the same. Maybe he handled the fruits and smelled them. Finally, after however long, God directed him to eat the produce of the trees.

The philosopher Immanuel Kant observed in the eighteenth century that the first man was an adult, able to stand and to walk, talk, and think. His ability to think is reflected by his ability to talk in coherent language and by his being assigned responsibilities requiring technical skills and the ability to make critical decisions. Since human experience teaches us that these abilities are learned and not instinctual, the first human must have learned them on his own through trial and error.[13]

Adam was formed as a naturally inquiring being, one capable of accepting instruction, but one who had to be warned that certain actions might have unforeseeable consequences.

11 THE FIRST SOCIAL WELFARE PROGRAM

(Gen 2:18–20)

Genesis 2

18a And YHWH god said:
          The human, being by himself is not good.
18b   I will make for him *'ēzer kenegdōw.*
19   And YHWH god formed from the soil every animal of the
      field and every flying creature of the heavens,
      and he brought [each] to the human to see what he would
      call it. And all that the human, the living
      soul, would call it, that is its name.
20   And the human called names to every herd animal and
      flying creature of the heavens and to every animal of the
      field;
          but for the human he did not find *'ēzer kenegdōw.*

Sometime after warning the man, God decided that it was not good for
him to be alone, that man lacked something, and so God determined to
make for man's benefit an *'ēzer kenegdōw* (Gen 2:18). The Hebrew word
'ēzer, usually translated as "help" or the like, does not imply inferiority in
and of itself. It is used to describe YHWH god as the helper of the tribe of
Judah (Deut 33:7), of the people of Israel (Ps 33:20), of the sons of Aaron
and those that fear him (Ps 115:9–11). It is not the word *'ēzer* that presents
difficulties to interpreters, but the expression of which it is a part.

Augustine of Hippo pondered the expression around 400 CE and wrote:

> If one should ask why it was necessary that a helper be made for man, the answer that seems most probable is that it was for the procreation of children, just as the earth is a helper for the seed in the production of a plant from the union of the two. . . . She was not to till the earth with him, for there was not yet any toil to make help necessary. If there were any such need, a male helper would be better and the same could be said of the comfort of another's presence if Adam were perhaps weary of solitude. . . . Surely no one will say that God was able to make from the rib of the man only a woman and not also a man if He had wished to do so. Consequently, I do not see in what sense the woman was made as a helper for the man if not for the sake of bearing children.[1]

Despite Augustine's commonsense explanation that acknowledges the sexual nature of the prelapsarian couple, the exact meaning communicated to readers of the Hebrew text is far from obvious.

The expression *'ēzer kenegdōw* is variously rendered "a help meet for him" (KJV), "a helper as his partner" (NRSV), "a helper" (NRSV), "a suitable partner" (NAB), "a fitting helper" (NJPS), or the like.[2] Everett Fox's renderings, "a helper corresponding to him" and "a helping counterpart," even though not idiomatic English, reflect what is generally considered the sense of the Hebrew more accurately than the others.[3] All these translations wrestle with the meaning of the second word.

THE FIRST ALTERNATIVE TRANSLATION

R. David Freedman advances an understanding of the *'ēzer kenegdōw* by assuming that the difficulty lies not in the combination of words but in the first word alone.[4] His argument is based on a fact known primarily to specialists in comparative Semitic linguistics: Iron Age Hebrew had more consonantal sounds than there were signs in the Phoenician alphabet that Israelites borrowed for writing. For example, the letter *shin* was used to represent two distinct consonants, one pronounced /sh/ and one pronounced /s/. This is comparable to the different pronunciations of English *th* in *this, that, thing,* and *thought.* Another letter, *'ayyin,* represented both the unvoiced guttural consonant 'ayyin, represented phonetically by /'/, and a second consonant, the voiced gutteral ghayyin, represented phonetically by /ġ/. (The term *voiced* refers to the vibration of the vocal cords involved when pronouncing the consonant aloud, as in English and Hebrew /g, b, d/. *Unvoiced* or *voiceless* refers to the absence of such vibrations, as in English and Hebrew /k, p, t/.)

This second consonant, *ghayyin*, unpronounceable to most speakers of Western languages without practice, is common in Arabic and was common in ancient Ugaritic, a language related to Hebrew. In written Arabic, 'ayyin and ghayyin share the same letter, but the /ġ/ pronunciation is signaled in the writing system by an overdot. In Ugaritic, each consonant had its own distinctive sign. In written Hebrew, no distinction was ever made between the two consonants.

Because of the statistical infrequency of the *ghayyin* in Hebrew, it came to be pronounced as an 'ayyin around 100 BCE. The transition in pronunciation was facilitated by their being represented by the same letter. This clarifies why *Gaza* in English, though spelled with an 'ayyin in the Bible and pronounced 'azzāh in contemporary Hebrew, is written with a consonant indicating a voiced sound, /g/. Jews translating the Bible into Greek during the third and second centuries BCE still knew and heard the *ghayyin* pronunciation even though they saw an 'ayyin spelling. They used the Greek letter *gamma* to transliterate the name. So, too, the name of Sodom's sister-city, Gomorrah, written with an 'ayyin once pronounced correctly as *ghayyin*, was transliterated into Greek by a *gamma*.

Freedman argues that '-z-r, the three-consonant root of 'ēzer, reflects two original, distinctive roots. The first, most frequently attested in biblical Hebrew, is '-z-r, with an original 'ayyin, meaning "rescue/save/help." The second, with an original ghayyin, is ġ-z-r, meaning "be strong," The second root, ġ-z-r, is attested in Ugaritic.[5]

His argument, based on word origins, is supported by the synonymous alternate names of the Judahite king Uzziah. Each *Uzziah* appears in both a short and a long form: 'uzziyāh, and 'uzziyāhūw (2 Kings 15:30, 32), as does the alternative *Azariah*: 'azaryāh, and 'azaryāhūw (2 Kings 14:21; 15:1, 7; 15:6; 2 Chron 21:2; 22:6). All mean "My strength is Yah(u)." This example virtually assures that the use of ġ-z-r to mean "strength" is not restricted to obscure poetic diction in Hebrew. On the basis of this

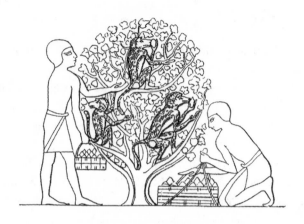

Monkeys Picking Figs in Egypt
(Reprinted from A. Erman, *Life in Ancient Egypt,* London: MacMillan, 1894, p. 199.)

evidence, Freedman suggests that the Hebrew expression *'ēzer kenegdōw* be translated as "a power equal to him."[6]

Drawing on the philological insights of Freedman and Fox, translators may render the expression *'ēzer kenegdōw* as "a powerful counterpart." Not only is this linguistically possible, but it is appropriate in context. The phrase occurs first in verse 18 after God places the human in the garden to commence his rounds of prescribed labor (Gen 2:15). God wanted to provide him with a co-worker, a partner.[7] And so, God first formed animals of the field and then birds of the heavens (Gen 2:19).

Although God brings the animals to the man for naming, God also parades the animals before the man to see if either the man or God—Genesis 2:20b is not quite clear—could find an *'ēzer kenegdōw* among them. The man, however, does not recognize one as appropriate for the designated role. Presupposing that Adam would instinctively recognize one when he saw it, the narrator does not clarify exactly what features were being sought in the *'ēzer kenegdōw.*

Animals and birds may all have been useful in the economy of the Garden. Some animals can be harnessed to pull loads. Grazing animals keep down weeds, provide natural fertilizer, and supply milk for cheeses and other secondary products. Some animals could have simply been interesting, distracting fauna to observe. Some may have been drafted for other tasks. Egyptians, for example, trained monkeys to pick fruit.[8] Not one, however, could serve as "a powerful counterpart," capable of sharing the load of labor and responsibility.

THE SIGNIFICANCE OF NAMING

This episode about the formation and naming of animals is significant for a number of reasons. It illustrates God's concern for the first human and, by extrapolation, for all people; it demonstrates God's ability to improvise; it provides an etiology for the superior status of humans over animals, which were created for the benefit of the first human; it indicates that the human possessed intelligence sufficient for distinguishing between the various animals and providing them with individual labels; and it provides an etiology for animal names. Generalizing from the fact that later in the story the human named his wife "woman," providing her with a generic name, it is regularly assumed—correctly, in my opinion— that the naming to which this chapter refers was generic. Practically speaking, this involved the man's being able to sort out the animals and to create logical categories into which they would fit, to distinguish monkeys from himself, and dogs from cats, from camels, from horses, from donkeys. The ability to create categories under which everything that existed could be filed was considered an important type of knowledge in ancient Mesopotamia and underlies analytic thought, ancient and modern.

The American poet Anthony Hecht (1923–2004) playfully imagined a somewhat confused Adam trying to figure out what he was supposed to do to fulfill God's command. He described Adam's first attempt in the second stanza of a short poem entitled "Naming the Animals":

> Before an addled mind and puddled brow,
> The feathered nation and the finny prey
> Passed by; there went biped and quadruped.
> Adam looked forth with bottomless dismay
> Into the tragic eyes of his first cow,
> And shyly ventured, "Thou shalt be called 'Fred.'"[9]

Beyond the naming, the scene is important for what it reveals about the author's comprehension of speech. He knew that many animals make sounds: some low, some bray, others whinny or bark or hiss. He most likely understood that each animal produces only a limited number of typical sounds, signaling the presence or absence of food, danger, pain, and the like. In contrast, he understood that only people were capable of generating a seemingly infinite variety of sounds to communicate the same concerns as animals, but also to reflect generally about actions, things not present, and abstract ideas. People could be innovative with language, generating new nouns and verbal forms.[10] Israelites did not consider communication with animals ordinarily possible. On the two instances when animals reportedly address people in the Hebrew Bible and converse with them rationally—the serpent in the Garden story and Balaam's ass (Num 22:28–30)—the occasion is extraordinary, the language is that of the humans, and the animals are the initiators of the short, informative conversations.

The significance of the naming motif should not, however, be overstated. It need not be read back or read against Genesis 1:26–28, where God assigns to humans dominion over fish, flying creatures, animals, and creeping creatures.[11] Although in some cases naming could be a political or a religious act, in most circumstances, naming in ancient Israel was simply naming.

In Genesis 4:1, Hawwa names Qayin, a declarative act that provided her son with a name, not one that gave her any control or dominion over him. In Genesis 2:23, Adam calls the new creature 'iššāh (woman), an act that hardly demonstrates any dominion over her; and in Genesis 3:20, he renames her Hawwa. He thus gave species and specimen names. Finally, in Genesis 2:20, Adam presumably called the belly-crawler and other fauna of his kind, nāḥāš, "serpent." If that was an exercise of dominion, the serpent sadly missed the point.[12]

WHY DID THE ANIMAL EXPERIMENT FAIL?

Determining why the animal parade failed to discover a powerful counterpart for Adam can be answered only indirectly by working back from response to stimulus, from what God eventually formed from a part of Adam's body to what God and Adam must have seen among the animals and birds before the surgery. They saw animals paired, male and female, somewhat similar in appearance, every exemplar of each species with its own powerful, gendered counterpart.[13]

The situation described in this episode of the Garden story is similar to the assumption in Genesis 1:20–22 from the Cosmic Creation story about other creatures: they were created capable of reproducing themselves. Genesis 1:20–21 describes the creation of creatures—"Let the waters bring forth . . . living creatures and birds that fly. And God created . . .

living creatures of every kind." The verses do not mention specifically the differentiation of creatures into genders. Nevertheless, the differentiation is presupposed by the command in verse 22: "be fruitful and multiply."

Although Israelites in the Iron Age were ignorant about how reproduction actually occurs, they understood the mechanics of procreation, at least among large vertebrate species. In the literary context of the Garden story, where gendering is taken as a given, the fact that no human female was immediately available suggests that initially the human was intended to be distinctly different from other fauna and a creature with its own biological history. Within the pragmatic frame of the story and the world of its author and his audiences, the only obvious distinction between the first person and limbed animals created for his benefit was that the other creatures were mostly quadrupeds and flying bipeds, whereas the man, like his later descendents, was a biped capable of producing and using a variety of tools regularly. The first man differed from his (future) descendents in that he was incapable of reproducing himself.

Among the animals, each partner was equal to the other, looked somewhat similar, and was able to do most of what the other could; yet each was specialized. And so God constructed, *wayyiben*, a woman as the man's specialized, powerful counterpart, and Adam recognized her as such immediately (Gen 2:22–23).

At least one nineteenth-century theologian, Adam Clarke, reached a similar conclusion in his comments on Genesis 2:18 after evaluating the Hebrew text: "Woman was formed a social creature . . . and therefore formed, as a companion for him, one exactly the counterpart of himself; of the same nature, the same constitution, and with equal powers, faculties, and rights."[14]

The translation of *'ēzer kenegdōw* by "a powerful counterpart" and the implications of this translation for understanding the narrative may be considered only the first of two alternatives.

DIFFICULTIES WITH THE FIRST ALTERNATIVE TRANSLATION

Comparative thematics supports questioning whether the *'ēzer kenegdōw* identified as Hawwa is properly understood as "a powerful counterpart." In the Mesopotamian *Gilgamesh Epic,* when the gods wished to create someone equal to the powerful, rambunctious, semi-divine Gilgamesh, they created Enkidu, a male. In an Old Babylonian hymn, when the god Enki wished to calm and pacify the fiercely impetuous goddess Ishata, he created Ṣaltu, also a female. The powerful counterpart for the male was male and for the female, female.[15] If the Garden story is read against these two traditions, then the very femaleness of Hawwa militates against her being a counterpart to the male Adam in the context of a patriarchal culture.

If the first analysis is correct, it appears that the author of the story purposely opted for convoluted, ambiguous language to introduce information that could have been presented simply. He could have employed the term *neqēbāh*, "female," in verse 18 to make his point directly about the feminine nature of the new creature (cf. Gen 1:27; 5:2): "I will make for him a female." He could have used a grammatically feminine participle, *'ōzeret*, "power," or a grammatically feminine noun such as *'ezrāh* (2 Chron 28:21) or *'ezrat* (Pss 60:13; 108:13) in phrases like *'ezrāh kenegdōw* or *'ezrat kenegdōw* to make his point subtly but unambiguously. These are significant but not compelling arguments against the first alternative. It is possible that the author may indeed have opted for a complicated way of providing the information, but I have been unable to determine his reason.

There remain two linguistic reasons for questioning the first alternative:

(1) The different interpretations of the expression overlook that *kenegdōw* is a compound word composed of a preposition followed by a noun (assumed to be a preposition) followed by the third-masculine singular pronominal possessive suffix indicating "his": *ke + neged + ōw* = "like + opposite/counterpart + his."

(2) The different interpretations likewise ignore the 149 other attestations of *neged* in the Bible. In biblical Hebrew, with only two exceptions, *neged* indicates a degree of adjacency, proximity, or nearness and may be rendered as "close to, before" —as in Genesis 33:12; Exodus 19:2; 34:10; Numbers 25:4. It also occurs in combination with the prepositions *le*, "to, toward," and *m/min*, "from," but not with the preposition *be*, "in." These combined prepositions do not appear to affect the meaning of *neged* in a significant way.[16]

Neged occurs twice with *ke*, "like, as," in the Garden story. Significantly, these two uses are unique in the Bible. They are the only ones in which *neged* does not mediate or indicate a positional relationship between two people, places, or things. They are most unpreposition-like.[17]

THE SECOND ALTERNATIVE TRANSLATION

The difficulties with the first alternative translation prompt me to propose an alternative translation and explanation for the expression *'ēzer kenegdōw*. I begin with the observation that in the Hebrew text of both verses where it appears, Genesis 2:18, 20, a disjunctive accent mark called a *ṭipḥāh*—it is shaped something like a reversed comma and means "small space"—is found under the first word, separating it from the second one. What is the significance of this disjunctive accent?

This accent is part of a system of quasi-musical notations developed by Masoretes between the sixth and ninth centuries CE to record a heretofore oral tradition of recitation. The objective of the system was to inform readers how to parse the text when reading it aloud: where to pause for shorter and greater breaks and where to stop completely before continuing. The disjunctive *ṭipḥāh* instructs readers to pause after the marked word, as if after an English comma, so that a sliver of silence separates it from the following word: *'ēzer* [helper] + disjunctive accent + *ke* [like] + *neged* + *ōw* [his].

The ancient interpretation of the verse implied by this Masoretic accent indicates that the words were not considered immediate constituents of the same phrase. The last word is a modifier, clarifying what sort of helper is intended. Accordingly, verse 18b may be translated: "I will make for him a helper, like his *neged*." This leaves only *neged* in need of clarification.

The significant difference between the woman and other creatures formed by God, many of whom could function as helpers, is that she was of the same species as the man. More empirically, she was like him in a way that the other animals, even the large mammals, were not. The meaning of *neged* is to be sought in this distinction. It can be found with the help of another Semitic language.

Ancient Ethiopic, Ge'ez, a language distantly related to Hebrew, provides an etymological cognate that fits the semantic bill: *nagad*, a word meaning "tribe, clan, kin." The Ge'ez word is also cognate to Hebrew *neked*, whose meaning as determined by context is "progeny" or "descendent" (Gen 21:23; Isa 14:22; Job 18:19).[18] I propose that in its two occurrences in the Garden story, *neged* is not the common preposition but, like its cognate in Ge'ez, a kinship term. *Neged* is distinguished semantically from the more common cognate *neked* in that *neked* indicates kin related through a vertical lineage (that is, from mother to children to grand-children), whereas *neged* indicates kin related horizontally (first cousin, second cousin, first cousin once removed, and so on).[19]

Recognizing *neged* in the Garden story as a noun belonging to the sphere of kinship terminology explains why it does not provide information about positional relationships as in the other 149 attestations of the word in the Bible. It is not a preposition.

Applying this conclusion to verse 18b yields: "I will make for him a helper like his kin." God could only make a helper "like his kin" because families, clans, and tribes did not yet exist for Adam in the isolated Garden. There was no common ancestry and no common descent.

This interpretation is less dramatic than "a powerful counterpart," but it accounts for the use of the preposition *ke*, "like," and rests on a more solid philological base as well. Additionally, it sets the scene appropriately for the story's next dramatic episode: the creation of Hawwa.

12 THE FIRST LADY

(Gen 2:21–23)

Genesis 2

21 And (so) YHWH god made a heavy slumber fall on the
human and he slept; and he took one *miṣṣalʿōtā(y)w*
and he closed flesh beneath it.

22 And YHWH god built the *ṣēlāʿ* that he took from the human
into a woman, and he brought her to the human.

23 And (then) the human said:
This one. This time. Bone from my bones and flesh
from my flesh. This one will be called *ʾiššāh* because
from *ʾīyš* this one was taken.

The three verses about the creation of Hawwa raise interesting questions:

(1) Why did God construct the woman from Adam's *ṣelaʿ*, commonly taken as referring to rib?

(2) Why does the narrator mention that God "closed the flesh beneath it," that is, at the place from which the rib was taken?

A third question derives from Israelite burial practices. In the Iron
Age, these consisted of placing bodies on raised benches in burial caves,
leaving them until only the skeleton remained, and then, when the bench
was needed again, removing the skeletal bones to a common storage
niche.[1] It is reasonable to assume that Israelites were familiar with both

137

Tomb of a Wealthy Jerusalem Family around the Seventh Century BCE

Bodies were laid out on stone shelves in a tomb until they decomposed. Afterward, the skeletons were disarticulated and the bones placed into a repository excavated either in the entrance chamber or under the shelf, as shown in this drawing of Ketef Himmom burial cave 25. This procedure enabled a family to reuse a tomb for generations. (Adapted from a drawing in Gabriel Barkay, *Ketef Hinnom: A Treasure Facing Jerusalem's Walls*, Jerusalem: Israel Museum, 1986, p. 24. Used with permission.)

human and animal skeletons and that they noticed that ribs are paired symmetrically. Were Adam a prototype, people, or at least males, should logically have had either one asymmetrical rib or a place on the skeleton where such a rib might have been situated.

(3) From where in Adam's body did God take the rib used to make man's helper?

The first and third of these questions are among the most asked about this part of the story, not to mention the basis of many jokes. The second question, as will be shown below, provides the key for interpreting this episode.

MESOPOTAMIAN AND EGYPTIAN PUNS

One response to the first question is that the choice of a rib may have been influenced by a motif attested in Sumerian myth and magic traditions. In Sumerian, a non-Semitic language once used in southern Mesopotamia, the word *ti* means both "rib" and "life," so *Ninti* in Sumerian means both "Lady of the rib" and "Lady of life."[2]

There are four difficulties with this clever explanation.

First, in the Sumerian myth of Enki and Ninhursag, where Ninti, "the Lady of the rib/life," is mentioned because she was created to heal Enki's rib, seven other goddesses were also created to heal his head, hair, nose, mouth, throat, arm, and side. The goddess Na*zi* healed Enki's throat, *zi*; Nin*siki*la healed his hair, *pa-siki*, and so forth. This pattern of punning, where the divine names indicate healed parts of the body, does not evoke ambiguity outside the Sumerian story.[3] Although this explanation of the choice of rib is theoretically possible, then, it is not ultimately satisfying.

Second, Sumerologists have not yet determined how the written form of Sumerian sounded when read aloud. It is possible that the words meaning "rib" and "life" were pronounced very differently.

Third, if punning was actually at work in the Sumerian, it is highly unlikely that a Sumerian pun would have been known to Israelites or mediated to them through another language. Sumerian was a known *written* language in Mesopotamia, but it was dead as a spoken one by the last quarter of the second millennium BCE. This was almost three centuries before Hebrew emerged as a distinct language around the beginning of the first millennium BCE.

Fourth, the biblical story does not associate the rib and the "mother of all life," as Hawwa is called in Genesis 3:20. The lady-from-a-rib in the Garden story is named *'iššāh*, "woman," a word associated with *'īyš*, "man," in verse 23, not with "rib."

Another response to the first question is that the reference to a rib may be based on a pun in Egyptian, where the word for "rib" and "clay" is *imw*. Furthermore, this word may be written in Egyptian hieroglyphics to look like the word for "flesh," creating a visual association.[4] Unfortunately, the Egyptian story about Khnum's creation of man from clay does not refer to the formation of a woman at all. This explanation, a partial response to the first question, must be deemed as inadequate as the

Sumerian one. At best, the two ancient Near Eastern stories indicate that just as the author of the Garden story punned—*īyš,'iššāh*, "man, woman"—so too did other authors in different cultures.

Another way of approaching the questions posed at the beginning of this chapter is to reevaluate the assumption that the word *ṣēlaʻ* refers to "rib."

REASSESSING THE RIB

The notion that *ṣēlaʻ* in this context might not refer to a rib is not new; it underlies a debate between Rav and Samuel, Jewish authorities who taught after the codification of the Mishnah, around 200 CE. One teacher—the Talmud does not indicate which scholar adopted this position—argued that it refers to "backside." Since the first human was created "male and female" (Gen 1:27; 5:2), and the two aspects of the human were attached back to back, as written in Psalm 139:5—"you formed me [or surrounded me] in back and in front, you lay your hand on me"—the second aspect, the female, must have been split off from the backside of the male. The second scholar stated simply and without elaboration that the word *ṣēlaʻ* indicates that the woman was formed from Adam's tail (*b. Erubin* 18a).

The "tail" interpretation is more covert in the earliest collection of rabbinic homiletic exegesis, *Bereshith Rabbah,* compiled sometime after the third century CE. Here we see comments relating to the words "and he closed the flesh *taḥtennāh*" (Gen 2:21b):

> Rabbi Hanina b. Isaac said, "The Holy One, Blessed be He, made a fitting organ/limb for his lower part, *nōwy letaḥtīytōw,* so that he wouldn't be disgraced like an animal."
>
> R. Ammi said, "He made for him a lock and a little chair attached to it so that he wouldn't despair when he sits."
>
> R. Yanai said, "He made for him pillows." (*Bereshith Rabbah* 17:6)

The circuitous reference is to the human anus, whose sphincter muscle, the "fitting organ" that has "a lock," is not exposed because it is concealed by the buttocks, the "pillows" that form a "little chair" on which he sits. The first interpretation is launched by Rabbi Hanina from a consideration of the letters *nh* at the end of the word *tḥtnh* in the biblical verse translated by NRSV and NAB by "in its place." The letters representing consonant sounds are associated with the same letters in the biblical word *nāwāh*, "pretty, pleasant" (Jer 6:2), which is then associated with the related word *nōwy*, "grace, beauty, decoration." The second and third interpretations by Rabbi Ammi and Rabbi Yanai accept the initial wordplay but amplify the meaning of "fitting organ/limb."

Underlying these various fanciful comments is the notion that even though God made humans animal-like by providing the male with a conjugal partner, he still wanted to distinguish humans from other animals with regard to inherent dignity by providing them with natural privacy in the performance of certain bodily functions. To do so God removed the original tail, consisting of flesh and bone, and performed reconstructive surgery to conceal the incision and benefit the human, and then he formed the removed appendage into something new.

Homiletics and punning aside, these far-fetched, etiological comments explained not only man's lack of a tail in comparison to other vertebrate mammals but also the presence of his coccyx, his tailbone, an obvious feature of human skeletons. (They failed to explain, however, why females possess a tailbone.)

One final rabbinic interpretation, most likely relying on Genesis 2:23, specifically refers to the material from which the woman was created:

> Why is it that a woman must perfume herself but a man does not need to perfume himself? He [Rabbi Judah] said: Man was made from earth and earth never stinks, but Hawwa was made from a bone, *'eṣem*. Consider! If you leave a bone three days without salt, it immediately begins to stink. (*Bereshith Rabbah* 17:8)[5]

Whatever doubtful value Rabbi Judah's statement may have for perfumers, its value for comprehending the biblical passage lies in its understanding of *ṣēla'* as a rare synonym for a more common Hebrew word, *'eṣem*, meaning "bone." Bone, not rib. Not one of these rabbis considered the "rib" interpretation.

Most episodes in the story of Genesis, chapter 2, are replete with etiological information. This helps ground a hypothesis that the closing up of the flesh in verse 21 is etiological, too. Its mention seems to indicate that somewhere on the male body there is either a scar or what appears to be a scar caused by an incision whose origin is explained by this story. Although most men are unaware of it, such a "scar" can indeed be found and seen on their bodies.

In a male fetus of ten weeks, edges of the urogenital groove begin to fold together over the urogenital sinus, forming the underside of the penis. Where the edges come together they form a seam, or raphé, which indicates its bilateral origin. A similar seam, though with a slightly different derivation, is found on the scrotum. Both are visible after birth and throughout life, appearing as a straight thread of fine scar tissue, slightly different in coloration from surrounding skin. A common anomalous development in which the urogenital groove fails to close completely anywhere along its length results in hypospadias, openings along the seam, which extends from the bottom of the scrotum to the tip of the penis.[6] Hypospadias would certainly have drawn attention to this usually covered and not readily visible part of the male anatomy and to the normal raphé along which they formed.

I hypothesize that the origin of this seam on the external genitalia of males was explained by the story of the closing of the incision.[7] This explanation for the mention of the closing of the wound indicates that Hebrew *ṣēlaʿ* is to be associated with the man's penis, not his rib.

Even as this explanation provides an answer, it raises another question: Where did the "rib" tradition emerge? The earliest rendering of *ṣēlaʿ* as "rib" is by the Greek translators of the Pentateuch in the mid-third century BCE. They used *pleura*, a word commonly indicating "rib," but also "side" as in the side of a person, an army, a place, or a triangle or rectangle. The "rib" understanding entered the European tradition through Jerome's use of Latin *costa*, meaning "rib" or "side," in the Vulgate—the Latin version of the Bible used by the Roman Catholic Church—and became fixed there by interpretive translations from Latin into other languages using unambiguous "rib" words in the target languages.

The specific conclusion associating *ṣēlaʿ* with the penis is anticipated by at least one midrash. Commenting on why other parts of the body were not used in the creation of the woman, Rabbi Joshua from Siknin (ca. third century CE) said:

God said, I shall not create her from the eye, so that she won't be be haughty, and not from the ear, that she won't be an eavesdropper, and not from the mouth, so that she won't be talkative. . . . From where

shall I create her? From the modest organ/limb, *min'ēber haṣṣanūwa'*,
that he has, from the *yārēk*, thigh. (*Devarim Rabbah* 6:11)[8]

The full explanation of Rabbi Joshua's *yārēk*-thigh explanation is clarified
by the following discussion.

Disassociating *ṣēla'* from rib has strong philological support. In biblical Hebrew, *ṣēla'* is employed to refer to a number of different items: the
sides of a structure, Exodus 25:12–14; chambers or rooms extending from
the side of another structure, 1 Kings 6:5; wooden planks or support
beams, 1 Kings 6:15–16; the side of a hill, 2 Samuel 16:13. In fact, the only
place in biblical Hebrew where it may refer to skeletal ribs is in the Genesis passages. Its Akkadian cognate *ṣēlû* means "rib, side, lateral wing of a
building," and by extension, "direction"; its Geʻez cognate, *ṣʾlle*, means only
"tablet, beam."[9] All these nouns refer to pleuric structures. Its Arabic verbal cognate, *ḍalaʻa*, means "to incline, to deviate." Provided with a slightly
different pattern of vowels, the same consonantal root is an intransitive
verb, *ḍaliʻa*, which means "to be crooked" or "to be bent," hence the Arabic
noun *ḍilaʻ*, "rib."[10] The core sememe (unit of meaning) clarifying these
various applications expresses a two-dimensional, geometric relationship
between something vertical or horizontal but lateral to a main axis.

Accordingly, "penis" is the referent of *ṣēla'* in Genesis 2:22—a penis is
lateral to the up-down axis of the male body viewed in profile. Both ribs
and penises reflect the basic sense, the core sememe, of the root *ṣ-l-ʻ*.[11]

EUPHEMISMS FOR *PENIS* IN BIBLICAL HEBREW

Other data must be considered as well. Although post-biblical Hebrew
refers to the penis clinically by the terms *'ēbār*, "organ/limb," or *'ēbar
hazzākār*, "organ/limb of the male," or *'ēbar qāṭān*, "small organ/limb"
(*b. Sukkah* 52b), no such term is known in biblical Hebrew.[12] Instead, biblical Hebrew regularly uses circumlocutions and euphemisms. The difficulty with the latter is that considering something a euphemism may be
the result of reading too much into a text: "sometimes a cigar is just a
cigar." Nevertheless, examination of the general or specific contexts of
certain passages indicates that the following words refer to a penis.[13]

regel, "foot/feet," in Exodus 4:25: "and Zipporah took a flint and cut off
the foreskin of her son and brought it next to his *raglā(y)w*." (The

meaning of the last part of this verse that I do not cite remains uncertain.)

regel in 2 Kings 18:27 (= Isa 36:12): "Did my lord send me to say these
words against your lord and to you, was it not to the people sitting
on the wall who will eat their dung and drink from the waters of
their *ragléyhem*" (reading with the Qeri; "their urine" [Ketiv]).

kelīy, "instrument(s), tool(s)," in 1 Samuel 21:5–6: "there is no common
bread at hand, only sacred bread if the young men have guarded
themselves from women. And David responded to the priest . . . :
'Indeed women are kept away from us as always when I go out, and
the *kēlīym* of the young men are holy even on a common journey.'"

qōṭen, "small one," in 1 Kings 12:10 (= 2 Chr 10:10): "My small one,
qoṭonniy, is thicker than the loin of my father."

'ēṣ, "stick," and *māqēl*, "staff," in Hosea 4:12: "My people, he inquires of
his stick and his staff tells him because a spirit of whoring made
them stray, and they whored away from their God."

yād, "hand," in Isaiah 57:8: "you mounted and you widened your bed . . .
you loved their bed, you saw a *yād*."[14]

yād in Isaiah 58:10: "you found the life-force of your *yād*."[15]

*šekōbet, "lying," in Leviticus 20:15: "and a man who gives/places
his lying in an animal will be put to death." See also Leviticus
18:20, 23.[16]

mebūwšĭym, "embarrassments," in Deuteronomy 25:11: "the wife of one
draws near to rescue her husband from his smiter, and she extends
her hand and grabs his embarrassments."[17]

bāśār, "flesh, meat," in Exodus 28:42: "let them make for themselves
linen pants to cover the *bāśār* of nakedness."[18]

bāśār, in Leviticus 15:2–3, 16: in a chapter dealing with genital discharges, *bāśār* refers to that member on the male from which flows
caused by illness (often identified with benign gonorrhea) and semi-
nal emissions occur.

bāśār, in Leviticus 18:6: "don't approach the relative of your *bāśār* to
reveal nakedness."

The expression *še'ēr bāśār* in the last verse, as well as in Leviticus 25:49,
is a technical term referring to kin within the extended family. It combines *še'ēr*, a word referring both to food (Exod 21:10; Ps 78:20) and to a
relative (Num 27:11) with one that refers to flesh and the male procreative

organ. The context of Leviticus 18:6, which deals with prohibited sexual liaisons, makes this use particularly poignant.

> *bāśār*, in Ezekiel 16:26: "and you whored with the sons of Egypt, your neighbors big of *bāśār*, and you multiplied your whoring to anger me."
>
> *bāśār*, in Ezekiel 23:20: "she lusted on account of their concubines, those whose *bāśār* is the *bāśār* of donkeys, and their flow the flow of stallions."

Rabbi Joshua, after asking "From where shall I create her?" came up with the answer *yārēk*, "thigh." What did he intend by using that word? It occurs in a number of places in the Bible (Exod 32:27; Judg 3:16; 15:8; Jer 31:19; Ezek 21:17; Ps 45:4). It is also used to refer to the side or to an area near the side of a building: the tabernacle (Exod 40:22, 24) or an altar (Lev 1:11; 2 Kings 16:14).[19]

In many passages, however, the singular *yārēk* is used to indicate penis: Genesis 46:26, "all people . . . who came from his *yārēk*"; Exodus 1:5, "And all the people, those who came out of the *yārēk* of Jacob"; Judges 8:30, "And Gideon had seventy sons who came out of his *yārēk*."[20]

Once the referent of *yārēk* in the preceding passages is clear, the euphemistic rather than literal usage in the following passages becomes obvious. In Genesis 24:2–3 (cf. verse 9), Abraham, concerned that his son Isaac has no wife gives his senior servant specific instructions about what sort of a wife he is to find for Isaac. He instructs the servant to take an oath: "Place your hand under my *yārēk* and I will make you swear" (that is, touch my testicles and testify to the effect that you will do such and such). See also Genesis 47:29, where the same expression involving a formal oath occurs. In Genesis 32:26, the narrator of Genesis describes a wrestling match in which Jacob will not release a mysterious man who asks to be released before the sun rises. Jacob refuses and the man takes action: "and he touched the hollow of his *yārēk*, and struck (a powerful blow at) the hollow of the *yārēk* of Jacob while struggling with him . . . and he [Jacob] limped on account of his *yārēk*."[21]

Two conclusions may be reached on the basis of this survey. Excluding *mebūwšīym*, "embarrassments," which may not refer to a penis at all but, if so, is clearly a euphemism, *kelīy*, "instrument/tool," which may be slang, and *qōṭen*, "small one," which may be a vulgarism, most of the words that biblical writers employed when referring to the penis are usually applied to limbs or parts of the body that are attached and protrude from the trunk. The single word on this list whose semantic range, exclusive of its use to refer to a penis, resembles that of *ṣēlaʿ* is *yārēk*, which happens to be the word that refers to a penis most often. It was the euphemism preferred by Rabbi Joshua. This does not prove, but does support, the contention that *ṣēlaʿ* also referred to penis in Jerusalemite Hebrew.[22]

Individuals were able to imagine the erect penis as a homunculus from which a human figure could be formed. More important, however, is the observation that the erect phallus, as opposed to the flaccid one, is the only protuberance on the male body lacking a bone. But if it lacks a bone, how is it that the man referred to the woman as "bone from my bones" in verse 23?

THE BACULUM

Among mammals, all insectivores, bats, rodents, all carnivores, and most primates have a bone called a baculum, or *os penis* and sometimes *os priapi*, that occurs as a stiffening rod in the penis. Human males (like spider monkeys) lack this bone and rely instead on fluid hydraulics to maintain erections.[23] The baculum is not necessarily a small bone. That of a large male dog can be almost four inches (10 centimeters) long, half an inch (1.3 centimeters) wide, and more than a third of an inch (1 centimeter) thick.[24] The largest mammalian baculum is that of a walrus, which can reach lengths of up to thirty inches (76 centimeters).

Israelites comparing skeletons of common male animals with those of deceased human males must have noticed the absence of a baculum on the human skeletons. In context, Adam's statement in Genesis 2:23 is etiological; it explains what happened to the bone: "This one. This time. Bone from my bones and flesh from my flesh. This one will be called Woman [*'iššāh*] because from Man [*'īyš*] she was taken."

Adam's statement is interesting for three reasons.

First, he uses the term *bāśār* meaning "flesh, meat," to refer to the woman. The word is one of the euphemisms for penis discussed above as well as a word connected to kinship terminology.

Second, Adam's declaration explains the literal, as well as the literary, origin of an idiom expressing blood kinship, *ʿaṣmīy ūwbeśārīy*, "my bone and my flesh," that recurs in the Bible (Gen 29:14; Judg 9:2; 2 Sam 5:1 [=1 Chron 11:1]; 19:13, 14).[25] This should not be confused with the familiar and

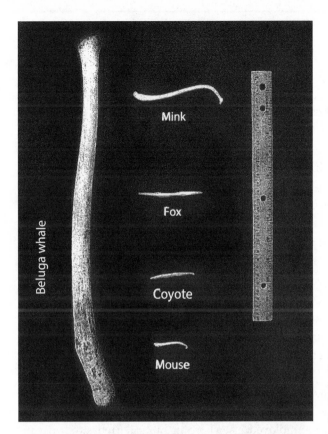

Bacula from Selected Mammals (Courtesy of Scott F. Gilbert, Department of Biology, Martin Biological Laboratories, Swarthmore College.)

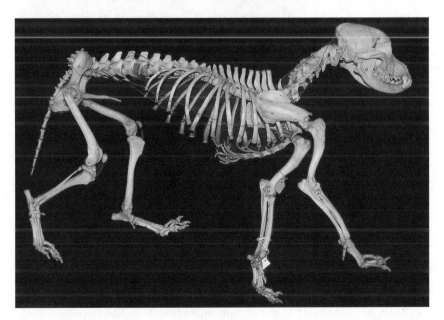

A Skeleton of a Male Dog
(Courtesy of Scott F. Gilbert and the Mütter Museum of the College of Physicians, Philadelphia.)

somewhat similar expression "flesh and blood," which originates in a phrase used in New Testament passages to refer to people in general, not to relatives (Mat 16:17; Gal 1:16; Eph 6:12). In contemporary expressions such as "he is my flesh and blood" meaning "my kin or family," "flesh and blood" is used as if it were the Hebrew expression "my bone and my flesh."

Third, in Adam's enthusiastic declaration about the woman, he articulates the distinction between human males and human females. Prior to the formation of the woman, a special term referring to a male human would have been meaningless, since he was the only show in town. The first creature was an *'ādām*, a sexually undifferentiated human. There is semantic truth in the folk expression "it takes a woman to make a man."

The distinction made by Adam between himself as a man, *'īyš*, and the woman, *'iššāh*, employs words that with one exception refer to humans alone. The exceptional reference in Genesis 7:2 refers to animals as mated pairs entering the ark: "the man and his woman." This contrasts sharply with the cryptic verse in Genesis 1:27 that describes a figure with both male and female characteristics: "And God [Elohim] created the human' [*ādām*] in his image, in the image of God he created him, male and female he created them." The clinical terms used there for male, *zākār*, and female, *neqēbāh*, are employed elsewhere in biblical Hebrew to distinguish animals by sex.[26] This usage suggests one additional implication of Adam's statement about the new creature.

The author of the Garden story could assume his readers' awareness of a widespread feature in Hebrew that serves to mark a noun as grammatically feminine: the suffix *-āh* (as in the word *neqēbāh*, meaning "female"). The same suffix is often used to distinguish between nouns referring to the male and female of a species: *par* (steer, young bull—Num 7:15) and *pārāh* (heifer, cow—Isa 11:7); *śūwś* (male horse—1 Kings 20:20) and *śūwśāh* (mare—Song of Songs 1:9); *kebeś* (ram lamb—Isa 1:11) and *kibśāh* (ewe lamb—Lev 5:6); *pered* (he-mule—2 Sam 18:9) and *pirdāh* (she-mule—1 Kings 1:33). So, he wrote, after Adam saw the creature that God had made from bone and declared her name, *'iššāh*, Adam was expressing that she was a female of the same species as he and was therefore sexually appropriate for him.

Humans can and regularly do copulate in the ventro-ventral (face-to-face) position, whereas most primates, owing to their anatomy, cannot do so. There are only two known exceptions to this. Bonobos (*Pan paniscus*), a distinct species of ape, conduct about one-third of their copulations in ventro-ventral positions. And Western lowland gorillas (*Gorilla gorilla gorilla*) in the Republic of Congo were first observed and photographed using this position in 2007; they usually adopt a dorso-ventral (back-to-front) position, in which both face the same direction.[27] Since Israelites in Iron Age Israel knew neither bonobos nor gorillas, Adam's statement may be understood as a positive comment on the sexual uniqueness and appropriateness of the female.[28] This provides a naturalistic etiology explaining why human males copulate with human females and not with animals.

A second-century CE teacher, Rabbi Elazar, pondered the words "this one, this time" in Adam's declaration and concluded: "This teaches that Adam cohabited with every animal and beast but his mind was not at peace until he cohabited with Eve" (*b. Yebamot* 63a). Elazar's explanation may strike contemporary readers as condoning bestiality, which our Western tradition considers a violation of, if not natural, then biblical law. In the Hellenistic world, though, bestiality was perhaps practiced occasionally or regularly in different locales. It is described in myths about Leda and the swan (who was actually Zeus), Olympia, mother of Alexander the Great, and a snake (Zeus again), and others, and in stories about satyrs born of goats but fathered by humans.[29]

Ancient Israelites were certainly aware of behaviors associated with bestiality. Laws against it were part of their tradition. Each of the three major collections of laws preserved in the Pentateuch proscribes bestiality without explanation: Exodus 22:19, "Whoever lies down with an animal, dying will be put to death"; and Leviticus 18:23; 20:16; Deuteronomy 27:21. In their literary contexts, unaccompanied by justifications, these laws represent the arbitrary will of the divine author vis-à-vis Israel. Zoophilia is something that God forbade Israelites because he desired to do so.

Elazar's interpretation accepts the story of God bringing the animals to the first person as an etiology for bestiality. It had been practiced by Adam and was not divinely forbidden to humans, only to Israelites after Sinai. In the twenty-first century, contemporary statutes outlawing human-animal sexual acts often do so on the grounds of animal cruelty. In many countries around the world, such acts are not considered illegal.

One additional etiological element may be seen, in the second half of verse 22, where God brings the newly made woman to Adam. In Israel, as in other parts of the ancient Near East, males arranged marriages for dependent women. Although the women may have been consulted and may have had some influence in determining the choice, the final decision was not theirs. In like manner, Rachel is obtained by Jacob (Gen 29:21), Zipporah is given to Moses (Exod 2:21), Achsah, the daughter of Caleb, is handed to Othniel (Judg 1:13).

A final etiological element may be inferred from the monogamy evident in Genesis: Adam and the overwhelming majority of the men have only a single wife. Most marriages in Israel and elsewhere in the ancient Near East were monogamous for practical reasons. Maintaining two women with the legal status of wives was a major expense involving many legal complications in matters of inheritance.[30]

This whole complicated story about the first lady of humanity, etiological implications and all, is completely ignored in the verse that follows, verse 24.

13 WHY "THEREFORE"?

(Gen 2:24)

Genesis 2

24 Therefore a man *ya'azōb* his father and his mother and clings to
his *'iššāh* and they become one flesh.[1]

Ostensibly verse 24 continues Adam's statement in verse 23: "This one.
This time. Bone from my bones and flesh from my flesh. This one will be
called Woman because from man this one was taken." However, when
the two verses are read consecutively, verse 24 immediately presents a
problem. The word "therefore," a correct translation of Hebrew *'al kēn*,
signals that what follows is a conclusion reached on the basis of what
precedes. The problem is that verse 24, with *ya'azōb* understood to mean
"leaves" or "will leave," does not seem to follow the previous verse logically or to present a conclusion drawn from any elements in the previous
narrative.

Genesis 2:24 may sound familiar even to those who have never read
the Garden story because the verse is often cited in wedding homilies. In
that context, it is treated as a scriptural instruction to young couples to
strike out on their own, leave their parents, and establish their own
families. In a thoughtful book, *Adam and Eve: Marriage Secrets from the
Garden of Eden*, Michael Shevack makes this exact point. He writes: "This
'therefore' feels so out of context in the story that it's hard to imagine why
it's actually there. It feels more like a commentary than part of the story

line. Indeed, that's what it is: a one-line editorial, designed to deliver one of the Garden's most indispensable lessons. Ignore this one and you condemn to exile not only your marriage, but the entire world."[2] Shevack, following a 2,200-year-old tradition, learns something from the passage after the "therefore" despite his lack of clarity on how it connects to what comes before. He is not the first to do so.

John Calvin's comment on the verse—written in the sixteenth century—addresses the question of the verse's relationship to verse 23: "It is doubted whether Moses here introduces God as speaking, or continues the discourse of Adam, or indeed, has added this in virtue of his office as teacher, in his own person. The last of these is that which I most approve." He explains that Moses could not possibly have meant that a man is to leave his father on account of his marriage, an idea that Calvin believed contradicted nature. Since it could not mean what it appears to mean, Calvin argued, it *must have another meaning*. He claimed that the verse teaches that in cases of conflict, a man should prefer his wife to his father, because the marriage bond is more significant than the bond of birth.[3]

Rabbi Shelomo ben Isaac (1040–1105) from Troyes, France, commonly known and referred to by the acronym Rashi, commented: "The Holy Spirit says this in order to prohibit incest among the descendents of Noah."[4] Rashi's concern about verse 24, no matter the merit of his somewhat far-fetched explanation, is triggered by his observation that since verse 24 does not continue Adam's speech from verse 23, a different speaker is responsible for these words; and since the words are not pertinent to Adam's circumstances, they *must address some other situation*. Calvin proposed that the verse be attributed to Moses; Rashi proposed God.

About twelve hundred years before Rashi, the author of *Jubilees*, an apocryphal book (ca. 125 BCE), explained the passage differently. He has the Angel of Presence explaining to Moses what happened in the Garden. The angel says that after the woman was presented to Adam and after he "knew" her, he addressed the "bone of my bones" speech (verse 23) to her. And then the angel, in commenting to Moses, provided the words for verse 24 (*Jubilees* 3:6–7). Moses simply recorded what he heard as if the angel's words were the continuation of Adam's speech to Hawwa and not the angel's comment to him.

Commentators who focus on the question of who may have written the verse tend not to observe that it is only the man who takes leave of his parents, not the woman. From this we can infer that he moves into her father's house. She seems to be—like the young wife in the American folk song "Where Have You Been, Billy Boy?"—a "young thing that cannot leave her mother."

My objections to common understandings of the verse are based on my answers to three basic questions:

(1) What does the verse mean? What can it mean?

(2) How is this meaning connected to what was said by Adam about the formation of the *'ēzer kenegdōw*? How is it connected to the whole prior narrative about that?

(3) Does the "therefore" address any social reality in ancient Israel?

TRANSLATING *YA'AZŌB* AS "LEAVES" OR "WILL LEAVE"

Calvin alone among the commentators cited above was bothered by the statement that men leave their fathers as a consequence of marriage, but then he explained the problem away eisegetically.

During the twentieth century, a few biblical scholars proposed that the statement is etiological and that it alludes to a type of matrilocal marriage described by nineteenth-century ethnographers working in Sri Lanka, who labeled it a "*beena* marriage."[5] In *beena* marriages, the male either leaves his family and takes up residence with his wife's family, or he gains rights to visit his mate, who is living with her family, while he continues to live with his own family. Biblical evidence in support of this explanation is not convincing.

Jacob's fourteen years of service to Laban and his residence with his wives' family involved paying off a debt to their father: the combined bridal prices of Leah and Rachel measured in years of service (Gen 29:15–30). Even though his father-in-law may have wanted Jacob to continue working for him, Jacob was legally free to leave once he had cleared his obligations. And when Jacob felt that the time was right, that is exactly what he did, taking his wives with him.

Moses, a refugee from Egypt, has no home to which he can take his wife; so he settles in the land of Midian with his father-in-law, who employs him as a shepherd. Exodus 2:21 suggests that Moses dwelled with Reuel as a condition of the marriage: "Moses agreed to stay with the man and he gave Zipporah, his daughter, to Moses." Although this arrangement appears to qualify as a *beena* marriage, it is more a case of the wealthy concerned father guaranteeing that his penurious refugee son-in-law be able to provide for his daughter and perhaps later for him in his old age.

Moses' independence is clear. After God tells him to go to Egypt, he returns home and announces: "I will indeed go . . . and I will indeed return to my brothers in Egypt." Moses declares his intention to leave, and he leaves with his father-in-law's blessing, taking his wife and his children with him (Exod 4:18, 24–26).

Apart from these three stories, there is no evidence that marriages of the *beena* type were known in ancient Israel.[6] Furthermore, societies in which *beena* marriage patterns are attested have a strong matriarchal element affecting lineage and inheritance. The idea that such an element was present in Israel is contradicted by what is known about marriage arrangements and inheritance laws in ancient Israel and generally throughout the ancient Near East.[7] Consequently, unless new data will compel a *beena* marriage interpretation, Genesis 2:24 cannot be interpreted as the origin of a nonexistent "leave and cleave" practice.

A HELPFUL INSIGHT ABOUT "CLINGING"

The Hebrew word translated as "cling" is from the root *d-b-q*, meaning "to cling, cleave to, to be or stay very close or firmly attached" (Deut 13:18; 2 Sam 23:1). By semantic extension, it is also associated with a sense of loyalty and devotion to individuals or to God. Although the word does not pose any difficulty in the verse, the verse itself is open to a number of possible interpretations because of the uncertainty about how "clinging" connects with the ideas of "leaving his father and his mother" and "becoming one flesh."

H. C. Brichto, like Calvin, considers verse 24 a statement explaining the loyalty of males to their exogamous wives over against their own parents and argues that it is to be understood as addressing the dynamics of the human family.[8] His view is supported by verses that employ verbs based on the root *d-b-q* in contexts dealing with human love, attraction, and marriage:

Genesis 34:3: "And his soul [*tidbaq*] attached to Dinah, daughter of Jacob, and he loved the young maiden, and he spoke appealingly to the young maiden."

Joshua 23:12: "If you turn away [ūwdebaqtem] and become very attached, to the remnant of those nations left with you and intermarry with them."

1 Kings 11:1–2: "King Solomon loved many foreign women . . . from the nations . . . Solomon [dābaq] became attached, to them for love."

Verse 24 traces the origin of such attachments to the founding ancestor, Adam. I conjecture that it also alludes to the social and legal independence of the married son from his own father and mother when the newlyweds become one flesh, a distinctive family unit.[9] Brichto's insight suggests a way for clarifying the placement of the verse at this juncture in the context of the story.

Triggered by Adam's "bone from my bones and flesh from my flesh" remark in verse 23, the authorial comment of verse 24 makes a point on the basis of the two referents of Hebrew 'iššāh, which means both "woman" and "wife." The authorial comment implies that the exogamous mating behavior of people with whom Israelites were familiar was modeled after the relationship of the first couple at the very beginning of humankind's sexual experience. In Israelite conception, Adam and Hawwa were, by default, an exogamous pair. She was unknown to Adam before God presented her, and she was not descended from either of Adam's nonexistent parents. Despite her unique origin, she could not be considered his sister or his daughter or a close blood relative in any way that Israelites might have imagined.

By the end of the story, Adam dwells with his wife and children outside the Garden and away from Eden. His lack of father and mother is of no consequence because his behavior with the woman established and exemplified the norm for all their descendents.

Drawing on the social experience of his readers, the author may have intended that verse 24 function as a foreshadowing of events about to be described. These would involve the man's being by his wife during the fruit incident, his clinging to her in fruitful cohabitation through which they would produce one flesh, and his remaining with her as they metamorphosed into the original family consisting of father and mother with children.

Although the preceding explanation constitutes a step toward a solution, it does not clarify the verse's disruptive heaviness or explain how the "therefore" fits in. It also fails to account for the problem of a man's leaving his father and his mother.

TRANSLATING *YA'AZŌB* DIFFERENTLY

Verbs from the root *'-z-b* are attested 216 times in the Hebrew Bible. In three passages where a meaning such as "leave" or "abandon" is inappropriate, they are translated differently.

The first passage is Exodus 23:5, "When you see the ass of your enemy lying under its load, and you refrain from *mē'azōb* [setting it right] for him [that is, for the donkey], *'azōb ta'azōb* [you will certainly set it right] with him." In other words, together with your enemy, you will reposition the load on the donkey's back. Deuteronomy 22:4 clarifies this. It instructs Israelites not to be oblivious when they sees a kinsman's donkey or ox fallen on the road (most likely under a load): "you will surely raise up with him"; that is, you will help your kinsman get the animal up on its feet. Both of these laws are concerned with the animals, not with their owners.

The second passage using the root is Nehemiah 3:8. In a description of work teams reconstructing gates and repairing breaches in the walls of Jerusalem, the following occurs: "Next to them Uziel son of Harhayah of the smiths strengthened [the wall], and next to him Hananyah of the perfumers strengthened [the wall], *waya'azebūw* [and they repaired] Jerusalem up to the broad wall."

The third passage is also in Nehemiah, 3:34. In a speech to fellow detractors of the wall-building project in Jerusalem, Sanballat asked: "What are the miserable Jews doing? *Haya'azebūw?* [Will they repair (it)] for themselves? . . . Will they restore the stones from piles of dust, burnt as they are?"

Medieval Jewish exegetes pointed out the distinctly different meanings of the verbs in these passages, and perhaps in Jeremiah 49:25. However, not until the twentieth century did scholars posit the existence of another root, identified as *'-z-b* II, and recognize that it has cognate verbs in Ugaritic, Epigraphic South Arabian, and Ge'ez.[10] On the basis of these cognates, the posited meanings of the newly discovered Hebrew root are "to help, fix, make whole, set right." Recognizing that Genesis 2:24 should be added to the list of verses demonstrating the new root makes the Ge'ez cognate, *'azzaba*, "to assist, uphold, help," particularly relevant. The verse now supports the following translation: "Therefore a man strengthens/supports/helps his father and his mother and clings to his woman/wife and they become one flesh."

Genesis 2:24 follows events narrated earlier in the story that perhaps justify the presence of "therefore": God brought Adam into the world, employed him, provided for his sustenance, and provided him with a wife that Adam recognized as kin. By fulfilling his work obligations properly, Adam had supported God and would continue to do so afterward; by presenting Adam with a wife, God had fulfilled an obligation to Adam. In this context, with the failed animal experiment behind them, "therefore" marks a conclusion that humans behave differently from animals that do not care or even recognize their mother and father after they mature, that mate (more or less) indiscriminately and casually, and that are unaware of their own offspring after they mature.

The verse implies that since parents birth sons and (may) provide those sons with wives (see Gen 28:2; 38:2, 6; Judg 14:2–3), every son is obliged to care for his father and his mother (Exod 20:12; Deut 5:16) and to cling to his wife simultaneously.[11] Understood this way, the verse also alludes to the formation of extended families embracing three generations in a single household that were typical of Israelite society.

In the Garden story, verse 24 concludes the first series of major episodes, even as it introduces a second series in which some consequences of "clinging" unfold.

14 HOW BARE IS NAKED?

(Gen 2:25)

Genesis 2

25 And the two of them were naked, *hā'ādām*, and his
'*ištōw*, but they were not ashamed of each other.

This verse, the logical continuation of verse 23, moves readers from the first to the second series of episodes constituting the story, from those about the formation of the Garden and its inhabitants to those about the encounter between cognizant humans and their world. It directs attention to the sorry sartorial state of the first couple even as it emphasizes, by repeating the word for woman/wife from verses 23 and 24, that the first two humans were married, a detail of consequence in the unfolding narrative. It is unclear to me what, if any, significance should be attached to the pairing of *hā'ādām*, "the human," with '*ištōw*, "woman/wife," as opposed to pairing '*īyš*, "man," with "woman/wife" at this point in the story.

Information in this verse foreshadows human sewing activities in Genesis 3:7 and the divine undertaking in low couture mentioned in Genesis 3:21.[1] Its contribution to the story lies in the author's aside to his readers that may be paraphrased: "We are shamed when completely naked in the presence of our spouses. Believe it or not, our ancestors in the Garden experienced no shame under similar circumstances."

From the author's perspective, the couple's behavior in the Garden is not innocently naive but atypically odd, quite indecent by the Israelite standards of his day, certainly noteworthy, and in need of explanation. Mention of their nakedness here foreshadows the story of how normal humans cover their bodies properly that begins in Genesis 3:7.

The word 'ištōw, "his woman/wife," has been taken as indicating possession, raising thereby issues of power, control, and authority. This interpretation, however, is questionable on four grounds:

(1) She was not formed to be a possession. She was formed, as were the animals, for some function relevant to the man. That is all.

(2) All interpretations of 'ēzer kenegdōw presented in Chapter 11 of this book militate against such an interpretation. Not one indicates that the 'ēzer was intended to be a possession. The author could have used the word 'ebed, "slave."

(3) The reference to Adam as "her man" in Genesis 3:6 contains the identical grammatical construction. The context there does not countenance the understanding that she possessed him.

(4) The nature of contracted marriages in Israel and the ancient Near East does not suggest that marriages granted the husband possession of the wife as if she were a chattel.

15 CLEVER CONVERSATION AND
CONSPICUOUS CONSUMPTION

(Gen 3:1–6)

Genesis 3

1a   And the *nāḥāš hāyāh 'ārūwm* than every animal of the field
1b   that YHWH god made, and he said to the woman:
          'ap, kīy, God said:
               lō' tō'kelūw mikkol 'ēṣ haggān
2   And the woman said to the *nāḥāš*:
          From the fruit of trees of the garden we eat
3   but from the fruit of the tree that is within the garden,
          God said:
               lō' tō'kelūw from it *welō' tigge'ūw bōw*
               pen temutūwn.
4   And the *nāḥāš* said to the woman:
          lō' mōwt temutūwn.
5a   Indeed, God knows that on the day of your eating
5b   from it your eyes *wenipqeḥūw* and you will be like God,
          yōde'ēy ṭōwb wārā'.
6a   And the woman saw the tree good for eating and appetizing
6b   for the eyes and the tree *neḥmād lehaśkīyl,* and she took from
     its fruit and ate and she gave also to her man [who was]
     with her, and he ate.

The event called the Fall, if indeed it was a fall, is covered at the beginning of chapter 3 of Genesis—more precisely, in verse 6. The drama occurs in the first five verses, however. They tell about a fatal conversation in the course of which one aspect of God's plan for the Garden was undermined.

ENTER THE SERPENT

The serpent, unmentioned until now, has actually been part of the narrative since Genesis 2:18–20, which described the "first social welfare program." In Genesis 3:1–6 he slides out of the crowd, no longer an extra in the background. He moves forward into the spotlight, a star, and into infamy.

The *nāḥāš*, "serpent," is cast as a generic figure. He is not identified with any of the specific species referred to elsewhere in the Bible: *ṣepaʿ* (Isa 14:29), *ṣipʿōnīy* (Jer 8:17), *ʾepʿeh* (Job 20:16), *qippōwz* (Is 34:15), *ʿakšūwb* (Ps 140:4), *šepīypōn* (Gen 49:17), *tannīyn* (Gen 1:21; Isa 27:1 [a sea creature]; Exod 4:3; 7:9 [a land creature]), *peten* (Deut 32:33; Ps 58:5), or *śarap* (Num 21:6; Deut 8:15; Isa 14:29; 30:6). The author's preference for the generic term *nāḥāš* over the more specific terms may have been influenced by its connotations: the word resonates with verbs and nouns from the root *n-ḥ-š* that refer to divining the future (Gen 44:5; Num 24:1). In and of itself, the word *nāḥāš* did not evoke anything sinister in Israelite culture. It was even a personal name in Israel (2 Sam 17:25) and among Israel's neighbors, the Ammonites (1 Sam 11:1–2).

Individual Israelite readers most likely imagined the serpent differently depending on their experience with glissading creatures, just as *snake* might evoke different images for people in England, India, Amazonia, and Arizona, who may smile or shudder at thoughts of garters, cobras, anacondas, and rattlers. An ancient Israelite may have imagined any of the forty species of snakes attested in Israel—from a blind worm snake to a black desert cobra to a Palestine saw-scaled viper—of which only six are poisonous.[1]

Genesis 3:1a alludes to Genesis 2:19 by its reference to the "every animal of the field" and through its formal syntax. The first allusion is obvious, the second much less so.

After the linking conjunction *and,* the Hebrew verse does not begin with a verb in the narrative tense but with the noun *nāḥāš*. This

Subject + Verb word order signals a break with the sequence of activities described in the immediately preceding verses, all of which begin, in Hebrew, with verbs in the first position. Genesis 3:1 introduces a new subject at the *beginning* of the sentence, the *nāḥāš*, and then employs a construction comprising a past tense form of the verb "to be," *hāyāh*, followed by a participle. A participle is a verbal noun used like an adjective—as in "galloping horse" or "sleeping sloth." With active participles, the noun being used as an adjective is in a transitive activity; it is giving, throwing, cooking—doing something that affects something or somebody. With passive participles, the noun being used as an adjective is in an intransitive state, such as thinking, sitting, or sleeping. The Hebrew word *'ārūwm* used to describe the serpent is the passive participle formed from a root, *'-r-m* II (1 Sam 23:22; Prov 15:5), whose meaning and nuances are crucial for understanding the story.

In Hebrew narrative prose, a syntactic pattern consisting of a new subject introduced into the narrative by the conjugation *we*, "and," + Subject followed by *hāyāh* + participle describes a situation or circumstance that had existed *prior* to the chronological onset of the narrative and that continued through the time of the narrative. This pattern inserts a touch of necessary background for what is about to be narrated.

For this reason Genesis 3:1a should be understood as indicating "And the serpent [*hāyāh 'ārūwm*] had been (and still was) more shrewd than every animal of the field."[2] This quality dominated his character from the moment God formed him along with every other animal of the field in Genesis 2:19. He was this way while the human was naming him and the other animals and when Adam and God were considering which of the creatures might be the sought-after *'ēzer kenegdōw*.[3] He was by nature preeminent among the animals with regard to a particular virtue highly esteemed by Israelites who appreciated "wisdom."

I use *wisdom*, here and in following chapters, in the technical sense defined by historians of Israelite and other ancient Near Eastern cultures. The word refers to writings that commented on the universality of human experiences as people related to each other individually and as they functioned in hierarchically organized societies; the literature contains pithy observations about happiness, suffering, life, and death. Its goals, as indicated by wisdom books in the Bible and elsewhere in ancient Near Eastern texts, were to employ clear language in expressing objective observations—not divine revelation. Its writers analyzed the ways of the world, discerned how people gain mastery over their lives, described how to behave in God's presence, and made concrete suggestions on how to succeed in many aspects of life. The biblical books of Proverbs, Ecclesiastes, and Job, despite their differences, are types of wisdom literature. The concerns of wisdom thinking, an ancient forerunner of American Pragmatism, are found also in the stories about the rise of David to power narrated in 1 Samuel and those about the court intrigues and manipulations described in Esther, as well as in the Garden story.

THE SERPENT'S PARTICULAR GIFT

The serpent was *'ārūwm*. People characterized as *'ārūwm* conceal what they feel and what they know (Prov 12:16, 23). They esteem knowledge and plan how to use it in achieving their objectives (Prov 13:16; 14:8, 18); they do not believe everything that they hear (Prov 14:15); and they know how to avoid trouble and punishment (Prov 22:3; 27:12). In sum, they are shrewd and calculating, willing to bend and torture the limits of acceptable behavior but not to cross the line into illegalities.[4] They may be unpleasant and purposely misleading in speech but are not out-and-out liars (Josh 9:4; 1 Sam 23:22).[5] They know how to read people and situations and how to turn their readings to advantage. A keen wit and a rapier tongue are their tools.

Nowhere in the Hebrew Bible is the serpent referred to as a *rāšaʻ*, a wicked or evil creature. In a popular book on Psalms, Nahum Sarna defines the "unlovely characteristics" of people to whom *rāšaʻ* is applied in both Psalms and Proverbs. Their "abhorrent portrait" reveals them marked by

> arrogance, pride, and vainglorious bluster. They are brazen-faced, insolent, derisive, and contemptuous of others. They plot evil even in bed and scheme against the innocent. They are enamored of injustice and deliberately pervert the administration of justice by means of bribery. . . . Their speech is deceitful and duplicitous, mendacious, fraudulent and treacherous. They abuse another's friendship, repaying good with hate.[6]

Although a few characteristics of the evil person are similar to those of the shrewd one, the two are not the same. Only in medieval interpretation was the devious fused with the evil, creating a devil. Thus a serpent in the Garden was transformed into Satan who rules in Hell.

By describing the serpent as *'ārūwm*, the Iron Age author signaled, *Caveat lector! Caveat auditor!* Reader, beware! Listener, beware! Attend carefully to the use and misuse of language in the story that is about to follow. Scrutinize closely what is said and what is omitted.

The author was not informing his readers of anything new because biblical stories often advance plot and illustrate character through the use of oblique responses to direct questions and by means of thoughtfully crafted, misleading statements. Here are some examples.

> In Genesis 4:9, Qayin, no stranger to conversational stratagems, avoids responding to God's query "Where is Hebel, your brother?" by posing a deflecting question of his own: "Am I my brother's keeper?" The underlying postulate of the question is true: since I am not his keeper, it is unreasonable of you to ask me, Qayin, about my brother's whereabouts.

> In Genesis 20:2, Abraham provides a misleading half-truth to the men of Gerar curious about his attractive female traveling companion. Fearful for his life, he informs them that Sarah is his sister, omitting to mention that she is his half-sister and wife as well (see verse 12).

> In Genesis 22:8, Abraham and Isaac ascend the mountain where Abraham is resolute to sacrifice his son. Isaac asks, "Here are the firestone and the wood, but where is the lamb for the burnt offering?" Abraham replies, "God will see for himself the lamb for an offering." His answer is intended to mislead the designated "lamb," his son, so he would proceed docilely, carrying wood up the mountain to his own slaughter.

> In Genesis 37:32, the brothers present to their father Joseph's tunic, which they had stained with goat's blood, and say truthfully, "We found this. Recognize it." Then they ask, "Is it the tunic of your son or not?" Jacob jumps to all the wrong conclusions about what happened to his beloved son, just as the jealous brothers anticipated. He concludes that an animal killed Joseph.

> In Exodus 3:18, God instructs Moses to request from Pharaoh permission to travel three days' journey into the wilderness in order to sacrifice to "the God of the Hebrews." The instruction conveniently omits mention of the intention of the Israelites not to return to Egypt.

In Judges 4:9, the prophet Deborah tells the military leader Barak that if she goes to battle with him, his glory of victory will be given to the "hand of a woman." She does not mention that it will not be credited to herself, a popular public figure with whom Barak might have been willing to share glory, but to Jael, an unknown, reclusive wife of a non-Israelite. Barak, reaching the wrong conclusion, invites Deborah along. When the battle is over, glory is assigned to Jael (Judg 4:22; 5:6, 24–27).

Nowadays, such attention to the nuances of what is said and how it is expressed, of what is left unsaid, is often restricted to the parlance of statecraft, diplomacy, courts, contracts, and the arguments of children. Subtle speech is largely absent from the popular culture of plainspoken America but is present in that of England and France. The frequency of nuanced language use in biblical tales shows that general Israelite culture recognized it as part of conversational strategy and narrative art. The skilled author of the Garden story appreciated linguistic nuance and knew how to exploit the subtleties of Hebrew in composing his work.

Sensitivity to the full semantic range of the word *'ārūwm,* obvious to author and audience, enables us to understand that the serpent's words are goal-oriented, measured, and hardly random. It does not enable us, however, to discern his underlying motivation. Why did he want to precipitate these specific actions and bring trouble to the first couple?

THE SERPENT'S MOTIVATION: THE BEGINNINGS OF A HYPOTHESIS

The cluster of images and motifs, serpent + animals + people + deceit + vegetation + sex + clothing + life, in the Garden story is found also in the Mesopotamian *Gilgamesh Epic.* There a water snake steals a plant called "old man becomes young" from the semi-divine Gilgamesh, who required it to revive his dead friend Enkidu.[7] Enkidu had once been a man-animal, playing and romping innocently with animals until "tamed" by a prostitute sent from the city to seduce—and thus to humanize—him, and to garb—and thus to civilize—him. After Enkidu had been seduced sexually by a woman, the animals would have nothing to do with him, so he came to live with people and became Gilgamesh's beloved companion. The water snake's action guaranteed that Enkidu remained dead.[8]

The Mesopotamian and Israelite stories are not strictly parallel. In the former a snake steals a particular rejuvenating plant; in the latter a serpent encourages the consumption of a particular fruit granting a particular type of knowledge. In *Gilgamesh* the prostitute is sent by people to diminish Enkidu's natural quality of life; in Genesis Hawwa is formed to enhance Adam's quality of life. In both stories, however, plants are associated with the theme of death, and in both, the female protagonist permanently affects the relationship between the male and animals. The snake in *Gilgamesh* may be understood as taking revenge on Enkidu, who abandoned animals, as well as on Gilgamesh, the ultimate beneficiary of Enkidu's actions; the serpent in Genesis may be understood as attempting to take revenge against the woman responsible for changing Adam's relationship with animals.

Whatever the obvious assets of the recently formed woman may have been for Adam, the sapient serpent, most shrewd of animals initially formed by God for Adam, had devised plans of his own for her. He would talk of trees, but would think of death.[9]

THE PLOT IN PROCESS

The serpent's inducement in Genesis 3:5 was that eating from the tree would result in the woman's knowing *ṭōwb* and *rā'*, good and bad. She would gain the acumen to distinguish between what is more and what is less appropriate, preferable, or desirable (cf. Isa 7:15–16; Lev 27:12–14). Although a type of wisdom underlying responsible actions, it was of a lesser, simpler quality than his own complicated attribute of shrewdness.

His first words to the woman were: "Even, indeed/though ['*ap, kīy*], God said, 'You [plural] will not eat [*lō' tō'kelūw*] from every tree of the garden [*mikkol 'ēṣ haggān*]." Evaluated with insight born of hindsight, they reveal his method. There is neither question nor complete sentence here. His words trail off into silence, a lingering, incomplete thought. All that emerges clearly from his non-sentence is the phrase "*every* tree of the garden." By placing an incomplete utterance in the serpent's mouth, the author left readers—or, within the narrative, the woman—to complete the thought.[10]

The serpent said nothing of substance. His grammatically incomplete sentence lacks content, but it shapes the following dialogue. Israelites sensitive to such ploys would have understood that the serpent purposely inverted the permitted and the forbidden—had gotten it all backwards— a point that the woman corrected impatiently, breaking into the serpent's incomplete sentence in Genesis 3:2. But the serpent had already introduced a critical theme into the conversation: God's instruction that Adam eat "from every tree of the Garden" (Gen 2:16).

In addition to inverting the facts, the serpent introduces a confusing, ever-so-slight grammatical variation that the woman fails to notice and correct. He uses a plural form in quoting God (Gen 3:1) that the woman adopts. She then continues using plural forms in her restatement, imaginatively inserting herself into a scene that had occurred before she was manufactured. In her amplification of God's statement to Adam, she changes God's words in verse 3: *tō'kelūw . . . tigge'ūw . . . temutūwn*, "you [plural] will eat . . . you [plural] will touch . . . you [plural] will die." "You" rather than "thou" will die, rather than "dying you [masculine singular] will die." The actual instruction to Adam, however, in Genesis 2:16–17, is in the singular, *tō'kēl . . . tō'kal . . . mōwt tāmūwt*, that is, with "thou" in contrast to the plural "you." Furthermore, in her misquotation, the woman embellishes, adding a prohibition against touching the tree.[11]

Carried away, she places an emphasizing, heavy suffix, the *nun energicum* (or energetic *nun*), on the final verb, *-ūwn*, so it means "you will *surely indeed* die," rather than the common suffix *-ūw*. This new suffix added oomph to her declaration: "You will DIE."[12] Perhaps for this reason she drops the adverbial expression *beyōm 'akolkā* "on the day of your [singular] eating" from her retort (cf. Gen 2:17). Sharp of mind and sharp of tongue, Hawwa unwittingly opens her mouth to speak and swallows the serpent's baited hook.

For this conversation between the serpent and Hawwa to have taken place, both must have known about God's instruction to Adam.[13] This indicates to the modern reader that the author compressed events in composing his narrative, skipping over a scene in which Adam told her about that meeting with God. For the serpent to have initiated the exchange with Hawwa, he, too, had to have been in the know. Since the serpent was formed after God had instructed Adam, the serpent must have overheard Adam's history lesson to Hawwa.[14] Like all smooth serpents, he knew how to use what he had heard.

In verse 4, the serpent corrects the woman patiently, rebutting her assertion: "No, dying will you [plural] *surely indeed* die [*lō' mōwt temūtūwn*]."[15] He negates the veracity of her statement. The difficulty usually perceived with his response is that either the serpent lies here or God lied in Genesis 2:17, but this comprehension of what the serpent meant is chimerical.

As the discussion of *mōwt tāmūwt* in Chapter 10 demonstrates, from inception the human was mortal, and at worst, God's words conveyed a veiled threat of an early death by some outside agent. His words were hardly a decree of summary execution.[16] Consequently, the serpent may be understood as stating truthfully that the woman's emphasis on dying is misplaced. Linguistic usage did not allow her to assume an automatic death by agent.

Although the serpent may have nurtured hope in all three chambers of his heart that her death would be sooner than later—after all, God had used the expression "on the day of your [singular] eating," which she seemed to have forgotten—he did not want her to think so. This, however, constituted only part of his rebuttal.

By negating her use of the emphatic plural and deflating the intensity of her statement, the serpent reminded the woman that God's words were phrased in the grammatical singular (a significant point reflected only in the KJV translation through the use of the archaic English singular "thou") and in the grammatical masculine to boot and that therein lay two loopholes for sidestepping the prohibition. Were she to act alone, or were they to act in concert, neither the warning nor the veiled punishment would be applicable on technical grounds.

How so?

The serpent, whose particular type of wisdom came to the fore in his subtle use of language (he was certainly on a linguistic par with the author), realized that the feminine is marked in Hebrew whereas the so-called masculine functions as a common gender.

Like other Semitic languages, Hebrew does not create a grammatical opposition between "feminine" and "masculine" but between what speakers of the language consider "absolutely feminine" and "not absolutely feminine." A group of girls would be absolutely "feminine"; a group of boys or a mixed group of boys and girls or a large group of girls including only one boy would be "not absolutely feminine." In the conventional terminology of grammarians, "not absolutely feminine" is described as "masculine." Moreover, just as feminine is marked, so is plurality. Consequently, on a theoretical level, because the original restriction was expressed using a grammatically singular verb, the woman *may* have fallen under the authority of God's qualifying restriction and could have been held culpable after ignoring it. ("So," thinks the serpent, "if she takes a bite of the fruit, just maybe, she will die, if only I can convince her to act.") But then, she may not have fallen under its authority.

In Genesis 3:5, the continuation of his speech, the serpent emphasizes that the restriction does not apply to her: "Indeed, God knows that on the day of your [plural] eating from it"—here the serpent reintroduces the adverbial phrase that the woman dropped and changes the original singular pronoun of Genesis 2:17 to plural—"your [plural] eyes will open themselves [*wenipqehūw*] and you [plural] will be like God, knowers of good and bad."[17]

His use of "to open the eyes" in addressing the woman appeals to the most common, concrete way people obtain knowledge. The expression, always with a verb formed from the root *p-q-h*, when not referring to actual vision—as in Genesis 21:19; 2 Kings 6:17–20; Psalm 146:8—refers figuratively to comprehension and understanding, as in Isaiah 42:7 and Jeremiah 32:19. So, also, "to open the ear" in Isaiah 42:20. Her achievement of "knowing" would occur as a somatic reflex to the swallowed fruit. Her eyes would open themselves.[18]

In colubrine calculation he hinted, "See, you shall understand." English has much the same meaning: "I see/hear what you mean." The ophidian's use of the "opening the eyes" metaphor may have been stimulated by the author's knowledge that the eyes of snakes are always open. They lack movable eyelids.

Considered as a unit, the serpent's discourse comprises a strategic ploy. Insinuating the plural form into the conversation, the scaly rhetorician manages to confuse and disorient the woman, and then, by hinting at the grammatical correction and its implications, he makes it necessary for her to weigh options quickly and to decide independently on a series of actions.[19] Otherwise, the conversation would have to stop with everything unresolved.

Reuven Kimelman suggests that the serpent's discourse punctured the awesomeness of the restriction. "By linking up the knowing of good and evil with becoming like God, the serpent dangles before Eve a grand future in order to persuade her that God is a god who begrudges their potential godliness rather than one who graciously grants them life and sustenance."[20]

THE CONTEMPLATED ACTION

After the serpent's remarks in verses 4–5, the author describes the tree from the woman's point of view as she ponders his suggestion. Even before indulging herself, the woman became aware that in addition to being both edible and aesthetically pleasing, the tree was *neḥmād . . . lehaśkīyl*, "desirable . . . for enwisening" (verse 6).[21] I coin an English word here, *enwisening,* to capture the Hebrew meaning: "to make wiser."

Hawwa discerned, even before she ate, how the tree differed from other trees that were merely *neḥmād lemar'eh* (Gen 2:9), "desirable for seeing," that is, pleasant to look upon. Such trees could slake only an aesthetic thirst. But the serpent had dangled the possibility of intellectual self-improvement before her.[22] Bernard Levinson observes thoughtfully that even as she responded by taking action, Hawwa was considering her relationship to God, to Adam, and to her freedom to choose.[23]

Convinced, but not fully comprehending the implications of the serpent's remarks, the woman "took from its fruit and ate and she gave also to her man, who was with her [*le'īyšāh 'immāh*], and he ate" (Gen 3:6). Acting in concert, they became part of a grammatically marked category: "plural." They both indulged, and what came to pass was exactly that which the soothsaying serpent had foretold. On the day of their eating, their eyes opened themselves (Gen 3:5, 7). They achieved a new type of consciousness—discerning self-consciousness. They did not die.

The conversation with the snake is often labeled "The Temptation of Eve" or "The Seduction of Eve." Such loaded terms are inappropriate, since most of what took place occurred within Hawwa's head as she processed cognitive information.

Adam can hardly be described as tempted on the basis of anything narrated. His action was rather abrupt and instinctive, like the actions of hungry Esau, who "ate, drank, rose, and walked away" (Gen 25:34). Adam did not participate in the conversation with the snake; he did not comment on it, though he may have been nearby, "clinging" to the woman. (See the discussion of Genesis 2:24.)

The species of tree with enwisening fruit remains unmentioned. The Western tradition that it was an apple tree arose because of the assonance between the Latin words for wrongdoing, *malum,* and apple, *malus.* The association of apples with the Tree of Knowing lacks any basis in the Hebrew text. Insofar as the tree is not identified with a particular species, it could have been any one. Moreover, there may have been many trees like it in the garden, only one of which was designated as special with regard to knowing good and bad.

Given fruit, Adam ate. Like an infant being spoonfed, asking no questions, he opened his mouth, chomped, chewed, and swallowed.

He may be considered an innocent bystander, a naive accomplice, or an accidental beneficiary. His later ability to discriminate between proper and improper at an abstract level is the fruit of his consumption. Adam's earlier exhibitions—naming animals and recognizing the woman as what he wanted or needed—reflect innate knowledge used to make spontaneous and instinctive decisions, not high-level reasoning. The author does not describe Adam engaging in any activities requiring abstract cognitive thinking until after he munched the fruit.

16 DRESSING UP FOR A DRESSING DOWN

(Gen 3:7–11)

Genesis 3

7 And the eyes of both opened themselves and they knew that
they were naked; and [then] they sewed fig leaves and made
ḥagōrōt for themselves.

8 And they heard the sound of YHWH god moving back and forth
in the garden at the wind of the day, and *yitḥabbēʾ* the human and his
woman from before YHWH god *betōwk ʿēṣ* of the garden

9 And YHWH god called to the human and said to him:
Where are you?

10 And he said:
I heard your sound in the garden and I feared because
I was naked so I hid myself.

11 And he said:
Who told you that you are naked? Have you eaten
from the tree concerning which I commanded you to
not eat from it?

The couple eat, and as the serpent had foretold, they do not drop dead
on the spot.[1] Likewise, just as he had stated in verse 5, their eyes open
themselves and they know the world differently. Verse 7 continues to
describe how their "eye opening" manifests itself in action: in sewing.
Although their rush to make loincloths is sometimes presented as a

demonstration of their guilt, it is actually about the rush of knowledge that follows a blush of shame. Shame is tied to understanding cultural values and to changeable individual behavior; guilt is tied to juridic, forensic contexts and can sometimes be expiated. For individuals to experience shame, they must know social codes and must be aware that they committed or were subjected to an impropriety related to a particular value or norm. They also must know what is required to rectify the situation.

SHAME

The significance of their fig leaf coverings in verse 7 harks back to the narrator's remark in Genesis 2:25 that though naked, "they were not ashamed of each other." As verse 7 makes clear, their first experience with the new wisdom was linked to a social convention. They perceived their nakedness as unacceptable, undesirable, and inappropriate (bad—*ra'*). They resolved the situation inventively, improvising appropriate garments from fig leaves (good—*ṭōwb*).[2] Not only was this the first cover-up, but the cover-up led to the most human of inventions—clothing. Then, as verse 8 tells us, they experienced fear because God was approaching (bad—*ra'*). They fled, concealing themselves from his gaze in the foliage of a tree (good—*ṭōwb*). Finally, in verse 11, confronting an implicit accusation of wrongdoing which they recognized as undesirable (bad—*ra'*), they tried to avoid its consequences by clever argumentation (good—*ṭōwb*), which I discuss in the following chapter.[3]

Hearing the sound of God in the Garden, the humans, newly gifted with a capacity for deeper insight and understanding than before, withdraw from public space to conceal themselves. The Hebrew verb describing this is *yithabbē*,' "to hide/conceal oneself," formed from the root *ḥ-b-'*. In a nineteenth-century study of this root in all its contexts, James Kennedy illustrated that it is always used with reference to persons prompted by a strong fear of perceived or actual danger, that it involves flight but not necessarily to a distant place, and that it involves thorough concealment and covering.[4] Verbs from the same root are used when Saul, not wishing to be elected king over Israel, conceals himself at the outskirt of a military camp among baggage carts (1 Sam 10:22); and again when Israelites, fearing discovery by Philistines, conceal themselves in caves and crannies near where they lived (1 Sam 13:6; 14:11, 22; see also Josh 10:16–17, 27).

Adam and Hawwa did not conceal themselves "among the trees," which would have been expressed clearly by *bēyn 'aṣēy haggan*, "among/between the trees of the garden" (cf. Isa 7:2; 45:12; Ezek 31:9, 16, 18).[5] According to the narrative, they retired "within a tree of the garden." The use of the singular "tree" makes sense if the author intended readers to imagine them crouching in a natural thicket formed by the drooping branches of a willow or the like, or as having clambered into the thick foliage of a convenient tree.

Although the narrative is clear that they exploited something in an arboreal part of the Garden to avoid the divine gaze—even if specifics remain unclear—it does not elucidate exactly what precipitated their desire to hide. Of whom or what were they so afraid that they scampered into concealment?

I hypothesize that their departure was motivated by the fear of being seen by God. They were not trying to keep him from knowing where they were. Had total concealment been their objective, as in the game of hide-and-seek, Adam would not have responded to God's question, "Where are you?" He would have kept silent. They were motivated by shame, not guilt. This is supported by verse 10. There, Adam's explanation that he hid because he was naked sounds reasonable—but only until we recall that he was wearing a covering secured around his midriff when he spoke. His statement makes more sense, however, once we recognize that Israelites distinguished between two different types or degrees of nakedness.

In contrast to Genesis 2:25, where Adam and Hawwa were absolutely naked and unconcerned, in Genesis 3:7, after the moment of comprehension—described by a common verb indicating cognition, *y-d-ʿ*, "to know"—they altered conditions so that they would no longer confront what had shamed them. We can infer from the couple's loincloths that they both experienced shame on seeing the other's genitals and buttocks and on comprehending that their own were visible also. To eliminate the discomfort of shame, they covered what the author's Israelite norms taught ought not to be seen.[6]

The girdling loincloths, *ḥagōrōt*, which they made for themselves from fig leaves, provided only the absolutely minimal cover considered acceptable between a man and his wife. Even when alone together in Iron Age Israel, a husband and a wife were partially covered.

NUDITY AND MODESTY

Total nudity, considered acceptable, normal, and natural in such situations by many in contemporary, non-traditional Western society, is not so considered in all traditional Christian, Muslim, and Jewish societies. In many parts of these societies, parts of the body remain draped even in very intimate moments. For example, early Muslim jurists allowed different types of female body exposure—face, arms, legs—depending on the relationship between the viewed and the viewers with regard to kinship and class and depending on whether the viewing occurred in a public or a private place. Certain kin had more access than others depending on what part of the body was viewed and where the viewing occurred. They considered areas of a woman's body part of the family's sphere of privacy. At the more intimate end of the scale, they allowed legally married couples to have contact with each other's genitals, not only for procreation but for pleasure as well. Some jurists, however, thought it inappropriate for couples to look at each other's genitalia.[7]

The preceding example from Islamic law shows that what constitutes appropriate attire—understood as the proper, modest draping of different parts of the body—is a matter of cultural codes, not natural law. Read with this in mind, the Garden story provides insights into what Israelite culture considered the minimal parameters of proper modesty. The author applies these standards to the first humans in the Garden story.

In Song of Songs 4:1–8 and 7:2–10, where the woman's body is described from the top down and then from the bottom up—eyes, hair, teeth, lips, mouth, brow, neck, breasts, feet, thighs, navel, belly, breasts, neck, eyes, nose, head, hair—and in 5:10–16, where the man's body is described, all three descriptions skip over buttocks and genitalia.[8] Furthermore, the story of Noah's drunkenness, presupposes that even in the privacy of his own domicile, an individual would have his private parts covered: "and he drank from the wine and became drunk and he revealed himself inside his tent" (Gen 9:21).

Noah's sons Shem and Japheth cover his *'erwāh*, "exposed, revealed, bared part, nakedness," so that even alone, unseen by others, he would be covered.[9] Remarkably, as they enter their father's tent to cover him, they hold the covering garment between them while walking backward in order not to view their father's nakedness.

But even a loincloth was insufficient to eradicate shame in the presence of a third party.

David's forceful twirling dance as Israelites brought the ark up to Jerusalem, described in 2 Samuel 6:13, exposes his private parts. His display both angers and disgusts his wife Michal. Before he enters his house, she goes out and reproaches him sarcastically: "How honored is the day, king of Israel who revealed himself today for the eyes of the maids of his servants like one of the *rēqīym* reveals himself" (2 Sam 6:20). The noun *rēqīym*, conventionally rendered "worthless ones," literally means "empty ones" and may refer to individuals who are not too bright or who are uncouth. Michal castigated David's overly enthusiastic public exposure as benighted: he allowed other females to view in public what convention disallowed her to see even in private, an act characteristic only of "empty ones," men lacking knowledge of proper behavior.[10]

In Song of Songs 5:3, when asked by her beloved to open the door after she had gone to bed, the coy maiden responds with a question, "I have removed my *ketōnet* [tunic], should I put it on?" Her beloved, taking her statement at face value as implying that it was too much bother for her to dress herself properly to receive him, turns and leaves before she opens the door (5:6). Similarly, when the brothers removed Joseph's *ketōnet*, tunic, and presented it bloodied to their father, both the characters in the story and the Israelite readers understood that it was not the type of garment removed casually in a public place (Gen 37:3, 23).[11]

Assuming that the *beged*—this is a general term for garment or body covering—that Joseph left in Mrs. Potiphar's grasping hand was a tunic, we can clearly see its incriminating nature in that narrative (Gen 39:11–15). It was hardly an optional accoutrement that Joseph, a house servant, might have removed during work on a hot day and left behind absentmindedly. Thus, the mere fact that Joseph had removed the *beged* sufficed as evidence, according to Mrs. Potiphar, that Joseph intended to assault her.

Adam's modesty problem in Genesis 3:10, then, is real. He hid himself from God's presence because he was naked. The presence of a third party, God, made it impossible, for reasons of modesty, to come out of hiding for a meeting, confrontation, or comeuppance.

God supplied the proper body covering for this situation later, in 3:21, when he gave Adam and Hawwa tunics of leather, *kotnōwt 'ōwr*, garments that cover both the upper and the lower body.[12] The Garden story provides etiologies for all of these cultural features and attitudes.[13]

A similar attitude to the humanness of clothing is found in the Meso-potamian *Gilgamesh Epic*. There, a prostitute first tamed the naked Enkidu, who romped wildly, innocently, and naively with animals, by seducing him sexually, marking him as a human. She then garbed him appropriately so that he could be introduced into human society. Both in *Gilgamesh* and in Genesis, Polonius's words in *Hamlet* apply: "the apparel oft proclaims the man."

From the cultural standpoint of Iron Age Israel, Adam's statement "I was naked," even though the couple wore basic attire, contrasts strongly with their infantile innocence about clothing in Genesis 3:1. It betrayed their earlier refection to the deity.

THE DAILY OPERATION OF THE GARDEN

More information may be teased out of Genesis 3:8–10 that bears on the author's understanding of the operations of the Garden and on his comprehension of God. These verses indicate that the humans were ac-customed to being in the presence of God at the breezy time of the day, perhaps the late afternoon, when he bestirred himself.

From Adam's response to God's question, it is possible to infer some-thing about these meetings. He did not say, "I saw you walking." Rather, he mentions a sound or a voice that indicated the presence of the invisible deity.[14]

God's question "Where are you?" indicates that Adam was not where God expected to find him. From this I infer that God used to meet with his gardener and his helper at this time and place regularly, perhaps to talk over what had to be done on the morrow. The question is important because the narrator is not portraying God in the Garden story as omni-scient. He does not know everything. Among the things that God does not know is what happened at the Tree of Knowing, although he will soon deduce this knowledge.

God's question in verse 11, using a second person masculine singular pronoun, indicates that it was directed only to Adam, the designated ag-riculturalist. Similarly, in Ruth 2:3–7, when Boaz comes to his Bethlehem field to check on the progress of his harvesters during the late afternoon, he speaks only with his appointed headman.

Adam's verbose response to "Where are you?"—delivered while he is wrapped in a loincloth and hiding under or in a tree—is informative.

It shows that he acknowledged the hierarchical supremacy of God over him and recognized that God was not family in the same way that Hawwa was. It also indicates that Adam comprehended intuitively that even though he was wearing a loincloth, it was inappropriate for God to see him.

17 INTERROGATION AND NEGOTIATION

(Gen 3:11–13)

Genesis 3

11 And he said:

Who told you that you are naked? Have you eaten
from the tree concerning which I commanded you to
not eat from it?

12 And the human said:

The woman that you gave [to be] with me, she gave to
me from the tree and [so] I ate.

13 And YHWH god said to the woman:

mah zō't 'aśīyt.

And the woman said:

The serpent *hiššīy'anīy,* and [so] I ate.

God asks two questions, but it is the second, simple, direct one that
he wants answered immediately: "Have you [second person masculine
singular] eaten from the tree concerning which I commanded you
[*ṣiwwīytīykā*; second person masculine singular] to not eat from it?"
(Gen 3:11). What triggers God's suspicion is that Adam has introduced the
concept of nakedness into a social context and appraised it negatively. On
prior occasions Adam appeared before him as he had been formed. The
idea of nakedness implies its correlative, the idea of being draped, covered, clothed. Adam implied in the previous verse that dressed properly, he

would not fear to be in God's presence. Now God wants to discover where Adam learned such notions.

The very first question—"Who told you that you are naked?"—may have caused Adam an "oh no" moment. God was not about to compliment him on his modesty. But God's second question, not the first, focuses the inquiry.

Parsing God's use of "which I commanded you," Adam comprehends that no matter the lack of formal, correct grammar in the original policy statement about fruit consumption in Genesis 2:16–17, God had intended that it be taken as a command. (The narrator cued readers, but not Adam, in his introduction to the original statement.) Moreover, with his heightened sensitivity to good and bad, Adam comprehends that the formulation of God's question makes it one to which he ought not respond directly. A "yes, but . . ." answer might not be well received, because God could stop listening after the "yes," or he could cut off conversation before an excuse could be presented. The better tactic was to begin directly with the excuse.

Adam defends himself in Genesis 3:12 with a red herring and a technicality. In his response, he makes a seemingly irrelevant observation about the woman: "you gave (to be) with me."[1] This phrase may be interpreted as expressing a total lack of awareness that any misdeed has been committed or could have been committed: God had given him the woman, and she could certainly be trusted.[2] The tactical objective of his response is to deflect the focus of God's question. It implies that he, the man, implicitly trusts the actions of the woman whom God has made for him. In contemporary terms, he is insinuating that the manufacturer is liable for damage caused by a defective product—in other words, that the manufacturer's reputation is so good that the woman must have come with an implied warranty.

Then he presents the technicality: "She gave to me from the tree and I ate." Adam's statement can be unpacked: You, God, gave something to me. She gave something to me. I did not eat from the tree; I ate what she handed me from the tree; I accepted what she gave. This defense can be interpreted in one of two ways: (1) "I ate from the tree only indirectly and hence did not violate what you are now characterizing as a command," a defense based on mitigated culpability; or, (2) what is more likely in light of the serpent's grammatical hints, "We both participated together and hence are not in violation of your instruction in the second person masculine singular," a defense challenging the applicability of the restrictive prohibition to the particular circumstances of the situation.

In considering the dramatic confrontation within a public reading of the story to an audience, it is useful to imagine a drawn-out dramatic silence after Adam's bold response. The narrative provides no inkling of how God processed what Adam had said. God's thoughts have to be inferred from what he did next and from what he did not do, and from what was said as well as from what was not said.

God does not advance a "yes . . . but" counterargument. He accepts Adam's defensive excuses, preferring to encumber his statement intended as a prohibition with the serpent's implied grammatical yet convoluted sophistries. By so doing he obviates dealing with any sanction involving death "on the day of your eating."

Breaking the silence that I imagine, God directs his next question to the woman. It contains no accusation of wrongdoing, suggesting thereby that the analysis of the prohibition that the serpent presented to Hawwa when both were by the Tree of Knowing was correct. This indicates God's implicit acceptance of Adam's contention that the so-called command had not been violated, at least technically. Consequently, the woman is not culpable for abetting.

Examination of the pattern of God's question to the woman—*mah zō't 'aśīyt/-tā/-tem/-nūw*, "what is this [*zō't*; feminine singular] that you [singular or plural] / we did?"—in biblical contexts reveals that it was not intended to elicit a response. Rather, this pattern was often used rhetorically when something bad and unexpected occurred and when the details were obvious and the identity of the responsible parties was beyond dispute. Some examples:

Genesis 12:18, where Pharaoh poses the question to Abraham after discovering that Abraham has passed off Sarah as his available sister

Genesis 26:10, where Abimelech of Gerar poses the question to Isaac after discovering that Isaac has passed off Rebecca as his available sister

Genesis 29:25, where Jacob poses the question to his father-in-law Laban after discovering that Laban has given him Leah, the older, nearsighted sister, as a wife rather than Rachel, for whom he had contracted and labored

Genesis 42:28, where Jacob's sons pose it of each other after discovering
in their grain bags the very silver that they have just disbursed for
grain in Egypt

Other examples are found in Exodus 14:5, 11; Judges 2:2; 15:11; Jonah 1:10.[3]

To solicit actual information, Israelites posed a slightly different form
of the question: *mah + zeh + 'aśiytā/tem*, "what is this [*zeh*; masculine sin-
gular] that you did?" Examples of this form of the question are infrequent
in the Bible, but occur in Genesis 44:15; Judges 8:1; 2 Samuel 12:21; Nehemiah 2:19; 3:17.[4]

So God's question to the woman is rhetorical, a plaint rather than a
request for information. Although the words translate as "What is this
that you have done?" they mean something like "How could you do such
a thing, upsetting the order that I established!" (Gen 3:13). Since the question is not a true one, the woman does not respond. Reacting only to the
implied issue of responsibility in God's pseudo-question, she declares
simply, "The serpent *hiššiy'aniy*, and (so) I ate."

Hawwa refers to what the serpent did using a causative Hiphil verb
formed from the root *n-š-'*, which may be translated with "tricked,
tempted, incited, or deceived." The verb indicates that his trickery involved using language to mislead somebody (2 Kings 18:29; Isa 36:14; 2
Chron 32:15; Jer 4:10; 29:8; 37:9; Obad 7). The import of her response is,
"the serpent misled me with his calculating, shrewd talking" or, more
simply, "the serpent beguiled me and I ate." Her true statement describes
events in the order of their occurrence while implying a causal connection between them. The serpent had employed his natural, God-given wit
to persuade the woman to exploit a technicality and do something that
she might not have otherwise done: look at a fruit, pluck it from the tree,
take a bite, and share the fruit with her husband. The story does not
indicate that she acted surreptitiously, eating furtively when God was not
around. She admits to acting consciously and openly, but identifies the
serpent as the catalyst for her deed.

When God interrogated Adam and Hawwa, they were not being
judged; rather, they were being deposed gently. God was collecting aver-
ments on whose bases he could reach decisions. Although the meeting
involved direct questions and indirect, oblique responses, the exchange
of words amounted to a negotiation between derelict laborers, an inter-
fering troublemaker snake, and the lord of them all, the master of the

Garden. The relationship between the humans and God differed from that between the serpent and God. There was no relationship between the humans and the serpent other than the knowledge, shared by God, Adam, and the serpent, that even though God had made the serpent for the benefit of Adam, the serpent had been found wanting through no fault of its own.

God possessed the power to do what he wished to the serpent, the woman, and the man. But he also had his Garden in mind along with the disposition of his creatures. He had custom-made each of the three: the man for his Garden and the serpent first and the woman second for the benefit of the man.

As the story was told, lying in the background of the negotiation were implicit rules about rights and obligations, conventional understandings of property rights, of distinctions between "what is actually mine" and "what I claim to be mine," and some sense of whether it was worthwhile to press a claim to the end. Some victories are Pyrrhic.

The story's author and its audience understood these implicit elements because they were part of their social, political, and juridical world. In this world, laws were not necessarily intended to be applied literally and harshly but were grasped as principles and precedents, rules intended to help people work through and settle disputes intelligently.[5]

There was no reason for God to inquire into the motive of the serpent. He knew. He knew that the serpent did not have an ethical leg to stand on; he knew that the serpent had acted directly and simply, in accord with his nature. God knew that he had made the man and the woman and that he had also shaped the serpent.

It is again useful to imagine a silence after the interrogation. God was silent, mulling over the situation, pondering its implications, ambiguities, and potential consequences. He was confronting an issue later framed as a question by Abraham in the story of Sodom and Gomorrah: "Will the judge of all the earth not deal justly?" (Gen 18:25). God, the character in the Garden story, had to consider what constituted justice in this case.

The narrator of the story had to resolve these issues in a manner that would resonate with the ethical notions of his readers and with their, and his, sense of fairness.

18 PROCREATION IN THE GARDEN

(Gen 3:14–19; 4:1–2)

Genesis 3

14 And YHWH god said to the serpent:

Because you did this, *'ārûwr 'attāh* than every
beast and than every animal of the field.
On your belly *tēlēk*, and *'āpār* you eat all the days
of your life,

15 and I place enmity between you and between the
woman, and between your seed and between her seed;
and he *yešûwpkā* (at the) head, and you *tešûwpennûw* (at the)
heel.

16a To the woman he said:

Multiplying, I will multiply your pain and your
pregnancy.
In pain you will birth children,

16b and *'el 'îyšēk tešûwqātēk*,
but he *yimšol bāk*.

17 And to Adam he said:

Because you listened to the voice of your woman and
you ate from the tree concerning which I
commanded you saying:

You will not eat from it,

'arūwrāh the soil ba'abūwrekā.

In 'iṣṣābōn you will eat from it all the days of your life.

18   And thorn and thistle it will sprout lāk;

but you will eat edible plants of the field.

19   By the sweat of your nose you will eat food until you

return to the soil because you were taken from

it.

Indeed, you are a clod, and to a clod you return.

Genesis 4

1   wehā'ādām yāda' 'et ḥawwāh 'ištōw, and she conceived and

birthed Qayin. And she said:

I have qāniytīy a man with YHWH god.

2   And she continued to birth his brother Hebel.

And Hebel was a shepherd, and Qayin had been a worker of the

soil.

God makes declarations, one after another, without interruption. Two aspects of his sentences stand out. First, not one indicates that the consequences of eating might be an untimely death by some agent.[1] Second, sentences addressed to both the serpent and to the woman focus on progeny and childbirth (Gen 3:15–16a). To comprehend the full significance of these sentences, we must skip ahead and discuss Genesis 4:1 first. God's other sentences of Genesis 3:14–19 are discussed in the next chapters.

WHERE DID HAWWA GIVE BIRTH?

Genesis 4:1 occurs in the narrative sequence *after* Adam and Hawwa have left the Garden but does not continue the narrative from that point chronologically. The verse actually refers back to an earlier period. An analysis of the first words in the verse confirms this assertion, although it contradicts most interpretations.

The great medieval scholar Rashi was the earliest to offer this retrospective interpretation as being the plain, simple, and obvious meaning of the verse. He commented on the words at the beginning of verse 1, *wehā'ādām yāda'*:

This happened before the preceding incident, before he sinned and was driven from the garden of Eden, and so also, the pregnancy and birth.

Had he written, *wayyēda' 'ādām*, it would have sounded as if he had children only after he went out.[2]

The inspiration for Rashi's comment appears to have been a midrash, a homiletic interpretation, cited in the Babylonian Talmud:

> The day consisted of twelve hours. In the first hour, Adam's dust was gathered; in the second, he was made into a crude shape; in the third, his limbs were formed; in the fourth, a soul was infused into him; in the fifth, he stood on his feet; in the sixth, he named [the animals]; in the seventh, Hawwa became his couple [that is, they became a pair]; in the eighth, the two of them went up onto the bed and four descended; in the ninth, he was commanded not to eat from the tree; in the tenth, he sinned; in the eleventh, he was judged; in the twelfth, he was banished and left. (*b. Sanhedrin* 38b)[3]

The midrash does not provide any grammatical basis for its sequencing of events. Rashi, however, observed that the word order at the beginning of Genesis 4:1, Subject + Verb, differed from the usual Verb + Subject order in which biblical narrative presents sequenced events and drew his conclusion accordingly. It is not clear from his statement, however, whether he was arguing on the basis of the apparent inner logic of the story or on the basis of grammar.

THE ANTERIOR CONSTRUCTION

Unlike Rashi, Abraham Ibn Ezra (1089–1164), whose commentary is characterized by close attention to grammatical detail, considered the events of Genesis 4:1 post-Edenic, as did most of his Jewish and all of his Christian contemporaries. He explained that once the man comprehended that he would not live forever, he understood that it was necessary to continue the species. Although this view prevails in most contemporary interpretations of the story, considerable grammatical data support Rashi's argument.[4]

When biblical authors wished to indicate that a given action or state in the past was anterior to another described action or state in the past, they employed a particular construction to express this chronological sequencing. In English, this collocation of events is expressed using pluperfect verbs (also called past perfect verbs). Consider the following sentence:

"Montgomery arrived for the rendezvous at the appointed time, but Elton had arrived twenty minutes earlier." Although mentioned later in the description of events, Elton's arrival preceded Montgomery's; it happened first. The sentence presents events out of chronological sequence but indicates the correct chronological order through the proper use of verbs.

The anterior construction is used in Hebrew to furnish similar information. A type of subordinate circumstantial clause, the anterior construction is connected to what precedes it by the conjunction *we-* (and), but then introduces a new subject followed by a verb in the past tense (in the *qatal* form).[5] This can be represented formulaically, *we-* + Subject + Verb (in the *qatal* form), and is demonstrated in the following examples.[6] In these, the conjunction *we-* is rendered mechanically by *and* to emphasize the Hebrew syntax. In a more elegant English translation, *but, so,* or *since* might be more appropriate, depending on the general context:

> Genesis 20:3–4: "and Abimelech *had not approached* her"
> Genesis 24:1: "and God *had blessed* Abraham"
> Genesis 31:33–34: "and Rachel *had taken* the teraphim"
> Judges 3:25–26: "and behold, their lord lying dead, and Ehud *had fled*
> while they tarried, and he had passed the Pesillim"
> Judges 4:21: "and he *had fallen asleep*"
> Judges 16:31: "and he *had judged* Israel"
> 2 Samuel 18:17–18: "and Absalom *had taken and set up* for himself in
> his lifetime the marker"

The third example in the preceding list, Genesis 31:33–34, illustrates this succinctly. Jacob leaves his father-in-law abruptly, taking with him his wives, Leah and Rachel, his children, and all his possessions. Rachel steals her father's teraphim, some sort of household images, before leaving her father's house (Gen 31:19). Later, when Laban returns home, he notices that his teraphim are missing, not to mention his daughters, grandchildren, son-in-law, and flocks of animals, so he sets out after Jacob. When he catches up with him, Laban accuses Jacob of stealing the images. Jacob, ignorant of his wife's thievery, denies the accusation angrily and invites Laban to search wherever he wishes. After going through a number of tents, Laban "came to the tent of Rachel, and Rachel *had taken* the teraphim and placed them in a camel saddle and sat on them" (Gen 31:34). As her father searches through her tent handling things, she apologizes for being unable to stand up, explaining that she is menstruating.

The narrative sequence of events indicates clearly that Rachel had stolen and later concealed the teraphim and that she had hatched her plan long before her father entered her tent. The theft, described in Genesis 31:34, is mentioned also in Genesis 31:19 as having occurred during the family's hasty flight from Laban just after Laban went off to shear his sheep.[7]

The same syntactic construction is used in Genesis 3:24–4:1. Accordingly, the verses must be translated to show the actions in this order: "He expelled the human and settled the cherubs and the flaming ever-turning sword to the east of the garden of Eden to guard the way to the Tree of Life; and [or: *but*] the human had known Hawwa his woman/wife, and she had conceived and birthed Qayin, and she said, 'I have created a man with YHWH god.'"[8]

Although the preceding discussion clarifies when Adam "knew" his wife, it does not explain why the author used a verb indicating "knowing," rather than one of two other common expressions that indicated sexual activity: *bā' + 'el*, " had come to," or *šākab + 'et/'im*, "had lain with." David Rothstein suggests that these common expressions and a few others that occur have legal implications and project information about the relationship between the man and women involved, whereas the euphemism "to know" is legally neutral.[9]

The use of the anterior construction expressing pluperfect at this juncture achieved two objectives: it clarified retroactively several aspects of the sentences pronounced by God in Genesis 3:14–16 even as it introduced the progeny of Adam and Hawwa, the main subjects of following stories.[10] Usually only the second function of this verse is considered; its first, however, is much more interesting.

Though only implicit in the text, a period of no less than the nine months of gestation but most likely two or three years were imagined to have passed between the mention of Adam and Hawwa's nakedness, in the last verse of chapter 2, and the serpent's appearance in the first verse of chapter 3. The consumption of fruit from the Tree of Knowing took place *after* what is described in Genesis 4:1: *after* Adam and the woman had had sexual relations and *after* she had borne at least her first child.

Had the author wished to announce that the woman would give birth in the future, linguistic resources were available for him to do so. He could have used a future-tense verb and written after Genesis 3:15, *wekiy tēldiy bāniym 'ēybāh 'āšiyt*, "and when you will birth sons, I will set enmity," but he did not, because that is not how he understood the actual sequence of events in his story to have unfolded.[11]

HAWWA AS CREATOR AND NAMER

In Genesis 4:1 Hawwa asserts either that she and God are partners in creation because, no matter the unique circumstances of her own origin, she was empowered to birth the species, or she asserts that she has creative power with God. Her words may be paraphrased: "Just as God manufactured me, woman/Isha, from man/Ish; I have *created* a man/Ish with God."

The Hebrew word translated here with "created" is *qānīytīy,* from the root *q-n-h.* Words based on this root are usually understood as relating to the control of property and are translated with "gain, acquire, purchase" or the like. But a cognate verb that occurs in Ugaritic has a significantly different meaning that is appropriate to the context of the Garden story. Ugaritic *q-n-y,* used often in a divine epithet, *qnyt ilm,* "creatrix of the gods," suggests that "create" or "form" is likely in Genesis 4:1, as well as in Genesis 14:22b, *'ēl 'elyōwn qōnēh šāmayim wā'āreṣ,* "El Elyon, creator of heavens and earth."[12]

Hawwa's statement contains an implicit etiology for all women for all time.[13] It indicates that although conception and birthing are natural phenomena requiring a male and female, they also require divine intervention or presence. Her assertion reflects an Israelite notion expressed elsewhere in the Bible that the inability of a woman to conceive is due to the absence of divine causation. This idea underlies Jacob's sharp retort to Rachel's nagging implication in Genesis 30:2 that somehow he is responsible for her lack of children: "Am I in place of God, who has withheld from you fruit of the womb?" It finds expression also in the prayer of childless Hanna in 1 Samuel 1:11—"do not forget your handmaid and provide your handmaid male seed"—and in Genesis 20:18, where the barrenness of the women in Abimelech's household is attributed to divine intervention.

Hawwa's explanation of why she named her first child Qayin does not explain what the name actually means. Hawwa's explanation, and the author's, associates the name, derived from the root *q-y-n,* with the Hebrew root *q-n-y,* referring to creating. Scholars observing that the name is actually based on the triliteral root *q-y-n* connect it (1) with an Arabic word for smith, *qayn*; (2) with the Qenites, *qēynīy*, a tribe of smiths (Num 24:21–22; Judg 1:16; 4:11); and (3) with the occupation of Qayin's descendent, Tubal-Qayin, "who forged all implements of iron and copper" (Gen 4:22). The validity of the final connection is supported by a Hittite-Hurrian bilingual inscription from Boghazköy in which the Hittite logogram for metalsmith, *lú* SIMAG, is identified with the Hurrian word *ta-ba-li-iš*. Removing the suffix *-iš* from the Hurrian word reveals the underlying *tabal*, which is most likely cognate to Tubal.[14]

Within Genesis 1–11, the primeval history of humanity, Qayin's name is predictive in that knowledge of metallurgy was essential for the technological development of the complex civilizations that began to flourish in the ancient Near East after 3000 BCE. His descendents built cities, became musicians, and forged tools (Gen 4:17–22). Qayin founded civilization by manufacturing items from materials found in the hard crust of the earth.

The pun relating the scientific etymology of Qayin's name and Hawwa's explanation of why she named him is not unique. In Genesis 5:29, the name Noah, derived from the root *n-w-ḥ*, meaning "to be at rest," is explained by his father, Lamech—"this one *yenaḥamēnūw*, will comfort us"—using a word derived from the root *n-ḥ-m*. This is typical of the Bible's explanations for punned names.[15]

That Hawwa determined her firstborn's name does not seem to have any particular significance: fathers named children (Gen 16:15; 21:4; 25:26; 38:3), and so did mothers (Gen 19:36–38; 29:32–30:24; 38:3; Judg 13:24; 1 Sam 1:20). Adam named Hawwa; she named Qayin, and he may have named Hebel/Abel (Gen 4:1–2); then she named Seth (Gen 4:25). Adam and Hawwa acted no differently in this regard than those for whom the tale was set down in writing. Of the forty-six reports about baby namings in the Bible, mothers name infants in twenty-five cases, fathers name them in fifteen, and both parents participate in one or two cases.[16]

CUSTOMARY MATING

Naming aside, the pragmatic setting of God's words in Genesis 3:15–16a with the references to "seed" presupposes within the story's frame that all characters know about birthing. The grammar of Genesis 4:1 indicates that the woman had given birth while in the Garden. The appellation used by Adam in Genesis 3:20, *'ēm kol ḥay*, "Mother of all kinfolk," discussed in Chapter 20 below, confirms this analysis, indicating unambiguously that motherhood was instituted in the Garden.

Awareness that the sequential presentation of events in the Garden story conflicts with the chronological sequence of their natural unfolding clarifies details in the divine sentencing of the perpetrators (Gen 3:14–19). This explanation still leaves unsettled a bothersome question: If this information is so important, why didn't the author provide it earlier in the narrative? In fact, he did so implicitly.

The sexual distinction between male and female is celebrated in the episode of Hawwa's formation and in Adam's naming of her as his female counterpart, 'iššāh. This distinction is implied by the juxtaposition of his declaration with the author's statement about clinging and becoming one flesh (Gen 2:22–24). Given the sexual difference, both the author and his readers would have taken for granted that the first couple had sexual relations once Hawwa entered the scene.

Israelites assumed that unless custom controlled, prohibited, or proscribed sexual intercourse, men could have it with certain women whenever they wished in an appropriate place. Moreover, aside from such rare exceptions as Potiphar's wife and seductive adulteresses (Prov 7:5–22), the culture assumed that males are usually the aggressors in sexual matters. This is reflected not only in narratives but also in the language used to frame laws dealing with sexual behavior: Leviticus 18:8–20; Numbers 5:13; Deuteronomy 21:10–11.

It is thus apparent that Genesis 4:1 reprises what was self-evident to the author and his readers. Genesis 4:1–2 provides details necessary for understanding the subsequent stories about the descendents of Adam and Hawwa. Structurally, the verses bridge the Garden story and the following narrative in the same way that Genesis 2:4a bridges the Cosmic Creation story and the Garden story.

That the narrator had this in mind is apparent from Genesis 3:20, as we shall see. In that verse, describing an episode that occurred before the couple was sent from the Garden, Adam refers to Hawwa as a mother.

19 NOT A LEG TO STAND ON

The Serpent's Sentence and the Israelite

Culture of "Curse"

(Gen 3:14–15)

Genesis 3

14a And YHWH god said to the serpent:
> Because you did this, *'ārūwr 'attāh* than every
> beast and than every animal of the field.

14b On your belly *tēlēk* and a clod you eat all the days
> of your life,

15 and I place enmity between you and the
> woman, and between your seed and her seed;
> and he *yešūwpkā* (at the) head, and you *tešūwpennūw* (at
> the) heel.

According to Martin Luther, "Before the sin, the serpent was a most beautiful little animal and most pleasing to man, as little mules, sheep, and puppies are today; moreover, . . . it walked upright. And so it is due to the curse and not to its nature that it now creeps on the ground, just as it is due to the curse that a women conceives with shame, gives birth in pain, and brings up her offspring in toil."[1] Luther's comment to verse 14 reflects Jewish and Christian interpretations since Late Antiquity. These held that as part of the serpent's punishment, he was partially dismembered so that he could no longer maintain an upright posture when moving on the earth. Luther's explanation, whether taken literally or metaphorically, anticipated what remains a widespread interpretation—an interpretation that is incorrect on both Hebrew and herpetological grounds.

After God concluded his questioning (Gen 3:11–13), he began to declare sentences to the silent Adam, Hawwa, and the serpent. Others, however, were also present: Qayin, an infant or a toddler, was one. And from God's declaration in Genesis 3:15, it is reasonable to infer that the serpent, like the humans, had reproduced in the Garden and that at least one serpentling was squiggling about.

The pronouncement of sentences, usually understood as curses, as punishment is a conceptually difficult section of the story for today's readers. Contemporary notions of blessing and cursing are not based on their meanings or applications in Iron Age Israel. Nor do contemporary understandings encompass an awareness of how Israelites—as represented in biblical narratives—reacted to being cursed or blessed.

THE CULTURE OF CURSE

God's first communication to the serpent in verse 14, "because you did *this*," employs the same feminine demonstrative pronoun, *zō't*, that he used when addressing the woman—"What is *this* that you did?"—in the previous verse (Gen 3:13). The significance of the author's choice of this Hebrew word over an available alternative, discussed in Chapter 17 above, signals the subject of God's concern. He is reacting to the perpetration of what he refers to as *this*, the perceived disruption and breakdown of his Garden project.

In Genesis 3:14, God states to the serpent, "'*ārūwr* [are] you from every [domestic] beast and every animal of the field"—that is, you are more '*ārūwr* than they. Structurally, this statement parallels the author's remark in Genesis 3:1 describing the serpent as "'*ārūwm* from every animal of the field," that is, more cleverly devious than they. Just as '*ārūwm* describes a state of being, so too does '*ārūwr*. Both nouns, in what grammarians label the *qātūwl* pattern, are stative, passive participles of the Qal conjugation used as predicate adjectives. English equivalents would be the adjectives in "Sally is beloved"; "You are grown"; "The papers are graded."

'*Ārūwr*, usually rendered as "cursed" or "cursed be" (with a verb of being added for clarity in English), lacks the range of negative associations attached to *cursed* in English. The English word includes the notion of a malevolent power triggered by some supernatural authority that wreaks destruction or vengeance.

In biblical Hebrew, in contrast, to be 'ārūwr is to be in a diminished, disempowered, weakened, impoverished state (Gen 49:7; Deut 27:16–26; 28:18–19; 1 Sam 14:24–28).[2] In only two passages is the exact nature of the diminution specified: servitude in Genesis 9:25 and the death of children in Joshua 6:26. In both, the time reference of the main verbs is the future: "in the future, you will be / may you be 'ārūwr with regard to such and such."

The stative sense of the participle may have developed from a more dynamic one. H. C. Brichto, basing his ideas on earlier work by E. A. Speiser, argued on the basis of Akkadian and Hebrew usage that the core sense of the root '-r-r indicated "to bind, hem in with obstacles, render powerless to resist." People against whom an 'ārūwr formula had been pronounced were considered barred or restricted from enjoying whatever particular good had been designated. They were constrained, held back, handicapped, lessened.[3] Consequently, 'ārūwr automatically suggests a distinction between ṭōwb, "good," and raʿ, "bad." The subjective emotional tones evoked by the word may have been detestation and loathing.

Ample data indicate that Israelites, along with just about all other ancient peoples, believed that words could have maleficent power, but few examples suggest that such power was associated with whatever was described by words based on the root '-r-r. In Deuteronomy 27:15–26, a so-called list of curses, the 'ārūwr series does not imply the worsening of any situation. It states that persons engaging in certain types of activities are already 'ārūwr by virtue of having so engaged themselves. Likewise, a thief is not a person called thief but one who thieves. The moment that anyone steals, he (or she) becomes a thief whether or not the theft is a matter of public knowledge. All sentences in Deuteronomy 27:15–26 are indicative; for example, in verse 15, "'ārūwr [is the state of being of] the man who will make a statue and molten image."

In contrast, Psalm 109:6–19 provides a list of dynamic curses, a wish list of calamities that the suffering psalmist hopes will befall an evil person in the future:

Psalm 109:6b: a prosecutor will stand at his right
Psalm 7b: his prayer will become a wrongdoing

Psalm 8b: his allotment, another will take
Psalm 9a: his sons will be orphans, his wife a widow

No word derived from the root '-r-r occurs in these verses.[4]

Deuteronomy 28:15 states that qelālōwt, "curses," could overtake people. Deuteronomy 28:20–68 provides a detailed list of calamities conditionally called down on Israelites should they violate the terms of their covenant with God. All are expressed through future, *yiqtol* verbs indicating a conditioned wish:

> May YHWH send against you the imprecation, the confusion, and the frustration against everything that you do until your speedy destruction and elimination . . . ; may YHWH cause the plague to cling to you until it finishes you off . . . ; may YHWH smite you by means of wasting disease, fever, ague, inflammation. . . . (Deut 28:20–22)[5]

Neither the passive participle 'ārūwr nor any verb formed from '-r-r occurs in these verses.[6]

Biblical narratives reveal conflicting Israelite attitudes toward imprecations couched in 'ārūwr terminology. The story of Joshua's conquest of the land contains a tradition that after Jericho was destroyed miraculously, Joshua pronounced an imprecation: "'ārūwr [is the state of being of] the man before YHWH god who will rise and rebuild this city, Jericho. At the cost of his firstborn he will establish its foundation and at the cost of his youngest he will set up its gates" (Josh 6:26). The historian who composed the book of Kings records that centuries later, in the days of Ahab, a certain Hiel from Bethel ignored the ancient warning and set out to rebuild Jericho: "at the cost of Abiram his firstborn he established its foundation and at the cost of Sagib his youngest he set up its gates, according to the word of YHWH god that he spoke by means of Joshua son of Nun" (1 Kings 16:34). For the ancient historian, this example demonstrates the dynamic nature of 'ārūwr. So far as the historian is concerned, Hiel paid no heed and paid the price. The historian's presentation of this story reflects a belief in the magical power of imprecation. The example, based as it is on the use of 'ārūwr, is exceptional, however.

Narratives in other books illustrate that the casual attitude of Hiel was more prevalent than the magical thinking of the historian. In fact, Hiel's story reveals that even after the death of his first son, he did not stop his project. His perspective, as a character written about in Kings, is captured by the modern phrase "Bad stuff happens."

According to Judges 21:18, Israelites were reluctant to give wives to Benjaminites because of the proclamation "'*ārūwr* [is the state of being of] he who gives a wife to Benjamin." They avoided the label through a subterfuge: Benjaminites were instructed to "snatch" and "steal" women for wives from among the dancers at the Shiloh festival (Judg 21:20–23). This story reflects Israelite respect for imprecations and illustrates their reluctance to become '*ārūwr*. It also reveals that they were not reluctant to engage in legalistic chicanery to undermine an imprecation's intent.

An even more casual attitude is revealed by a third story. In the course of a battle, Saul declared to his army "'*ārūwr* [is the state of being of] he who eats food before sunset" (1 Sam 14:24). Although his conditional imprecation frightened most of his army, it did not faze his own son Jonathan, who ate. Jonathan's self-indulgence had no ill effect on the successful outcome of the battle or on himself (1 Sam 14:27–31).

The continuation of this story in 1 Samuel 14:36b–45 involves Saul's anger at his imprecation's being ignored and his authority challenged, even though it was by his son. He uttered a *mōwt tāmūwt*, "dying you will die," formula considered far more ominous by the gathered people, since Saul appeared willing to rush natural death along. The army intervened, and the popular Jonathan was not executed. Significantly, the historian who composed the story indicates that the imprecation was *not* self-fulfilling. Nothing happened. Moreover, it appears that even Saul did not think that anything would happen, which is why he decided to take action.

The only passage, other than those dealing with the rebuilding of Jericho, where an imprecation involving a word from the root '-r-r is deemed to have had a deleterious effect is Genesis 5:29, alluding to Genesis 3:17.[7] This passage is discussed below. More commonly, X, a person or object, entered into the passive state of being '*ārūwr* through a speech act in which somebody declared X to be '*ārūwr*. Jeremiah 20:14–15 demonstrates this clearly: "'*ārūwr* [is] the day on which I was born, on which my mother bore me. Let it not be *bārūwk*, blessed. '*Ārūwr* [is] the man who reported to my father saying 'a male child has been born to you'" (cf. also Job 3:1–9, but especially verse 8).[8]

When Jeremiah was born, the day was declared *bārūwk*—that is, aus-picious, strengthened, empowered—most likely by Jeremiah's parents; thirty years or so later, Jeremiah himself declared it *'ārūwr,* and likewise the bearer of tidings to his father. Clearly, nothing happened to the day, long past, and to the man, most likely long dead. Jeremiah thus called for a retrospective radical devaluation and formulated a new way of ob-serving this event in his own life. Psychologists refer to this process as the "framing" or "reframing" of an event. The serpent engaged in refram-ing when describing the virtues of the tree. Political handlers and publi-cists call it "spin."

The change in status was brought about through a declarative act. Verbs formed from '-r-r and b-r-k are *performatives,* speech acts that achieve their objective at the moment of utterance. Similarly, the declara-tion of the *verba solemnia,* "I now pronounce you man and wife," imme-diately achieves a change of status if pronounced by an empowered person under the proper circumstances, as do the words "I divorce you, I divorce you, I divorce you" in Islamic jurisprudence. Similar to these is the di-vorce formula in Hosea 2:4, "She is not my wife and I am not her hus-band." Another example is the expression "We find the defendant not guilty," uttered at the end of a criminal trial by a jury foreperson.

In the same way, the very recitation of the words *'ārūwr* and *bārūwk* describes what the words are intended to accomplish.[9] Similarly, when Israelites wished to "praise" God—the Hebrew verb is *hallēl*—they either called out *hallelūwyāh* (cf. Pss 113:9; 115:18; 116:19, etc.) or said *hallēl* (cf. Ezra 3:11; Jer 10:23; Prov 27:2).[10]

THE PROBLEM OF TRANSPORT

God's saying *'ārūwr 'attāh* to the serpent in Genesis 3:14a was a perfor-mative act. The content of the statement is descriptive: you are in the permanently intransitive state of having been declared diminished, downgraded, and the like, more than any other animal. Verses 14b–15 continue by describing the nature of the serpent's *'ārūwr*-edness: "on your belly *tēlēk* and a clod you eat all the days of your life."[11] The import of this half-verse is that by virtue of what the serpent is and how he trans-ports himself, he is declared to be devalued retroactively, as in the case of Jeremiah's birthday.

Egyptian Nehebkau with Feet
(Composite figure based on multiple sources,
drawn by Debby Segura.)

The present-future verb *tēlēk* in verse 14b is derived from the root *h-l-k,*
which regularly indicates walking. It has much the same literary and figurative associations as *walk* in English. Unlike the English word, however,
the Hebrew verb is used also to describe the motion of suspended mist
(Hosea 13:3), wind (Eccles 1:6), wheels (Ezek 1:19; 10:16), shadows (2 Kings
20:9), and flowing water (Isa 8:6; Ps 105:41; Eccles 1:7).[12] In Leviticus 11:42
it refers to the type of locomotion employed by "each that moves on its
belly and each that moves on four."[13]

Some commentators think, as did Luther, that God's words to the serpent indicate that he had feet, like the Egyptian serpent god Nehebkau.[14]
Nehebkau, a powerful, benign deity who helped the deceased king by
functioning as his intercessor, was represented variously with feet—a
conventional, positive sign of high status in Egyptian art—and arms, but
sometimes also without feet. Although details about his functions remain vague, images on Egyptian artifacts and paintings and on Phoenician seals from the Levant suggest that he was very popular there also,
perhaps as a protective deity for common folk.[15]

If Nehebkau lies in the background of the story, then the account has
to be explained as clarifying how and why a protective intercessory figure
became a hostile, threatening one that lost its feet and high status. That
theme, however, is not part of the story line in the biblical narrative. Al-
ternatively, if the story was just about a serpent that once had feet, then
the story would be etiological, explaining why serpents crawl. There is a
problem with this approach as well. A proper interpretation of this incident must begin with the observation that neither the Hebrew word for
foot, *regel,* nor any other word suggesting limbs that the serpent may

Egyptian Nehebkau without Feet
(After Christian Herrmann, "Fünf phönizische Formen für ägyptische Fayencen," *Zeitschrift des Deutschen Palästina-Vereins* 105 [1989]: 33.)

have used for locomotion occurs in the narrative. Nothing in the statement to the serpent suggests that he moved or would move differently after the pronouncement than he had before his conversation with Hawwa.

A PRESSING MATTER

The serpent's ill will toward the woman, whatever its basis and however rationalized, antedated the events narrated in Genesis 3:1. Consequently, the "enmity" element of the divine sentence emphasizes that the relationship will not change. The innovation is the extension of the enmity to Hawwa's progeny and the way that enmity would be acted out: "I place enmity between you and the woman and between your seed and her seed. He presses you (at the) head, and you press him (at the) heel."

Both verbs translated here as "press" are formed from the root *š-w-p*, "to press, rub against." Their meaning is established on the basis of postbiblical Hebrew, where the root is used in verbs that describe rubbing. The author may have used this rare word because it resonates with the name of a type of serpent, *šepīypōn*, mentioned once in the Bible (Gen 49:17).[16]

Thus, to translate the verb with "bruise" (KJV), "strike" (NRSV, NAB, NJPS), "crush," or "stomp" may be misleading and inconsistent with attestations of the verb in somewhat clearer contexts. Hostile action directed by humans against serpents is better expressed with the verb *d-r-k*, "tread" (cf. Ps 91:13), and by serpents against humans, with *n-š-k*, "bite"

(Num 21:6; Prov 23:32). One biblical passage describes a serpent biting a horse's heel, suggesting that the heel was a strategic place to wound a horse: "Dan shall be a serpent by the road . . . that bites the horse's heel so that his rider is thrown backward" (Gen 49:17). Another verse that does not contain a word for "bite" indicates, nevertheless, that humans were considered vulnerable at the heel: "Gad shall be raided by raiders, but he shall raid their heels" (Gen 49:19). The author of the Garden story, however, used the same word to describe seemingly different activities by two different subjects—or did he use the same word intending it to mean the same thing?

Difficulties notwithstanding, two dissimilar explanations are possible for this sentence in Genesis 3:15. According to the first explanation, the circumstances may involve immobilization, not killing. This interpretation adequately accounts for the human activity. Humans render snakes harmless by grasping them or placing a forked stick or even a foot just behind their heads and pressing. Once immobilized, they can be picked up and handled. So long as their heads are grasped from behind, they cannot bite. Ground snakes, the only species living in the Near East, attack threatening humans by biting whatever limb menaces them, usually a foot. If the reference to 'āqēb, "heel," included the calcaneus (heel bone) and the attached Achilles (calcaneal) tendon, which anchors the main calf muscles to the heel bone, a vulnerable point, then a sharp blow somewhere behind or below the ankle may have been capable of immobilizing a person for a while.[17]

If what is described is a roughhouse activity in which children race after harmless snakes to catch them and then let them go, what the imprecation adds is an interpretation of the game as a reflection of mean-spirited enmity.[18] The verbs meaning "press, push" in Genesis 3:15 do not justify considering the activity to be seriously harmful to either serpents or people. No biting or treading is involved, no beheading or poisoning. At worst, pressing could involve risk of injury.[19]

According to the second explanation, the language in this sentence describing actions of both serpents and humans may reflect idioms known from the Mesopotamian legal tradition. Texts dated to the eighteenth century BCE from Alalakh in northwest Syria and from Mari, also in Syria, contain the Akkadian expression qaqqadam maḥāṣum, "to strike the head." Although the contexts are somewhat opaque, the idiom apparently refers to a ritual act in which a person accused erroneously or sued by a plaintiff struck the head of the accuser before witnesses, indicating that accused was innocent of wrongdoing. This interpretation of the phrase is supported by the legal ritual act of *pūtam maḫāṣum*, "to strike the forehead," by which a debt holder publicly indicated the debtor. The person deemed by law to occupy the advantageous position performed the symbolic act. Moreover, in some Mesopotamian legal texts, Akkadian *šēpu*, "foot," is used to indicate a person's power or authority in matters of inheritance.[20]

With this information as background, the divine sentence may be interpreted as meaning that in the future, the serpent's seed will attempt to strike or push aside the feet of the woman's seed—serpents will attempt to undermine human authority and to usurp humans' standing with God—but the woman's offspring will strike the head of the serpent's offspring in triumph. If correct, this interpretation exposes beyond cavil the scheme of the serpent: it was a plot to supplant humans from their position in the divinely established hierarchy of authority on earth. This interpretation might explain why enmity was extended to progeny in the context of the story. The serpent-human relationship would not change in the future, but it would be recognized and called by its proper name.[21]

Unfortunately, this interpretation, like the preceding one, does not explain everything in the story. The significance of some details escapes us still. The introduction of the enmity theme in verse 15 may not arise from anything in the narrative. It may simply be tagged onto the story to explain actual human behavior around serpents. Daniel C. Dennett, a philosopher of cognition, meaning, and consciousness, observes that some primates raised in captivity who have never seen a snake react very negatively when presented with one. He suggests that human dislike of snakes may have a biological source in the transformation of primal aversion reactions developed during the course of evolutionary history. If so, the sentence of enmity may be taken as an etiology for a common human tendency to fear and avoid snakes.[22]

None of these explanations is bound strictly to the language of the text. All are more speculation than explanation.

THE SERPENT'S DIET

The reference to a daily diet of clods—large or even very small clumps of soil, like that from which Adam was formed—is peculiar. It may allude to snakes' method of eating: they neither tear nor chew their prey but swallow it whole. Owing to some modifications in the skull bones, ligaments, and mandibles, a snake can distend its mouth to swallow prey larger than the diameter of its own body. The meal remains an obvious clod-shaped lump in the body, visible to all during early stages of digestion.

The allusion may also be to snake behavior prior to casting off an old skin. The snake repeatedly rubs its nose and chin against a stone or something else hard to weaken the skin at these points. To a casual observer maintaining a safe distance, this may appear to be feeding behavior.

A third possibility, quite distinct from the preceding suggestions, is based on a description of Israel's suffering after the destruction of Jerusalem: "He will sit alone and be silent because he imposed it on him; he will place his mouth in a clod; perhaps there is hope" (Lam 3:28–29). If "eating a clod" is the same as "placing a mouth in a clod," that is, filling one's mouth with clumps of soil, so as to bear a punishment in silence, then possibly the allusion in Genesis 3:14 is to the silence of serpents in the real world. If so, the sentence has an etiological overtone: once a crafty, loquacious serpent spoke, but now all serpents are silent.

GUILT OF THE SERPENT

All these attempts to clarify God's sentence leave a major question unanswered: Of what was the serpent guilty? He was not responsible for entrapment, because he did not eat the fruit to set an example for her, nor did he actually suggest that Hawwa eat or that Adam partake. But even had the serpent eaten to set an example, the story presents no prohibition against his consuming fruit from this particular tree. Moreover, his particular knowledge was innate. It would have been unaffected by fruit from the tree. Still, there is no doubt about his responsibility for catalyzing a connected series of events. But wherein lies his culpability?

Nothing explicit in the story addresses this issue, but the woman's statement directing attention to the serpent bears on the question implicitly.[23] His fault lay in the mischievous application of the very particular type of wisdom with which he had been well endowed. Through unfinished sentences, devious assertions, and a dollop of truth, he successfully misrepresented the intent of God and directed the woman toward a course of action with irreversible consequences. He instigated and created a climate within which she indulged a particular, benign desire. But even that does not seem to have been a violation of any social or legal norm.

For example, in the story of Abraham and Sarah first in Egypt and then at Gerar, Abraham, too, is an instigator. But he committed no perceived wrong and was, consequently, not culpable (Gen 12:11–13, 17–19; 20:2, 9). Abraham did not instruct Pharaoh or Abimelech to take Sarah into the harem; the serpent did not say, "Disregard what YHWH god told your husband; eat to be wise." And even had he said it, of what would he be blameworthy? Even if it appears to contemporary sensibilities that the serpent's instigation was unethical, in Israelite jurisprudence it was not illegal.

Thus, the not-so-innocent serpent was not guilty of anything. This explains why the divine sentences in verses 14–15 do not impart a real punishment. The verbal diminution of status through the ʾāruwr, "diminished/weakened," formula involved an apparent change of status in the hierarchy of animals, but nothing physical: there was no loss of feet or voice. The change was entirely psychological. One can imagine the serpent slithering off, forked tongue darting, head low in mock contrition, a smile well hidden. Observant Israelites may have thought that the serpent failed to hear a word that God said because snakes lack external ears.

SEXING THE SERPENT

This study consistently refers to the nāḥāš as a masculine creature. Linguistic, naturalistic, and literary arguments, however, may be advanced to contend that it was perceived as either androgynous or female.

(1) There is no word in biblical Hebrew for a female serpent/snake.

(2) Hebrew is marked for feminine only. It treats subjects considered unqualifiedly feminine, for whatever reasons, in a special way, using unique forms of nouns, pronouns, adjectives, and verbs. Were the creature androgynous—either not completely feminine or both feminine and masculine—Hebrew would have employed not-feminine verbs and adjectives—verbs and adjectives that grammars and lexicons traditionally label as masculine.

In English, all that is left of a similar, though hardly identical, system is the pronoun she. Two contrasting English sentences suggest how this common Hebrew feature works:

All the waitresses are beautiful.

All the waiters are good-looking.

The first sentence employs a noun marked feminine by the *-ess* suffix and a predicate adjective, "beautiful," conventionally applied to feminine subjects. The second sentence could refer to a group of exclusively male waiters or to a mixed group of waiters. In twenty-first-century American English, it could also refer to a group of females.

(3) Israelites could not distinguish the gender of serpents since snakes lack obvious, definable external indicators. A technique for determining gender, called "cloacal probing," was first described only in 1933. Nonetheless, it is reasonable to assume that Israelites in the Iron Age knew that snakes lay eggs (Isa 59:5). Reasoning analogically from birds to snakes, they might have concluded that what lays eggs is a mother and female.[24] In the absence of recognizable males, however, they may have thought that snakes were androgynous. Since the serpent was not completely female, Hebrew required grammatically masculine nouns and verbs when referring to "him."

(4) The word rendered as "seed" in Genesis 3:15 is *zeraʿ*. The noun can refer to plant seed or semen. When it is applied to people, with the meaning of "progeny," it is sometimes used with a singular sense and sometimes with a collective sense. English words demonstrating the same linguistic behavior are *sheep, head,* and *fish*—and, indeed, *offspring, progeny,* and *seed.* Usually context suffices to determine how it is to be understood.[25]

In Genesis 3:15, the third person masculine singular pronoun *hūwʾ* refers to "her seed," that is, the woman's son, and the associated verb form is likewise third person masculine singular. When applied to the serpent's seed, however, the term could theoretically refer to a number of crafty crawlers. Unfortunately, the single reference leaves the matter of number unresolved. In nature, young animals are usually cared for by their mothers.

The parallel reference to the serpent's *zeraʿ* and the woman's *zeraʾ* suggests, but does not prove, that the two seed bearers occupied parallel roles in procreation, since the "mothers" are both chastised through the evocation of some ill on their brood. Although this last point constitutes an argument for considering the serpent female, Hebrew grammar disallows this. Though a mother, the serpent was not completely female.

The Serpent as Female

This sketch of a fourteenth-century wall painting in the monastery at Wienhausen, Germany, shows the serpent of Eden as female. The motif can be traced back in European art to the twelfth century. (Drawing courtesy of Izak Cornelius, University of Stellenbosch, South Africa; from I. Cornelius, "Some Pages from the Reception History of Genesis 3: The Visual Arts," *Journal of Northwest Semitic Languages* 23 [1997]: 232 [fig. 2].)

Hebrew notwithstanding, the snake is represented as female in a number of Renaissance paintings.[26]

A CURIOUS HERPETOLOGICAL AFTERWORD

Since the middle of the twentieth century, biologists have known that the elongated body and loss of appendages in snakes are an evolutionary feature found also in various vertebrate groups other than snakes: in eels and morays among fishes and in "worm lizards" and "glass snakes" among lizards. Vestiges of a pelvic girdle and hind limbs are found in both pythons and boas, which are fairly primitive snakes, although the most primitive are blind snakes (scolecophidians) found worldwide and South American pipe snakes (*Anilius scytale*).[27] Genetic studies of lizards and snakes, along with fossil finds of seagoing snakes with small hind legs, lead biologists to conclude that around 150 million years ago snakes evolved on land, not in the sea, as previously thought.[28] That is when they "lost" their legs.

20   NO BUNDLE OF JOY

Hawwa's Sentence and Israelite Predilections

in Legal Reasoning

(Gen 3:16)

Genesis 3

16   To the woman he said:
> Multiplying I will multiply *'iṣṣebōwnēk* and your
> pregnancy.
> In *'eṣeb* you will birth children,
> and *'el 'īyšēk tešūwqātēk*,
> but he *yimšol bāk*.

Contemporary Western society tends to view childbirth—or the process of childbirth—as a positive experience despite the acute pain and discomfort that accompany it. Those who prefer or must endure natural childbirth view the pain as a test of womanhood, a private, bittersweet experience, and an act of motherhood.[1] This was not always the case.

"THE CURSE"

In contemporary English, "the curse" is sometimes used in place of the more clinical "menstruation." The phrase was also widely used to refer to childbirth until 1853, when Queen Victoria gave birth to Prince Leopold, using chloroform to alleviate her birth pains. As the practice of using anesthesia gained acceptance in both Protestant and Catholic countries, overcoming the initial objections of clerics, fear of birth pains receded, as did the application of the expression "the curse" to birth. Nowadays, birth pains can be masked with opioids and blocked with an analgesic delivered through a catheter into the epidural space between vertebrae of the lower back and the spinal column.

One early Jewish source connecting the pains of childbirth and many other feminine pains and discomforts with "the curse" on Hawwa is *Aboth d'Rabbi Nathan* (The Fathers According to Rabbi Nathan), first of the minor tractates of the Babylonian Talmud. Though compiled into its extant form sometime between 700 and 900 CE, it is based on traditions reaching back to the second century. *Aboth d'Rabbi Nathan* interprets Genesis 3:16 as containing many curses on womankind, among which are listed: two painful discharges of blood, one during menstruation and one with the termination of virginity; pain at conception; pain at childbirth; yearning for a husband when he is about to set out on a journey; and being subject to a husband's commands (*b. Aboth d'Rabbi Nathan* 17a; *b. Erubin* 100b).[2]

This and similar interpretations of God's words to Hawwa lack any basis in the Hebrew text.

Pain in childbirth is part of the birthing process. In late pregnancy, generally painless contractions of the uterus help soften and thin the cervix, a band of muscles and connective tissue at the bottom of the uterus. At full term, the strongest muscle in the female body, the uterus, begins a series of contractions that become regular, frequent, of increasing duration, and increasingly painful. They cause the cervix to thin, stretching pelvic ligaments and the vaginal wall as the downward pressure slowly expels the mature fetus through normally small apertures.[3] Isaiah 26:17 describes birthing: "Like a pregnant woman approaching birth, she writhes, she shouts in her pains." Birth hurts. Women experience pain.

Iron Age Hebrew used three words to refer to pains associated with childbirth:[4]

(1) The word *ḥebel* (singular) / *ḥabālīym* (plural) refers mainly to the pains of childbirth (Isa 13:8; 66:7; Jer 13:21; 22:23; Hosea 13:13). The root *ḥ-b-l* forms verbs meaning "to writhe in birth" used in Psalm 7:15 and Song of Songs 8:5, 9. This Hebrew word is related etymologically to others meaning "binding, tying." If so, it may refer to the pain caused by contractions.[5]

(2) The word ṣiyr (singular)/ṣiyriȳm (plural) also refers to birth pains (1 Sam 4:19; Isa 13:8; 21:3). This noun appears connected to its Hebrew homophone ṣiyr meaning "messenger" (Isa 18:2; 57:9; Jer 49:14), which is connected with the Arabic verb ṣāra from a root ṣ-y-r, "to go, walk." If this is the correct etymology of the Hebrew word, ṣiyr may refer to shooting, moving pain.

(3) Verbs based on the root ḥ-y-l refer to experiencing pain in general (Isa 13:8; 26:17; 66:7; Ezek 30:16), while the noun ḥiyl refers to the strong pain usually felt at childbirth (Jer 3:43; 22:23; Mic 4:9). Its context in Psalm 48:7, "shaking took hold of them there, ḥiyl, pain like one birthing," hints that it may refer to a sudden throbbing pain. See also Exodus 15:14–15.[6]

The common nouns indicating general hurt, ache, and pain, both physical and psychological, are ke'ēb (Isa 65:12; Job 2:13; 16:6) and mak'ōb (Exod 3:7; Ps 32:10; Lam 1:12, 18). Verbs referring to experiencing or causing such pain are derived from the same root: k-'-b (Gen 34:25; Ezek 28:24; Ps 69:30). When Israelite authors described severe pain, they used similes drawn from descriptions of childbirth. For example, Jeremiah imagines a man in the throes of birth pangs: "Inquire, please, and see, does a male give birth? Why? I saw every male, his hands on his thighs like a birthing mother and all faces turned pale green" (Jer 30:6; see also Jer 48:41; 49:22).[7]

Had the author of the Garden story wished to inform readers that Hawwa's sentence was about throbbing or shooting birth pains or writhing contractions, or had he wished to say simply that it was about pain in general, he had an ample supply of nouns and verbs with which to work. He ignored them all. God's sentencing of the woman does not involve any malediction. He did not say, "From this day I add throbbing and shooting pains to your discomfort so that you will birth in anguish."

God's sentence in verse 16 is about 'iṣṣābōn and 'eṣeb, physical sensations with which the woman formed to assist Adam is presumably already familiar. Biblical verses using these and other words derived from the same consonantal root, '-ṣ-b, illustrate what these sensations are.[8]

In Genesis 5:29, Lamech names his son Noah because "this one will comfort us from our works and from the 'iṣṣebōwn yādēynūw [exhaustion of our hands]." That is, our hands are tired; we are exhausted from working the soil. Isaiah 14:3 uses a related word from the same root. It states that God will grant respite from the "'ōṣeb [exhaustion], agitation, and hard labor" that Israelites were compelled to perform in exile. An abstract plural form, 'aṣṣābiym, in Psalm 127:2 is used in a phrase referring to the "food of exhaustion," food produced through physical toil. This recurs in an abbreviated form in Proverbs 5:10: "lest encroachers feast on your strength and on your exhaustion in the house of a stranger." Here in Genesis 3:17, in God's address to the woman, both iṣṣābōn and 'eṣeb refer to tiredness and fatigue due to her physical efforts.

When God speaks to the man in Genesis 3:17 (discussed in the next chapter), iṣṣābōn is used to describe the man's physical state when he sits down to eat.[9] Here in verse 16, God tells the woman that she will always be drained, weary, pooped. In that state of continuous exhaustion she will conceive many times and give birth while totally fatigued.

Cross-cultural studies of pain perception, including those of childbirth, indicate that although individuals experience and describe similar degrees of pain, sociocultural context affects the perception of pain. Consequently, women surveyed about birth pains respond differently based on cultural factors. For example, Chinese women having unmedicated births in hospitals said that it was shameful to scream and that such actions used up energy required for the physical exertion of giving birth. Bedouin women in Kuwait reported experiencing pain but did not demonstrate pain behavior. Muslim women sometimes cried and screamed, but devout women were less inclined to do so and instead asked God to help them give birth safely.

A study from western Canada indicated that Anglo women had the highest perception of pain, women from east India the second highest, Hutterite women the third highest, and Ukrainian women the least. Mayan women living in Guatemala tended to accept pain stoically as the lot of women. Their coping mechanism for pain was to use a special mantra during birth and to call out "My God! I can't bear it any more!" The shouting women and the quiet women all indicated that they were experiencing similar degrees of pain. They were simply treating it differently.[10]

Through his words, God transformed the birth culture of Hawwa from one in which draining birth pain was a fact of life to one in which this specific pain bore a negative valence.[11]

God's pronouncement played on Hawwa's knowledge of her world. It gave a name to her physical sensations at the end of a day's work in his Garden, to her perception of the tiring nature of pregnancy and of the exertions and labor pain associated with birth. He characterized her life as consisting of drudgework and projected it into a bleak future. Her anticipation that in the future all births would occur in a state of extreme fatigue would alter the reality. That was the sentence. God took part of her world and colored it blue.

No word such as *'āruwr*, "being in a lowered state," or *qallēl*, "curse," that can be translated, mistranslated, or misconceived as "curse" is to be found in the statement.

DESIRE, DESIRABILITY, AND CONTROL

The second part of verse 16, *we'el 'iyšēk tešūwqātēk,* but he *yimšol-bāk,* may be interpreted in three different ways.

First, it can be read this way: "Your desire [is] to your husband and he rules / shall rule you." The noun rendered as "desire," *tešūwqāh,* derives from the root *š-w-q,* which, when conjugated in the Hiphil verbal conjugation, refers to being full of liquid (Joel 2:24; 4:13). The meaning of *tešūwqāh,* however, is connected to a secondary development of the root *š-q-q,* which is used to form verbs with an almost opposite meaning: to thirst for water in Isaiah 29:8 and for solace in Psalm 107:9. In both attestations, the mind directs the person experiencing thirst, desire, or longing to whatever it wants or requires. This interpretation, leaning more to a psychological desire than to a physical, instinctual urge, suggests that *tešūwqāh* itself does not necessarily imply a sexual need, although it does not exclude such a possibility. In verse 16, the word could refer to a desire or longing to be with her man/husband.

A second interpretation revolves around the noun *tešūwqāh,* which recurs in Genesis 4:7 and Song of Songs 7:11, where it is interpreted as having a sexual overtone. In our verse, coming in an utterance whose first sentence deals with childbirth, a sexual overtone may also be present. This possibility allows for a more restricted understanding.

A. J. Bledstein suggests that *tešūwqāh* in the Garden story means "desirable" and that verse 16 can be translated as "your desirability is your husband's"—that is, he is attracted to you.[12] Bledstein's interpretation works well with Song of Songs 7:11—"I am for my beloved [*we'ālay tešūwqātōw*], and his desirability is over me," or, in other words, he is attractive to me—but is forced in Genesis 4:7, where sexual desire or attraction is not readily apparent. There, God tells Qayin that the *tešūwqāh* of

Sin personified—as the problematic word *ḥaṭṭā't* is usually translated—is directed toward him but that he may rule over it: *'ēleykā tešūwqātōw we'attāh timšol bōw*, "its desirability is to you"—that is, it is attractive to you—"but [despite this] you will rule it."[13]

A third interpretation takes its point of departure from the final words of Genesis 4:7, God's counsel to Qayin, where the palliative to the force of Sin's *tešūwqāh* is ruling authority, expressed through the verb *timšōl*, "you will rule." W. Vogels suggests that *tešūwqāh* refers to a desire for power and control.[14] This sense can also be applied to Genesis 3:16: "your will for power is directed toward your man, but he will rule you"—that is, he will have the final word. It can also be applied in Song of Songs 7:11, but its appropriateness there is not so apparent, since the male figure never controls the female one.

Though differing as to who desires whom, the first two interpretations conclude with the man having some vague authority over the woman, however this is to be understood. Bledstein's interpretation is more in keeping with the fact that the woman was created to benefit Adam. The third interpretation leads to the same conclusion, but what is at issue there is clear: influence, power, and control.[15]

Hawwa's sentence, then, does not mark any significant change in her circumstances. There is no indication that when the woman gave birth the first time it was painless and that she was not exhausted, or that her need for her husband, or vice versa, did not exist. In fact, the semantics of *'ēzer kenegdōw* implies some sort of mutual dependence. Even God's concluding remark that her husband will rule her does not introduce an innovation. The only change involves her perception of intensified exhaustion before and after childbirth. Because exhaustion will be perceived differently, she will respond to it differently.

ISRAELITE HABITS OF THINKING LEGALISTICALLY

Unlike the serpent and Adam who are both implicated in wrongdoing, the woman is not. So why did God sentence her? At best, she may have been responsible for abetting a questionable violation of an utterance that lacked the gravitas of a command. Her situation would be similar to Sarah's, first in Egypt and then at Gerar (Gen 12; 20). In those cases, where adultery was involved, nobody accused Sarah of having done anything wrong. She was given a pass.

Although this sounds like legalistic hairsplitting, details related to social norms, rules, and law must be comprehended within the cultural milieu within which the Garden story was told and the literary and social setting within which it was preserved. To be unaware of this aspect of Israel's culture is akin to watching a police or court drama with no knowledge of the basic principles and rules governing criminal law, legal investigative procedures, and nuanced jurisprudence.

Israelite tribes, clans, and extended families shared a worldview embodying beliefs, concerns, commitments, and norms that loosely defined their sense of a common fate, religion, and identity. Laws within this worldview were meant to reinforce and maintain what their society valued: order, security, and stability. Because the laws articulated and helped reinforce norms that clarified both the collective social identity and the identity of individuals within kin groups, they provide contemporary readers access to the ancient culture that helps clarify elements in the Garden story.[16]

The distinction between a crime and a noncriminal but still wrongful or blameworthy act is crucial for understanding the motivations of characters and the development of plots in a number of biblical narratives. An awareness of what constituted proper behavior, common legal traditions, and localized social norms informs many biblical narratives. Three examples—one short and simple and two longer and somewhat complicated—illustrate these shared understandings. The examples illustrate legal principles and subterfuges in Israelite culture that can be brought to bear on the interpretation of the Garden story.

Example 1. Before dying, David instructs Solomon to get rid of Shimei, a person whom he, David, motivated by political considerations at a particular time, has promised not to harm (2 Sam 19:24). He counsels acting wisely to avoid incurring any blame: "*You* must also deal with Shimei . . . *I* swore to him by YHWH, '*I* will not kill you by the sword.' But now, *you* do not leave him unpunished. Indeed, *you* are a wise man and *you* know what *you* will do to him and *you* will bring down his white hair in blood to Sheol" (1 Kings 2:8–9).

Solomon, a patient man, lays down a rule compelling Shimei to build himself a home in Jerusalem and restricting him to the city on pain of death: "dying you will die [*mōt tāmūt*], and your blood will be on your own head." Shimei accepts these restrictions as fair.

Three years later, Shimei leaves the city to reclaim runaway slaves in Gath, thinking, perhaps, that Solomon's declaration is not to be taken too seriously or that he has a valid excuse. After Solomon learns of the brief excursion, he confronts Shimei and then has him executed (1 Kings 2:36–46). David's honor as a man who kept his word remains intact.

Example 2. The narrative about the rape of Tamar by her half-brother, Amnon, in his house (2 Sam 13:1–22) makes perfectly clear that a great wrong was committed. If so, the lack of any legal procedure against Amnon requires explanation. The only known Israelite laws possibly applicable to Tamar's particular case are found in part of a tenth–ninth-century BCE collection of laws incorporated into Deuteronomy 22:23–29:

> If there is a girl of marriageable age, a virgin, pledged to a man, and a man finds her in the city and lies with her, you shall take the two of them out to the gate of that city and stone them with stones so that they die— the girl because she did not call out in the city, and the man because he afflicted his neighbor's wife, and you will get rid of the evil from your midst.
>
> But if the man found the pledged girl of marriageable age in the open field, and the man grabs her and lies with her, only the man who lay with her shall die. To the girl you will do nothing; the girl is not culpable for a capital offense, because this case is like that of a man rising up against his neighbor and murdering him. He found her in the open field, the pledged girl of marriageable age called out, but there was nobody to rescue her.
>
> If a man finds a girl of marriageable age, a virgin, who is not pledged and he seizes her and lies with her and they are found, the man who lies with her will give to the father of the girl fifty [sheqels of] silver and she will be his wife. Because he forced her, he will not be able to send her away all of his days.[17]

The circumstances of the case of Tamar are not congruent with any of the preconditions delineated in these laws. What was done to her was done in the city, not in the country. Amnon and Tamar were not found together, there were no eyewitnesses and there was no cry for help and nobody who could or would attest that he or she had heard such a cry.

The first two laws are concerned with the rape of betrothed women, while the intent of the third one is to protect men from unsubstantiated accusations that they are responsible for deflowering a young woman known to have been a virgin. Each law posits a particular scenario based on the status of the involved parties and the circumstances of the alleged criminal event. None of the circumstances or conditions considered relevant by the legislator applied to the case of Tamar and Amnon, so the wrong committed did not constitute a crime. Since no law had been violated, there could be no guilty person and no punishment.

Had Tamar been raped in the countryside, her word would have sufficed to make a case against Amnon; had she been found together with him in the city, there might have been a shotgun wedding. But neither of these conditions was met. Consequently, as Isaac Abarbanel observed in his commentary on this story in the fifteenth century, no legal action could be taken.

Example 3. Absalom, Tamar's only full brother, construes the incident as a family matter that has to be resolved to restore honor and respect to his mother's family, for it had been shamed, as in the case of his ancestor Dinah and the Canaanite prince Shechem. Then, Simon and Levi, Dinah's full brothers by the same mother, Leah, avenged the family honor when their father, Jacob, and their other brothers desisted (Gen 34).

Absalom may have waited for David, the paterfamilias, to take action. But when David chose not to act against his firstborn son and possible heir to his throne, Absalom orders his men to kill Amnon publicly in an act of vengeance and then flees, most likely because he knows that his deed can be construed as murder (2 Sam 13:28–29, 34).[18] Absalom fled to the protection of his mother's father, Talmai, king of Geshur, a small kingdom north of Israel (2 Sam 3:3; 13:37). Three years later, David allows Absalom to return, effectively granting him amnesty (2 Sam 14:21–23).

This story raises a number of interesting questions: Was Absalom a murderer? If yes, why didn't David punish him? On what basis could David grant amnesty in a case of premeditated murder carried out before witnesses? These questions may be answered once we see that Absalom returned only after David had established a legal precedent in the hypothetical homicide revenge case presented by the Tekoite widow (2 Sam 14:1–11).

The widow pleaded before David on behalf of her fratricidal son to stay the hand of blood avengers. Were the fratricide avenged, she would be left childless. The fact that she pleaded before David indicates that the ruler was implicitly empowered by the tribal elders who had elected him their king to adjudicate cases when extenuating circumstances or the limitations of existing norms or conflicting legal traditions or political interests could lead to a perceived injustice or to social destabilization.

The Tekoite's situation was like that of Adam and Hawwa after the death of Abel; unlike them, however, the Tekoite's husband was dead, so a new heir could not be produced. Were her second son to be executed, her husband's real property would be lost and his name blotted out. Had there been an unmarried daughter, a solution along the lines of the ruling made for the daughters of Zelophahad might have been possible—they were permitted to inherit their father's estate on condition that they marry within their tribe (Num 36:2–12)—but no daughter is mentioned.[19]

David ruled in favor of the widow, ordering that her living son not be killed by relatives for murdering his brother. In stopping the regular process of blood vengeance in a matter not linked to his own family, David created a legal administrative precedent.

Applying this precedent to the case of Absalom was easy, since the rules of blood vengeance operated as a traditional norm and, as David's ruling indicated, took precedence over other laws. The norm did not compel; it permitted action that under other circumstances was considered criminal. Should the avenger opt to exercise his prerogative, tradition protected his right by defining his action so that it did not constitute murder.

David's decision in the case of the Tekoite established that the king could halt the process by virtue of his authority. The implication of this decision for Absalom's circumstances was that unless the king actively stopped the process, the rights of the avenger were not annulled and the tradition remained an active, operative norm.

David's silence and inaction after the rape—no matter the reasons— had neither cleared Amnon of the offense nor abrogated Absalom's right of revenge. It did, however, leave Absalom's act in limbo in that David or one of his other sons was empowered by extra-legal convention to kill him in avenging the family honor. Absalom's uncertainty about whether David might take action against him explains his flight. Thus, even though Absalom had had Amnon killed, a fact complicating the question of culpability, a wrong had undoubtedly been committed, but Absalom himself had violated no law. There had been a homicide, but no murder.[20] By publicly allowing Absalom to return to Judah, David signaled effectively that as king, he had abrogated his own right as father and the rights of his other sons to exact vengeance.

These examples indicate that some biblical narratives presuppose their audience's familiarity with common legal norms and judicial procedures, no less than do contemporary novels, plays, and films. They attest that the system of Israelite law allowed for ad hoc and ad hominem innovation in unusual or ambiguous situations.

A different set of examples illustrates that the Israelite legal system included a principle under which indirect causation of an act with an undesirable outcome subjected the perpetrator to a less severe sanction than that imposed on perpetrators who intentionally brought about the outcome.

Genesis 9:7 presents a general norm: "He who sheds the blood of man, by man his blood will be shed." Exodus 21:12–13 restates the norm while establishing a qualifying principle: "He who smites a man and he dies, dying will be put to death; but concerning him who did not lie in wait and whose hand God forced, I will designate for you a place to which he can flee."[21] While unclear as to details, this principle apparently establishes a rule whereby death due indirectly to an act of God does not eliminate culpability but does restrict the avenger's response by providing the accidental killer a safe haven.

Deuteronomy 19:4 introduces the category of "one who smites his fellow unknowingly without having hated him" to clarify what Exodus 21:12–13 was trying to express. Deuteronomy 19:5 provides a hypothetical case illustrating how the principle might be applied:

> Concerning one who comes into a forest with his friend to cut wood, and his hand swings the ax to cut a tree and the iron [ax head] slips from the shaft and strikes his friend who dies—he will flee to one of these [cities of refuge] and live.

In both the Exodus and the Deuteronomy cases, the killer can avoid the avenger by fleeing to an asylum city. The avenger's rights are thereby restricted, not abrogated. Comparing the laws in Exodus and Deuteronomy reveals that Israelite legal thinking differentiated between cases in which the killer knew his victim and premeditated his act and those in which he did not. What remains unclear from the available material is how this worked itself out in the application of law.

Laws in the book of Numbers sort out all the principles implicit in these early laws. Numbers 35:16–21 defines what sort of act constitutes murder under law by considering such different factors as the delivery of a blow, the nature of the relationship between killer and victim at the time of the incident, and the presence of an intent to do harm. Numbers 35:22–24 addresses factors that exclude a killing from the category of murder: lack of malice, lack of intent to do harm, and the possibility of accident. Numbers 35:30 permits the testimony of one reliable witness for a person to be judged guilty of manslaughter but requires two witnesses for him to be adjudged a murderer.

Even a casual reading of Numbers 35 shows that the general principle of Genesis about the penalty for spilling human blood is intact but that a second principle accompanies it. The difference between the two principles manifests itself practically in the legal definition of "spilling human blood" such that rules for distinguishing between a manslayer and a murderer can be set in place and norms for treating each established. This differentiation did not eliminate the theoretical right of the blood avenger, but it rather severely restricted that right in cases where the law determined that the killer was not a murderer.[22]

In the narrative examples cited above, dramatic tension is created by a conflict between a defined norm or law and the cultural preference for leniency. The story of Absalom shows this in action. Absalom's servants were not culpable as a group because they were doing what servants did, acting in a subordinate capacity and following instructions. Conspiracy and abetting were not defined as crimes, and the concept of an accessory to an act did not exist in Israelite jurisprudence. Absalom, the instigator, considered as an individual, had not actually done anything, nor had he expressed aloud any hatred of Amnon, a point emphasized in the story (2 Sam 13:20–22).

Applying the reasoning implicit in resolving the Tekoite woman's hypothetical case to the case of Absalom, David worked through the multifaceted Absalom-Amnon-Tamar events involving servants, the questionable obligations of brothers to avenge half-brothers, rape, his personal honor, and the honor of his family. He then exercised his authority to act in a spirit of leniency to achieve the outcome that he preferred. The author of the David story trusted his readers to infer the legal reasoning on the basis of a few clues planted in the narrative and their awareness of the legal workings of their own society; so, too, the author of the Garden story assumed that his readers could follow the logic of God's sentencing of Hawwa and the serpent.

HAWWA'S GUILT

In the Garden story, the legal tension is resolved by disproving the applicability of the eating prohibition in the circumstances.

In Genesis 3:16, God pronounces a sentence but does not announce a punishment. Since nothing in the circumstances of Hawwa's actions constituted a direct violation of any rule, her actions do not warrant a penalty. There has been no crime and no misdemeanor; therefore, there can be no punishment. Hawwa is guilty of nothing other than irritating God.[23]

21 TOIL AND TROUBLE

Adam's Sentence and the Rights of Laborers

(Gen 3:17–19)

Genesis 3

17 And to Adam he said:
> Because *šāma'ta leqōwl* of your woman/wife and
> you ate from the tree concerning which I
> commanded you saying:
>> You will not eat from it,
> *'arūwrāh* the soil *ba'abūwrekā*.
> In *'iṣṣābōn* you will eat from it all the days of your life.

18 > And thorn and thistle it will sprout *lāk*;
> but you will eat edible plants of the field.

19 > By the sweat of your nose you will eat food until you
> return to the soil because you were taken from it.
> Indeed, you are a clod and to a clod you return.

Translations of Genesis 3:17 employ words indicating that Adam is indicted for listening to his wife. They faithfully represent the Hebrew word *šāma'ta*, derived from the root *š-m-'*, which in most of its 1,159 attestations in the Bible refers to hearing and listening. These translations of verse 17 are problematic, however, for a rather embarrassing reason. In the description of what happened in Genesis 3:6, the woman said nothing to her husband. She gave fruit to him and he ate.

This anomaly raises the following question: Was God misrepresenting what actually occurred at the tree?

THE SILENCE OF THE MALES

Accepting a translation involving "hearing" or "listening" implies that we are missing either a brief speech—something along the lines of "Adam, at least taste it!"—or a more extended dialogue during which the woman successfully cajoled Adam into eating. That conversation, implied by this verse, constitutes what has become known as the Temptation of Adam. John Milton (1608–74) caught the moment in *Paradise Lost*:

> He scrupled not to eat
> Against his better knowledge, not deceived
> But fondly overcome with female charm. (book IX, lines 997–99)

A second possible translation does not require inventing a conversation or interpreting unmentioned silence and inaction as crucial to the comprehension of the story. It is based on a tiny linguistic clue. As elsewhere in the Garden story, attention to prepositions sometimes yields useful dividends.

The Hebrew preposition in verse 17 used with the verb for listening, *šāma'ta,* is *le,* not the more common *be.* Whereas *š-m-'+ be + qōwl* refers to listening and obeying, acquiescing, or following instructions 107 times in the Hebrew Bible, *š-m-'+ le + qōwl* (or *qōl*—a slightly different orthography), occurring only 16 times, is occasionally used differently.[1] In four passages, including Genesis 3:17, there is no preceding speech. All four, however, use the word *qōl,* "voice/sound." Two examples are in Exodus 4:8–9:

> And it be, if they do not believe you and will not pay attention to [*we lō' yišme'ūw leqōl*—literally "and will not hear/listen for the sound/voice of"] the first sign, they will believe the last sign. And it will be that if they do not believe in both these signs and will not pay attention to you [*welō' yišme'ūn leqōlekā*— literally "and will not indeed hear/listen for your sound/voice"], you will take from the waters of the Nile . . . and they will become blood on the dry ground.

The "signs" to which these verses refer were acts performed in silence. They are described in Exodus 4:2–8. In the first, Moses turned his staff into a snake and then back into a staff; in the second, he made his hand turn leprous and then returned it to its prior healthy state. There was nothing to be heard.

A third example occurs in Jeremiah 18:19: "Attend, YHWH god, to me and pay attention to my opponents [*ūwšemaʿ leqōwl yerīybāy*—literally "and hear/listen to the sound/voice of my opponents]." Jeremiah does not indicate that his opponents said anything; rather, they did something: "they dug a pit for me" (Jer 18:20).

The string *š-m-ʿ* + *le* + *qōwl / qōl*, "hear/listen + to/for + sound/voice," in all three examples considered in context is defined linguistically as a syntagm, pronounced /sin-tam/. This word refers to a sequence of individual words that in combination constitute a single unit with its own meaning. In other words, the syntagm is other than the sum of its parts. Its meaning is not readily accessible if only its component elements are considered; the meaning can be determined only by studying how the syntagm is used in context. An example of an English syntagm is "How do you do?" No study of all the words in this question could possibly indicate that it functions as an expression of informal greeting and is the equivalent of "Hello."

In all examples of the syntagm *š-m-ʿ* + *le* + *qōwl / qōl* considered above, it refers to acting or evaluating a situation on the basis of an observed action or object or person. This understanding of the syntagm's import clarifies the meaning of what God said to Adam in Genesis 3:17: "because you paid attention to your woman's behavior." God sentences Adam for acting in imitation of his wife. He emphasizes the possessive—"*your* woman/wife"—thus sweeping aside in a less than subtle manner Adam's implicit excuse in Genesis 3:12—"the woman that *you* gave." It leaves the matter of how she encouraged his eating opaque and irrelevant so far as God is concerned. Perhaps Ralph Waldo Emerson's words capture God's sentiment here: "What you do speaks so loudly that I cannot hear what you say."

ADAM'S GUILT

Because the woman was not censured for listening to the serpent or being (mis)guided by him, these factors were clearly not considerations in ascertaining her diminished culpability. God did not refer to any specific act of malfeasance when addressing Hawwa. Absence of any such reference with the woman emphasizes its presence with the man. As God saw it, the man ought not to have followed the woman's lead; he ought not to have allowed her actions to influence his. After all, God did not ask *them* where they were; he sought out Adam, spoke to him first, and inquired whether or not he had eaten. The helper, Hawwa, remained silent on the side until addressed directly.

The preconception here is that because the woman was Adam's helper, not his partner, he had responsibilities, obligations, and authority that she did not, including authority over her with regard to certain matters. This interpretation indicates that the phrase "he rules / shall rule you" did not alter the woman's status, only made it explicit. Furthermore, these circumstances clarify why the woman could not be indicted. She had no legal standing in this affair.[2]

Adam's sentence in verse 17 echoes one element from Hawwa's in verse 16, the reference to *'iṣṣābōwn*, "exhaustion," and one from the serpent's in verse 14, the phrase "all the days of your life." Like the sentences of the other two, Adam's resulted in little change. He was a hard-working agriculturalist before, and so he remained.[3] In light of the analysis of *'ārūwr* earlier, the expression "*'arūwrāh* [is] the ground" in verse 17 means that the ground appears diminished in productive strength "on account of" the man (cf. Deut 28:16–18; Pss 106:32; 132:10).[4]

Adam was mortal before he tasted the fruit, and so he remained. The only slight change was that now the man would notice that among the natural plants of the field the ground produced thorns and thistles that were particularly difficult to deal with (cf. Gen 2:5). God focused Adam's attention on the thorns and thistles by saying that the ground would sprout them "for you" (*lāk*; Gen 3:18). The statement introduced nothing new into nature.

Tending the Garden had always involved dealing with weeds and other unwanted plants. These had to be uprooted by hoeing, digging, and pulling and then destroyed by burning. This work came in addition to the regular rounds of cultivating, raking, pruning, pinching, watering, and harvesting.[5] Despite all this labor, God told Adam he would "eat edible plants of the field" (Gen 3:18). These were the plants that sprouted after the first rains and had always been in and about the Garden. Readers of this story, basing their understanding of how Adam had lived on how they lived, would have assumed that he had eaten such plants regularly all along.

Though not part of the Garden story, Genesis 5:29b clarifies the nature of Adam's sentence. There, Lamech explains the role that his son Noah will play in the history of humankind: "This one will comfort us from our works and from the exhaustion of our hands from the earth that YHWH declared diminished."[6] His statement implies that were it not for the divine sentence pronounced over Adam, working the land would entail less toil and exhaustion. The comment about relief anticipates God's statement after the flood in Genesis 8:21a: "I will not continue to curse the ground on account of the human [*leqallēl 'ōwd 'et hā'adāmāh ba'abūwr hā'ādām*]." Notice how the narrator has God use a stronger word, *qallēl*, in this narrative than the *'ārūwrāh*, "diminished," used in the original sentence to Adam in verse 17.

Assuming that God kept his word, we may ask what improved as a result of removal of the status of cursedness or of *'ārūwr*-edness from the ground. To what relief might Israelite farmers point that ancient tradition identified with the fulfillment of Genesis 8:21a?

Thorns and thistles and all manner of hard work had been the lot of Adam in the Garden and outside it, the same lot experienced by Israelite agriculturalists who read and heard the Garden story during the Iron Age. If this remained the situation after the departure from the Garden and after the flood, then it had nothing to do with God's sentence to Adam. The sentence in Genesis 3:17 declaring the soil diminished intended to have Adam, who had achieved the ability to distinguish between preferable and not preferable, think about his work and way of life as gloomy, dulling, and tedious. God's statement five chapters later ameliorated the negative perception for all humanity and likely reflects the common Israelite attitude. For the Israelite audience, the message of Genesis 8:21a was that agriculture does not involve struggling with the ground or overcoming cursed earth. It is simply work, and people must work if they are to succeed in raising what they require to eat. Israelite farmers hearing the Garden story sustained no myths of effortless agriculture. They knew neither Arcadia nor Cockaigne.

The author of Proverbs makes a rustic observation that Israelite farmers must have appreciated, just as their ancient ancestor would have:

I passed the field of a lazy man, by the vineyard of a person lacking sense.

Here, it was all coming up thorns; its surface covered with nettles and
    its stone fence destroyed.
I gazed and I reflected; I saw, and learned a lesson.
A little sleep, a little napping, a little folding of the hands to rest
And your poverty and privation stride and enter like a man of riches.
    (Prov 24:30–34)

EXISTENTIAL GUILT

Consideration of all three sentences of God's pronouncement to Adam
indicates that their main thrust was to reframe and to reinterpret behaviors, experiences, and situations. They were not punishments in the
sense that they worsened or altered any particular situation, but rather
heightenings of awareness that took advantage of the human's acquired
knowledge.

The serpent that crawled and appeared to swallow clods of soil would
continue to crawl, but now he would observe himself as diminished because of what he had done. Isaiah 65:25 indicates that even in an imagined ideal future, serpents will not change their eating habits: "A wolf and
a lamb will graze like one, and a lion, like cattle, will eat straw; and a
serpent, a clod is its food." (See also the expression "they will lick a clod
like the serpent" in Micah 7:17.)

The woman who had toiled, carried a child to term, and experienced
labor would do so again, only now she would focus more on the discomforting pains of childbirth, perceive them as unnaturally exhausting, and
recall what she had done. The man formed to labor would continue to do
so, only now, every thorn and thistle and every bead of sweat dripping
from his nostrils would remind him of his misguided, unthinking, imitative behavior at the tree.[7]

Where once life had only been lived, now life was lived and evaluated.
The penalty for being alert, having open eyes, and knowing the difference
between the acceptable, the desirable, and the appropriate and their
opposites was that the man and the woman would have to live with this
knowledge, experiencing it in mind and body. God's sentences were, in
essence, introductions to what we in the twenty-first century call existential guilt. They were God's way of demonstrating what it meant to know
good and bad, to distinguish between proper and improper. They were
the aftertaste of the fruit.

Although I use "existential guilt" anachronistically, the notion is not eisegesis bred in the post-Freud, post-Sartre, post-modern world. The same phenomenon is attested in Genesis 3:5–6, discussed earlier. There, the serpent's description of the intellectual benefits to be gained by eating the dangling fruit of the tree resulted in the woman's perceiving it differently. Nothing changed physically. The story's author depicted how words created a new perception of reality on which the woman chose to act.

The absence of any real punishments from this story is also understandable in terms of the Israelite law that composed part of the legal background of the author and many generations of his audience.

ADDITIONAL LEGAL ISSUES

Adam, his wife, and at least one son were resident caretakers on a large estate. In return for labor, they had the run of the estate and drew their sustenance from it. Although the landlord had given orders regarding a specific tree, he had not set it apart or isolated it in any way from the other trees in the garden. Furthermore, in addressing serpent, man, and woman, the landlord never referred to the tree possessively as "my tree" nor in any way indicated that it was a different type of property. In the employer-employee context all trees were his trees.

Under these circumstances, the following question is significant for understanding the story: Is it likely that the author of this story and his audience would have perceived that a norm or law had been violated?

The laws of theft in Exodus 21:37–22:3 presuppose that a thief attempted to remove property or livestock belonging to others from a grazing area or building. In these laws, the thief was understood to be either a rustler or a burglar. The laws do not address the theft of produce or the issue of servants or slaves who steal, and we do not know how, or even if, such exigencies were classified or treated under law.

Closer to the case at hand are the laws of Deuteronomy 23:25–26, part of a seventh-century BCE collection reflecting earlier customs. These allow people passing by a vineyard or a stand of ripe grain to pluck grapes or kernels by hand and eat to satiety, but prohibit them from removing any produce for consumption elsewhere.[8] Removal alone, according to these laws, constituted a violation of the owner's property. Resident workers would probably have had even greater rights.

Absent contrary evidence, the case in Eden does not involve theft, misappropriation, or mishandling; there is no mine-yours dichotomy. If the actions of the couple did not fall under the rubric of any particular legal norm within the framework of the story or in the cultural world of the author and his audience, then norms from some other cultural setting should not be imported into the text.[9]

All that was involved in terms of Israelite norms was the willful circumvention of the seemingly arbitrary instruction of a powerful employer-landlord. We may assume that employer-landlords would express displeasure and anger to their employees and dismiss those who did not follow instructions. But that did not happen in the Garden story. Presumably Adam and his wife were still the best gardeners around.

The scene with God did not involve accusations of perpetrating sin or dishonoring God. There was no groveling, confessing, or performing acts of contrition. There was no declaration of forgiveness, no benign action by God that could be considered kind, loving, or merciful. The narrative makes no mention of what happened after the sentences were pronounced.

Imagining the scene, we can see the verbally diminished characters depart: the serpent and its seed into the underbrush, off to hunt for rodents; Hawwa, baby Qayin in her arms, off to take care of his needs, and Adam, head bent after the tongue-lashing, off to conclude his day's labor in the Garden. Aside from the oral castigation, the couple were not disciplined in any way. They maintained their position in God's garden.

The notion that no punishment was meted out despite Adam's wrongdoing underlies a medieval rabbinic midrash, which reads in part: "In the twelfth hour he was pardoned. The Holy One, Blessed is He, said to Adam: 'This is a sign for your children. Just as you stood before me to be judged this day and went out with a pardon, so too will your children stand before me in judgment on this day and will go from before me with a pardon'" (*Leviticus Rabbah* 29:1).[10]

After God sentenced Adam, some time passed until the concluding episode of the Garden story. Life in the Garden went on much as before until God saw the emergence of a potential problem.

22 OUT OF THE GARDEN

(Gen 3:20–24)

Genesis 3

20a   And the human called the name of his woman *ḥawwāh*,
20b   because she was *'ēm kol ḥāy*.
21   And YHWH god made leather tunics for Adam and for his woman;
      and (then) he dressed them.
22   And YHWH god said:
              Behold! The human *hāyāh ke'aḥad mimmennūw* for
                      knowing proper/good and improper/bad; and now,
                      lest he send forth his hand and take also from the
                      Tree of Life and (then) eat and live forever. . . .
23   And YHWH god sent him away from the garden of Eden to
      work the soil from which he was taken.
24   And he expelled the human and settled to the east of the garden
      of Eden the cherubs and the flaming ever-turning sword to
      guard the way to the Tree of Life.

No material in the Garden story suggests that the thought of gaining
immortality ever flitted across a human mind. Had it done so, we have no
reason to think that Adam and Hawwa would have considered it desirable to eat from the Tree of Life, especially after eating from the Tree of
Knowing and learning the implications of that.

The author may have imagined that time elapsed between the Tree of Knowing incident (Gen 3:19) and Adam's renaming of his wife (Gen 3:20)—two years, maybe three. In any event, emerging developments and their attendant circumstances over an extended period of time brought about the couple's abrupt deportation.

In Genesis 3:20, Adam names his wife *ḥawwāh*, that is, Hawwa, providing an etymology in a phrase conventionally translated as "she was the mother of all living" or "the mother of all life." Adam explains this name in the same manner as he clarified why the new creature would be called *'iššāh*, "woman," in Genesis 2:23. What is not obvious from the context here is the event that precipitated his impulse to name her again.

The new sobriquet and Adam's accompanying explanation, including a past tense verb and the word *kōl*, "all/totality/every," would have made no sense within the framework of the story or from an author's perspective if Adam or the author had just Qayin in mind. The new name becomes meaningful, however, if Hebel was conceived and born soon after the couple achieved new insight from the fruit.[1]

The name *ḥawwāh*, derived from the root *ḥ-w-y*, is sometimes associated with the Aramaic word for snake, *ḥiwyā'*. Though possible etymologically, two better explanations are more likely. The snake explanation is unlikely because the word is not part of biblical Hebrew's extensive vocabulary for types of serpents and because widespread Aramaic influence on Hebrew vocabulary began only after 539 BCE, when the land of Israel became part of the Persian empire, which used Aramaic as its official language in conquered lands.

The name *ḥawwāh* is formed in a nominal *qattāl* pattern sometimes used to indicate a person who engages intensively or repeatedly in some activity. For example, *rakkāb*, "charioteer," is one who rides regularly (*r-k-b*); *sabbāl*, "porter," is one who bears a burden regularly (*s-b-l*); *dayyān*, "judge," is one who judges (*d-y-n*); *ḥammāh*, "sun," is always very hot (*ḥ-m-m*); and *ṭabbāḥ*, "butcher," is one who dresses meat regularly (*ṭ-b-ḥ*). The English use of *-er*, reflected in *teacher, preacher, healer,* and *baker*, is comparable. Accordingly, the woman's name may be understood in terms of her procreative role as "one who makes life regularly." It has a parallel in the name of the Phoenician goddess *'štrṯḥwt*, Ashtarthawwat, which means "Ashtart [is] life maker."[2] This possibility, however, does not clarify the explanation of the name provided in the story by the author.

The conventional translation "mother of all living/life" is problematic in that *ḥay* is morphologically singular, suggesting that it is a collective noun. It cannot refer to all living things or every living creature because Hawwa was the mother of humans only.

The word *ḥay* in this expression is cognate to an Arabic noun *ḥayya*, meaning "kin, related members of a clan, descendents of a father or ancestor." The Hebrew and Arabic words are derived from a root *ḥ-y-y*, meaning "to collect, bring, or draw together."[3] This meaning is attested clearly in 1 Samuel 18:18, where David, a Judahite, says to King Saul, a Benjaminite, "who am I and who is *ḥayyay mišpaḥat 'ābīy*, my *ḥay*, the clan of my father, in Israel that I will be the son-in-law of the king." In this verse, the word *ḥay* is glossed by the expression "the clan of my father."[4] It is also attested in 1 Samuel 25:6, where David instructs his men how to address Nabal, a fellow Judahite, "*wa'amartem kōh leḥāy* . . . and you will speak thus to a kinsman: and you are peace and your house is peace, and all that you have is peace."[5] That the editor of 1 Samuel 18:18, the first example in this paragraph, had to provide a definition for the word *ḥāy* indicates that in his day, in the late sixth or early fifth century BCE, he was unsure that his readers would know what it meant.

The proposed etymology clarifies not only the explanation provided for the name but also the name itself. Hawwa's name, *ḥawwāh*, is derived from *ḥ-w-y*—also cognate to *ḥ-y-y*—and refers to related people. Its translation should reflect that fact, and verse 20a, paraphrased expansively, reads: "And he called her Hawwa, that is, Kin-maker, because she was the mother of all kinfolk."[6] Her renaming indicates that as Adam saw his growing sons, he imagined their progeny and their progeny's progeny. His statement places a lock on the meaning of *'ēzer kenegdōw*. Adam's grandchildren would have what he had once lacked: relatives, people who help each other. The owner of the Garden, God, also saw Adam's growing sons and became apprehensive.

The growth of the first family triggered God's concern, expressed in Genesis 3:22, that man might wish to become immortal. (The idea had not yet occurred to the humans in the Garden and never did.) The basis for this concern, not explicit in the Genesis story, is clarified by Mesopotamian epic traditions about the creation and primal history of humans that told of their increase over the face of the earth.[7]

The Atrahasis myth, a literary distillation of Mesopotamian traditions, demonstrates this clearly. It says that after men and women were created by the mother goddess, and the bed prepared, and the wife and husband lay together, and there were people working at their assigned tasks building shrines and canal banks, people multiplied, and "the land was bellowing like a bull."

The racket disturbed divine beings. To lower the decibel level, the gods decided to thin the crowd. They seeded disease in people, decreased vegetation, withheld rain, and sent desiccating winds. After considering the results, they concluded that there were still too many humans. So they tightened the muscles of the birth canal so that babies would die in utero. People were reduced to cannibalism.[8] According to the Gilgamesh story, barren women were created along with an Eradicator demon that snatched babies from the laps of mothers.

In a penetrating study of the juxtaposed themes of human fertility and the divinely ordained culling of humans in these and other myths, Anne D. Kilmer demonstrates that the myths express an embedded Mesopotamian anxiety about overpopulation.[9] The point of the myths, Kilmer concludes, was to justify all forms of infertility, death, and natural disasters as divine winnowing processes that maintained population at an optimal level.[10]

Traces of a similar pattern of thinning population and a concern with overpopulation have been isolated in the primeval history of the Bible: the death of Abel (Gen 3:8), the boast of Lamech (Gen 4:23), and, most important, the flood in the days of Noah (Gen 6–9).[11] This pattern is essentially covert because the moral and uncapricious reasons that justified the flood dominate the Israelite story. The flood was brought because of human violence and corruption and humankind's focus on inappropriate things (Gen 6:3, 5, 11, 12).

The pattern left an overt trace only in Genesis 6:1–3: When "mankind began to increase on the earth and daughters had been born," all of them potential mothers, "YHWH said, my breath will not abide in mankind forever, in that he is flesh; and his days will be one hundred twenty years."[12] Only after humans were living out of the Garden for approximately seven generations—ten generations separate Adam from Noah—was a maximum life span determined. Thus, although elements of the "controlling overpopulation" theme are present in the Israelite material, their function and meaning in the narrative differ from those of similar elements in Mesopotamian literature because of the worldview that nuanced their use.

The theme is latent in the narrative after Adam named his wife the second time. Concern for an overpopulated world, which might lead to the types of miseries that preoccupied the Mesopotamians, led God to make it impossible for self-procreating humankind to achieve immortality.

God's statement in Genesis 3:22 does not express concern that people will become divine; nor does he say that humans became semi-divine by eating of the Tree of Knowing. Verse 22 does not use the construction *hāyāh + le*, "became"; rather, it employs *hāyāh*, a simple past-tense form of the verb "to be" followed by the preposition *ke*, "like," and should be rendered, "Behold, the human was like one of us." He was "like" the category of being to which God and his anonymous addressees belonged, but not identical to those beings. People looked like God because he made them that way. People shared a certain attribute with God: knowing good and bad. If achieved, immortality would simply have been another such attribute.[13] Even Gilgamesh, one-third divine by descent, died, as did other partially divine characters in Mesopotamian mythology.[14]

Martin Buber proposed that God had every reason to assume that humans might eventually wish to find the Tree of Life. After encountering death and experiencing it as undesirable, *rā'*, they might decide to avoid it and replace it with something preferable, *ṭōb*.[15] Since the fruit from that tree had not been prohibited, there would have been no reason not to experiment with it. In attempting to avoid one *rā'*, humans might have achieved immortality, resulting, according to God's calculus, in an even greater *rā'*. Instructing the people not to eat from the tree would have been difficult. With what could he threaten them? Death? A life of labor? Besides, humans knowing *ṭōb* and *rā'* had turned into rhetoricians and lawyers before his eyes.

Immortality was not achieved and never would be. The prophet Ezekiel, speaking in the sixth century BCE against the king of Tyre, imagined the king in a bejeweled Eden (very unlike the one in the Garden story), declaring, "I am a god" (Ezek 28:2, 13). Ezekiel quoted YHWH's condemnation of this king: "Because you have deemed your mind like the mind of God, I swear I will bring strangers against you . . . they shall unsheathe their swords against your wonderful wisdom . . . they shall bring you down to the Pit . . . you shall die. . . . Will you still say 'I am a god' before your killers and 'you are a human and not a god' against the hands of those striking you down?" (Ezek 28:7–9). The Israelite comprehension of the nature of things was that humans die.

The first humans were sent into the world beyond Eden not in anger and not as punishment, but in an act of kindness. Buber referred to God's act as a "stern benefaction" that saved man from "eating himself into aeons of suffering."[16]

In *The Annals of the World*, James Ussher (1581–1656), archbishop of Armagh, calculated that Adam and Hawwa departed from their original homeland on Monday, November 10, 4004 BCE, just when winter begins in the land of Israel. In anticipation, even before declaring his concern aloud, God acted preemptively. No sooner had Adam renamed his wife than God prepared skin tunics for them.

People know where leather comes from. Genesis 3:21 implies that God slaughtered and skinned the animals, dressed and softened the hides, and cut and sewed the hides into tunics, thereby modeling the use of animal hides for the good of humans and solving their dual problem of public nakedness and protection from the elements. In the world beyond the Garden, the place into which he was about to send them, there were other people, and the fig-leaf solution, questionably adequate for private nakedness, necessitated serious refinement. Adam's exercise in renaming may have provided God with an additional consideration for clothing them: since children were multiplying and growing up, it was necessary that the adults be covered properly.

This particular detail gains poignancy when considered in the light of an Akkadian expression in legal wills from Nuzi in the seventeenth century BCE: "to strip the garment and to drive out / go out naked." This expression refers to the ritual dismissal of the wife of the deceased if she committed some offense when the husband was still alive, such as living with another man, or declaring that he was not her husband. Her punishment was public shaming through nakedness even as she was expelled from the family unit.[17] This custom persisted in the ancient Near East, and Israelites continued it. It is reflected in a speech of the prophet Hosea from the middle of the eighth century BCE: "she is not my wife and I am not her husband. Let her put aside her harlotry . . . and her adultery lest I strip her naked and leave her as on the day of her birth" (Hosea 2:4–5).

Read against this background, God's garbing of the humans before compelling the family's move into the wide world indicates that his motivations were neither hostile nor aggressive but concerned and caring. His was not an act of retribution or repudiation. The story of their departure into the world also provided ancient Israelite readers an etiology, not for the origin of death, since the first human was formed as a being that would eventually die, but for the lack of access to immortality.

A similar comprehension of immortality is attested in Canaanite culture before the onset of Israelite history. The Ugaritic myth of Aqhat relates that the goddess Anat tried to tempt Aqhat into giving her his magnificent, divinely constructed bow by offering him "deathlessness." He responded that she must be lying because mortals are destined to die:

> Do not lie to me, O Virgin. Stop.
> For a hero, your lies are disgusting.
> What does man receive at his end?
> Whiteness is poured on his head;
> Whiteness on top of his skull.
> The death of all I will die.
> Indeed I will die.[18]

A like attitude is reflected in the Old Babylonian version of the Gilgamesh story where the alewife, Siduri, explains the facts of life to the hero:

> The alewife spoke to him, to Gilgamesh,
> "Gilgamesh, where do you roam?
> You will not find the eternal life you seek.
> When the gods created mankind,
> They appointed death for mankind,
> Kept eternal life in their own hands."[19]

This attitude contrasts with the one in other Mesopotamian tales of frustrated attempts by partial humans, Adapa and Gilgamesh, to achieve immortality. In both the Adapa and the Gilgamesh myths, the hero almost gained immortality but failed to achieve it through lack of either prowess or wit. The presupposition of these two stories is that the lot of every person, even of heroes, is to be mortal, because people cannot partake of mortality's antidote.

The myth of Adapa deals with the question of immortality, but the fragmentary nature of extant text makes interpretation uncertain. The tale hinges on whether or not Adapa, a wise man who introduced proper cultic rites to the ancient Sumerians, would gain eternal life. At one point in the story, the god Anu proffers Adapa the bread and water of life, but advised by his father Ea that these would be the bread and water of death, Adapa refuses. The story is open to various interpretations.

Either the god Ea tricked Adapa, wanting to retain control over him, or the god Anu, anticipating Adapa's refusal to accept death, fooled him by substituting the bread and water of life for the bread and water of death. The tablet on which the tale is inscribed is broken one line after the following exchange between a laughing Anu and a bewildered Adapa:

> Come, Adapa, why didn't you eat? Why didn't you drink?
>> Didn't you want to be immortal?
>> Alas for downtrodden people!
> (But) Ea my lord told me: You mustn't eat! You mustn't
>> drink![20]

No matter how Ea's intention is interpreted—Ea was a trickster—the supposition of this myth is that a certain human in the past had an opportunity to become immortal, though not divine, and acted on it unsuccessfully.[21] Trying to achieve immortality is not a theme in the Garden narrative or in any other biblical story.

One final example from Mesopotamian lore reflects the same motif. In the standard, seventh-century BCE version of the *Gilgamesh Epic,* based on many earlier Gilgamesh traditions, a silent serpent stole Gilgamesh's plant of rejuvenation—not immortality—from him. Gilgamesh, however, unlike Adapa, was bringing the plant back to the city of Uruk, where he planned to share it with people and then eat of it himself.[22]

Gilgamesh spoke about the plant to the boatman Ur-shanabi:

"Ur-shanabi, this plant is a plant to cure a crisis!
  With it a man may win the breath of life.
  I shall take it back to Uruk the Sheepfold; I shall give it to an elder to eat,
    and so try out the plant.
  Its name (shall be): 'An old man grows into a young man.'
  I too shall eat (it) and turn into the young man that I was once."
  At twenty leagues they ate their ration.
  At thirty leagues they stopped for the night.
  Gilgamesh saw a pool whose water was cool,
  And went down into the water and washed.
  A snake smelt the fragrance of the plant.
  It came up silently and carried off the plant.
  As it took it away, it shed its scaly skin.

Thereupon Gilgamesh sat down and wept.
His tears flowed over his cheeks.[23]

   This story contrasts with the Genesis account on a crucial point. In Genesis there was no quest for immortality, just as there had been no initial quest for knowledge. Within the frame of the Garden story, the issue of immortality was raised and decided before it dawned in human awareness. The first family was never informed about the reasons for their coerced exodus.

   Although individual scholars interpret these Mesopotamian myths somewhat differently, a common theme underlies most interpretations. Arvid S. Kapelrud suggests that in the ancient Near East the lack of immortality placed humans in a tragic situation. On the basis of clues from the stories of Gilgamesh and Adapa, he infers that the pains of mortal life are illness, loneliness, lack of helpers, hopelessness, poverty, and fatal events.[24] N. Vulpa interprets the Gilgamesh story as expressing a coming to terms with mortality and its attendant woes, but with moments of comfort.[25] Thorkild Jacobsen sees in these and other stories a range of attitudes toward death from the fatalistic acceptance of the unavoidable to a bewildering lack of comprehension about what death implies.[26] These encapsulated statements distill into a consensus. Individuals who wrote these stories, and the Mesopotamian societies that told them, accepted their lot, but it was the lot of losers.

   In the Garden story, however, mortality of the individual is perceived as a prerequisite for the species to live. That Israelite culture considered God's decision a good one is evident in the woman's comment after the birth of her first child in Genesis 4:1: "I have created a man with YHWH." Her comment in Genesis 4:25 after the birth of her third son, Seth, also reflects a positive approach to a life lived with the knowledge of eventual death. Explaining why she named her third son Seth, Hawwa is cited as saying: "God has set for me another seed in place of Hebel because Qayin killed him." She recognizes that younger can replace older, that generations overlap, and that information and knowledge gained through experience can be transmitted.

   After quoting Hawwa, the author comments that Seth had a son Enosh, whose name means "humanity," and that in Enosh's lifetime people "began to invoke the name YHWH" (Gen 4:26). Prior to that, only Hawwa had uttered the name aloud after the birth of Qayin (Gen

4:1). Somehow—the text does not explain how—the private name of God had become known to people generations before the flood. From the author's perspective, these were all human steps in the right direction.

God set cherubs to guard the entrance to the Garden to be sure that his plan would work, that the first family would live and fend for themselves outside the Garden, away from the Tree of Life. Cherubs, known in Akkadian as *kāribu* or *kiribu*, had the bodies of winged lions and human heads. Mesopotamian archaeologists have unearthed their images flanking entrances to important rooms in palaces and temples, where they served usually as paired stone sentries. To prevent brazen trespassers or lost wayfarers from happening upon the path to the Tree of Life, God also blocked the way with a deadly sword. From the vantage point of Israelites, the world in which they lived, the world beyond Eden, was God's gift to humanity, appointed for people in a decision based on his concern for their well-being.

Adam and Hawwa left the Garden, traveling in the direction of the rising sun, and they never looked back.

PART THREE

Then and Now

Now and then there are readings that make the hairs on the neck, the non-existent pelt, stand on end and tremble, when every word burns and shines hard and clear and infinite and exact, like stones of fire, like points of stars in the dark—readings when the knowledge that we *shall know* the writing differently or better or satisfactorily, runs ahead of any capacity to say what we know, or how. In these readings, a sense that the text has appeared to be wholly new, never before seen, is followed almost immediately, by the sense that it was *always there*, that we the readers, knew it was always there, and have *always known* it was as it was, though we have now for the first time recognised, become fully cognisant of, our knowledge.

—A. S. Byatt, Possession (1990)

23 THE ESSENTIAL PLOT OF THE GARDEN STORY

The analyses in the preceding chapters give us a revised plot of the Garden story, one stripped of its Greek and later accretions. Reprised in modern English, the story goes like this.

THE PLOT

God planned a garden for himself in a place called Eden, a name meaning "Bountiful," located in the most distant northern corner of the world as it was known to ancient Israel. Far off the beaten track in what is now eastern Turkey, the Garden contained many fruit-bearing trees, among which two were special: the Tree of Knowing Good and Bad and the Tree of Life. Grains such as wheat and barley and other edible field plants grew around the Garden (Chapters 7–8).

God made Adam as part of his original plan to have a resident gardener. Formed by God from a clod of wetted soil and vivified by his breath, the human differed from all the inanimate objects that filled God's garden. As an individual, he was a special focus of God's attention (Chapters 6, 9).

The human was set to work in God's garden, employing his innate skills and natural ability to figure things out. Presumably, in addition to caring for the trees in God's garden, Adam provided his own necessities by cultivating cereals and gathering edible plants around the garden.

God told his gardener to eat fruit from all the trees but qualified his words with an oblique instruction that Adam not eat from the Tree of Knowing. To this qualification, God appended a vague threat of death if Adam were to ignore the instruction not to eat from that tree. Although the narrator describes the instruction and qualification as a command, the actual words that Adam heard did not constitute a formal command (Chapters 7, 10).

Time passed. God, observing the singularity of the human, concluded that it was not good for him to be by himself. So he decided that Adam required a reliable helper, like a kinsman, but he was unsure exactly what this helper might be. God first made animals, hoping that Adam would find such a helper among them, but the human found them all unacceptable as his helper. God then constructed a creature from Adam's baculum that he accepted as his helper, a woman whom Adam eventually called Hawwa, a name translatable as "Kin-maker."

Adam and Hawwa worked in the garden oblivious to their nakedness. They cohabited sexually and had at least their first son, Qayin. Adam experienced the hard work of a gardener and a grain farmer, and Hawwa experienced natural childbirth (Chapters 11–14, 18).

Time passed. The serpent, one of the creatures formed by God for Adam when he was trying to find a helper for him, engaged Hawwa in a conversation in the vicinity of the Tree of Knowing. With clever rhetoric and linguistic sophistication, the serpent mentioned the intellectual benefits that Hawwa would gain if she were to eat fruit from the tree that God had instructed Adam not to eat from. To clinch his argument, the serpent indicated that despite what God had said about dying to Adam, she would not die if she consumed this fruit. Driven by a desire for the knowledge of good and bad and convinced by the serpent that she would suffer no ill, Hawwa ate. Then she wordlessly gave the fruit to nearby Adam, who, following her example, ate also (Chapter 15).

Both Hawwa and Adam gained knowledge, as the serpent had said. Now understanding that it was inappropriate for them to be stark naked, even though they were alone, they devised girdles of fig leaves to conceal their genitals and buttocks from each other's view.

Later, when they heard the sound of God moving around in the garden, they concealed themselves because they knew that it was inappropriate to be seen by a third person wearing only their makeshift girdles, a sort of underwear. More appropriate raiment was required before they could be seen in public by a third party.

God understood from their self-concealment and from Adam's words, "I feared because I was naked," that they had eaten from the tree. When queried, Adam admitted eating the fruit but implicated God by pointing out that he had given him the woman, the very Hawwa who had handed Adam the fruit. She had misappropriated the fruit; he had not.

The woman in turn implicated the serpent, who had informed her in a roundabout way that she would not be in violation of the instruction directed to Adam were she to take and eat fruit from the tree, nor would Adam be in violation of it were they to eat together. Each pointed finger constituted more than an attempt to deflect blame; it also constituted an implicit defense against charges of culpability based (1) on the language of God's original instructions to Adam and (2) on the specific circumstances of what had actually occurred at the Tree of Knowing (Chapters 16–17).

Distraught at having his plans upset, yet accepting the convoluted arguments of the couple, God addressed sentences to the serpent, Hawwa, and Adam. These did not result in any physical change or harm but did compel each to perceive some element of her or his life differently and somewhat negatively. Though chastised, they were not punished. They had not done nothing deserving of punishment (Chapters 18–21).

Time passed. Adam and Hawwa continued to work in the Garden and eventually had another child. God became concerned. The Garden that he had designed with only a single human gardener in mind was now home to four people. Moreover, it also contained the second special tree, the Tree of Life, about which the humans had not yet thought. It was theoretically possible for his Garden to become overpopulated, a circumstance that would devastate the people about whom he cared and destroy his garden. So he provided the adults in the first family with proper attire and sent them out of his Garden into the large world east of Eden, where other people were already living. He did so not in anger and not as a punishment, but out of concern for their future well-being (Chapter 22).

IMPLICATIONS

This skeletal retelling of the Garden story in a most non-traditional manner rests on the justifying details provided in Part II. Those details provide the cultural and linguistic matrix within which the Garden story was originally told and understood. They substantiate the argument that the Garden story was not the story of a Fall.

A new translation based in these details is presented in the next chapter.

The final chapters of this book, based on this new interpretation and on the new translation, cite evidence in the form of biblical passages illustrating that ancient Israelites understood the Garden story as a positive and optimistic one.

24 A LITERAL TRANSLATION OF A LITERARY TEXT

Genesis 2

4a These are the generation of the heavens and the earth
in their being created.

4b On the day of YHWH's making earth and heavens
5 and every plant of the field was not yet in the earth
and every edible plant of the field had not yet sprouted
because YHWH had not made it rain on the earth
and no human existed to work the soil
6 but a surge of water ascending from the earth
and it watered all the face/surface of the soil
7 and (then) YHWH formed the human,
a clod from the soil,
and he blew into his nostrils the breath of life,
and the human became a living soul.
8 And YHWH planted a garden in Eden, at the east,
and placed there the human that he had formed.

9 And YHWH caused to sprout from the soil every tree
desirable for seeing and good for eating,
and the Tree of Life within the garden,
and the Tree of Knowing proper/good and improper/bad.

•

10 And a river goes out from Eden to water the garden.
And from there it divides and becomes four head(water)s.

11 The name of the first, Pishon.
> It (is the one) that curves by all the land of
> Havilah where there is gold.

12
>> And the gold of that land is good.
>> Bdellium is there and onyx stone.

13 And the name of the second river, Gihon.
> It (is the one) that curves by all the land of Kush.

14 And the name of the third river, Hidekel (Tigris).
> It (is the one) that flows east of Ashur.
And the fourth river, it is Perat (Euphrates).

15 And YHWH took the human
and placed him in the garden of Eden
to work it and to guard it.

16 And YHWH commanded restraining the human saying:
> From every tree of the garden, eating you will eat,

17
> but from the Tree of Knowing proper/good and
> improper/bad—you will not eat from it;
> because, on the day of your eating from it,
> dying you will die.

18 And YHWH said:
> The human, being by himself is not good.
> I will make for him a helper like his kin.

19 And YHWH formed from the soil
every animal of the field
and every flying creature of the heavens,
and he brought each to the human to see what he would call it.
And all that the human would call it, the living soul,
that is its name.

20 And the human called names to every herd animal
and flying creature of the heavens
and to every animal of the field;
but for the human he did not find a helper like his kin.

21 And (so) YHWH made a heavy slumber fall on the
human and he slept;
and he took one of his lateral limbs and he closed flesh beneath it.

22 And YHWH built the lateral limb that he took from the
human into a woman,
and he brought her to the human.

23 And (then) the human said:
> This one. This time.
> Bone from my bones and flesh from my flesh.
> This one will be called "Woman"
> because from man this one was taken.

24 Therefore a man supports his father and his mother
and clings to his woman/wife, and they become one flesh.

25 And the two of them were naked,
the human and his woman,
but they were not ashamed of each other.

Genesis 3

1 And the serpent had been more shrewd than every animal
of the field that YHWH made, and he said to the woman:
> Even, indeed/though, God said:
>> You will not eat from every tree of the
>> garden . . .

2 And the woman said to the serpent:
> From the fruit of trees of the garden we eat
3 but from the fruit of the tree that is within the
garden, God said:
>> You will not eat from it
>> and you will not touch it
>> lest you will surely die.

4 And the serpent said to the woman:
> No dying you will surely die.
5 Indeed, God knows that on the day of your eating from it,
your eyes will open themselves
and you will be like God,
knowers of proper/good and improper/bad.

6 And the woman saw (that) indeed the tree (is) good for eating
and appetizing for the eyes,
and the tree (is) desirable for enwisening.

And she took from its fruit and ate,
and she gave also to her man (who was) with her,
and he ate.

7   And the eyes of both opened themselves
and they knew that they were naked;
and (then) they sewed fig leaves
and made for themselves loincloths.

8   And they heard the sound of YHWH moving back and forth
in the garden at the wind of the day.
And the human and his woman concealed themselves from
before YHWH within a tree of the garden.

9   And YHWH called to the human and said to him:
> Where are you?

10   And he said:
> I heard your sound in the garden
> and I feared because I was naked
> and (so) I hid myself.

11   And he said:
> Who told you that you are naked?
> Have you eaten from the tree concerning which I
> commanded you to not eat from it?

12   And the human said:
> The woman that you gave (to be) with me,
> she gave for me from the tree
> and (so) I ate.

13   And YHWH said to the woman:
> What is this that you did?
And the woman said:
> The serpent beguiled me,
> and (so) I ate.

14   And YHWH said to the serpent:
> Because you did this, you are diminished/weakened from
> every herd animal and from every animal of the field.
> On your belly you move,
> and a clod you eat all the days of your life.

15   > And I place enmity
> between you and between the woman,

and between your seed and between her seed.

He presses you (at the) head,

and you press him (at the) heel.

16 To the woman he said:

Multiplying I multiply

your exhaustion and your pregnancy.

In fatigue you will birth children.

And to your man is your desirability,

but he will rule you.

17 And to Adam he said:

Because you paid attention to your woman

and you ate from the tree concerning which I

commanded you saying:

You will not eat from it,

Diminished/weakened is the soil on your account.

In exhaustion you will eat from it

all the days of your life.

18 And thorn and thistle it will sprout for you;

but you will eat edible plants of the field.

19 By the sweat of your nostrils you will eat food

until you return to the soil

because you were taken from it.

Indeed, you are a clod and to a clod you return.

20 And the human called the name of his woman "Hawwa"
because she was the mother of all kinfolk.

21 And YHWH made leather tunics for Adam and for his
woman; and (then) he dressed them.

22 And YHWH said:

Behold! The human was like one of us for knowing

proper/good and improper/bad;

and now, lest he send forth his hand

and take also from the Tree of Life

and (then) eat and live forever. . . .

23 And YHWH sent him away from the garden of Eden
to work the soil from where he was taken.

24 And he expelled the human
and settled to the east of the garden of Eden the cherubs

and the flaming ever-turning sword
to guard the way to the Tree of Life.

Genesis 4

1   But the human had known Hawwa, his woman, and she had
    conceived and birthed Qayin.
    And she said:
            I have created a man with YHWH.
2   And she continued to birth his brother Hebel.
    And Hebel was a shepherd,
        but Qayin had been a worker of the soil.

The typical artistic and structural features of biblical narrative discerned and described by biblical scholars for almost a century characterize this narrative.[1] It contains alliterative patterning throughout:
śīyaḥ haśśādeh (edible plant of the field—Gen 2:5), *'ādām, 'adāmāh, 'ēd*
(human, soil, surge of water—Gen 2:5-6), *wayyippaḥ be'appā(y)w* (blew
into his nostrils—Gen 2:7), *'īyš, 'iššāh* (man, woman—Gen 2:23), *hannāḥāš*
hiššīy'anīy (the serpent beguiled me—Gen 3:13), *pen yišlaḥ . . . welāqaḥ* (lest
he send forth . . . and take—Gen 3:22), *wayyešalleḥēhūw . . . luqqaḥ* (he
sent him away. . . . he was taken—Gen 3:23), and *lahaṭ haḥereb hamithap-
peket* (the flaming, ever-turning sword—Gen 3:24),

Considered broadly, following an introduction (Gen 2:4b-7), the story
is enveloped by the theme of humanity's placement in (Gen 2:8-15) and
expulsion from the Garden (Gen 3:22-24). It is framed by repetitive or
echoing phrases that provide verbal definitions of its boundaries, recurring key words that emphasize—perhaps too obviously for modern taste—
what the narrator considered important, and some repeated expressions
that provide cohesive compactness to the tale. For example, the story
is framed by the motif of the "garden at the east." In Genesis 2:8, it is
planned and planted somewhere in the *east* of a territory known as Eden.
The human made and brought from elsewhere was placed in it as worker
and guard. In Genesis 3:24, cherubs are settled *east* of the Garden to
guard it from the expelled humans should they try to return to the Tree
of Life within the Garden.

Similarly, Genesis 2:5, 6, 7, and 8 narrate that the human formed from
the *'adāmāh,* "soil," somewhere outside the Garden was destined to work
the soil in the Garden; Genesis 3:17, 18, and 19 indicate that this very human

was then sent from the Garden to work soil elsewhere until he died and returned to the soil from which he was taken.

Genesis 2:5 and 3:23 both contain the expressions "YHWH" and "to work the soil." They create a thematic envelope, or *inclusio*, around the story through the striking echo of their vocabulary.

Word order in the two sentences describing the watering of the soil to make it malleable (Gen 2:6) and the watering of the garden to make it fruitful (Gen 2:10a) is identical. Similar vocabulary in both sentences reinforces their thematic coherence as well as the link between the human as artifact and the Garden as artifice.

Clod is the key word linking the motif of the formation of the human, Genesis 2:7, with that of his eventual demise, Genesis 3:19, as well as with the judgment of the serpent in Genesis 3:14. Words for "seeing" and "eating," more the latter than the former, resound throughout different scenes of the story—Genesis 2:9, 16; 3:1, 2, 3, 5, 6, 11, 12, 13, 14, 17, 18—weaving it into a patterned, thematic unity. Through consumption humans enhanced perception.

Genesis 2:17, God's instruction to Adam, employs the phrase, "the day of your [singular] eating," while Genesis 3:5, the serpent's prognosis of what will occur after ingestion, modifies it: "the day of your [plural] eating."

The expressions "every animal of the field" and "every flying creature of the heavens" in Genesis 2:19 recur chiastically, that is, in reverse order, in verse 20, with the reference to "herd animals" thrown in to soften what might appear a clunky mechanical repetition. However, in Genesis 3:12 and 3:13, the mechanical repetition of the phrase "so I ate" augments the banality of the human responses within the staccato dialogue of inquiry and buck-passing.

During the sentencing episode of the story, Genesis 3:9–19, interviews proceed from Adam to Hawwa, skipping the serpent; sentences to the perpetrators, however, are delivered in reverse order, beginning with the serpent, thus balancing and rounding out the scene. The word *zō't*, "this," referring to what the woman had done, is used first in Genesis 3:13, the last interview scene, and is repeated with the same referent in 3:14, the serpent's sentence.

The author follows the divine name YHWH throughout with the descriptor *'elōhīym*, "god." These words are translated "YHWH god" (see also Gen 2:4, 5, 7, 8, 9; 3:1, 8). The characters in the narrative, however, differ in their forms of reference to God. The serpent never uses the personal name, but refers to his maker, perhaps deferentially, by the term *'elōhīym,* alone (Gen 3:1, 5). Hawwa, responding to him, follows suit (Gen 3:3); but in Genesis 4:1, after giving birth to Qayin, she makes a very personal statement that bespeaks intimacy and closeness: "I have created a man with YHWH."

These aesthetic and structuring elements were part of the conventional array of devices used in ancient Israelite narrative. The author of the Garden story used them to construct a didactic literary tale that instilled in its Israelite audience an implicit anthropology of humanity. It taught them that the life they lived as agriculturalists able to fend for themselves was natural. Shakespeare expressed it this way in *Hamlet:* "There is no ancient gentlemen but gardeners, ditchers, and grave-makers; they held up Adam's profession." The story instructed Israelites that their basic social unit, the extended family within a clan, their standards of modesty, their living, their birthing, and their dying was like the life of all people.[2]

Despite unavoidable peculiarities owing to the unique formation and manufacture of the primordial ancestors of all living humanity known to ancient Israelites, Adam and Hawwa, now long dead, had lived that life also.

25 ALLUSIONS TO THE GARDEN STORY IN THE HEBREW BIBLE

The Garden story, told in the book of Genesis, is alluded to in other parts of the Bible. Indeed, favorable allusions to the story illustrate clearly that a wide range of biblical authors knew it and understood it positively.

PROPHETS AND PSALMS

Isaiah of Jerusalem, a prophet of the late eighth to early seventh centuries BCE, describes a future in which a descendent of David will put evil to death by proclamation (Isa 11:3). As a consequence, predation, a feature of created nature, will cease; the natural order will be reformed:

> A wolf will dwell with a lamb,
> and a leopard will lie down with a kid,
> and a calf and lion and fatling, together [will lie down],
> and a small lad leads them.
> And a cow and bear will graze together;
> their young will lie down;
> and the lion will eat hay like cattle.
> And a suckling will play by the hole of an asp;
> and over the adder's den, a weaned child
> will stretch out his hand. (Isa 11:6–8)

The concluding lines that connect infant humans with asps and adders alludes to the natural, even innate enmity—whatever its roots—between serpents and humans spelled out in Genesis 3. In this futuristic nature, Isaiah imagined that serpents would no longer be perceived as enemies of humans, just as predators would no longer attack their "natural" prey.

The anonymous sixth-century BCE prophet whom scholars call Second Isaiah or Isaiah of the exile undertook to comfort his people after the destruction of Jerusalem and the exile of 586. In one speech he describes restored Jerusalem in language evoking images of Eden and its garden:

> Indeed, YHWH comforted Jerusalem,
> comforted all her ruins;
> and he made her wilderness like Eden,
> her grazing land like the garden of YHWH;
> gladness and joy will be found within her,
> thanks and the sound of music. (Isa 51:3)

In another prophecy, Second Isaiah alludes to Adam's labor, Hawwa's giving birth, Hebel's meaningless death, and the serpent. He combines them with the image of an idealized Eden created by Isaiah of Jerusalem that is cited at the beginning of this section. In the words of Second Isaiah, the sentences represented desired outcomes for human undertakings:

> They will not toil for nothing;
> they will not give birth for misfortune,
> because they are the blessed seed of YHWH
> and their descendents with them.
> And it will be; before they call, I will respond;
> they are yet speaking and I hear.
> A lamb and a kid will graze like one;
> and the lion, like cattle, will eat straw;
> and the serpent, a clod is his food. (Isa 65:23–25)

In a rather difficult verse, the prophet Zechariah, who spoke circa 520–500 BCE, describes a prophet who denies that he is a prophet and asserts that he is a farmer:

> I am not a prophet.
> I am a man working the soil like Adam.
> He created me [thus] from my youth. (Zech 13:5)[1]

The prophet alludes to Genesis 2:5, 7, and 4:1–2 to justify being a farmer. The reference to Adam as the prototypical agriculturalist is positive.[2]

Similarly, the book of Job, written sometime between 550 and 350 BCE, contains a mention of Adam as a prototypical laborer in a passage whose exact meaning remains unclear but seems positive overall:

> From *'āpār* [a clod], iniquity does not go forth;
> and from *'adāmāh* [soil], labor does not sprout;
> for *'ādām* [Adam], was born to labor
> as the sons of Resheph fly high. (Job 5:6–7)[3]

The image of Eden, "Bountiful," as a place from which nurturing rivers flow in different directions is developed by the prophet Ezekiel, who spoke circa 592–570 BCE. In a vision of the restored Temple, he apparently refers—the verses are not clear—to two streams flowing from under the Temple platform to the Sea of the Arabah, the Dead Sea. Their waters give rise to verdure and animal life and turn the Dead Sea into a living sea (Ezek 47:1–12). In Ezekiel's imagery, the Temple in Jerusalem functions as a relocated Eden. This parallels an image in Psalm 46:5 of "a river whose branches make God's city happy, the holy dwelling of the Most High."

Zechariah, who spoke approximately two generations after Ezekiel, developed the same image and spoke about two rivers that one day would continually flow from Jerusalem, one east to the Dead Sea and one west to the Mediterranean. They were destined to turn the whole country into a garden spot (Zech 14:8–11).

The river images in Psalm 46:5, Ezekiel, and Zechariah are not based on an exaggeration of any artesian well in Jerusalem or of any rivulet that flowed through the city. The sole natural source of water in Jerusalem during the First Temple period was the Gihon Spring, which still flows in the Kidron Valley, at the bottom of the city's eastern slope, far from the Temple. Since the Gihon does not gush up within the city and is not mentioned by name, the images cannot be based on it. The only Israelite story known to me whose imagery could have fructified the imaginations of the ancient poets is the Garden story.

Some psalms refer to the Garden story. One mentions the natural mortality of Adam and refers to the divine beings of Genesis 3:5b—according to the interpretation of *'elōhīym* as divine beings—and Genesis 3:22–23, where God expressed his concern about eternal life:

> I thought you were divine beings;
> and sons of the Most High, all of you.
> However, *ke'ādām* [like Adam], you will surely die,
> and like one of the officers, you will fall. (Ps 82:6–7)

Another psalm refers to the status of man vis-à-vis divine beings, directly mentioning God's statement in Genesis 3:22: "Behold, the human was like one of us." The psalm unabashedly compares humans to divine beings:

> What is a human that you are mindful of him
> and a son of Adam that you take account of him?
> You made him slightly less than divine beings.
> You crowned him with glory and majesty.
> You set him as ruler over what your hands made.
> Everything you placed under his feet. (Ps 8:5–7)

Psalm 103:14, Jeremiah 1:5, and Isaiah 44:2, 24 allude to Genesis 2:7: God's forming, *y-ṣ-r*, of the human. Psalm 104:14 refers to the situation described in Genesis 2:5 and 3:18b–19 and employs the same vocabulary in a context of divine beneficence: You cause the fodder to sprout for animals, and the edible plants for the work of the human (*hā'ādām*).

Psalm 139:13 alludes to Genesis 4:1b, the formation/creation (*q-n-h*) of a person as due to both God and his mother. Psalm 144:3–4 alludes generally to the Garden story and the death of Hebel. The psalmodic allusions emphasize the createdness of humans and their natural mortality.[4] Although Psalms 22:10 and 71:6 do not allude to the story, they express the notion that God is involved in protecting children even in the womb, an idea congruent with Hawwa's statement in Genesis 4:2.[5]

WISDOM TRADITIONS AND LADY WISDOM

Savants of the Israelite wisdom traditions—scholars seeking the universal principles of deportment that lead to what both people and God consider worldly success—eisegeted the *waw* in Genesis 2:9b as a *waw explicativum*, the Hebrew equivalent of Latin *id est* or of the English expression "that is (to say)": "and a Tree of Life in the middle of the garden, that is, a Tree of Knowing proper/good and improper/bad." Construing it for their own reasons *against* the overt sense of the narrative and fusing the two trees into one enabled them to refer to "Wisdom" as a "Tree of Life" (Prov 3:18; 11:30; 13:12; 15:4).

> Happy is a human who finds Wisdom
>> and a human who achieves insight.
>
> .   .   .
>
> Length of days is in her [Wisdom's] right hand,
>> and in her left hand, wealth and honor.
> Her paths are paths of pleasantness
>> and all her ways are peaceful.
> A Tree of Life is she for those who grasp her,
>> and whoever grasps her is happy. (Prov 3:13, 16–18)

Proper acts are likened to a "Tree of Life." In Proverbs 11:30, "the fruits of a righteous person," that is, the acts of a person who acts within the law, are like such a tree. In Proverbs 15:4, "a healing tongue," that is, the words of one who speaks gently and honestly to others, is "a Tree of Life."[6]

Psalm 1, also a wisdom composition, employs the image of "a tree planted by streams of water, which gives fruit in season, whose leaves do not shrivel," as a simile for the good man who shuns evil and desires only the teachings of God (Ps 1:3), as does Jeremiah 17:8 for the man who trusts God. These appropriations of a one-tree motif do not allude directly to the story, but they illustrate how the verdant tree image developed into a powerfully positive image for people who distinguish between good and bad.[7]

These examples indicate that the Israelite wisdom traditions with their universalistic orientation considered the Garden story to be about cultural heroes. If so, it would have been easy for those attuned to wisdom themes to create associations between the Garden story and Hawwa out in the world. She could have been seen as chastised by but reflective of her experiences, as wisdom personified—as ḥokmāh, sometimes rendered "Lady Wisdom," in Proverbs 8. Throughout Proverbs 8, Lady Wisdom's ruminations could be understood as harking back to prior experiences as if she were Hawwa:

> To you men, I call out.
> My voice is for the children of Adam.
> Understand shrewdness, naive ones
> and stupid ones, understand [the contents of a] mind.

I Lady Wisdom dwelt with shrewdness.
I find knowledge of plots.
Fear of YHWH [is] hating badness,
pride and arrogance, and the way of badness.
And I hate the duplicitous mouth. (Prov 8:4–5, 12–13)

Lady Wisdom is not atypical in the Bible. Women, much more than men, appear as wise characters in biblical narratives, and their wisdom seems to owe more to the serpent, perhaps a feminine creature, than to the woman's attainments. Rebecca (Gen 27), Tamar (Gen 38:11–30), Rahab (Josh 2:1–21), Achsah (Josh 15:16–19; Judg 1:12–15), Jael (Judg 4:17–22), Abigail (1 Sam 25:14–42), the woman from Abel (2 Sam 12:10–22), the woman from Tekoa (2 Sam 14:1–20), Bathsheba (1 Kings 1:1–40), Jezebel (1 Kings 21:1–16), and Lady Folly (Prov 7)—these women are all examples. They are not relevant to my analysis, however, because no key words or allusions connect them explicitly to the Genesis narrative, but they are a form of social commentary. With the exception of Jezebel and Lady Folly, all are portrayed positively.[8] As portrayed by the author of the Garden story, Hawwa emerged from the same cultural milieu that generated literary presentations of these other wise women.

The Garden story's connection with wisdom is not merely thematic. Wisdom is actually embedded in the vocabulary of the story with its words and syntagms for knowing, understanding, perceiving, influencing, craftiness, and verbal deception. The faults of all its characters are explained through words, words that beget understanding and misunderstanding, words that frame and focus perceptions of reality, and words that mitigate and transform situations from *ra'* to *ṭōwb*, from bad to good.

ECCLESIASTES

Only one book in the Bible may be considered an extended meditation on the theme of human life in the world after God's sentences: Ecclesiastes, composed between the late fourth and early third century BCE. The author of this book accepted the story's conceptualization of human destiny as anchored in physical labor, but he extended it to include all manner of human pursuits. He was concerned with ethical and moral questions created by human behavior in society and puzzled by the lack of an automatic connection between doing right and being requited for it.

Although he does not allude to the Garden story and does not employ its terminology (except perhaps in Ecclesiastes 12:7 [see below]), the author of Ecclesiastes is both impressed and depressed by the sheer repetitiveness and apparent meaninglessness of human activity. So far as he is concerned, the endless rounds of labor and the pursuit of novelty, pleasure, and wisdom are unfulfilling because at the end there is nothing. Food is eaten, pleasure is forgotten, and wisdom is taken to the grave.

With some imagination, it is possible to hear Adam as an old man speaking in selected verses from Ecclesiastes:

What is a human's gain from all his labor that he labors under the sun?
A generation goes, a generation comes, and the earth remains forever.
All things are exhausting. A man is unable to speak. An eye is
    never satiated with looking and an ear does not fill itself with
    hearing.
What was is what will be, and what was done is what will be done,
    and there is nothing new under the sun.
Concerning what befalls children of Adam and what befalls
    animals, one thing befalls them. As this one dies, so that one dies.
    There is one lifebreath for them. There is no advantage to the person
    because everything is [hebel] fleeting breath.
I congratulate the dead who died more than the living who are still
    living. But better than both is he who has not been, who has not
    seen the bad deed done under the sun.
Look forward to life with the woman you love all the days of your
    life of fleeting breath that he gives you under the sun. All the days of
    your fleeting breath—indeed, that is your portion in life, and in your
    labor that you labor under the sun.
And the clod will return to the ground as it was; and the lifebreath will
    return to God, who gave it. (Eccles 1:3–4, 8–9; 3:19; 4:2–3; 9:9; 12:7)

The seventeenth-century poet Thomas Traherne (1636–74) captures Adam's wistful reflections about what he thought life was before he gained knowledge. This is the first stanza of his poem "Eden."

A learned and a happy ignorance
Divided me
From all the vanity,
From all the sloth, care, pain, and sorrow that advance
The madness and the misery
Of men. No error, no distraction I
Saw soil the earth, or overcloud the sky.[9]

For those who thought like the author of Ecclesiastes, quiet death and its accompanying oblivion were a welcome solution and harmonious resolution to the exhausting unfairness of life. Traherne's gentle realistic pessimism reflects Near Eastern philosophical trends during the late Persian and early Hellenistic periods.

Others with like concerns did not consider natural death so benignly. They did not anticipate oblivion (or eternity in Sheol or Hades) as a soft comfort during eternal sleep. The very idea frightened them. Some among them began to speculate about the issues of fairness, sin, and hope.

CONCLUSIONS FROM THE ALLUSIONS

As these biblical citations, excluding those from Ecclesiastes, indicate, the Garden story was known in ancient Israel and alluded to by authors writing in different literary genres and directing their words to different audiences. The earliest datable allusions are from prophets in the eighth century BCE (Amos, Isaiah of Jerusalem), the latest from the sixth (Jeremiah, Ezekiel, Second Isaiah). Amos is the earliest of the Israelite prophets whose writings have come down to us.

Unfortunately, experts in Hebrew and in Semitic linguistics have not yet figured out how to date texts in Classical Hebrew to particular periods within the almost four centuries of its use, 1000–539 BCE. Consequently, although the allusions to individuals and events in such self-dated texts as the books of Amos and Isaiah allow historians to assign dates to their composition, the allusions in Psalms and Proverbs might come from any time within this broad period.

The allusions presuppose that those hearing them are capable of making the appropriate connections and drawing the correct inferences. Prophets spoke in streets and public places to passersby. Psalms were part of public or private temple liturgies, sung aloud in the hearing of other participants. Proverbs and wisdom texts were part of the oral and written literature of elite groups with a particular orientation to reality. Considered together, all these texts inform us about what ancient Israelites, at least some of them, thought about the Garden story. A story about beginnings, it could be used to suggest a new beginning after defeat and exile. A story about the acquisition of wisdom, it could be used to refer to a new leader who would be characterized by divinely granted wisdom.

What is not reflected in the Hebrew Bible and what was not known in ancient Israel was a Garden story that expressed the myth of a Fall.[10]

26 CONTRA THE COMMON INTERPRETATION

The translation and interpretation of the Garden story in Part II of this book do not support the common interpretation, described in Chapter 1. The common interpretation so entrenched in Western culture reflects, in mild form, attitudes about gender attested as early as the eighth–seventh centuries BCE among the Greeks. As Tikva Frymer-Kensky observes:

> The Greeks considered females to be inherently so different from males that they spoke of a *genes genaikon*, "a race of women," in effect calling women an entirely different species from man. The Greek philosophical systems viewed the male-female polarity as the major axis of their thinking. In this dichotomy, women were the reflex of men in all aspects. . . . Man embodied all those characteristics that the Greeks considered the highest achievement of their civilization, and women, by contrast, had all the characteristics that the Greeks denigrated and discarded.[1]

In different ways, these attitudes filtered into and found expression within religions that evolved in the Hellenistic ethos of the Greco-Roman world. This included the ethos of early rabbinic Judaism and early Christianity. Paul, sensing that the "time is short," counseled the Corinthians that sexual abstinence was preferable to limited sexual contact between male and female, but that limited, controlled contact was preferable to burning with passion (1 Cor 7:1–8, 36–38). Jewish sages counseled, "Whenever a man engages in much conversation with a woman, he brings evil to himself, neglects the study of Torah, and in the end will inherit Gehenna" (*m. Aboth* 1:5). The Garden story was not written under the sway of any notion close to these.

In its own historical time it was not a story about sin—no word for sin, rebellion, disobedience, or the like occurs in it—although it does deal with the circumvention of a divine instruction. It was not a story about death or redemption. It was a story about the origins of humanity and human nature, about proper comportment, dignity, the acquisition of knowledge, and, ultimately, ethical self-awareness.

The interpretations presented in Part II justify rejection of the prevalent common interpretation as unfounded philologically and as misrepresenting the story's sense within the context of Israelite culture during the Iron Age. Concomitantly, they do not support a general misogynist reading of the story (see Chapter 2). The Garden story reflects the belief that although women are men's helpers, they lack authority in certain areas of life. In Genesis 21:9–12, Sarah insists that Abraham throw out his concubine and the concubine's son, his legal heir, in an apparent violation of accepted Near Eastern norms. Abraham is reluctant to do so until instructed by God to "do whatever Sarah tells you." This instruction is a clear indication that under normal circumstances, Abraham, as head of the household, would have had the final say-so. Some form of men's authority over women is to be expected because it was a story told in a patriarchal society.

In an important, pioneering study of patriarchy, Gerda Lerner, a leading American social historian and founder of the discipline of women's history, reports that she does not find any historical society in which patriarchy was nascent or developing. Her research indicates that in all historical societies, that is, societies for which we possess adequate documentation, patriarchy was well developed. She therefore posits patriarchy's origin in a time before the emergence of historical societies, during the Neolithic period, the New Stone Age, 8000–4000 BCE.

The purported period of patriarchy's origin is reconstructed, or reimagined, by combining archaeological data interpreted through systematic extrapolations of information from historical societies read back into prehistoric societies. Lerner assumes that it was in the newly emerging agricultural societies of the Neolithic period that women were first subjugated and then traded not only as a way of avoiding warfare through marriage alliances but also as a way of breeding healthy stock to work the fields. She argues that the subjugation of women came about when they were perceived as another type of human being, an "other," but a useful other. She argues further that only following the subjugation and enslavement of women did male slavery evolve.[2]

I refer to Lerner to take Israel off the hook. Whatever the origins of patriarchy, it did not emerge in ancient Israel or in the historical, pre-Israelite ancient Near East of the second millennium BCE. It was integrated into native worldviews long before then. Lerner's conclusion disallows argument that the Garden story was created to bolster patriarchy; rather, it justifies Athalya Brenner's conclusion, discussed in Chapter 2, that patriarchy was a social given within the milieu that produced the narrative and is reflected within it.[3]

Patriarchy, an ill-defined term, should not be understood as reflecting any particular modern understanding of gender and power relations. Power relationships, the comprehension of gender and gender roles, and the social distribution of domestic obligations had many forms and styles in the different cultures of Early Antiquity, even as they do today. At best, the Garden story distills some Israelite attitudes relevant to understanding the social mechanics of patriarchy in ancient Israel.[4]

The only overtly patriarchal feature of the Garden story, if treated as a universal metaphor, is in God's sentence to Hawwa that her husband "rules" her, whatever that term is intended to cover. Noticeably absent from the story is any discussion of or allusion to nonbiological male and female roles and tasks. The man and the helper could engage in similar workaday and some domestic tasks.[5] To a great extent this nondifferentiation reflects ancient Israel's agrarian society, which was partially or generally indifferent to gender distinctions unless size and strength figured critically into efficient performance of a specific task, such as construction. Both men and women could work in the fields, shepherd flocks in pastures adjacent to villages, and draw water (Gen 24:15–20; 25:12–14; 20:4–10; Exod 2:16–17; 3:1; Ruth 2:4–9).

Some tasks, however, appear to have been thought of as traditional "women's work," among them baking bread and cooking food, spinning yarn, sewing clothing, and possibly creating household pottery. These domestic activities kept women in the village. Consequently, providing care for the very young and providing their practical early education were also thought to be women's responsibilities. Most information about specifically female roles is learned directly or inferred from biblical texts, but recently archaeology has contributed significantly to our knowledge about their tasks.[6] None of these topics are addressed or alluded to in the story, reflecting perhaps the idea that the rustic nature of the first couple marked them as less developed socially and culturally than those telling stories about them.

The story does reflect patriarchism in that it—and the whole sequence of stories about the world and humanity before the flood—presents its account primarily in terms of prestigious males.[7] In the story's description of the expulsion, it mentions Adam alone (Gen 3:23–24). This orientation toward men is typical of the Hebrew Bible as a whole.[8]

Aside from this bias, the Garden story was neither archetypal nor paradigmatic nor prescriptive for Israel's Iron Age society. Because no evidence suggests that it functioned as a myth, it cannot be considered a myth. Furthermore, it is unlike myths that maintain story lines through sequenced but not chronologically anchored events. Myths usually take place in some vague "way back when." One biblical allusion to a myth is found in Psalm 74:12–14. The psalmist knows a myth describing the ordering of the cosmos by God's defeat of hostile powers:

> God, my king from of old
>> who does saving deeds in the midst of the land!
> You drove back Sea with your might;
>> you shattered the heads of Tanniynim on the waters.
> You crushed the heads of Leviathan;
>> you gave him as food to people of the wilderness.

The psalmist refers here to an ancient Israelite myth known to him and his audience but unknown to us. The authors of Psalm 89:10–11 and Job 26:12–13 also knew it. In Psalm 74 its contents and its lack of chronological setting characterize the description of events as myth. The contrast with the Garden story is sharp.

The Garden story is anchored chronologically into a broader context. The author's use of the anterior construction in Genesis 4:1 indicates that it was important for him that the unfolding of events be comprehended chronologically as well as thematically. Its characters are portrayed as having lived in real time. Hebel died (Gen 4:8, 25), Adam's death is reported (Gen 5:4–5), as is Seth's (Gen 5:7–8), and genealogical lists interspersed with mini-narratives create a loosely wrought chronological frame. The whole flows, with many streams, into the more focused and developed Noah story and then into the Abrahamic narrative cycle.[9] The non-myth character of the Garden story may explain why there are only a few allusions to it in the Hebrew Bible. It was not a particularly important story, nor did it have any direct bearing on the historical, covenantal, and other theological themes of interest to most authors of texts included in the Bible.

The Garden story was a tale about something that happened a long time ago in a place located far to the north of Israel. It clarified some details about how and why all people within the purview of Israelite observation, not only Israelites, lived and acted as they did. Its many etiologies explained agriculture, the origin of animals, the human origin of animal names, the origin of women, a man's support for his parents even as he clings to his wife, and the different types of clothing worn. What it had to teach concerned humanity's role within the shared social world known to ancient Israel.

Perhaps the most significant etiological feature of the Garden story is its explanation of how all humanity, not only Israelites, obtained the knowledge to discriminate between the more and the less preferable when making choices. This knowledge conferred on people the ability to make legal, ethical, and moral choices consciously, an ability that the species was obligated to exercise thereafter. All these developments underlie the stories that follow in Genesis, from the foundation of cities, to the flood, to the tower of Babel, to the confusion of languages, to the establishment of urban civilizations around the ancient Near East.

Considered as a wisdom story, Genesis 2–3 is not about loss but about gain. It is not the story of a decline but of a rise. Within the traditions of Israelite society, whose anthropology it reflects, the path out from Eden led to all places in the known world. But one path conducted a small part of humanity to dusty roads leading from Mesopotamia to Canaan to Egypt to Sinai and from there through the Sinai wilderness back to Canaan, a land promised by God to Abraham, Isaac, Jacob, and their descendents.

It was a homely story, not a cultic, or ethnic, or tribal legend. It originated in the very human quest for knowledge about what is known through experience and observation. Its author assumed that there are rational explanations for what is knowable about the physical and social world within which Israelites lived.

27   BEYOND THE TOWER OF BABEL

When Alexander the Great conquered the Levant in 323 BCE, the cultural world of the ancient Near East began to give way slowly to Hellenism. More by seduction than by force, more through evolution than through revolution, Hellenism influenced, indeed invited, change. An ill-defined cultural movement, it made an impact more like that of the printing press or tourism than the computer. It posed new issues to religious thinkers and provided new ways of thinking about them. The social dislocations caused by wars and political ferment in what had been the Iron Age kingdom of Judah, destroyed in 586 BCE, exacerbated discontent with old views and frustration with old answers to what appeared to be new questions. Under the influence of Hellenism, people began to interpret the Garden story, an internally coherent story that fit its original cultural milieu, in ways that subverted its original meaning.

In the age of cosmopolitan and trans-ethnic Hellenism, tribalism and the old social cohesion of a communitarian society were no longer significant factors in the lives of its readers and interpreters. All talk of kith and kin and large extended families was felt to belong to another time and place. People who thought in terms of Hellenistic mores and laws administered by non-natives no longer comprehended the legal and rhetorical traditions of the Iron Age culture or the politics of judicial administration. People speaking the Hebrew of Late Antiquity used a grammar and vocabulary different from those of Classical Hebrew. The meanings of rare words and uncommon expressions barely understood at the end of the Iron Age were lost to Hellenistic readers, as were uncommon grammatical constructions. Such readers translated and interpreted as best they could.

Philosophically, the ability of wisdom teachers like Ecclesiastes to live in discomfort with unresolved ethical questions about life and death and moral uncertainties was rejected. Hellenistic philosophers sought complete answers in closed systems. Jewish thinkers who were culturally engaged looked for the same and tried to construct those answers out of their own tradition. People who comprehended the Garden story as being about death linked it to the view that any deliberate disobedience of God's instructions constituted a sin deserving punishment. They hunted for sin, not mentioned in the Hebrew text, and found it.

A lone voice against this drift is found in the apocryphal book of Tobit, a second-century BCE composition. It still presents a positive attitude toward the events in Eden, filtered through Ecclesiastes' notion of sharing a good marriage.

Tobit marries his relative Sarah, who had already been married seven times to men who all died on their wedding night. After the formalities of the marriage contract and the celebration, Tobit is led to his bride in the marriage chamber. He rises from the bed and says, "Get up, my love; let us pray and implore our Lord to grant us mercy and keep us safe." In his prayer, Tobit refers to the Garden story:

> You made Adam and Eve his wife as a helper and support; and those two were parents of all humans. You said: "It is not good for the man to be alone; let us make him a helper like himself." I now take this relative to wife, not out of lust but in sincerity. Grant that she and I may find mercy and that we will grow old together. (Tobit 8:4–9)

The optimism of Tobit's author had no influence during his time. The darker interpretations against which he wrote were more attuned to the atmosphere of late Hellenistic Palestine. People lived in political uncertainty under a debilitating pall of failed confidence and aimlessness. They turned inward. God was perceived as being more transcendent, more distant; people, more blemished and naturally perverse.

One contemporary writer, an anonymous figure identified by scholars as Pseudo-Philo, was a Jew who wrote in Hebrew around 100 CE. His work is known to us incompletely in a Latin translation of a Greek translation of a work written in Hebrew. Pseudo-Philo retold Bible stories to suit the temper of his times and his community. His recasting of Genesis 4:19–22 reflects the mood of the Jewish community within which he lived and for whom he wrote. Here, first, is the passage in the Hebrew Bible:

> Lamech took to himself two wives: the name of the one was Adah, and the name of the other was Zillah. Adah bore Jabal; he was the ancestor of those who dwell in tents and amidst herds. And the name of his brother was Jubal; he was the ancestor of all who play the lyre and the pipe. As for Zillah, she bore Tubal-cain, who forged all implements of copper and iron. (Gen 4:19–22a, NJPS)

In Pseudo-Philo's retelling, the story has a different tone:

> At that time, when the inhabitants of the earth began to do evil deeds, every man against his neighbor's wife and they defiled them, God became angry. And men began to play the lyre and cythern and every instrument of sweet music and to corrupt the earth. Sella bore Tobel . . . this is the Tobel who showed men arts in lead and tin and iron and copper and silver and gold. Then the inhabitants of the earth began to make sculpted objects and to worship them.[1]

Many welcomed such new interpretations, which clarified a state of mind that could be understood in metaphysical terms as a profanation of the soul. Increasingly popular in the final decades of the Second Temple and flourishing after its destruction by the Romans in 70 CE, these ideas gained some influence through the teachings of certain early rabbis but spread with greater rapidity to larger audiences through the teachings of Paul and the early Christianity within which they jelled into a doctrine. They were filtered through the cultural mores of the Middle Ages, during which both Christian and Jewish scholars and homileticians gave them oral and written expression.[2] Eventually they were perceived as basic to understanding the enigma of salvation. Read back into the Hebrew Bible, these alien notions settled into the Garden story and have never left it.

After partaking of the fruit, the first couple devised proper, minimal attire and used their newfound knowledge throughout their conversations with God. Their story is about how human curiosity begat more awareness, consciousness, and conventional behavior and how awareness begat creative inventiveness, a distinguishing feature of civilized humanity. Not everybody had to eat the fruit—the new knowledge could be transmitted by speech and by example, through formal and informal education.

In the chapters of Genesis after the Garden story, the descendents of Adam and Hawwa applied the knowledge they had acquired. People devised ways of thanking God through offerings and discovered that they could call on his name (Gen 4:1, 4, 26; 8:20); they founded urban centers (Gen 4:17), established pastoral nomadism (Gen 4:20), learned to fashion musical instruments (Gen 4:21), and forged metal tools (Gen 4:22). They learned how to use wood and how to construct large ships (Gen 6:14), how to practice modesty in dress and how to honor parents (Gen 9:22), and how to hunt (Gen 10:8–9). They established kingdoms and colonies (Gen 10:10) and devised construction techniques involving manufactured rather than natural materials (Gen 11:3).

The increase of knowledge outside the Garden led to the emergence of social, ethical, and technological knowledge that, in the eyes of Israelites, characterized all known humanity in the latter half of the Iron Age. The increase of knowledge seems to have been the point of Israel's story about the first people within its historical, linguistic, social, legal, and intellectual contexts as these are known and understood today. One of the story's meanings was to be found in its lesson that humans possess the ability to create knowledge.

To be sure, such knowledge is not foolproof. It is objective in that it is based on evidence and its conclusions are derived through reason. It is objective in that it may be corrected on the basis of new evidence and better reasoning presented in open discussion. Changes that such evidence and reasoning introduce into human knowledge expose the time-boundedness of such knowledge but also its improvability.

When Adam and Hawwa, children in tow, left the Garden, they took seeds from the fateful fruit with them.

Appendix:

Transliterating Hebrew for Tourists

in the Garden

In transliterated Hebrew, graphemes, the letters of written Hebrew, are represented by English equivalents. Thus, the Hebrew letter בּ, or *bet,* pronounced like English *bee,* is represented by *b,* and ג, or *gimmel,* pronounced like the *g* in *God,* is transliterated by *g.* Hebrew ד, or *dalet,* sounded like English *dee,* is represented by *d.* This is very intuitive.

Consonantal sounds indicated by *ḥ, ṭ,* and *ṣ,* all with an underdot, are similar to the sounds without the underdot but more emphatic. The *ḥ* is similar to a polite clearing of the throat; the *ṭ* is like the double *t* in *bottle* and *mutton* pronounced slowly with an exaggerated British English accent. The consonant *ṣadey,* צ, indicated by *ṣ,* originally sounded like the double *ss* in *hiss* and *kiss.* Although many Sephardic Jews from the Middle East continue to pronounce it this way when reading the Torah in synagogue, most Jews today pronounce it in the Ashkenazic manner, like the *ts* in *tsunami* and *cats.*

The *š* transliterates the Hebrew letter *shin,* which sounds like English *sh* in *shall* and *hush,* and both *s* (= Hebrew letter *samekh*) and *ś* (= Hebrew *śin*) are equivalent to English *s* in the words *sister* and *suspense.* Though originally distinct consonants, each with its own written sign, the letters came to be pronounced much the same. Somewhat similar developments in English account for *fun, photograph,* and *enough,* and *king, queen,* and *cat.*

Some Hebrew letters represent consonants lacking clear English equivalents. For example, the first letter of the Hebrew alphabet, *aleph*, transliterated by a mark (') that looks like an apostrophe as typeset in this book, represents a glottal stop, a sound similar to that before the first vowel of English *uh* in the expression of assent, *uh huh*, or before the first vowel of the sailor's "Ahoy there!" Likewise, Hebrew *'ayyin*, transliterated by a mark (') that looks like an opening single quotation mark as typeset here, represents a sound close to the initial sound of the choked "ahhh" uttered by the gagging patient after a physician depresses the back of the tongue.

Hebrew spelling in the biblical period did not usually indicate vowels. Thus, the word spelled with the three consonants *bgd* could be pronounced /beged/ or /bāgad/, meaning, respectively, "apparel" or "he betrayed." The consonants *šmr* could be pronounced /šāmar/ or /šāmūr/ or /shimmēr/, meaning, respectively, "he guarded," "he is in the state of being guarded," or "he preserved." Context is usually adequate for determining the intended meaning. Were English written the same way, a typical sentence might look like this: "Th dg ws n th hs" (The dog was in the house).

Sometimes, however, the letter *waw*, transliterated as *w*, functions as a vowel-letter for the sound *ō* as in English *show* and *mow* or for the sound *ū* as in English *blue* and *brew*. Where this occurs, the transliterations are *ōw* and *ūw*, respectively. Likewise, the consonant *yod*, which usually indicates the consonant sound /y/ as in English *yell*, sometimes functions as a vowel-letter. When it marks the same long vowel as in English *sleepy* and *weepy*, the convention transliteration is *īy*; but when it represents the same long vowel in English *whey* and *prey*, it is transliterated as *ēy*. (In transliterating Hebrew, *ā* is not used to indicate vowels sounds such as those in "fade" and "day." Rather, it is used for a vowel that sounds like the *a* in *aha*.)

*

Our knowledge of Hebrew vowels is based on vowel markings invented and placed in codex or booklike versions of the Bible from the sixth through the ninth centuries CE, more than one thousand years after the latest books of the Hebrew Bible were composed. These markings were devised by scholars called Masoretes after a Hebrew word meaning "transmitters." These scholars, recognizing the fallibility of memory, were intent on preserving, to the best of their ability and knowledge, the most authentic text of the Bible and in recording the most archaic way of reading it aloud that was accessible to them. Until the Masoretes invented their system of notation, the tradition of pronunciation remained oral, and readers in each generation had to learn pronunciations by heart. To this day, when the Torah is read in the synagogue, readers must have memorized the pronunciations, since no vowel notations may be written in the synagogue scroll. To learn the pronunciations, however, Torah readers no longer rely on an oral tradition but memorize the vowels and text divisions from printed books based on Masoretic codices.

The scholarly research of the Masoretes was very successful. Their system of vowel notations may reflect how the text was pronounced in the first century BCE, if not even earlier. It certainly does not reflect pronunciation patterns of the later rabbinic Hebrew of the first–second centuries CE.

The largely intuitive system adapted for this book follows most general conventions of contemporary biblical and Semitic linguistic studies. It is readily comprehensible to Hebraists, even as it does not burden readers who wish to pronounce the words intelligibly even though they do not know Hebrew. Despite the consonantal convention, this book usually provides a broad transcription that includes all vowels so that readers will have a sense of how the word sounds when read aloud.

Where indicated, vowels are pronounced roughly as in English. Hebraists will recognize the subtle distinctions in vowel quality and length indicated by *ā, ē, ō*, and the like. These conventional markings need not distract readers unfamiliar with Hebrew.

I do not indicate what Hebraists call ultra-short vowels. The so-called mobile *shewa* (schwa), an indistinct vowel pronounced like the *e* in *quiet*, is indicated by *e*, as is the *seghol* vowel notation, pronounced like the *e* in *let*.

Notes

Abbreviations

BDB   Brown, Driver, and Briggs, *A Hebrew and English Lexicon of the Old Testament*

CAD   *The Assyrian Dictionary of the Oriental Institute of the University of Chicago* (= *Chicago Assyrian Dictionary*)

KTU   Dietrich, Loretz, and Sanmartin, *Die keilalphabetische Texte aus Ugarit*

A Preface about "Really"

1. *Divino Afflante Spiritu* is accessible online at the Vatican Web site, http://www.vatican.va/holy_father/pius_xii/encyclicals/documents/hf_p-xii_enc_30091943_divino-afflante-spiritu_en.html (viewed April 25, 2012). See paragraphs 35–36.

2. W. S. LaSor, D. A. Hubbard, and F. W. Bush, *Old Testament Survey: The Message, Form, and Background of the Old Testament,* Grand Rapids, MI: Eerdmans, 1982, pp. 5–6. In the second edition of this book (1996), the citation is at the back of the book, on p. 590.

3. Similar concerns appear to have led Harold S. Kushner to use "What Really Happened in the Garden of Eden?" as a chapter title in his book *How Good Do We Have to Be? A New Understanding of Guilt and Forgiveness,* Boston: Little, Brown, 1996. Assuming that the story is about responsibility and forgiveness, not guilt and punishment (pp. 21, 22, 24–25, 31), Kushner, writing from a liberal, Jewish perspective, suggests that the Garden story is really about how the humans left the world of animal existence behind to enter the problematic world of being human (pp. 16–26). To achieve his interpretation, he draws on personal, humanistic assumptions. These enable him to suggest his benign interpretation that he contrasts with what he

considers "superficial" New Testament interpretations of "what happened" questions about the story.

Clayton Kendall used "really" in the title of his *What Really Happened in the Garden of Eden? And Rebuttal to: Eve, Did She or Didn't She?* New York: Vantage Press, 2007. This book was, as of April 25, 2012, the only one with this title listed in the catalogue of the Library of Congress.

Writing from an isolatable, conservative Christian perspective, Kendall approaches the Garden story through the New Testament. For him, "really" refers to an understanding of the story promoting "seedliner" theology. He lays bare the real story by asking interesting literary questions while imposing questionable, figurative, symbolic interpretations to problematic words, passages, or elements in the narrative. For example, the Tree of Knowledge is understood as a metaphor for Satan (see p. 15). Seedliners assume on the basis of their interpretations of the Garden story and other passages, such as Matthew 3:7; 12:33–34; 2 Corinthians 11:1–3; 1 John 3:12; Revelation 12:9; 20:2, treated out of context, that Eve's sin consisted of a single sexual act with Satan in human form. This led to the birth of Cain, from whose line of descendents many groups of people alive today are descended (pp. 74–75, 109–44, 177–78).

Introduction

1. The historian A. S. Finstuen describes how and why doctrines of the Fall rose to prominence in American Protestant thought in the first half of the twentieth century and flourished during the 1950s and 1960s. Many considered original sin to be the only verifiable doctrine of Christian faith. See A. S. Finstuen, *Original Sin and Everyday Protestants: The Theology of Reinhold Niebuhr, Billy Graham, and Paul Tillich in an Age of Anxiety*, Chapel Hill: University of North Carolina Press, 2009, pp. 69–90.

Finstuen's analysis combined with Rodney Stark's findings in a survey of religious belief in America suggests just how significant such beliefs may be in influencing conduct associated with reward and punishment. When people were asked if they believed that Satan absolutely exists and if they believed that Heaven absolutely exists, the results were as follows: Satan: all liberal Protestants (Unitarians, United Church of Christ, Episcopalians, Methodists, Presbyterians, and Lutherans), 52 percent; all conservative Protestants (Church of Christ in God, Pentecostals, Baptists, Assemblies of God), 88 percent; Mormons, 87 percent; Roman Catholics, 52 percent; Jews, 8 percent. Heaven: liberal Protestants, 66 percent; conservative Protestants, 92 percent; Mormons, 98 percent; Roman Catholics, 69 percent; Jews, 27 percent. See R. Stark, *What Americans Really Believe: New Findings from the Baylor Survey of Religion*, Waco, TX: Baylor University Press, 2008, p. 8.

2. C. G. Ellisson and J. P. Bartkowski report the influence of gender ideology on women's household labor in "Conservative Protestantism and the Division of

Household Labor among Married Couples," *Journal of Family Issues* 23 (2002): 974–76. Books addressing marital problems apply humanistic therapies with cultural sensitivity to those who comprehend power relationships in marriage on the basis of the story of the Fall. See M. A. Yarhouse and J. N. Sells, *Family Therapies: A Comprehensive Christian Appraisal*, Downers Grove, IL: InterVarsityPress Academic, 2008, p. 20. Florence Littauer and Fred Littauer—in a chapter entitled "Were Adam and Eve Mature?"—use the Bible story as a paradigm for explaining some of what goes wrong in contemporary marriages. See F. Littauer and F. Littauer, *After Every Wedding Comes a Marriage*, Eugene, OR: Harvest House, 1981, pp. 97–105.

3. M. Rotenberg, *Damnation and Deviance: The Protestant Ethic and the Spirit of Failure*, New Brunswick, NJ: Transaction Publishers, 2003 (first published in 1978), pp. 1–76, 172–89; Rotenberg, *Christianity and Psychiatry: The Theology behind the Psychology* (Hebrew), Tel Aviv: Ministry of Defense, 1994, pp. 17–48, 99–106. See also the philosophical investigation of theories concerning the definition and origin of "criminality" from a Marxist perspective by F. Werkentin, M. Hofferbert, M. Baurmann: "Criminology as Police Science or 'How Old Is the New Criminology?'" *Crime and Social Justice* 2 (1974): 29 and notes 12–14 (for original sin), 34 (for a discussion of social-ideological contexts within which deviant behavior is identified and labeled); J. L. Sundt and F. T. Callen, "The Correctional Ideology of Prison Chaplains: A National Survey," *Journal of Criminal Justice* 30 (2002): 380–82.

Chapter 1. The Fall in Interpretation

1. English *Adam* approximates the Hebrew pronunciation; *Eve*, however, does not. It reflects the inability of Greek speakers to pronounce her Hebrew name—Hawwa—which is used in this book. The first *h* is pronounced as a guttural, like the *ch* in Scottish *loch* or the *J* in the Spanish name José.

Ashkenazic Hebrew that evolved in German-speaking countries renders "Hawwa" as "Havva." This is due to the lack of the /w/ sound (heard in English *win, water*) in the dialects where this type of Hebrew pronunciation emerged during the Middle Ages. Sephardic Hebrew preserved the original ancient /w/ pronunciation because it evolved where Arabic dialects that have a /w/ sound were spoken.

2. M. H. McEntire, *The Blood of Abel: The Violent Plot in the Hebrew Bible*, Macon, GA: Mercer University Press, 1999.

3. The terms BCE and CE are used in biblical and historical scholarship and, increasingly, in general publications rather than BC and AD since it was discovered that because of reckoning errors in establishing the calendar, Jesus was born in 4 BC.

4. Nehemiah reverses the order of these two stories as they are presented in the Pentateuch, the first five books of the Bible.

5. Brevard S. Childs suggests that it is still useful to refer to this story as "the fall." Even if it does not indicate a stage in evolution, he argues, it may portray "basic distortions of human existence in respect to God by means of a theological aetiology."

Childs points to Genesis 3:19, "by the sweat of your brow you will eat bread," as confirming the etiological thrust that justifies maintaining the term since this passage emphasizes the anthropological and cosmological consequences of disobedience. See B. S. Childs, *Biblical Theology of the Old and New Testaments*, Minneapolis, MN: Fortress, 1993, pp. 121, 570–71.

What was comprehended by "the Fall" and what its implications were for Christian anthropology varied among Christian groups in the first centuries of the church and even in the early Orthodox Church over time. See E. H. Pagels, *Adam and Eve and the Serpent in Gen 1–3* [= Occasional Papers of the Institute for Antiquity and Christianity, no. 12], Claremont, CA: Institute for Antiquity and Christianity, 1988, pp. 1–11; and Pagels, *Adam, Eve, and the Serpent*, New York: Vantage, 1989, pp. 62–77, 106–26. An important study tracing late medieval notions of the Fall from Paul through confessions of faith and the dogmatics of contemporary Protestant and Catholic theologians is W. S. Towner, "Interpretations and Reinterpretations of the Fall," in F. A. Eigo, ed., *Modern Biblical Scholarship: Its Impact on Theology and Proclamation*, Villanova, PA: Villanova University, 1984, pp. 53–85. Towner, however, does not discuss the thought of contemporary evangelical theologians or of some contemporary Jewish movements influenced by a sixteenth-century kabalistic notion that because of sinning under the influence of Adam's sin, the people of Israel cannot be redeemed until the coming of the Messiah. The desire to maintain the notion in a modern philosophical, not theological, context is problematic. As L. Wieseltier observes: "If I am originally and essentially guilty, if my guilt precedes what I do, then I may do as I please. What a license such guilt is! Ontological guilt is an immoralist's dream" (L. Wieseltier, *Kaddish*, New York: Knopf, 1998, p. 220).

6. Quintus Septimus Florens Tertullian, "The Apparel of Women," cited from L. A. Bell, *Visions of Women*, Clifton, NJ: Humana Press, 1983, p. 78.

7. J. L. Kugel, *Traditions of the Bible: A Guide to the Bible as It Was at the Start of the Common Era*, Cambridge, MA: Harvard University Press, 1998. See the sections addressing sinfulness, pp. 97–98, 130.

8. Kugel, *Traditions of the Bible*. See the sections entitled "Blaming the Woman," pp. 100–102, 108–10, 128–29.

9. Ben Sirah's conception of the "evil wife" may have been modeled on the very negative image of Pandora, a female creature introduced into a world inhabited only by males. The Greek poet Hesiod, who lived around 700 BCE, wrote in his *Works and Days* (67–78) that Pandora, given by Zeus to the brother of Prometheus as a punishment for the theft of fire, was endowed with "a dog's mind and . . . guileful ways and a thievish character." See T. A. Ellis, "Is Eve the 'Woman' in Sirach 25:24?" *Catholic Biblical Quarterly* 73 (2011): 335–41.

10. H. C. Kee, "Testaments of the Twelve Patriarchs," in J. H. Charlesworth, ed., *The Old Testament Pseudepigrapha: Apocalyptic Literature and Testaments*, Garden City, NY: Doubleday, 1983, pp. 782–84.

11. An exalted Adam was necessary for Paul's exegesis as a typological counterpoint for the risen Christ (Rom 5:12–21; 1 Cor 15:21–22, 45–49). A Jewish tradition about exalted Adam is preserved in the Latin "Life of Adam and Eve" (first century CE). In chapters 13–14, Satan informs Adam that when God made him a living creature, the angel Michael compelled all of the other angels to worship him in the presence of God. See M. D. Johnson, "Life of Adam and Eve," in J. H. Charlesworth, ed., *The Old Testament Pseudepigrapha*, vol. 2, Garden City, NY: Doubleday, 1985, pp. 252, 262. Indeed, were it not for Paul, it is uncertain whether or not the figure of fallen Adam would have been featured so significantly in post-Pauline thought and theology. See J-M Maldamé, "Adam, Ève et le serpent: Péché du monde et péché l'Adam," *Cahiers Disputatio* I (2008): 18–19; and P. C. Bouteneff, *Beginnings: Ancient Christian Readings of the Biblical Creation Narratives*, Grand Rapids, MI: Baker Books, 2008, pp. 39–46.

12. Anxieties about sexuality were expressed in homiletic elaborations of the biblical story, and many attempts to resolve them can be traced in early Christianity and Judaism interacting with each other. See D. Boyarin, *Carnal Israel: Reading Sex in Talmudic Culture*, Berkeley: University of California Press, 1993, pp. 31–106.

13. Shammai's notion that it would have been better had man not been born is found also in 2 Esdras 7:116, a first-century composition.

14. An early philosophical-theological study of the idea of the Fall that was unfortunately ignored by scholars during most of the twentieth century is that of F. R. Tennant, *The Sources of the Doctrines of the Fall and Original Sin*, New York: Schocken, 1968 (first published in 1903), pp. 106–234. Although the book is incomplete by contemporary standards and the author is unaware of ideas in the Dead Sea Scrolls discovered almost fifty years after he wrote, Tennant provides useful analyses of the idea's development until Augustine. See also the analyses in Bouteneff, *Beginnings*, that cover the first four Christian centuries, pp. 55–168.

15. The following paragraph is cited from section 27 of "The Jewish People and Their Sacred Scriptures in the Christian Bible," a document issued by the Pontifical Biblical Commission in 2001. It represents official, considered Roman Catholic thinking about the matter: "It is common place to speak in one phrase of the 'greatness and wretchedness' of the human person. These terms are not found in the Old Testament to characterize the human condition, but equivalent expressions are encountered: in the first three chapters of Genesis. Man and woman are, on the one hand, 'created in the image of God' (Gen 1:27), but are also 'sent forth from the garden of Eden' (Gen 3:24) because they disobeyed the command of God. These chapters set the tone for reading the entire Bible. Everyone is invited to recognise therein the essential traits of the human situation and the basis for the whole of salvation history." Section 28 begins: "*Human wretchedness* finds its exemplary Biblical expression in the story of the first sin and punishment in the garden of Eden" (italics in the original). (This document is quoted from the Vatican Web site:www.vatican.va

/roman_curia/congregations/cfaith/pcb_documents/rc_con_cfaith_doc_20020212
_popolo-ebraico_en.html [March 20, 2012]).

16. P. Giller, *The Enlightened Will Shine: Symbolization and Theurgy in the Later Strata of the Zohar*, Albany: State University of New York Press, pp. 34–40; Giller, "The Common Religion of Safed," *Conservative Judaism* 55:2 (2003): 28–29.

17. T. N. D. Mettinger, *The Eden Narrative: A Literary and Religio-historical Study of Genesis 2–3*, Winona Lake, IN: Eisenbrauns, 2007, pp. xii, 27–28, 36–38, 41, 47–52, 63–64.

18. J. Berlinerblau, *The Secular Bible: Why Nonbelievers Must Take Religion Seriously*, New York: Cambridge University Press, 2005, p. 141.

Chapter 2. The Fall in the Hebrew Bible

1. Claus Westermann observes this in his famous commentary. Despite his rejection of the notion of a "Fall" with all its theological baggage, Westermann maintains that the story was told and appreciated in ancient Israel as a response to the question "Why is a person who is created by God limited by death, suffering, toil, and sin?" See C. Westermann, *Genesis 1–11: A Commentary*, Minneapolis, MN: Augsburg Publishing House, 1984, pp. 276–77.

2. These stories were expanded, details added, and their characters developed in the literature originating during the Hellenistic and Roman periods, particularly in apocryphal and pseudepigraphical writings: *The Apocalypse of Moses*, 15–21; *The Life of Adam and Eve*, in which Eve assumes total responsibility ("transfer his pain to me since it is I who have sinned"; 35:3); the *Book of Adam*; *2 Esdras* 3:4–7; 4:30; 7:11, 48; *Jubilees* 3:28–29, as well as in tannaitic, amoraic, and medieval midrashim. See the translations in L. Ginzberg, *The Legends of the Jews*, vol. 1, Philadelphia: Jewish Publication Society, 1909 (and reprinted often), pp. 49–102; H. Freedman and M. Simon, *Midrash Rabbah: Genesis*, vol. 1, London: Soncino Press, 1939, pp. 119–79. Relevant translations and analyses are found in P. Morris, "Exiled from Eden: Jewish Interpretation of Genesis," in P. Morris and D. Sawyer, eds., *A Walk in the Garden: Biblical, Iconographical, and Literary Images of Eden* (= Journal for the Study of the Old Testament Supplement Series 136), Sheffield, England: JSOT Press, 1992, pp. 117–66; J. R. Levison, *Portraits of Adam in Early Judaism from Sirach to 2 Baruch*, Sheffield, England: Sheffield Academic Press, 1988; L. L. Bronner, *From Eve to Esther: Rabbinic Reconstructions of Biblical Women*, Louisville, KY: Westminster John Knox, 1994.

An independent line of development originating within the same milieu but generating a rather different anthropology of women is found in the New Testament: Romans 5:12–20; 1 Corinthians 11:2–12; 15:20–22, 45–50; 2 Corinthians 11:3; Ephesians 5:22–33; 1 Timothy 2:8–14. See W. E. Phipps, *Genesis and Gender: Biblical Myths of Sexuality and Their Cultural Impact*, New York: Praeger, 1989, p. xiii. Although Phipps claims to be recovering the original intent of the myths in Genesis 1–4, his useful book actually traces major exegetical traditions from Late Antiquity through contemporary feminist criticism.

3. P. Trible, *God and the Rhetoric of Sexuality*, Philadelphia: Fortress, 1978, pp. 72–73. The relevant chapters on Genesis 2–3 were originally published as an article, "Depatriarchalizing in Biblical Interpretation," *Journal of the American Academy of Religion* 41 (1973): 30–48; see also Trible, "If the Bible Is So Patriarchal, How Come I Love It?" *Bible Review* 8:5 (1992): 45–47, 55, cf. p. 47. In my presentation of Trible's list I combine and paraphrase some items.

4. Trible, *God and the Rhetoric*, pp. 94–102, 109–11, 117–18, 126–35. Phipps presents a minor tradition of philogynistic interpretations that anticipate Trible in his *Genesis and Gender*, pp. 26–35. Trible's work alone, however, precipitated discussions during the late twentieth and early twenty-first centuries. Written clearly, simply, and without rancor, it appealed to feminist theologians as well as to scholars who study the Bible as literature and has clearly influenced my understanding of the story.

Trible's approach may be characterized as a feminist response employing "the historical-critical method with appropriate feminist modifications," which means comprehending the story without its patriarchal and hence ideological/political overtones. See M. A. Tolbert, "Protestant Feminists and the Bible: On the Horns of a Dilemma," in A. Bach, ed., *The Pleasure of Her Text: Feminist Readings of Bible and Historical Texts*, Philadelphia: Trinity International Press, 1990, pp. 12–13, 21 n. 22. A critique of some of Trible's conclusions on the grounds of historical plausibility is found in P. J. Milne, "Feminist Interpretation of the Bible: Then and Now," *Bible Review* 8:5 (1992): 42–43. An analysis of her work within the context of diverse feminist approaches to the Bible is found in I. Pardes, *Countertraditions in the Bible: A Feminist Approach*, Cambridge, MA: Harvard University Press, 1992, pp. 20–25. Pardes, whose study is self-consciously anchored in the traditions of general and feminist literary theory informed by biblical studies (see pp. vii–viii), analyzes and critiques a range of scholars, including their methods, conclusions, and agendas, from the pioneering work of Elizabeth Cady Stanton in the 1890s to that of Harold Bloom in 1990s.

5. G. A. Yee, *Poor Banished Children of Eve: Women as Evil in the Hebrew Bible*, Philadelphia: Fortress, 2003, pp. 1–20, 29–33, 59–68.

6. Yee, *Poor Banished Children*, pp. 169–77.

7. Yee, *Poor Banished Children*, p. 1.

8. Yee, *Poor Beloved Children*, pp. 29–31. Yee may not be faulted for not considering why the Garden story is not alluded to in a negative way elsewhere in the Hebrew Bible because the theoretical frameworks within which she worked assumed oppression, control, and subjugation to be operative at all levels of Israelite society and hence present throughout the Bible. For a partial critique of the social-historical theory adopted by Yee and the historical reconstructions of emerging Israel on which it is based (without reference to the Garden story), see Z. Zevit, *The Religions of*

Ancient Israel: A Synthesis of Parallactic Approaches, London: Continuum, 2001, pp. 57–62, 69–73, 86–89, 91–121; and for a characterization of her work as "Marxist-feminism," see R. T. Boer, "Twenty-Five Years of Marxist Biblical Criticism," *Currents in Biblical Research* 5:3 (2007): 307.

9. A. Brenner, *The Israelite Woman: Social Role and Literary Type in Biblical Narrative,* Sheffield, England: JSOT Press, 1985, pp. 128–29. Although this work may appear dated from a twenty-first-century vantage point, I am unaware of new data that challenge the soundness of Brenner's general conclusions. Brenner, like Yee, sees Hawwa as a retrojected prototype. Yee writes that women became the incarnation of evil in Genesis 2–3 by being represented by "the primordial Eve, by whose agency man was expelled from paradise and became mortal" (*Poor Banished Children,* p. 161).

10. Brenner, *Israelite Woman,* pp. 135–36. Yee might agree with this statement in principle.

11. D. L. Carmody, *Biblical Woman: Contemporary Reflections on Scriptural Texts,* New York: Crossroad, 1988, pp. 12–13. B. J. Stratton discusses the epistemological bases for different feminist readings and reading strategies of the story. See Stratton, *Out of Eden: Reading, Rhetoric, and Ideology in Gen 2–3* (= Journal for the Study of the Old Testament Supplement Series 208), Sheffield, England: Sheffield Academic Press, 1995, pp. 74–108.

12. Trible's work remains a vital benchmark for feminist readings. A. O. Bellis summarizes nine discussions of the story starting with Trible and comments on the others in relation to her work. See Bellis, *Helpmates, Harlots, Heroes: Women's Stories in the Hebrew Bible,* Louisville, KY: Westminster John Knox, 1994, pp. 45–62; and Stratton, *Out of Eden,* pp. 85–106.

13. H. N. Wallace provides a convenient summary of major approaches in mainline historical philological study through the early 1980s in *The Eden Narrative* (= Harvard Semitic Monographs 32), Atlanta, GA: Scholars Press, 1985, pp. 1–25. The bibliography in D. Carr, "The Politics of Textual Subversion: A Diachronic Perspective on the Garden of Eden Story," *Journal of Biblical Literature* 112 (1993): 577–95, covers pertinent discussions through 1990.

Chapter 3. Who Wrote the Garden Story and When?

1. Biblical data useful for supporting the tradition of Mosaic authorship are surprisingly sparse. They are collected and analyzed in A. Rofé, *Introduction to the Literature of the Hebrew Bible,* Jerusalem: Simor, 2009, pp. 159–62. The tradition is supported mainly by the assumptions and declarations of authorities in Jewish and Christian communities from the medieval through the modern period.

2. A. Clarke, *The Holy Bible: Notes and Practical Observations,* London: Fisher, Son, and Co., 1847, p. 5. This thoughtful popular commentary still enjoys wide circulation in certain quarters.

3. According to a rabbinic statement preserved in the Talmud, "Moses wrote his own book, the story of Balaam and Job" (*b. Bab Batra* 14b). The expression "his own book" refers to Deuteronomy despite apologetic demurrers by some Jewish medieval scholars who ignored the possessive pronoun "his" in the statement, claiming that "book" referred to the complete Torah. See M. M. Kasher, *Torah Shelemah: The Complete Torah Talmudic-Midrashic Encyclopedia of the Pentateuch* (Hebrew), vol. 19, New York: American Biblical Encyclopedia Society, 1992, pp. 363–65; A. J. Heschel, *Heavenly Torah as Refracted through the Generations*, London: Continuum International, 2006, p. 611.

4. Z. Zevit, "The Gerizim-Samarian Community In and Between Texts and Times: An Experimental Study," in C. A. Evans and Sh. Talmon, eds., *The Quest for Context and Meaning: Studies in Biblical Intertextuality in Honor of James A. Sanders*, Leiden: Brill, 1997, pp. 547–72.

5. The change is similar to those occurring in English during the sixteenth and seventeenth centuries from a mixed humanist-Gothic to a modern-appearing English alphabet and in German by the end of the twentieth century from a Gothic to a more Latinized alphabet. The older forms of these Western alphabets are still seen in dedicatory inscriptions on public buildings.

6. S. E. Fassberg, "Which Semitic Languages Did Jesus and Other Contemporary Jews Speak?" *Catholic Biblical Quarterly* 74 (2012): 270–80.

7. See essays published in C. Miller-Naudé and Z. Zevit, eds., *Diachrony in Biblical Hebrew*, Winona Lake, IN: Eisenbrauns, 2012, including my article: Zevit, "Not-So-Random Thoughts Concerning Linguistic Dating and Diachrony in Biblical Hebrew," pp. 469–81.

8. M. S. Smith, "Why Was 'Old Poetry' Used in Hebrew Narrative? Historical and Cultural Considerations about Judges 5," in M. J. Lundberg, S. Fine, and W. Pitard, eds., *Puzzling Out the Past: Studies in Northwest Semitic Languages and Literatures in Honor of Bruce Zuckerman*, Leiden: Brill, 2012, pp. 210–12.

9. T. Longman III, *How to Read Genesis*, Downers Grove, IL: InterVarsity Press, 2003, pp. 20–21. Longman discusses with approval the Reformation notion of the perspicuity of scripture, the idea that the Bible is sufficiently clear so that it can be broadly understood. He points out, however, how research and evaluative scholarship contribute to making what was clear in the distant past accessible to contemporary readers.

10. V. A. Hurowitz, "'Proto-Canonization' of the Torah: A Self-Portrait of the Pentateuch in Light of Mesopotamian Writings," in H. Kreisel, ed., *Study and Knowledge in Jewish Thought*, Beer Sheva: Ben Gurion University of the Negev Press, 2006, p. 32.

11. For a succinct, popular presentation of this approach, see R. E. Friedman, *The Bible with Sources Revealed*, San Francisco: HarperSanFrancisco, 2003, pp. 1–31. The Yahwist also used the word *elohim* as a common noun referring to the deity, god, but

not as a proper name. *Elohim* as the divine name, according to this hypothesis, differentiates the Elohist only until the story of the burning bush in Exodus 3. After that, the Elohist also uses YHWH, the name revealed to Moses at the bush.

12. The following examples are drawn from J. H. Tigay, ed., *Empirical Models for Biblical Criticism*, Philadelphia: University of Pennsylvania Press, 1985. Tigay assembled and edited essays dealing specifically with the question of whether any empirical evidence supports the idea that scribes/authors could take compositions written at different times and combine, conflate, or blend them into a single composite text. His collection demonstrates conclusively that such evidence does exist. The examples convince because the earlier source documents can be viewed alongside the later composite redactions. In addition to examples cited in this book, the essays in his compilation present examples from rabbinic literature and the Septuagint, the Greek translation of the Hebrew Bible.

13. G. F. Moore, "Tatian's Diatessaron and the Analysis of the Pentateuch," *Journal of Biblical Literature* 9 (1890): 201–15. According to Moore, the Diatessaron contains 50 percent of Mark, 66 percent of Luke, 76.5 percent of Matthew, and 96 percent of John. One example illustrates Tatian's method. The story of Jesus stilling the waters on the Sea of Galilee contains the following sequence of sources and consists of eleven joins (indicated by +): Mark 4:35a + Luke 8:22b + Mark 4:36a + Luke 8:22a + Mark 4:36b + Matthew 8:24a + Luke 8:23b + Mark 4:38a + Matthew 8:25 + Luke 8:24b + Mark 4:39b–41a + Luke 8:25b–27a. See Moore, "Tatian's Diatessaron," p. 207. An English translation of the Diatessaron (from an Arabic version) made in 1886 by Hope W. Hogg shows the sources for the complete work. It is available at http://mb -soft.com/believe/txua/diatess.htm (viewed March 8, 2013).

14. J. H. Tigay, "Conflation as a Redactional Technique," in Tigay, *Empirical Models for Biblical Criticism*, pp. 68–78.

15. J. H. Tigay, "The Evolution of the Pentateuchal Narratives in the Light of the Evolution of the Gilgamesh Epic," in Tigay, *Empirical Models for Biblical Criticism*, pp. 31–50; and A. R. George, *The Babylonian Gilgamesh Epic: Introduction, Critical Edition, and Cuneiform Texts*, vol. 1, Oxford: Oxford University Press, 2003, pp. 4–33, 39–47. A thirty-eight-line fragment of the *Gilgamesh Epic* in Akkadian was discovered in northern Israel at Megiddo by a kibbutz shepherd leading his flock. On the basis of names used in the fragment, scholars believe that it is a copy of one version of the story as it was known among Hittites of Asia Minor sometime after 1400 BCE. See George, *Babylonian Gilgamesh Epic*, pp. 83–84; and W. Horowitz, T. Oshima, and S. Sanders, *Cuneiform in Canaan: Cuneiform Sources from the Land of Israel in Ancient Times*, Jerusalem: Israel Exploration Society and the Hebrew University, 2006, pp. 4, 14–19, 102–5. Some crucial details from this epic figure into the following analysis of the Garden story.

16. A medieval example of such a composition was discovered in the work of two medieval chroniclers, Benedict of Peterborough and Roger of Hoveden, who wrote

accounts of Thomas Becket's return to England in 1170. Benedict combined two earlier accounts, one by John of Salisbury and an anonymous one entitled *Passio Sancti
Thomas*. Roger used the *Passio*, citing it more often than did Benedict, but he also
used Benedict's work in order to cite from John of Salisbury's. Roger of Hoveden thus
combined three sources to produce his narrative: *Passio*, John of Salisbury's, and
Benedict's. Detailed proof of the process is presented by T. R. W. Longstaff, who then
applies insights from his investigation of the medieval chronicles to the Gospel of
Mark. See Longstaff, *Evidence of Conflation in Mark? A Study in the Synoptic Problem*, Missoula, MT: Scholars Press, 1977, pp. 42-111. Repeated attempts by students to
combine and blend old, purchased, or downloaded term papers into a new one on the
same topic represent the same process.

17. On the dating of P, see Zevit, *Religions of Ancient Israel*, pp. 45-47; Friedman,
Bible with Sources Revealed, pp. 21-24. A small group of researchers argue on lin-
guistic grounds that the complete Pentateuch, along with most of the Hebrew Bible,
should be dated to the fifth-fourth centuries BCE; that is, it was written, at the
earliest, almost a century after the destruction of Solomon's temple and the exile of
Jerusalem's elite classes in 586 BCE. The strongest statement of their position is I.
Young, R. Rezetko, and M. Ehrensvärd, *Linguistic Dating of Biblical Texts*, vol. 2:
A Survey of Scholarship, a New Synthesis, and a Comprehensive Bibliography, London:
Equinox, 2008. Their claims—published in many articles before the release of this
volume—have been critically analyzed and found wanting on linguistic grounds. See
the articles and bibliographies published in three volumes of the journal *Hebrew
Studies* 46-48 (2005-2007); and essays in Miller-Naudé and Zevit, *Diachrony in Biblical Hebrew*.

18. "Ptolemy to Flora," in B. Leyton, *The Gnostic Scriptures: A New Translation
with Annotations and Introduction*, Garden City, NY: Doubleday, 1987, p. 309. I thank
Harold Attridge for this reference (August 2006). The spellings "god" and "savior"
with lowercase letters are copied from the translation. Ptolemy's conclusions were
based on contradictions within the Pentateuch itself and on contradictions between
New Testament and Pentateuchal passages addressing the same topic—for example,
divorce.

19. See the general discussion, citations, and references cited in Heschel, *Heavenly
Torah*, pp. 610-40.

20. K. A. Kitchen, *On the Reliability of the Old Testament*, Grand Rapids, MI:
Eerdmans, 2003, pp. 304-6. Scholars can only speculate on what the original script
may have looked like. A discussion of relevant pre-tenth-century alphabets that may
support such speculation is in G. J. Hamilton, *The Origins of the West Semitic Alphabet
in Egyptian Scripts*, Washington, DC: Catholic Biblical Society, 2006. A thoughtful
critique of the conclusions reached by the literary-historical approach—referred to collectively as the Documentary Hypothesis—from a conservative Christian perspective
is found in R. S. Hess, *Israelite Religions: An Archaeological and Biblical Survey*,

Grand Rapids, MI: Baker Academic, 2007, pp. 47–80. Although Hess points out perceived problems with the hypothesis and issues that its contemporary advocates have not addressed, he recognizes that many of its historical insights are useful and important for understanding the thought of ancient Israel in its cultural setting. Hess, unlike Kitchen, is a scholar who dedicates all of his research to biblical topics.

21. M. Breuer, "The Study of Bible and the Primacy of the Fear of Heaven: Compatibility or Contradiction?" in S. Carmy, ed., *Modern Scholarship in the Study of Torah: Contributions and Limitations*, Northvale, NJ: Jason Aronson, 1996, pp. 159–80.

22. Breuer, "Study of Bible," p. 164. A thoughtful evaluation of the Documentary Hypothesis from the perspective of an Orthodox Jew is that of J. L. Kugel, *How to Read the Bible: A Guide to Scripture Then and Now*, New York: Free Press, 2007, pp. 45–46. Kugel considers the development of the hypothesis in its historical context (pp. 29–42) and compares its conclusions with those of traditional Christian and Jewish interpretations of many texts (pp. 47–363). Along the way, he points out how both the literary-historical and the traditional approaches leave certain types of questions unanswered, and he concludes that neither approach can be discarded (pp. 667–89). At the end, Kugel is unable to resolve the tension between the two but remains unwilling, despite the difficulties that the literary-historical approach poses for the tradition, to dismiss it as illegitimate, unwarranted, and useless even though he believes it problematic for Jewish tradition. His compromising approach is not so neat as Breuer's, but unlike Breuer, Kugel, like Richard Hess, is a scholar who has dedicated his career to the study of the Bible. He possesses an appreciation and understanding of those textual and ideational difficulties in the Bible that conservative Jewish and Christian approaches have been unable to explain and of the important questions that they prefer to ignore.

23. A sophisticated conservative Christian analysis reaching almost similar conclusions is that of Longman, *How to Read Genesis*, particularly in his chapter "Who Wrote Genesis?" (pp. 43–57). Longman identifies shortcomings in both explanations and proposes an explanation based on his estimation of the strengths of both. He would disagree, I suspect, with what I write in the next paragraph.

Chapter 4. What Is a Reader-Response Approach to Interpreting the Garden Story?

1. J. P. Tompkins, "An Introduction to Reader-Response Criticism," in Tompkins, ed., *Reader-Response Criticism: From Formalism to Post-Structuralism,* Baltimore: Johns Hopkins University Press, 1980, p. ix. Tompkins points out that reader-response criticism is applied to many methodologies. What unifies them under the umbrella term is a focus on the meaning of the text in the mind of the reader. See also Stratton, *Out of Eden,* pp. 18–22, for a precise, lucid description of reader-response criticism.

2. Frank H. Polak describes syntactic criteria which can be used to distinguish between classical narrative of the ninth–eighth centuries BCE, post-exilic narrative of the fifth century BCE, and late pre-exilic and exilic prose of an "interval" period. Within his scheme, Genesis 2–4 is part of a small group of late classical narratives sharing both classical and some interval features. According to his criteria, the extant written form of the story dates to the eighth–seventh centuries BCE. See F. H. Polak, "Development and Periodization in Biblical Prose Narrative (First Part)" (Hebrew), *Beit Mikra* 152 (1997): 37, iii (English abstract); Polak, "Style Is More Than the Person: Sociolinguistics, Literary Culture, and the Distinction between Written and Oral Narrative," in I. Young, ed., *Biblical Hebrew: Studies in Chronology and Typology*, London: T & T Clark, 2003, p. 64; and Polak, "Sociolinguistics: A Key to the Typology and Social Background of Biblical Hebrew," *Hebrew Studies* 47 (2006): 115–62.

Chapter 5. Reading, Presenting, and Evaluating the Garden Story

1. J. L. Lowes, "The Noblest Monument of English Prose," in *Essays in Appreciation*, Boston: Houghton Mifflin, 1936, pp. 3–31. In addition to demonstrating the influence of the King James Version on English prose since the seventeenth century, Lowes points out that the translators took advantage of such earlier English translations as those of John Tyndale and Miles Coverdale in order to capture the cadences and phraseology of the original languages, Hebrew and Greek. He therefore views the KJV as the end of a development in Bible translation that occurred fortuitously at a particular juncture in the history of the English language when writers were exploiting its flexibility and layers of vocabulary. This circumstance enabled the translators to improvise with their English in order to render subtle nuances in the Hebrew (pp. 22–29). Lowes's gracefully composed essay contains many insights that lead to a deep appreciation of the translator's achievement.

2. Scripture quotations identified as NRSV throughout this book are from the New Revised Standard Bible, copyright 1989 by the Division of Christian Education of the National Council of the Churches of Christ in the U.S.A., and are used by permission. All rights reserved. Unidentified translations of Hebrew and other texts are my own.

3. Scripture texts identified as NAB throughout this book are taken from the *New American Bible with Revised New Testament* © 1986, 1970 Confraternity of Christian Doctrine, Washington, DC, and are used by permission of the copyright owner. All Rights Reserved. No part of the *New American Bible* may be reproduced in any form without permission in writing from the copyright owner.

4. Scripture quotations identified as NJPS throughout this book are reprinted from the *Tanakh: The Holy Scriptures* by permission of the University of Nebraska Press. Copyright 1985 The Jewish Publication Society, Philadelphia.

Chapter 6. A Down-to-Earth Story

1. The formula occurs outside Genesis with a similar function in (1) Numbers 3:1, where it bridges genealogies of the tribes and of the Levites that incorporate special instructions for them alone, and (2) Ruth 4:18, where it bridges a general statement about David's descent from Ruth and specific details supporting the claim.

2. See *The Assyrian Dictionary of the Oriental Institute of the University of Chicago*, edited by Martha T. Roth, Chicago: Oriental Institute of the University of Chicago, 1956– (hereafter *CAD*, for *Chicago Assyrian Dictionary*), s.v. *edu*. The dictionary is accessible online at http://oi.uchicago.edu/research/pubs/catalog/cad (viewed October 27, 2011).

3. M. Luther, *Lectures on Genesis 1–5*, vol. 1 of *Luther's Works*, edited by Jaroslav J. Pelikan, St. Louis, MO: Concordia Publishing House, 1958, p. 215 (and see p. 84). Luther is clear about this when discussing Genesis 3:19 but not when commenting on Genesis 2:7.

4. In Deuteronomy 31:2, the expression "I am no longer able to exit and to enter" refers to engaging in military activity. Moses' admission is an indication of his physical inability to participate in such campaigns, but not of total decrepitude. See J. H. Tigay, "*lōʾ nas lēḥōh* 'He Had Not Become Wrinkled' (Deut 34:7)," in Z. Zevit, S. Gitin, and M. Sokoloff, eds., *Solving Riddles and Untying Knots: Biblical, Epigraphic, and Semitic Studies in Honor of Jonas C. Greenfield*, Winona Lake, IN: Eisenbrauns, 1995, pp. 345–50.

5. See *CAD*, s.v. *eperu*; E. A. Speiser, *Genesis*, Garden City, NY: Doubleday, 1964, p. 16; and V. A. Hurowitz, "The Expression *ûqsāmîm bᵉyādām* (Numbers 22:7) in Light of Divinatory Practices from Mari," *Hebrew Studies* 33 (1992): 9.

6. M. Malul, *Studies in Mesopotamian Legal Symbolism* (= Alter Orient und Altes Testament 221), Neukirchen-Vluyn: Neukirchen Verlag; Kevelaer: Butzon und Bercker, 1988, pp. 79–93, 92 (citation). Contemporary parents will recognize in this ritual something akin to the worry dolls that are given to children in some cultures.

7. J. E. Hartley, *The Semantics of Ancient Hebrew Colour Lexemes*, Louvain: Peeters, 2010, pp. 107–18.

8. A. Reifenberg, *The Soils of Palestine: Studies in Soil Formation and Land Utilization in the Mediterranean*, London: Thomas Murby, 1947, pp. 21 (fig. 2), 73–91; A. Singer, *The Soils of Israel*, Berlin: Springer, 2007, pp. 90–94, 102–4.

9. This conception of the location of the *nepeš* gives rise, in Israelite cultic lore, to the notion that blood is, on the one hand, a source of ritual impurity that may not be consumed but, on the other hand, a necessary ingredient in rituals involving purification (Lev 4). The culinary concern was most likely addressed by allowing hunted or slaughtered animals to bleed out and by roasting or grilling meat to get rid of the blood.

10. Z. Zevit, "The Two-Bodied People, Their Cosmos, and the Origin of the Soul," in S. L. Jacobs, ed., *Maven in Blue Jeans: A Festschrift in Honor of Zev Garber*, West

Lafayette, IN: Purdue University Press, 2009, pp. 465–75; B. Pongratz-Leisten, "Divine Agency and the Astralization of the Gods in Ancient Mesopotamia," in B. Pongratz-Leisten, ed., *Reconsidering the Concept of Revolutionary Monotheism*, Winona Lake, IN: Eisenbrauns, 2011, pp. 138–39.

11. James Weldon Johnson, "The Creation," in *God's Trombones: Seven Negro Sermons in Verse*, New York: Penguin Classics, 2008 (first published in 1927), p. 17; reproduced by permission.

Chapter 7. Why Eden? Why a Garden? Where Were the Trees?

1. After 500 BCE, Aramaic began to supplant Akkadian as the main spoken language in the Near East, maintaining that position, despite the penetration of Greek around 300 BCE, until Arabic replaced Aramaic in the seventh century CE. Akkadian most likely continued to be spoken in some rural areas and was still a learned language in its Late Babylonian form in some cult centers until the end of the first century CE. Aramaic remains a spoken, but rapidly dying, language among Kurdish Jews from northern Iraq, most of whom now live in Israel; among Chaldean and Assyrian Christians from northwest Syria and northeast Turkey, many of whom now live in the United States; and among the older generation in a few northern Christian Lebanese villages.

2. J. C. Greenfield, "A Touch of Eden," in P. Lecoq, ed., *Orientalia J. Duchesne-Guillemin emerito oblata*, Leiden: Brill, 1984, pp. 219–24; A. R. Millard, "The Etymology of Eden," *Vetus Testamentum* 34 (1984): 103–5; J. C. Greenfield and A. Shaffer, "Notes on the Akkadian-Aramaic Bilingual Statue from Tell Fekherye," *Iraq* 43 (1988): 109–16. Millard provides the history of the discussions since the Akkadian etymology was first suggested in the nineteenth century; my remarks are based on those discussions.

Interestingly, the Aramaic inscription contains two words rendered as the Akkadian word *ṣalmū*, "statue/image": *ṣlm'* and *dmt'* (lines 12, 15). These are cognate with the Hebrew words *ṣelem* in Genesis 1:26, 27; 9:6, often rendered as "image," and *demūwt* in Genesis 1:26; 5:1, rendered as "likeness." Fekheryah usage indicates that these words are almost synonymous and refer to a three-dimensional likeness: the statue. Accordingly, their use in the creation account in Genesis 1 and in other parts of the primeval history should be interpreted as indicating that some Israelites—not just the author of Genesis 1—understood that humans looked something like what they believed their invisible deity would have looked like had he been visible. This is the plain meaning of Genesis 5:3, which mentions that Adam fathered a third son *bidmūwtōw keṣalmōw*, "in his likeness like his image." Just as the newborn Seth bore a generic resemblance to Adam, so, too, did Adam look like God. This in fact is what a certain R. Hoshayah who lived around 250 CE thought. Commenting on the words "in the image of God he created him," the ancient sage said, "At the moment that the Holy One, Blessed is He, created the first man, the ministering angels erred and were about to say 'Holy' before him [i.e., the man]. What did the Holy One, Blessed is He, do? He caused a deep sleep to come over him so that all would know that he was but a man" (*Bereshith Rabbah* 8:10).

This comment leaves open whether or not anybody thought that YHWH, though usually conceptualized as masculine, was imagined to be male anatomically. Insofar as *none* of the metaphors applied to him in the Hebrew Bible suggest that he was sexed, it is likely that only the human was considered sexed and capable of procreation. If so, despite general, or specific, physiognomic similarities, this difference marked a major distinction between the human male and the conception of the nonhuman divine as "masculine" in Israelite imaginings.

Anthropomorphic images of deity, loaded with physicality, characterize most descriptions of deity in the Hebrew Bible, not because of a lack of theological imagination but because humans were conceived as theomorphic. The paradox of the physically present but usually invisible deity was of no concern to Israelite authors. Moreover, a consequence of the belief that humans of both genders were theomorphic was the innovative employment of feminine metaphors after 586 BCE in the writings of Second Isaiah: 42:13–14; 45:10; 49:14–15. See M. Gruber, *The Motherhood of God and Other Studies*, Atlanta, GA: Scholars Press, 1992, pp. 3–15; T. Frymer-Kensky, *In the Wake of the Goddess: Women, Culture, and the Biblical Transformation of Pagan Myth*, New York: Free Press, 1992, pp. 162–67. See also G. Gilmore, "An Iron Age Pictorial Inscription from Jerusalem Illustrating Yahweh and Asherah," *Palestine Exploration Quarterly* 141:2 (2009): 99–100.

In contrast to this picture based on biblical literature, mythic texts from Ugarit, a city near the Mediterranean coast of modern Syria, indicate that prior to 1200 BCE, Ugaritans believed that their divinities were male and female, that male deities had testicles and females a vulva, and that they engaged in sexual intercourse. See M. C. A. Korpel, *A Rift in the Clouds: Ugaritic and Hebrew Descriptions of the Divine*, Münster: Ugarit Verlag, 1990, pp. 123, 129–30.

3. D. Sivan and Z. Cochavi-Rainey, *West Semitic Vocabulary in Egyptian Script of the 14th to the 10th Centuries BCE* (= *Beer Sheva* 6 [1992]), Beer Sheva: Ben Gurion University of the Negev Press, 1992, p. 79.

4. H. C. Brichto, *The Names of God: Poetic Readings in Biblical Beginnings*, Oxford: Oxford University Press, 1998, p. 73.

5. See also Deuteronomy 11:15; Jeremiah 14:5–6 (paralleling *deše'*, "grass") and Psalm 106:20. Those plants that humans eat could also be fodder for animals, but not necessarily vice versa.

6. In Arabic, cognate words such as *'ušb*, "grass, herbage, plants," and *'ušbi*, "herbal, vegetable," demonstrate a similar range of meanings. In a few Egyptian texts a word *'=s=ba* may mean either "grassy patch" or "well-watered vegetable garden." See J. E. Hoch, *Semitic Words in Egyptian Texts of the New Kingdom and Third Inter-

mediate Period, Princeton, NJ: Princeton University Press, 1994, p. 79, no. 88) and the discussion here of Genesis 3:18, where the word recurs.

7. It is possible to determine how much land would have been required to provide adequate essential nourishment for the first couple. An average well-fed western European consumes about 2,500 calories/day; a fed human in India functions adequately on 2,000 calories/day, an intake recommended by Western dieticians. To achieve this number of calories, the former requires 616 pounds (280 kilograms) of cereal grain and dry legumes (peas, beans, lentils) per year. The latter requires about 495 pounds (225 kilograms). Cereals and pulses provide between 75 and 90 percent of the nutrition requirement with the remainder made up by fruits, vegetables, and meat. Depending on the water and soil quality in antiquity, a good yield for 2.5 acres (1 hectare) would be 2,200 pounds (1,000 kilograms) of cereals and pulses. See H. J. Bruins, *Desert Environment Agriculture in the Central Negev and Kadesh Barnea during Historical Times,* Nijkirk, The Netherlands: Midbar Foundation, 1986, pp. 178–80. This harvest could feed 4–5 people adequately. The first couple, before the blessed event, would have required 1.25 acres (0.5 hectare) to meet their annual needs. For the sake of comparison, an NFL regulation (American) football field is 100 x 53.3 yards = 5,330 square yards = 1.1 acres (0.45 hectare), excluding the end zones. The optimum size for a regulation soccer field is 120 x 75 yards = 9,000 square yards = 1.9 acres (7.7 hectares).

8. B. Rosen, "Subsistence Economy in Iron Age I," in I. Finkelstein and N. Naaman, eds., *From Nomadism to Monarchy: Archaeological and Historical Aspects of Early Israel,* Jerusalem: Yad Izhaq Ben Zvi and the Israel Exploration Society; Washington, DC: Biblical Archaeological Society, 1994, p. 342; C. Grigson, "Plough and Pasture in the Early Economy of the Southern Levant," in T. E. Levy, ed., *The Archaeology of Society in the Holy Land,* London: Leicester University Press, 1995, pp. 248–58; O. Borowski, *Daily Life in Biblical Times,* Atlanta, GA: Society of Biblical Literature, 2003, pp. 63–73; Borowski, "Eat, Drink and Be Merry: The Mediterranean Diet," *Near Eastern Archaeology* 67:2 (2004): 96–107; N. MacDonald, *What Did the Ancient Israelites Eat? Diet in Biblical Times,* Grand Rapids, MI: Eerdmans, 2008, pp. 19–40. Diets in ancient Israel and Anatolia (in modern Turkey) overlapped during the same period. The cereals cultivated widely during the first millennium were macaroni wheat, bread wheat, and hulled barley; the pulses were lentils, peas, chickpeas, bitter vetch, grass peas; the oil and fiber crop was flax; the fruits and vegetables included olives, grapes, and figs. See M. Nesbitt, "Plants and People in Ancient Anatolia," *Biblical Archaeology* 58 (1995): 75.

9. See Z. Zevit, *Matres Lectionis in Ancient Hebrew Epigraphs,* Cambridge, MA: American Schools of Oriental Research, 1980, pp. 5–6.

10. J. L. Ska refers to the syntactic phenomenon that I call "gapping" as "interrupted coordination" in his discussion of this verse. See J. L. Ska, "Genesis 2–3: Some

Fundamental Questions," in K. Schmid and C. Riedweg, eds., *Beyond Eden: The Biblical Story of Paradise (Gen 2–3) and Its Reception History*, Tübingen: Mohr Siebeck, 2008, pp. 9–11.

11. Although a major Oxford scholar clarified this sentence structure as a stylistic feature and thereby solved this problem more than a century ago, for many it remains a problem. See S. R. Driver, "Grammatical Notes: On Genesis II, 9b" *Hebraica* 2 (1885–86): 33. Driver presented over twenty examples where a second subject or object was added.

12. Westermann, in *Genesis 1–11*, pp. 211–14, summarizes the so-called one tree–two tree problem in the exegesis of this chapter. The verse might also be interpreted as indicating that the Tree of Knowing was also the Tree of Life in the sense that the knowledge is life. Although there might be good material for sermons in this interpretation, it is based on a problematic exegesis.

13. Additional examples of incompletely integrated story lines and motifs in Genesis are the following: the presence of created humanity unrelated to the first family of Eden (Gen 4:14–16), the snippet about the daughters of men and divine beings not mentioned previously (Gen 6:1–4), and the incongruous image of Abraham the aggressive warrior in Genesis 14 among stories in which he appears passive, fearful, and sometimes irresolute. All are explicable thematically, but the explanations cannot mask the unevenness that they introduce into the narrative flow for no recognizable purpose or rhetorical effect.

Chapter 8. Where in the World Was Eden?

1. Luther, *Lectures on Genesis 1–5*, p. 88. For the date of these lectures, see p. ix.

2. Luther, *Lectures on Genesis 1–5*, p. 99.

3. Luther, *Lectures on Genesis 1–5*, pp. 97–101. The quotation is from p. 101.

4. For a brief discussion of notions about world geography and maps in the ancient Near East and during Late Antiquity in the context of the Garden story, see B. E. Scolnic, *If the Egyptians Drowned in the Red Sea, Where Are Pharaoh's Chariots? Exploring the Historical Dimensions of the Bible,* Lanham, MD: University Press of America, 2005, pp. 15–19.

5. This point is emphasized in Y. T. Radday, "The Four Rivers of Paradise," *Hebrew Studies* 23 (1982): 31.

6. Wallace, *Eden Narrative*, pp. 75–76.

7. 2 Kings 14:23–15:7; 2 Chronicles 26:3–21.

8. Speiser, *Genesis*, pp. 14, 16–20. Making this suggestion more convincing was Speiser's acceptance of the proposal that the noun *Eden* derived from a Sumerian word meaning "steppe." He took this as a reference to the Plain of Babylon or the like, some flat region near the Persian Gulf. Speiser did not mention that the word occurs only in Sumerian, a non-Semitic language, that it never occurs in Akkadian, a Semitic language; that had Sumerian *e-di-in* been borrowed into Akkadian or another

Semitic language, it would have appeared with an initial *aleph* as *'ēden,* not with an initial *'ayyin* as *'ēden.* This proposal, which influenced Speiser, is no longer accepted for the reasons adumbrated. Kenneth Kitchen, supporting a southern Eden, maintains Speiser's claim that in Genesis 2:10, the narrator is looking upstream. In other words, although the narrator imagined himself seeing a single flow of confluent rivers moving toward him in a southern location, he described it in reverse as if the single flow had resulted from the convergence of four "head" rivers. See Kitchen, *On the Reliability of the Old Testament,* pp. 428–29.

9. S. N. Kramer, "Enki and Ninhursag: A Paradise Myth," in J. P. Pritchard, ed., *Ancient Near Eastern Myths Relating to the Old Testament* (second and revised edition), Princeton, NJ: Princeton University Press, 1955, p. 38.

10. J. A. Sauer, "The River Runs Dry," *Biblical Archaeology Review* 22:4 (1996): 52–57, 64.

11. Z. Sitchin, "Rivers of Eden? The Four Rivers Identified," *Biblical Archaeological Review* 22:6 (1996): 15–16.

12. Esther 1:1 mentions that Ahasuerus, king of Persia, reigned over a hundred twenty-seven provinces from Hodu, understood today as northern India, to Kush, possibly this northern Kush. Usually, however, Kush is understood to be Ethiopia, at the southernmost border of the Persian empire.

13. A connection between the Gihon River of the narrative and the Gihon spring outside Jerusalem appears unlikely unless some story not preserved in the Bible told of an ancient river connected to the flow from the spring. In any event, such a connection would not account for the Pishon.

An interesting and humorous chronicle of major views on the subject among critical and traditional scholars, from the medieval through the modern period, is available in Radday, "Four Rivers of Paradise," pp. 23–32.

14. See H. G. Gütterbock and H. A. Hoffner, *The Hittite Dictionary,* vol. P, fascicle 3, Chicago: Oriental Institute, University of Chicago, 1997.

15. *CAD,* s.v. *gaḫḫu.*

16. In Joshua 6:4, 11, 14–15 the verb refers to walking a complete circuit; in 1 Samuel 7:16, to traveling a circuit; and in 2 Kings 6:15, to surrounding a city, but these are atypical of its 162 occurrences. In most cases, when used to describe actual, not metaphorical, movement, the motion is nonlinear, involving a turning, wending, or weaving pattern: Exodus 13:8; Deuteronomy 2:3; 1 Samuel 15:12, 27; 1 Kings 21:4; 2 Kings 8:21; Ezekiel 47:2; Song of Songs 3:3, 5:7.

17. *CAD,* s.v. *kašašu.*

18. T. Stordalen combines elements from Speiser's approach but reads Genesis 2:10–14 as a myth that reverses the image of rivers flowing out from Jerusalem (Ezek 47:1–11; Joel 4:18; Zech 14:8–11). Arguing that the Gihon is the Nile, and the Pishon the combined Indian Ocean and Red Sea, he maintains that the four rivers mentioned flowed from the corners of the world "toward the center of the biblical world," which

he identifies with Jerusalem. See T. Stordalen, "Heaven on Earth or Not? Jerusalem as Eden in Biblical Literature," in K. Schmid and C. Riedweg, eds., *Beyond Eden: The Biblical Story of Paradise (Gen 2–3) and Its Reception History*, Tübingen: Mohr Siebeck, 2008, p. 43.

19. L. Coleman, *An Historical Text Book and Atlas of Biblical Geography*, Philadelphia: J. B. Lippincott, 1862, cols. 9–10.

20. The Akkadian identification allows the assumption that the putative Hittite or proto-Hittite *hattus means "silver." (The asterisk indicates that this form of the word has been reconstructed by scholars on the basis of other attested forms.) See E. H. Sturtevant, *A Hittite Glossary* (second edition), Philadelphia: Linguistic Society of America and University of Pennsylvania, 1936, p. 48; J. Tischler, *Hethitisches etymologisches Glossar* (Fascicle 2), Innsbruck: Institut für Sprachwissenschaft der Universität Innsbruck, 1978, p. 211, #229.

21. I thank Gary Beckman of the University of Michigan for information about the status of the Hittite etymology (private communication, September 4, 2007).

22. C. W. H. Merril, "Gold," in W. Van Royen and O. Bowles, eds., *The Mineral Resources of the World*, vol. 2, New York: Prentice Hall, 1952, p. 125.

23. C. W. Ryan, *Guide to Known Mineral Deposits of Turkey*, Ankara: Office of International Economic Cooperation, Ministry of Foreign Affairs, 1960, pp. 1, 15, 17, 281. The map at the back of the volume indicates one additional gold source on the Aras River north of Lake Van and two others by the Euphrates southeast of the modern town of Elazig.

24. For ancient translations, see the entry *šōham* in E. Ben Iehuda, *Thesaurus Totium Hebraitus* (Hebrew), vol. 14, Tel Aviv: LaAm, 1952, p. 6925. In antiquity, Asia Minor was known as a center for trade in gemstones, as the names of ancient cities linked to types of gems attest: Albanda, Chalcedon, and Sardis. The sources of these stones, however, are not clear. I was able to find information about the locations of gemstones in Turkey only at the Bir Damla Su Web site, citing work by M. Sezai Kṣrṣkoğlu of Istanbul Technical University: http://www.birdamlasu.com/gemstonesof Turkey.htm (viewed November 16, 2009; February 7, 2012).

25. Coleman, *Historical Text Book*, col. 10.

26. By the end of the tenth century BCE, northern tribes such as the Scythians (Herodotus's later name for them) were drifting into this area, which became known as Ishkuza to the Assyrians and as Ashkenaz to the author of Genesis 10:3. In the sixth century BCE, Jeremiah charged the kingdoms of Ararat, Minni (a small kingdom south of Lake Van whose people were known as Minneans), and Ashkenaz to attack Babylon (Jer 51:27).

27. B. E. Scolnic presents philological arguments and geographical considerations similar to these and concludes that Eden was somewhere around Lake Van. The Garden story, he says, "is a reflection of a memory of a very special place, a region near a freshwater lake in what we now call Turkey." My research, completed before I discov-

ered his work, covers much of the same material, differing from his in small details. Considered in combination, our independent analyses of relevant data provide a very strong, but not conclusive, argument for the northern Eden. See Scolnic, *If the Egyptians Drowned in the Red Sea*, pp. 19–32. The citation is from p. 30.

28. See the maps of trade routes in M. A. Beek, *Atlas of Mesopotamia: A Survey of the History and Civilization of Mesopotamia from the Stone Age to the Fall of Babylon*, New York: Nelson, 1962, p. 9; E. R. M. Dusinberre, *Aspects of Empire in Achaemenid Sardis*, Cambridge: Cambridge University Press, 2003, p. 3, fig. 2; N. B. Hunt, *Historical Atlas of Mesopotamia*, New York: Checkmark Books, 2004, p. 77.

29. See R. H. Hwesen, *Armenia: A Historical Atlas*, Chicago: University of Chicago Press, 2001, pp. 24–26, and note the broad distribution of Hurrian language and culture on map 10. The Plain of Ararat in this region is arid, receiving about twenty inches (fifty centimeters) of rain a year, but its soil is fertile. All agriculture there demands intensive cultivation (p. 16).

30. Ample evidence exists for a direct connection between Hurrian purification and expiation rituals using the blood of sacrificed animals and similar ceremonies prescribed in Exodus, Leviticus, and Numbers. The significance and meaning of these rituals as described in Hurrian and Hittite texts were changed when they were "translated" into the conceptual language of Israel's religious culture and accommodated to Israel's worldview. Questions about how and why these rituals were borrowed are complex, and so are the answers (and beyond the scope of this note), but the conclusion about a direct connection emerges clearly from a critical evaluation of the relevant data. See Y. Feder, *Blood Expiation in Hittite and Biblical Ritual: Origins, Context, and Meaning*, Atlanta, GA: Society for Biblical Literature, 2011, pp. 115–43, 147–65, 243–72. I hypothesize something similar for the narratives.

31. Early Israelite traditions knew of the Hittite presence in and integration into the populations of regions eventually controlled by Judah. Abraham negotiated with Hittites in Hebron for a cave in which to bury his wife (Gen 23); Esau married the daughter of Elon the Hittite (Gen 36:2); Uriah the Hittite, husband of Bathsheba, and Ahimelek the Hittite were among David's elite fighting men (1 Sam 23:38; 26:6). The Jebusites who resided in or around Jerusalem before and after David conquered the city were most likely also descendents of Indo-Europeans who had migrated down into the region from northern climes, bringing their traditions with them. For an evaluation of relevant data, see I. Singer, "The Hittites and the Bible Revisited," in A. M. Meier and P. de Miroschedji, eds., *Archaeological and Historical Studies in Honor of Amichai Mazar on the Occasion of His Sixtieth Birthday*, Winona Lake, IN: Eisenbrauns, 2006, pp. 736–50.

32. M. Ottoson, "Eden and the Land of Promise," in J. A. Emerton, ed., *Congress Volume: Jerusalem, 1986* (= Vetus Testamentum Supplement 40), Leiden: Brill, 1988, pp. 178–81. Radday considers the text "a piece of subtle and superb irony." For him, Eden is nowhere. Radday believes that the purposefully misleading and nonsensical

information was intended to bring a smile to the faces of readers and focus their attention on the real world encountered in the following chapters and on the commandments intended to guide people living in it. See Radday, "Four Rivers of Paradise," pp. 31–32.

Chapter 9. The Gardener and His Tasks

1. The word translated "garden," *gan*, occurs forty-one times in the Bible. In forty it is treated as a grammatically masculine noun, and only once is it treated as a feminine noun, in this passage, Genesis 2:15. Feminine treatment is indicated in Hebrew by the pronominal suffix indicating the object of verbs translated by "work" and "guard": the letter *hé* with a *mappiq*, a dot inserted in the letter by Masoretes to mark it as a consonant, the third feminine singular pronominal suffix. Two related forms of the word for *garden* are formally marked as feminine by the suffixed-*āh*: *gannāh* (e.g., Isa 1:30; Amos 9:14) and *ginnāh* (only in a construct in Song of Songs 6:11; Esther 1:5; 7:7–8). Since the author repeats *gan* in the story, it is unlikely that he intended to write one of the grammatically feminine forms.

The difficulty lies with the pronominal suffixes and is due to an error in the reading tradition preserved by the Masoretes that misconstrued the significance of the letter *hé*. It is actually an early vowel letter indicating a final vowel sound /ō/ that Israelite scribes began to replace with a *waw* in the eighth century BCE. (This point is determined on the basis of extra-biblical Hebrew inscriptions.) It remains, for example, in the Hebrew spelling of Solomon's name, *šelōmōh*, which means "his peace." The reading tradition misconstrued this early, rare usage of *hé*, rendering it as used commonly in late orthography.

2. D. J. Wiseman, "Mesopotamian Gardens," *Anatolian Studies* 33 (1983): 138, 142–43; T. Stordalen, *Echoes of Eden: Genesis 2–3 and Symbolism of the Eden Garden in Biblical Hebrew Literature*, Leuven: Peeters, 2000, pp. 82, 112–16; A. K. Thomason, "Representations of the North Syrian Landscape in Neo-Assyrian Art," *Bulletin of the American Schools for Oriental Research* 323 (2001): 63–96.

3. I. Cornelius, "The Garden in the Iconography of the Ancient Near East: A Study of Related Material from Egypt," *Journal for Semitics* 1 (1989): 206–9, 211–12.

4. On the importance of gardens in Mesopotamia in domestic, royal, and cultic settings, compare J.-J. Glassner, "À propos des Jardins mésopotamiens," in R. Gyselen, ed., *Jardins d'Orient* (= Res Orientales, vol. 3), Paris: Groupe pour l'Étude de la Civilisation du Moyen-Orient, 1991, pp. 9–17; and see K. Starodoub-Scharr, "The Royal Garden in the Great Royal Palace of Ugarit: To the Interpretation of the Sacral Aspect of the Royalty in the Ancient Palestine and Syria," in R. Margolin, ed., *Proceedings of the Twelfth World Congress of Jewish Studies, Jerusalem, July 29–August 5, 1997: The Bible and Its World*, Jerusalem: World Union of Jewish Studies, 1999, pp. 265–68; R. C. Steiner, *Stockman from Tekoa, Sycomores from Sheba*, Washington, DC: Catholic Biblical Association of America, 2003, pp. 48–64, 120–22.

5. L. Stager, "Jerusalem and the Garden of Eden," *Eretz Israel* 26 (1999): 185. Major studies of Mesopotamian gardens are mentioned in the bibliography of this study.

6. See A. Frisch, "The Biblical Attitude toward Human Toil," in I. Kalimi, ed., *Jewish Biblical Theology: Perspectives and Case Studies*, Winona Lake, IN: Eisenbrauns, 2012, 111–15.

7. See R. W. Moberly, "The Mark of Cain—Revealed at Last?" *Harvard Theological Review* 100 (2007): 13–18.

8. Anne D. Kilmer connects this fragment with the Mesopotamian myth about the seven *apkallu*, semi-divine, pre-flood sages. These creatures born of divine-human parentage could also mate with humans. Despite being semi-divine, they all died. See A. D. Kilmer, "The Mesopotamian Counterparts of the Biblical Nepilim," in E. W. Conrad and E. G. Newing, eds., *Perspectives on Language and Texts: Essays and Poems in Honor of Francis I. Andersen's Sixtieth Birthday, July 28, 1985*, Winona Lake, IN: Eisenbrauns, 1987, pp. 39–43.

Chapter 10. The Second Commandment

1. Genesis 50:16; Exodus 1:22; 16:34; 2 Samuel 17:23; Isaiah 23:11; Esther 3:12; 8:9.

2. Exodus 1:22; Numbers 32:28; 1 Samuel 20:29; 2 Kings 20:1 (= Isaiah 38:1); Isaiah 13:3; Jeremiah 32:23; 47:7; Psalms 105:8; 111:9; Lamentations 1:17; Nehemiah 9:14; 1 Chronicles 16:15.

3. Genesis 2:16, 12:20; 2 Samuel 14:8; 1 Kings 2:43; 11:11; Isaiah 5:6; Jeremiah 35:6; 39:11; Nahum 1:14; Job 36:32; Esther 2:10; 2:20; 4:8; 4:17; 1 Chronicles 16:40; 2 Chronicles 7:13; 19:9.

4. This harsh construction with *'al* does not occur in any of the Pentateuchal sections where Moses or Israel are commanded to do anything.

5. Other examples of the infinitive absolute + finite *yiqtol* forms where an imperative could be used are Deuteronomy 6:17; 7:18. Commonly, this construction is employed to intensify or emphasize the idea of the verb after the infinitive. Less rare is the use of the infinitive absolute alone where context indicates that a command is intended: Exodus 13:3; 20:8; Leviticus 2:6; Numbers 4:2; 25:17; Deuteronomy 5:12; 2 Kings 5:10; Isaiah 14:31; 38:5. In all these cases, exegetes should consider why authors opted for ambiguous infinitive forms rather than formal imperatives.

6. Aspects of this grammatical analysis and its implications for the interpretation of the story are anticipated by B. M. Levinson, in *"The Right Chorale": Studies in Biblical Law and Interpretation*, Tübingen: Mohr Siebeck, 2008, p. 44.

7. This interpretation is in concert both with the Qal morphology of the verb expressing a simple intransitive sense and with the contexts in which it is used. A good example is found in 2 Samuel 12:13–18, a conversation between David and the prophet Nathan over the Bathsheba affair. In verses 13–14, Nathan presents an oracle and declares "YHWH passed over your sin, you will not die [*lō' tāmūwt*]. . . . indeed, the son born to you, dying he will die [*mōwt yāmūwt*]." In verse 15, the omniscient narrator

informs readers that God afflicted the infant. From David's perspective, however, he had a mortally ill child who could still be rescued, and that explains his beseeching God on behalf of the infant and his fasting for seven days (verses 16–18). The child did not die immediately, and so long as he lingered, there was hope. Nathan's words, *mōwt yāmūwt*, were a sentence not of immediate but of eventual doom; they bespoke an unknown yet inevitable premature termination of life without indicating how premature it might be. His language contrasts with the language of the prophet Ahijah to the wife of Jeroboam: "when your foot enters the city, the child dies [*ūwmēt hayyeled*]" (1 Kings 14:12). No *mōwt yāmūwt* language here!

The contexts of three passages in which the expression occurs indicate clearly that a specific individual will be dispatched very soon by a human agent (1 Sam 22:16; 1 Kings 2:37, 42; Jer 26:8). In each of these, the speaker employs the expression sardonically, purposely confusing its common, overt, explicit "meaning" with that of *mōwt yūwmat* for ironic effect. For example, in 1 Samuel 22:16, the paranoid Saul tells Ahimelech, a priest whom he suspects conspired with David against him, that he will surely die (*mōwt tāmūwt*) along with his complete family; then he turns and orders his men to execute Ahimelech and all the priests.

In contrast to *mōwt tāmūwt*, *mōwt yūwmat* (in third person masculine singular), "he will be caused to die"—in other words, "be put to death"—unambiguously denotes almost immediate execution (Gen 26:11; Exod 19:12; 21:12; Lev 20:10, 11, 12; Num 15:35; 35:16, 17, 18; Deut 24:16; cf. Judg 21:5; 2 Kings 11:15, 16). This meaning is in concert with its Hofal morphology indicating a passive, causative sense and the contexts in which it is used. (The expression *mōwt tūwmat* in the second person masculine singular is unattested in biblical Hebrew.)

Therefore, because *tāmūwt* is used in God's statement to the human, we cannot be absolutely certain whether or not the announced consequence of eating from the tree was to be a natural death or an untimely one at the hand of some agent. Both grammar and attested usage suggest that the former is much more likely than the latter.

The preceding analysis expands on the observation of Jacob Milgrom that in P's legislation, *mōwt yāmūwt* always refers to death by natural causes that can be interpreted as execution by God, whereas *mōwt yūwmat* always refers to execution by human agents. See Jacob Milgrom, *Studies in Levitical Terminology,* Berkeley: University of California Press, 1970, pp. 5–8, 22.

8. R. Westbrook, "A Matter of Life and Death," *Journal of the Ancient Near Eastern Society* 25 (1997): pp. 64–68.

9. See B. S. Jackson, *Wisdom-Laws: A Study of the Mishpatim of Exodus 21:1–22:16,* Oxford: Oxford University Press, 2006, pp. 131–32, for a discussion of this formula by a legal historian.

10. To justify the punishment, Solomon described his warning as a ceremony in the course of which Shimei had sworn by YHWH not to leave the city on pain of

death—a description contradicting the narrative in verse 37—and had agreed to the fairness of the penalty (1 Kings 2:42–43).

11. With regard to this point, Israel's beliefs were similar to those in Mesopotamia as reflected in the names of some important mythic figures. Umul, the first baby born of the first woman capable of reproducing, bears a name meaning "My day (of death) is far." Ziusudra, hero of the Sumerian flood story, bears a name meaning "Life (of) prolonged day(s)." These indicate that the best humans could achieve was a long life. See A. D. Kilmer, "Speculations on Umul, the First Baby," in B. Eichler, ed., *Kramer Anniversary Volume: Cuneiform Studies in Honor of Samuel Noah Kramer*, Neukirchen-Vluyn: Neukirchener Verlag, 1967, p. 267.

K. Schmid presents arguments somewhat different from mine in reaching the same conclusion about the mortality of the first person. He also provides a list of major scholars writing from 1883 (Karl Budde) through the twenty-first century (Jan Gertz, Erhard Blum, and André LaCocque) who maintained that the first man lost immortality as a result of what happened. See K. Schmid, "Loss of Immortality? Hermeneutical Aspects of Genesis 2–3 and Its Early Reception," in K. Schmid and C. Riedweg, eds., *Beyond Eden: The Biblical Story of Paradise (Gen 2–3) and Its Reception History*, Tübingen: Mohr Siebeck, 2008, pp. 59, 62–64.

12. J. Calvin, *Commentary on Genesis*, translated and edited by John King, vol. 1, part 6 (Latin, 1554; English, 1578). This Calvin Translation Society Edition of 1847 is cited from http://www.iclnet.org/pub/resources/text/m.sion/cvgn1-06.html (viewed February 13, 2012). This idea can be traced back to Philo of Alexandria in the first century (see Chapter 16, note 1). It seems, however, to be an interpretation that has been (re)discovered independently by many who ponder this particular issue.

13. I. Kant, *On History*, edited by L. W. Beck, Indianapolis: Bobbs-Merrill, 1963, pp. 54–55.

Chapter 11. The First Social Welfare Program

1. Augustine, *The Literal Meaning of Genesis*, vol. 2, translated and annotated by J. H. Taylor, New York: Newman Press, 1982, book IX: 3, 5, pp. 73–75.

2. A. Brenner's translation, "a helper against him," reflects a traditional, and perhaps the best known, Jewish interpretation, based on Rashi, the most popular of the medieval Jewish commentators; see Brenner, *Israelite Woman*, p. 126. Rashi himself cited it from a midrash in *Bereshith Rabbah*: "If he is worthy, she will be a helper; if he is not, she will be against him for strife." The interpretation in the midrash, originating sometime between 200 and 300 CE, was based on the common use of *keneged* in Tannaitic Hebrew, where it meant "opposite, hostile," or where it could even be employed as a noun referring to an opponent in a legal matter (*b. Ketubot* 44:2; 94:2). See S. Naeh, "*'zr kngdw, kngd mšḥytym*: Forgotten Meanings and a Lost Proverb" (Hebrew), *Leshonenu* 59 (1996): 101–2.

3. E. Fox, *In the Beginning: A New English Rendition of the Book of Genesis*, New York: Schocken, 1983, pp. 12–13. R. Alter proposes "a sustainer beside him" as a proper translation. Alter's phrase manages to avoid Fox's wordy circumlocution but is not necessarily clearer. See R. Alter, *Genesis*, New York: W. W. Norton, 1996, p. 9. Both renderings are based on a more common meaning of the preposition, "parallel to, corresponding with, juxtaposed with," found in post-biblical Hebrew that developed from the sense "opposite." See Naeh, "Forgotten Meanings," p. 101.

4. R. D. Freedman, "Woman, a Power Equal to Man," *Biblical Archaeology Review* 9:1 (1983): 56–57.

5. In support of his argument, Freedman points to a number of passages in biblical Hebrew where the sense of "help/rescue" is not appropriate but that of "strength" is, for example: "Who is like you, people saved by YHWH,/shield of [*'ezrekā*] your strength/who is sword of your power?" (Deut 33:29). In this verse, *'ezrekā* parallels *ga'awāh,* a word meaning "power/pride/majesty" that elsewhere parallels *'ōz* meaning "strength" (Pss 68:34; 93:1). This chain of inner-Hebrew poetic parallelisms warrants positing some semantic connection between *'-z-r* in Hebrew and the notion of "power and strength." See R. D. Freedman, "Woman, a Power," pp. 56–57.

6. R. D. Freedman, "Woman, a Power," pp. 56–57.

7. Arguing that God may have thought that two workers could do the job better than one or that he anticipated that man alone would be utterly bored goes far beyond a philologically controlled explication. This consideration comprises an argument against a proposal that *'ēzer* is to be connected with an Arabic cognate meaning "virgin" in Arabic that might have referred to a woman in Hebrew. Were that the correct etymology, parading the animals before Adam would have made little sense. See Z. Ben-Hayyim, "'*zr kngdw*: A Proposal" (Hebrew), *Leshonenu* 61:1–2 (1998): 47–50. Ben-Hayyim's proposal is acceptable on linguistic grounds but not on contextual ones. I thank Gary Rendsburg of Rutgers, the State University of New Jersey, for bringing this article to my attention (private communication, November 2007).

8. On the basis of archaeologically derived evidence, it is possible to conclude that in the Iron Age, cattle were used primarily as draft animals and then for food; sheep and goats yielded milk for cheeses, fibers for weaving, and leather (Grigson, "Plough and Pasture," pp. 256–59). Applying this bioecological explanation to the conceptual world of ancient Israel is not anachronistic. The ordering of events in Genesis 1—first bodies of water and land, then plants, then fish, birds, and land animals—indicates that at least one taxonomy of the visible world distinguished between mineral, vegetable, and animal. In addition, those producing the lists were able to combine data from different lists, viewing them in general categories and coordinating them into a hierarchy based on consumption. All life forms were made only after their place of locomotion existed—bodies of water, sky, land—and only after what they would need for sustenance was in place. There were no cattle before there was appropriate fodder; their food grew in a place on which they could walk. There were no fish before there

were bodies of water in which they could survive. Only after all was complete were human omnivores introduced into the world.

9. Anthony Hecht, "Naming the Animals," in *The Transparent Man*, New York: Knopf, 1990, p. 58; reproduced by permission.

10. N. J. Jacobs, *Naming-Day in Eden: The Creation and Recreation of Language* (revised edition), London: Collier-Macmillan, 1969, pp. 4–5.

11. See the discussion of this motif in L. A. Turner, *Announcements of Plot in Genesis*, Sheffield, England: JSOT Press, 1990, pp. 42–43.

12. Naming is essentially an a posteriori expression of an a priori perception of separating out, individuating, and classifying. In Iron Age Israel, it was an accepted social activity belonging to the realm of human interactions. The narrative in Genesis 29:33–30:24 indicates that Rachel and Leah named all of their children. In Genesis 38, Judah named his firstborn Er (verse 3); his wife named the next two sons Onan and Shelah (verses 4–5). His sons born of Tamar he named Perez and Zerah (verses 29–30). The act of naming did not grant the namer preternatural or political control over the one named. See G. W. Ramsey, "Is Name-Giving an Act of Domination in Genesis 2:23 and Elsewhere?" *Catholic Biblical Quarterly* 50 (1988): 34–35.

13. Like these verses, Genesis 1:26–27 also addresses the natural pairing of humans for the purpose of procreation. See C. Meyers, *Discovering Eve: Ancient Israelite Women in Context*, New York: Oxford University Press, 1988, p. 86.

14. Clarke, *Holy Bible*, p. 7. Compare this analysis with Phyllis Trible's analysis, discussed in Chapter 2.

15. T. Frymer-Kensky, "The Ideology of Gender in the Bible and the Ancient Near East," in H. Behrens, D. Loding, and M. T. Roth, eds., *DUMU-E$_2$-DUB-BA-A: Studies in Honor of Ake W. Sjöberg*, Philadelphia: Samuel Noah Kramer Fund, 1989, pp. 187–88. A better case for "counterpart" could be made on the basis of Genesis 1, where an originally androgynous figure is made.

16. With *le*, there is no apparent difference in meaning between the word with and without the preposition (Num 22:32; 2 Sam 22:25; 2 Kings 1:13). My difficulty in distinguishing between *neged* and *leneged* may be because the languages in which I think lack the subtlety necessary to slice the semantics of Hebrew's prepositional pie. In contrast, *minneged* indicates a distance farther away than *neged* (Gen 21:16; Num 2:2; 1 Sam 26:20). In most passages where *neged* occurs, it can be replaced by *lipnēy*, meaning "before."

17. The adversative senses "opposite, over against, corresponding to," on which the interpretation of the phrase *'ēzer kenegdōw* rests, are first attested clearly only in Tannaitic Hebrew of Late Antiquity and thereafter in all later periods of the language, including Modern Hebrew—for example, in *Ethics of the Fathers*, 2:1: "Reckon the loss (incurred in the fulfillment) of a commandment against [*keneged*] its reward, and the reward of its transgression against [*keneged*] the loss (incurred by not fulfilling it)." There is, however, an indirect indication that the semantic change occurred

as early as the second century BCE. The Greek preposition *kat,* "opposite, over against," was used to translate the phrase in Genesis in the Septuagint, around 250 BCE. Since the Greek translation (most likely made in Alexandria) represents a Jewish understanding of the text at the time of the translator, it is likely that the shift in meaning had occurred by then.

These late meanings of *neged* that evolved as part of a complicated extension of earlier uses and a remapping of its semantics and applications gave rise also to the senses "hostile" and "legal adversary." They may not be read back into a story written about a thousand years before in a much earlier form of Hebrew. Such backreading results in an anachronistic comprehension of what was meant.

Hebrew underwent significant changes after 586 BCE, when Jerusalem was destroyed and its elite groups of temple officials, royal administrators, and scribes were deported to Babylonia. The evolved form of the spoken language that emerged as a literary language circa the first century CE is usually referred to as Rabbinic, Tannaitic, or Mishnaic Hebrew even though it was in use before there were Tannaim, rabbis, or the written Mishnah. Hillel and Jesus and Paul may have read and studied biblical Hebrew, but when speaking to their followers and fellow Jews, shopping in the market, and conversing about religious ideas, if they spoke in Hebrew, and not Aramaic or Greek, they spoke this evolved form of the language. See E. Y. Kutscher, *A History of the Hebrew Language,* Jerusalem: Magnes Press; Leiden: Brill, 1982, pp. 87–146; M. Bar-Asher, "Mishnaic Hebrew: An Introductory Survey," *Hebrew Studies* 40 (1999): 115–51.

18. W. Leslau, *Comparative Dictionary of Ge'ez,* Wiesbaden: Otto Harrassowitz, 1987, p. 391.

19. The difference between the two words involves a slight change in the point of articulation of the middle consonant on the hard palate. The different pronunciations arose to distinguish between the significantly different types of kin referred to by the original *neged.* In other words, when used to refer to descendents, *neged* became *neked.* From Rabbinic through Modern Hebrew, *neked* refers to a direct descendent of the third generation, a grandchild.

Chapter 12. The First Lady

1. See E. Bloch-Smith, *Judahite Burial Practices and Beliefs about the Dead* (= Journal for the Study of the Old Testament Supplement Series 123), Sheffield, England: Sheffield Academic Press, 1992; G. Barkay, "Tombs and Entombment in Judah during the Biblical Period" (Hebrew), in I. Singer, ed., *qbrym wmnhgy qbwrh b'rṣ yśr'l b't h'tyqh* (*Graves and Burial Customs in the Land of Israel in Antiquity*), Jerusalem: Yad Yitzhaq Ben Tsvi, 1994, pp. 96–164.

2. T. H. Gaster, *Myth, Legend and Custom in the Old Testament,* New York: Harper and Row, 1969, pp. 21, 330 (where the literature covering the history of this proposal and arguments both for and against it are cited). S. N. Kramer continued to cham-

pion this interpretation in *History Begins at Sumer* (third revised edition), Philadelphia: University of Pennsylvania Press, 1981, pp. 141–47.

3. According to some Sumerologists, this particular myth is both humorous and pun-filled, but apparently not with regard to the rib = life equation. See K. Dickson, "Enki and the Embodied World," *Journal of the American Oriental Society* 125 (2005): 505.

4. H. Goedicke, "Adam's Rib," in A. Kort and S. Morschauser, eds., *Biblical and Related Studies Presented to Samuel Iwry*, Winona Lake, IN: Eisenbrauns, 1985, pp. 75–76.

5. This citation from *Bereshith Rabbah* is excerpted from one of the harshest descriptions in rabbinic literature of disadvantages accruing to women as a result of Hawwa's actions. For an extensive discussion of the larger text in the context of rabbinic culture, see J. R. Baskin, *Midrashic Women: Formations of the Feminine in Rabbinic Literature*, Hanover, NH: University Press of New England, 2002, pp. 65–73.

6. L. B. Arey, *Developmental Anatomy*, Philadelphia: W. B. Saunders, 1954, pp. 332–35; K. L. Moore, *Clinically Oriented Anatomy* (third edition), Baltimore, MD: Williams and Wilkins, 1992, pp. 149, 297, 313. Hypospadias occurs in one out of five hundred newborn males. A similar, readily observable raphé is found along the join where the two parts of the hard palate meet in the roof of the mouths of both males and females. This may be checked with a mirror.

7. S. F. Gilbert and Z. Zevit, "Congenital Human Baculum Deficiency: The Generative Bone of Genesis 2:21–23," *American Journal of Medical Genetics* 101:3 (July 2001): 284–85. Information from this publication combined with data from a lecture that I presented to the Catholic Biblical Association in 2004 were worked into a humorous treatment of the story of Hawwa's origin. See J. Kaltner, S. L. McKenzie, and J. Kilpatrick, *The Uncensored Bible: The Bawdy and Naughty Bits of the Good Book*, New York: HarperOne, 2008, pp. xi–xiii, 1–11.

8. This midrash also occurs in a slightly different formulation in *Bereshith Rabbah* 18:2, where it is quoted in the name of R. Levi, the teacher of R. Joshua, and where the language has been changed: "and not from the hand . . . and not from the foot . . . but from the place which is modest [*mimmeqōwm šehūw' ṣānūwa'*] in man. Even when man stands naked, that place is covered." Here R. Joshua's midrash has been combined with that of R. Hanina. My late colleague Eliezer Slomovic drew my attention to R. Joshua's midrash after perusing a very early draft of this chapter.

A thematically similar interpretation is found in Thomas Aquinas (1224–74) but to a different end: "It was right for the woman to be made from a rib of man. First, to signify the social union of man and woman, for the woman should neither use authority over man, and so she was not made from his head; nor was it right for her to be subject to man's contempt as his slave, and so she was not made from his feet. Secondly, for the sacramental signification; for from the side of Christ sleeping on the Cross the Sacraments flowed—namely, blood and water—on which the Church was established" (from *Summa Theologica*, Question XCII, third article, cited in L. A. Bell, *Visions of Women*, Clifton, NJ: Humana Press, 1983, p. 106).

9. *CAD*, s.v. *ṣēlû*; Leslau, *Comparative Dictionary of Geʿez*, p. 54. The Geʿez word for rib is *gabo*.

10. The Arabic consonant *ḍ* sometimes corresponds to Hebrew *ṣ*. This sense for the Arabic is confirmed by another Hebrew cognate, the verb *ṣālaʿ*, "to limp," which refers to a type of hobbling gait involving lateral deviation from the direction of movement.

11. For comments on the methodology of this lexicographic analysis within the broader discussion of the semantics of dead languages, see P. Fronzaroli, "Componential Analysis," *Zeitschrift für Althebraistik* 6 (1993): 79–86; J. H. Hospers, "Polysemy and Homonymy," *Zeitschrift für Althebraistik* 6 (1993): 117–21.

12. Similar circumlocutions are attested in Hittite. The vulva is referred to by an expression that translates literally as "what she has below," while the penis is referred to by one word that translates as "manhood" and another as "stem" or "stalk." See H. A. Hoffner, "From Head to Toe in Hittite: The Language of the Human Body," in J. E. Coleson and V. H. Matthews, eds., *"Go to the Land I Will Show You": Studies in Honor of Dwight W. Young*, Winona Lake, IN: Eisenbrauns, 1996, p. 249.

13. A number of the passages cited below in the chapter are difficult with regard to both their syntax and lower critical issues; commentaries should be consulted.

14. See also Ugaritic *yd*, "hand" with the sense of "penis," in M. Dietrich, O. Loretz, and J. Sanmartin, *Die keilalphabetische Texte aus Ugarit*, Neukirchen-Vlyun: Neukirchener Verlag, 1976 (hereafter *KTU*), 1.10:III.7; 1.23:33; 1.24:8, and *ʾuṣbʿt*, "finger," with the same meaning in *KTU* 1.10:III.8.

15. M. Delcor, "Two Special Meanings of the Word *yd* in the Hebrew Bible," *Journal of Semitic Studies* 12 (1967): 234–40; S. Paul, "The 'Plural of Ecstasy' in Mesopotamian and Biblical Love Poetry," in Z. Zevit, S. Gitin, M. Sokoloff, eds., *Solving Riddles and Untying Knots: Biblical, Epigraphic, and Semitic Studies in Honor of Jonas C. Greenfield*, Winona Lake, IN: Eisenbrauns, 1995, p. 593 n. 30.

16. Z. Zevit, "Syntagms in Biblical Hebrew: Four Short Studies," in G. Geiger and M. Pazzini, eds., *En pāsē grammatikē kai sophiā: Saggi di linguistica ebraica in onore di Alviero Niccacci, ofm*, Jerusalem: Franciscan Printing Press, 2011, pp. 397, 402. The asterisk before the word indicates that it is a reconstructed form based on attested forms with prefixes or suffixes and slightly different patterns of vowels.

17. This noun, occurring only once in the Bible, is derived from the root *b-w-š*, "to be embarrassed, ashamed." In Deuteronomy 25:11 it appears in a form that may be either plural or dual with a possessive pronominal suffix. It could be translated as "his testicles" (if dual) or "his genitals" (if an abstract plural). It is a stretch to render it "penis." Martin Luther rendered it *Scham*, "shame," in the singular. The Samaritan Pentateuch reads *mbšrw* in this passage that may refer to "his meat." See the next word on the list. I thank Mordechai Rotenberg of the Hebrew University for reminding me of this word (private communication, March 11, 2008).

18. See also Ugaritic *bšr*, "meat, flesh" with the sense "penis" in *KTU* 1.24:9. It refers to female genitalia in Leviticus 15:19.

19. In a form derived from the base **yarekāh* or **yerēkāh*, it occurs once in the singular (Gen 49:13) and twenty-seven times in the dual absolute—for example, Exodus 26:23; 36:28; Ezekiel 46:19—and construct to indicate distance or remoteness, for example, Judges 19:18; 1 Samuel 24:4; Isaiah 14:15; Amos 6:10; Jonah 1:5. Although the masculine dual, referring to "hips" or "loins," occurs twice (Exod 28:42; Song of Songs 7:2), this is rare. The dual of **hālās, halāsayim* is used for this more commonly, a total of ten times—for example, Isaiah 5:27; 32:11; Jeremiah 30:6. The word *halāsayim* is also used figuratively, referring to the male source of virility (Gen 35:11; 1 Kings 8:19; 2 Chr 6:9), but not specifically to the penis. (The asterisk above indicates that this form of the word has been reconstructed by scholars on the basis of other attested forms.)

Such observations lead A. T. Reisenberger to conclude that "side" was the primary meaning of *sēla'* and that the noun indicates that the woman was created as the man's equal. Reisenberger is the first contemporary scholar of whom I am aware to question the rib meaning of *sēla'*, but her conclusion as to what it means is inexact. See A. T. Reisenberger, "The Creation of Adam as Hermaphrodite and Its Implications for Feminist Theology," *Judaism* 42:4 (1993): 449, 451–52.

20. The word *yārēk* may refer to female genitalia in the prescriptive ritual of the "cursing waters" ordeal (Num 5:21, 22, 27), but the details of what happens to the woman suspected of adultery as a consequence of that ritual are far from clear.

21. This interpretation of the expression was first ventured by S. Gevirtz, who supported it with his provocative suggestion that the term *gîyd hannāšeh* (Gen 32:33)—usually taken as a reference to the sciatic nerve or a muscle in the thigh—may contain a pun between the sound /nš/ in *nāšeh*, "sinew," and words for man—in Hebrew, *'enōš;* in Ugaritic, *bnš;* and in Aramaic, *'enāš*—and that the term referred to penis, that is, the "sinew of the male." See S. Gevirtz, "Of Patriarchs and Puns: Joseph at the Fountain, Jacob at the Ford," *Hebrew Union College Annual* 46 (1975): 52–53.

22. Among pre-classical Greeks, some myths attest to the notion that it was possible to be born from various parts of the male body: head, thighs, and knees. An underlying idea seems to have been that "seed" was located either in body cavities or in parts of the body filled with fluid or with marrow. See R. B. Onians, *The Origins of European Thought*, Cambridge: Cambridge University Press, 1988, pp. 174–84. In Hittite, an Indo-European language connected both to Greek and to Sanskrit that was used in what is now central Turkey, the word *genu*, connected etymologically to English *genuflect,* means both "knee" and "penis." The notion may have also originated from the observation of extraneous limbs or attached birth—Siamese twin—phenomena in which it appears that one body part or even a whole body grows out of another part. This is referred to technically as polymelia.

23. The human system involves increased blood flow into the corpora cavernosa, two tubes of spongy tissue that extend the length of the penile shaft.

24. Gilbert and Zevit, "Congenital Human Baculum Deficiency," p. 284. See also S. Sisson and J. D. Grossman, *The Anatomy of Domestic Animals*, Philadelphia: W. B. Saunders, 1953, p. 604; H. Scheibeitz and H. Wilkins, *Atlas Radiographic Anatomy of the Dog and Cat* (third edition), Philadelphia: W. B. Saunders, 1978, pp. 66–67; D. P. Sarma and T. G. Weilbaecher, "Human *os penis*," *Urology* 35 (1990): 349–50.

25. My daughter called me one evening to share a story about my then three-year-old grandson. Earlier that evening, while bathing, he examined his penis closely, looked up to her, and commented, "You know, Eema, my penis doesn't have a bone." Could the etiological story have its roots in a similar conversation that took place three thousand years ago?

26. Genesis 6:20; 7:3, 9, 16; Leviticus 3:1, 6.

27. For bonobos, see Frans B. M. de Waal, "Bamboo Sex and Society," *Scientific American* (March 1995): 82–83, available at http://www.songweaver.com/info/bonobos.html (viewed June 26, 2009). For the western gorilla, see Wildlife Conservation Society, "Unique Mating Photos of Wild Gorillas Face to Face," *Science Daily*, February 13, 2008, http://www.sciencedaily.com/releases/2008/02/080212134818.htm (viewed July 12, 2012).

28. Monkeys were known only as rare, exotic imported animals (1 Kings 10:22). They were most likely imported either overland from Lower Egypt or via the Red Sea trade routes.

29. Robinson Jeffers portrayed male animal–female human sex as a mystical union in his powerful poem "Roan Stallion." Jeffers's stark, powerful, and somewhat unsettling work may be used imaginatively to try to grasp intuitively how such unions may have been understood by Greek mythographers when thinking religiously, not raunchily.

30. Hennie J. Marsman, *Women in Ugarit and Israel: Their Social and Religious Position in the Context of the Ancient Near East*, Leiden: Brill, 2003, pp. 707–8.

Chapter 13. Why "Therefore"?

1. Technically, the first italicized Hebrew word in the passage should be vocalized as *ya'azob*, indicating a short o-*qāmaṣ*, as in the Hebrew text, where it is bound with the following noun: *ya'azob-'îyš*. I transliterate it as a freestanding form for the sake of convenience.

2. M. Shevack, *Adam and Eve: Marriage Secrets from the Garden of Eden*, New York: Paulist Press, 2003, p. 196. For the complete homily, see pp. 193–200.

3. Calvin, *Commentary on Genesis*.

4. Rashi's "incest" interpretation is prompted by eisegetical comments in the Babylonian Talmud, edited about four centuries before his time:

Rabbi Eliezer said, "*His father* means his father's sister; *his mother* means his mother's sister."

Rabbi Akiba said, "*His father* means his father's wife; *his mother* means his mother. *And he shall cling,* but not to a male; *to his wife,* but not his neighbor's wife; *and they shall become one flesh* applies only to those who can become one flesh. It excludes domestic and wild animals that cannot become one flesh with the male. (*b. Sanhedrin* 58a)

The rabbinic interpretations were intended to solve a problem in the story about Noah's drunkenness after the flood. The writers understood the story of Noah and Ham in Genesis 9:20–25 to have involved sexual misconduct and knew that Canaan was punished for violating some prohibition. If there was a punishment, they reasoned, the act must have been prohibited, but where? According to Rashi, Rabbi Eliezer and Rabbi Akiba found the source through their eisegesis of Genesis 2:24.

5. W. Robertson Smith, *Kinship and Marriage in Early Arabia*, Cambridge: Cambridge University Press, 1885, pp. 70–71, 176; E. B. Cross, "Traces of the Matronymic Family in the Hebrew Social Organization," *Biblical World* 36 (1910): 411–12; J. Skinner, *A Critical and Exegetical Commentary on Genesis*, New York: Charles Scribner's Sons, 1910, p. 70; U. Cassuto, *A Commentary on the Book of Genesis,* Part I, Jerusalem: Magnes Press, 1991, p. 137 (Hebrew original, 1944); R. de Vaux, *Ancient Israel: Its Life and Institutions*, New York: McGraw-Hill, 1961, p. 29. Cyrus H. Gordon identified a similar type of marriage in the ancient Near East. See C. H. Gordon, "Erēbu Marriage," in M. A. Morrison and D. I. Owen, eds., *Studies on the Civilization and Culture of Nuzi and the Hurrians*, Winona Lake, IN: Eisenbrauns, 1981, pp. 155–60.

6. The Samson stories are not relevant to this discussion because Samson never actually married the woman from Timnah. He abandoned her at the marriage party— at the altar, so to speak—and she was then quickly married off to another man (Judg 14:1–20). Nor did Samson's delightful dalliance with Delilah achieve the status of a marriage. Although he frequented her domicile, the relationship between the two was private, she being a woman of wily ways and independent means (Judg 16:4–22).

7. Gordon proposed that the verse refers to an *erēbu* arrangement known from the Middle Assyrian Laws of about 1076 BCE. All of the evidence cited in support of the existence of such arrangements indicates that a male of no or little means entered into the household of his wife's family, where he was supported. The cases of Moses and Jacob match only part of the pattern. However, insofar as such arrangements were exceptional and insofar as the legal texts and contracts cited in support of the hypothesis are not clear on the husband's lack of rights to his father-in-law's property, Genesis 2:24 fails to support the burden that Gordon would like it to bear. He would have the verse describe as common and widespread a practice treated as infrequent and rare in both biblical and cuneiform sources. See Gordon, "Erēbu Marriage," pp. 155–60.

8. Brichto, *Names of God*, pp. 77–79. I accept Brichto's general conclusion about the meaning of the verse, but not his analysis of its grammar on which his conclusion rests. My own analysis is presented later in this chapter.

9. This is a conjecture because neither biblical narrative nor law provides data that help spell out the nature of the legal relationship between married sons who live away from their parents.

10. L. Koehler and W. Baumgartner, *The Hebrew and Aramaic Lexicon of the Old Testament* (revised edition), Leiden: Brill, 1995, p. 807; M. Z. Kaddari, *A Dictionary of Biblical Hebrew* (Hebrew), Ramat Gan: Bar Ilan University Press, 2006, p. 787; Leslau, *Comparative Dictionary of Ge'ez*, p. 80, with reference to Jeremiah 49:25. See also A. Cooper, "The Plain Sense of Exod 23:5," *Hebrew Union College Annual* 59 (1988): 22, but see pp. 1–2 also.

11. Claus Westermann, in his study of verse 24, observed that it does not use the sociological term "house of his father," which refers to an institutionalized kinship group. The "institutional" reading is what led scholars in search of the institution and to the *beena* marriage model discussed earlier. Consequently, Westermann read the passage as referring simply to the loosening of social bonds in the nuclear family, an interpretation of which, I think, Calvin would have approved. See Westermann, *Genesis 1–11*, pp. 233–34.

Chapter 14. How Bare Is Naked?

1. The remarks in this note address a long-standing problem in the Hebrew text. The word translated as "naked," *'arūwmmīym*, in Genesis 2:25 is modeled after substantives such as *'ādōm/'adummīym*, "red," and *nāqōd/nequddīym*, "spotted," and is based on the substantive *'ārōm*, "naked," attested in 1 Samuel 19:24. The same word is written *plene*, with a *waw* to mark the long vowel /ō/ in Isaiah 20:2, 3, 4; Amos 2:16; Micah 1:8. In plural forms of this noun, the long /ō/ vowel of the singular is reduced to a short /u/ because the accent shifts from the final /rōm/ syllable to the new final syllable of the word. Then, because Hebrew habits of pronunciation did not tolerate a short, unaccented vowel in an open syllable, /u/ in this case, the /m/ consonant was geminated (doubled) and pronounced like the double *m* in English *yummy* to close the syllable. Thus, this word should not be confused, as it often is, with *'ārūwm*, the word meaning "crafty" that describes the serpent in Genesis 3:1. Nevertheless, it is suggested occasionally that the word in Genesis 2:25 be understood as referring or alluding to the fact that the male and female humans were wise or crafty as well as naked and, further, that this understanding creates a natural link with Genesis 3:1.

Although the two words are written alike, Masoretic vowel signs instructing readers which vowel to pronounce after each consonant and Masoretic diacritics indicating *how* consonants are to be pronounced distinguish between them. They are quite different. That the word indicating "naked" describes the first couple before their invention of body covers is apparent from the vowels and diacritic marks used in the word in Genesis 2:25: *'arūwmmīym*. The *daghesh* in the *mem* indicates a doubling of the consonantal /m/ following what is ostensibly a long vowel written with a *waw*: *ūw*. If the vowel were a true long vowel, Hebrew phonetics—that is, habits of pronunciation—could not have given rise to the doubling of the following consonant. The doubling indicates that what at first sight appears to be a long /ū/ because of the *waw* was actually pronounced as a short /u/ vowel derived from an original /ō/. Another example is found in Job 22:6. The extraneous *waw* was most likely inserted as a *mater lectionis* by a late copyist who no longer distinguished between short and long vowels in his reading. (*Mater lectionis*, literally "mother of reading," is a term applied to four graphemes that usually indicate the consonants /', h, w, y/. These were also employed to inform readers which vowels to use so that the text would be comprehensible.)

A different form of the word indicating nakedness is *'ēyrōm*, a substantive of the *qittōl* pattern. It is spelled *plene* with a *yod* in Genesis 3:10, 11, and Deuteronomy 28:48: *'yrm* = *'ēyrōm*. This spelling is in contrast to the defective orthography of the word written without the *yod* in Ezekiel 16:7: *'rm* = *'ērōm*. Both are the same word. The /ē/ vowel of the word's first consonant is a consequence of the compensatory lengthening of an original first vowel /i/ owing to the post-vocalic, non-geminate consonant *reš*. In other words, a theoretically original */'irrōm/ became /'ērōm/ automatically because the *reš* was not (usually) "doubled" in Classical Hebrew. The *reš* forms a regular plural on this base, *'ēyrummīym*, used in the discussion of Genesis 3:7. This variation in the choice of nouns may be attributed to the author's stylistic flair.

In conclusion, the words for "naked" in biblical Hebrew were *'ārōm* and *'ērōm*. For "crafty," the word was *'ārūwm*, with a long /ū/ that was retained in all forms of the word. See F. Delitzsch, *A New Commentary on Genesis*, vol. 1, Edinburgh, T & T Clark, 1888, p. 146.

Chapter 15. Clever Conversation and Conspicuous Consumption

1. None of these species named in the Bible have been identified with certainty. Some proposals are viper for *ṣepa'*, *ṣip'ōnīy*, and *peten*; horned viper or adder for *'akšūwb*; cobra or asp or adder for *peten* and *śarap*; crocodile for *'ep'eh* and *tannīyn*. The general term *nāḥāš* occurs in poetic parallelism with *'akšūwb* (Ps 104:4) and *peten* (Ps 58:5), indicating a semantic connection between the words. Hebrew *śerāpīym*, English "seraphs," a word also referring to winged creatures in the heavenly court (cf. Isa 6:2), occurs as an appositive of *neḥāšīym*, "serpents," in Numbers 21:6 and Deuteronomy 8:15, indicating perhaps that the *śārāp* is a species of *nāḥāš*. For a useful orientation, see K. R. Joines, *Serpent Symbolism in the Old Testament*, Haddenfield, NJ: Haddenfield House, 1974, p. 1.

2. See 1 Samuel 25:20; 2 Samuel 3:6. My remarks here are only provisional. This construction is treated in greater detail in my discussion of Genesis 4:1, where the stakes are much higher.

3. The serpent is referred to as male because Hebrew, like all Semitic languages, divides nouns into only two grammatical categories labeled "feminine" and "masculine." They lack a "neuter" category such as the one that exists in Latin, Greek, and some Romance languages. The Hebrew word for serpent is grammatically masculine, and I follow the convention of assuming that the creature involved was masculine. It may not, however, have been male. This possibility is explored in my analysis of Genesis 3:14–15.

4. See R. N. Whybray, *The Intellectual Tradition in the Old Testament* (= Beihefte zu Zeitschrift für die altestamentliche Wissenschaft 135), Berlin: Walter de Gruyter, 1974, p. 148. The word *'ārūwm* has a negative valence in Job 5:12, 13, only because of the objectives to which such people may aspire. They are so clever that divine intervention is needed to confound their plans. A person might wish for an attorney defending him in a criminal procedure or in an aggressive contract negotiation to have such a characteristic. M. V. Fox provides a sensitive discussion of the related noun *'ormāh* as part of the semantic field of terms for wisdom, pointing out that it is morally neutral. See M. V. Fox, "Words for Wisdom: *tbwnh* and *bynh*, *'rmh* and *mzmh*, *'ṣh* and *twšyh*," *Zeitschrift für Althebraistik* 6 (1993): 158–60.

'Ārūwm, used to describe the serpent, is a substantive of the *qātūwl* pattern that maintains its long vowel in the second syllable in all attested forms: in Proverbs 12:23; 13:16; 14:8, 15, all forms are singular; in Proverbs 14:18; Job 5:12; 15:5, all are plural. Other words in this pattern are *bārūwk/berūwkīym*, "blessed," and *ḥālūwṣ/ḥalūwṣīym*, "equipped (for war)." (See the discussion of *'arūwmmīym*, "naked" in Genesis 2:25 in Chapter 14, note 1.)

5. Exodus 21:14 may contain an exception. The situation hypothesized there presupposes a murder thinly disguised as an accident through *'ormāh*. Compare Deuteronomy 19:11–12.

6. N. Sarna, *On the Book of Psalms: Exploring the Prayers of Ancient Israel*, New York: Schocken, 1993, pp. 32–33. Few of the passages used by Sarna are drawn from Proverbs, whose general observations about people tend to be objective (Prov 10:6, 11, 31; 12:5–6; 18:3; 19:28; 29:26). Most of the passages, thirty-one in all, that Sarna uses to construct his definition are drawn from psalms of complaint whose poetic observations are both personal and subjective (see pp. 219–20). The speaking voices in these psalms are of individuals convinced beyond doubt that their cause is just and that they are righteous; consequently, they are just as positive that their opponents are evil enemies.

7. The editors of the *Chicago Assyrian Dictionary* (*CAD*, vol. 16, p. 122) associate the plant's name with rejuvenation, perhaps because after snakes shed their old skins, they do appear younger. If both the plant's name and the snake's theft reveal the plant's true function, we may infer that it may have been a skin conditioner.

8. J. R. Rosenberg, "The Garden Story Forward and Backward," *Prooftexts* 1 (1989): 7–8.

9. Additional ideas that contribute to an incomplete hypothesis about the serpent's motivation, comprehended as an element of plot in the cultural context of Iron Age Israel, are presented in Chapter 19.

10. Everett Fox's translation indicates the lack of clarity in the statement of Genesis 3:1: "Even though God said: You are not to eat from any of the trees in the garden . . . !" See E. Fox, *In the Beginning*, pp. 12–13. In Genesis 4:15a, where God promises to protect Qayin, he says, "Therefore, anyone who kills Qayin . . . ," but does not explain what will happen. Qayin could imagine whatever he wished. Other examples are found in Genesis 14:23; 21:23; 26:29; 31:50. Usually the pattern of incomplete utterances seems to imply an oath or a threat. For example, in English, "If you do that again, I'll . . ." or "I promise . . ." The proper reaction to such utterances, as smart children know, is to pause and then inquire, "What? You'll what?" or "You promise what?" The woman might have asked, "What did he say?"

11. The woman's addition of "don't touch" gave rise to midrashic tales that either the serpent himself shook the tree to bring down fruit and thus demonstrate that Adam had misled her, or that the serpent nudged her against the tree. When she discovered herself to still be alive after contact, convinced that her words had been God's, she believed the serpent and ate—becoming a victim not of appetite but of misquotation. See Freedman and Simon, *Midrash Rabbah: Genesis*, pp. 149–50.

12. The short form, without the emphasizing *nun energicum,* occurs fifty-two times in the Hebrew Bible with the second person plural "you will die" and the third person plural "they will die" forms. The long form with the emphatic suffix occurs only six times. This count is based on the data in A. Even-Shoshan, *A New Concordance of the Bible*, Jerusalem: Kiryat Sepher, 1980. All counts in this book are based on data from Even-Shoshan's concordance.

13. The narrative is silent about why the restriction was made. See J. Barr, *The Garden of Eden and the Hope of Immortality*, Minneapolis, MN: Fortress, 1993, p. 14.

14. Logically, this scenario or something similar must be posited to make sense of the unfolding plot. Absence of this information in the form of a sentence akin to "and Adam told Hawwa what YHWH had said to him about the tree, and the serpent had been moving through the grass nearby" may be deemed a fault in the narrative.

15. In constructions of this sort, the negative particle usually appears after the infinitive but before the finite form of the verb—for example, Exodus 5:23; Judges 1:28; 15:13; 1 Kings 3:26; Isaiah 30:19; Jeremiah 13:12; 30:11. The use of the negative *lō'* before the absolute infinitive is uncharacteristic of this construction and hence may have some emphatic function. Two other examples following this pattern are attested: Amos 9:8; Psalm 49:8.

16. On the originally mortal nature of man as represented in this story, see Barr, *Garden of Eden*, pp. 14–19.

17. In Genesis 3:5a, *'elōhīym* is masculine singular, as indicated by the masculine-singular participle *yōdēa',* but in 3:5b, the construct (or bound) form of the participle

yōde'ēy referring to the couple is masculine plural—that is, not "absolutely feminine." Verse 5b, considered a-contextually, could also be translated "and you will be like divine beings, knowers of *ṭōwb wārāʿ*." This would then connect easily with the anonymous group (of divine beings [?]) addressed by God in Genesis 3:22. Since, however, the anonymous group is not addressed as *'elōhīym* in the story and since the serpent used *'elōhīym* once in his discourse with the woman referring to God, the masculine singular is most likely the intended sense in the second half of the verse also. For a well-known plural usage see Psalm 82:1, 6.

18. The Niphal conjugation in biblical Hebrew is most commonly used to indicate a reflexive action, something one does to oneself, and that is how I render the verb. Most translations interpret it according to the much less frequent use of Niphal as a passive verb: "will be opened." However, had the author intended the passive sense of the verb, he would have indicated either explicitly or implicitly who or what would open the eyes.

19. Reuven Kimelman interprets the interchange between woman and serpent as one in which the serpent extended the woman's thinking; that is, he did not instigate it. His psychological reading is congruent with the characterization of the serpent as *'ārūwm*. The serpent would have known that a good salesperson is a good listener and that a leader knows how to follow. See R. Kimelman, "The Seduction of Eve and the Exegetical Politics of Gender," *Biblical Interpretation* 4 (1996): 6–8; Kimelman, "The Seduction of Eve and Feminist Readings of the Garden of Eden," *Women in Judaism: A Multidisciplinary Journal* 1:2 (1998), at http://www.utoronot.ca/wjudaism/journal/vol1n2/eve.html (viewed November 3, 2009).

Contrary to the widespread notion that the serpent is always a chthonic figure in Greek mythology, some sources identify it as a symbol for the perennial renewal of life, not immortality. This comprehension of the serpent clarifies its presence as a guardian of the golden fruit tree within the hidden garden of the Hesperides—goddesses charged with taking care of the tree whose fruit symbolized children. In view of a growing awareness among classical scholars that many elements of ancient Aegean mythology have their roots in the ancient Near East, this identification may help explain the presence of the serpent at the tree and link the serpent to the motif of natural reproduction. Similarly, in a Greek vase painting the snake is coiled around a tree growing over a gushing spring with double mouths; see J. E. Harrison, *Themis: A Study of the Social Origins of Greek Religion*, London: Merlin Press, 1977 (first published in 1912), pp. 271, 431–32. This portrayal may be connected to the Near Eastern tradition of two or four streams of life. See also Kimelman, "Seduction of Eve and Exegetical Politics," pp. 30–34.

20. Kimelman, "Seduction of Eve and Feminist Readings."

21. The Hebrew root *ḥ-m-d* in the word translated as "desirable" refers to a powerful, viscerally driven want, an urge to possess; see Deuteronomy 7:25; Joshua 7:21; Proverbs 6:25; 12:12. The same root is used in the verb rendered "covet" in both ver-

sions of the Ten Commandments (Exod 20:17; Deut 5:21). See R. N. Whybray's discussion of the semantics of *ś-k-l* in relation to other wisdom terms in *The Intellectual Tradition in the Old Testament*, pp. 137–38.

Enwisening is coined after a common pattern in English: enlighten, enrich, entangle, envision. It renders the causative *Hifil* infinitive of *ś-k-l* in this context. The connection of *lehaśkīyl* with wisdom is attested in a number of verses: Jeremiah 9:23; Psalms 32:8; 119:99; Proverbs 17:3; Daniel 1:17; 9:22.

22. Carol Meyers comments, "The woman's dialogue with the prudent reptile should be considered not a blot on her character but rather a comment on her intellect." See Meyers, *Discovering Eve*, p. 92.

23. Levinson, *"The Right Chorale,"* p. 43.

Chapter 16. Dressing Up for a Dressing Down

1. In his history of the interpretation of the Garden story, James Kugel illustrates how the perception of a contradiction between what God said in Genesis 2:16–17 and what happened as a consequence—Adam and Hawwa did not die—was one of the important factors influencing the formation of what we have identified as the common interpretation. See Kugel, *Traditions of the Bible*, p. 94.

Theologians explain that the "death" intimated was of the soul, not the body. Philo of Alexandria (20 BCE–50 CE), who used allegorical eisegesis to bring the teachings of scripture into line with logic and Greek philosophy, may have been the first to propose this solution: "And yet after they have eaten, not merely do they not die, but they beget children and become authors of life to others. What then is to be said to this? That death is of two kinds, one that of the man in general, the other of the soul in particular. The death of the man is the separation of the soul from the body, but the death of the soul is the decay of virtue and the bringing in of wickedness" (Allegorical Interpretation I: 105–7). See F. H. Colson and G. H. Whitaker, *Philo*, vol. 1 (Loeb Classical Library), London: William Heinemann; New York: G. P. Putnam's Sons, 1939, p. 217 (see chapter 33, commenting on Gen 2:7). Underlying Philo's explanation is Plato's understanding of the relationship between body and soul, a notion that would have been inconceivable to Israelites eight hundred years before Philo, well before the emergence of abstract Greek and Hellenistic metaphysical speculation.

2. Their use of fig leaves for clothing gave rise to a Jewish interpretation that the tree in which they later hid (verse 8) was a fig tree and that it may have been the tree from which they ate. See Freedman and Simon, *Midrash Rabbah: Genesis*, 15:7, p. 123.

3. This broad interpretation of the expression *ṭōwb wārā'* that combines socially grounded ethics with pragmatic comportment implicitly rejects the idea that the expression was restricted to sexual matters. as proposed by I. Engnell, in "'Knowledge' and 'Life' in the Creation Story," in M. Noth and D. W. Thomas, eds., *Wisdom in Israel and in the Ancient Near East* (= Vetus Testamentum Supplement 3), Brill: Leiden,

1955, pp. 115–16; R. Gordis, "The Knowledge of Good and Evil in the Old Testament and the Qumran Scrolls," *Journal of Biblical Literature* 76 (1957): 123–38; Jacob Milgrom, "Sex and Wisdom: What the Garden of Eden Story Is Saying," *Bible Review* 10:6 (1994): 21, 52. My interpretation does not imply that the expression could not be applied to sexual relations; rather, I maintain that the expression did not evoke that particular topic automatically. Were this not the case, its use in Genesis 3:22 would be senseless.

One verse commonly paraded to support the sexual interpretation is 2 Samuel 19:36. David, returning to Jerusalem after the death of Absalom, invites Barzilai, a loyal supporter, to join him in the city. Barzilai, an octogenarian, responds elliptically to King David, refusing the invitation by suggesting that he could not serve the king's interests: "I am a son of eighty years today. Do I know [the difference] between good/preferable and bad/not preferable if your servant [referring to himself in a courtly manner] tastes that which I eat and that which I drink; if I hear the sound of male singers and female singers?" Barzilai observes that with his failing senses he no longer distinguishes between tasty and poor food, good and bad drink, and good and bad music. He is not discussing his sexual prowess.

Other absolutist interpretations of *ṭōwb* and *raʿ* in the Garden story propose that the words refer to theological insight, or ethical wisdom, or knowledge of good and evil, or knowledge of magic. See Sekine, *Transcendency and Symbols in the Old Testament* (= Beihefte zu Zeitschrift für die altestamentliche Wissenschaft 275), Berlin: Walter de Gruyter, 1999, pp. 233–36.

4. J. Kennedy, *Studies in Hebrew Synonyms*, Oxford: Williams and Norgate, 1898, pp. 65–80. For the syntax of the singular verb with a compound subject, see M. B. Shepherd, "The Compound Subject in Biblical Hebrew," *Hebrew Studies* 52 (2011): 109.

5. Such an interpretation may be maintained if the singular form of the word *ʿēṣ* in the verse possesses a collective sense referring to the totality of trees, as in Genesis 1:11, where "fruit-bearing tree" clearly refers to a multiplicity of fruit-bearing trees.

6. On the humiliation of having buttocks exposed in public, see 2 Samuel 10:4; Isaiah 20:4; 47:2.

7. E. Alshech, "Out of Sight and Therefore Out of Mind: Early Sunni Islamic Modesty Regulations and the Creation of Spheres of Privacy," *Journal of Near Eastern Studies* 66 (2007): 286, 290. Some mountain tribes of New Guinea present a contradictory case. Males can go about their daily life completely bare except for a phallocarp, a decorated sheath that conceals their penis from public view.

8. The attitude reflected in biblical literature contrasts significantly with that in some Mesopotamian literature in which sexual organs are referred to both straightforwardly and pornographically. See V. A. Hurowitz, "An Old Babylonian Bawdy Ballad," in Z. Zevit, S. Gitin, and M. Sokoloff, eds., *Solving Riddles and Untying*

Knots: Biblical, Epigraphic, and Semitic Studies in Honor of Jonas C. Greenfield, Winona Lake, IN: Eisenbrauns, 1995, pp. 545-47, 553-55.

Song of Songs 7:3, *šorrēk 'aggan hassahar*, "your *šōr* [is a] crescent-shaped bowl; let it not lack mixed wine," has been interpreted as referring to the vulva, even though in Ezekiel 16:4 *šorrēk* (with a *daghesh* in the *rēš*) refers unambiguously to "your umbilical cord" that has not yet been cut. In Song of Songs, where the term occurs after mention of her thighs and just before a reference to the young woman's belly, it most likely refers to her navel. See M. Pope, *Song of Songs*, Garden City, NY: Doubleday, 1977, p. 617.

9. It is grammatically possible, though unlikely, that the revealed *'erwat nōaḥ*, "nakedness of Noah" (Gen 9:22), refers to his wife's private parts, not his own. Leviticus 18:8 refers to the "nakedness of the wife of your father" as the "nakedness of your father." According to this interpretation, the "nakedness of Noah" on which Ham gazed and commented to his brothers refers to the exposed genitalia of his own mother. In either case, whether Noah or his wife was seen naked, that which was exposed in domestic privacy ought not to have been visible, no matter the circumstances. At the literary level, lack of any mention of Mrs. Noah in the narrative is not easily overcome if she was the victim of voyeurism.

Similarly, Ezekiel first speaks of Jerusalem as a rejected, unwanted baby girl in the field, where God left her to grow like a plant. He then describes the city as a naked post-pubescent girl with breasts and pubic hair. At that stage, Ezekiel reports, God covered her "nakedness" with his robe and adorned her (Ezek 16:7-8). As a physically mature female—in the metaphoric address of the sixth-century BCE prophet—God would not allow her to be shamed. She, however, a wanton, later removed her own garments in public and shamed herself (Ezek 16:16). As a female adult unattached to a father or a husband, she could do as she pleased and bore complete responsibility for the consequences of her actions.

10. The book of Daniel narrates that when King Nebuchadnezzar became insane his behavior changed from that of a man to that of an animal. His *lēbāb*, literally "heart"—the heart was considered the seat of the intellect—and his *manda'*, knowledge/understanding, left him. Driven from men, he ate grass like an ox, and his body was wetted by heavenly dew (Dan 4:13, 30, 33 [in English translations, Dan 4:16, 33, 36]). I take the reference to his wetted body as an indication that he was naked, like an animal. Though composed centuries after the Garden story and in Aramaic, not Hebrew, this late story preserves the equation between knowledge/understanding and appointed apparel. Hence, it comments obliquely that knowledge of how and when to don appropriate body coverings distinguishes humans from other creatures.

11. After Amnon raped his half-sister, Tamar, and had her put out of his house into the street, she tore her *ketōnet happassīym*, a long-sleeved tunic worn by the virgins of the royal house, exposing part of her body that should have been covered, as a public sign of having been humiliated (2 Sam 13:17-19). Similarly, in Jeremiah 13:26,

when YHWH threatens Judah, who is personified as a woman, he declares: "I will pull the edge of your garment over your head and reveal your shame." Sensitivity to this comprehension of the humanness of clothing suggests an interpretation for YHWH's final words at the end of the book of Jonah (Jonah 4:11): "should I not pity Nineveh . . . in which there are more than one hundred twenty thousand *'ādām* [people], . . . and also *behēmāh rabbāh* [much livestock]?" God's response to the penitent behavior of people and livestock is foregrounded by the narrative in Jonah 3:7–8. There, the king of Nineveh orders people and livestock: "do not taste anything, do not graze, and do not drink water." In verse 8: "and they covered themselves with sackclothes, the people and the livestock." Although the narrative fails to clarify the nature of the animals' wrongdoing and culpability—bestiality comes to mind easily—they were deemed worthy of pity and forgiveness because they acted, or were made to act, humanlike in a public display of pious contrition involving proper clothing.

12. The motif of these garments became significant during and after the Hellenistic period and evolved through the combination of various biblical and post-biblical Eden allusions, including those in Ezekiel. See S. N. Lambden, "From Fig Leaves to Fingernails: Some Notes on the Garments of Adam and Eve in the Hebrew Bible and Select Early Post Biblical Jewish Writing," in P. Morris and D. Sawyer, eds., *A Walk in the Garden: Biblical, Iconographic, and Literary Images of Eden* (= Journal for the Study of the Old Testament Supplement Series 136), Sheffield, England: JSOT Press, 1992, pp. 74–94.

13. Deuteronomy 22:5 raises the question of whether or not Israelites imagined the first couple to be wearing leather tunics that looked exactly alike: "A *kelīy geber* [male apparel] will not be on a woman, and a male will not don *śimlat 'iššāh* [the garment of a woman], because anybody doing these [things] is abhorrent to YHWH your god." Although the specific referent of *kelīy*, translated "apparel" in Deuteronomy 22:5, NRSV and NJPS, is uncertain—it could refer to jewelry (see Gen 24:53; Exod 3:22)—Deuteronomic law distinguished between the *śimlāh* of a male (Deut 10:18) and that of a female (Deut 22:17). The prohibition of Deuteronomy 22:5, then, would not refer to a garment belonging to a female that looks just like that of a male but rather to a garment that by virtue of its cut or color or some other identifying feature was conventionally recognized as one donned by females. If so, mention of the fact that YHWH made the first couple their first tunics may also provide an etiology for what contemporary scholarship recognizes as a socially or culturally constructed rather than an essential/natural distinction between male and female clothing.

14. In fact, verse 8a could be translated as "and they heard the sound of YHWH god moving back and forth in the garden for the wind of the day" and interpreted as indicating that his movement in the garden created the wind that made the sound. This translation depends on interpreting the preposition *le* as emphasizing "the

significance of the occurrence in question for a particular subject." See W. Gesenius, *Gesenius' Hebrew Grammar as Edited and Enlarged by the Late E. Kautzch* (second English edition), London: Oxford University Press, 1910, par. 119s. Other passages where the *le* may be interpreted as marking who or what gains from some previously mentioned action are Genesis 1:11 (for the benefit of its species), 16 (for the ruling of the day); 22:7 (for the offering); 37:4; Leviticus 4:26. Although I consider this interpretation of verse 8 possible, I am unsure that it is appropriate to the context.

Chapter 17. Interrogation and Negotiation

1. This translation purposely preserves a sense of the Hebrew *nātattāh*, based on the verbal root *n-t-n*, "give." The line could also be rendered, "the woman whom you placed with me" (see Gen 1:17; Exod 40:7). The verb recurs immediately afterward in the same verse with the sense "give." The verb also occurs earlier in this chapter, in verse 6b, where it describes Hawwa giving the fruit to Adam.

2. This interpretation was suggested to me orally by Rabbi Yonah Geller of Portland, Oregon (private communication, May 1997).

3. A. Bartor suggests that some rhetorical questions, such as those discussed here, are part of a literary pattern that she terms the "juridical dialogue." See A. Bartor, "The Juridical Dialogue: A Literary-Judicial Pattern," *Vetus Testamentum* 53 (2003): 460–64.

4. In biblical Hebrew, the most common form of interrogation is through use of an interrogative particle, *ha-*, attached to the beginning of the first word of a declarative sentence. It indicates that what follows is a question. An English example clarifies this. Rather than write, "Are you going to the store?" with an inversion of the first two words and a graphic indication of rising tone at the end of the sentence, biblical Hebrew marks the question with the interrogative particle—here a question mark: "?you are going to the store." The Spanish "¿" serves the same function.

Since Iron Age Hebrew preferred to signal questions by attaching the *ha*-particle, the phrase *mah zō't* was freed for some other use. It became semantically distinct and may be compared to the question "Why me/us?" posed by people in times of tragedy or misfortune. The *why* of this question differs from the *why* in such questions as "Why does metal expand when subjected to heat?" "Why me?" is the equivalent of "Woe to me." It is less a question expecting an immediate response than an expression used when confronting adversity in circumstances perceived as ordered by design. See H. M. Schulweis, *For Those Who Can't Believe: Overcoming the Obstacles to Faith*, New York: Harper Perennial, 1994, 95–97.

As an interrogative, *mah zō't* raises issues of blame, guilt, and responsibility. For a more extensive discussion of *mah zō't* questions, see Zevit, "Syntagms in Biblical Hebrew," pp. 400–402.

5. Jackson, *Wisdom Laws*, pp. 29–39.

Chapter 18. Procreation in the Garden

1. S. M. Paul draws attention to two idioms that refer to an untimely death, *belō' yōwmōw*, "in not his day" (Job 15:32), and *belō' 't*, "in not time" (Eccl 7:17). Both terms, and others that he provides, are from a culture with some notion of a normal life span even though everybody dies (2 Sam 14:14). See S. M. Paul, "Untimely Death in the Semitic Languages," in *Divrei Shalom: Collected Studies of Shalom M. Paul on the Bible and the Ancient Near East, 1967–2005*, Leiden: Brill, 2005, pp. 226–238.

2. This is partially intuited also by J. Barr, who deals with this passage in a discussion about the awareness of sexuality but does not consider it linguistically. In contrast to Rashi, Barr concludes only that Adam and Hawwa were sexually active in the garden, not that she bore a child. See Barr, *Garden of Eden*, pp. 66–69.

3. Rabbi Yohanan's cramming all events into twelve hours of daylight reflects a creative, homiletic attempt to pack the Garden story into the sixth day of creation as described in Genesis 1:24–31 and appears to have been based on Psalm 49:13a, understood as meaning "Adam does not overnight in splendor."

4. A later scholar, Simeon Ben Zemah Duran (1361–1444, from Algeria), did not support Ibn Ezra's position but did not quite value Rashi's either. Duran allowed that both *wayyēda' 'ādām* and *hā'ādām yāda'*, the two alternative structures that Rashi compared, refer to past time. Duran, however, defended Rashi's interpretation, pointing out that had the text read *wayyēda' 'ādām*, it would have suggested that the "knowing" was subsequent to the exit from Eden. Duran cited Exodus 4:18 as a parallel case: *wayyēlēk mōšeh wayyāšāb 'el yeter ḥōtnōw*, "and Moses went and returned to Jethro his father-in-law." Following Hebrew word order, this can be translated literally: "and-he-went Moses and-he-returned to Jethro his-father-in-law." However, comparing the Subject + Verb ordering of elements in the Hebrew of Exodus 3:1, *ūwmōšeh hāyāh rō'eh*, "and-Moses was (a) shepherd," which Duran understood to mean that Moses had been a shepherd even before the king of Egypt died and before the Israelites called out to God, as described in Exodus 2:23–25, Duran argued that Rashi had inferred the correct meaning of Genesis 4:1. Duran argued additionally that this interpretation derived "from the manner in which the events are arranged and not because of grammar." See Shimon Ben Zemach Duran, *Sefer Hatashbetz*, part 2 (Hebrew), Lemberg: U. W. Salat, 1891, par. 222; A. Steinsaltz, *Torah Commentary in Responsa Literature from the Eighth through the Sixteenth Century* (Hebrew), Jerusalem: Keter, 1978, p. 5. Contrary to Duran's opinion, Rashi's linguistic view of Genesis 4:1 is correct. See the discussion in Chapter 18.

5. The *qatal* form distinguishes them semantically from nominal clauses with a participle whose time reference is the same as that of the verb in the main clause.

6. This topic is treated extensively on the basis of more than one hundred examples in Z. Zevit, *The Anterior Construction in Classical Hebrew*, Atlanta, GA: Scholars Press, 1998, 15–32.

7. The Garden story is not so succinct as the Jacob-Laban story; rather, it is a lengthy and convoluted one. It is therefore advantageous to see how the anterior construction clarifies the disjointed chronological presentation of crucial events narrated in Genesis 20:17–21:2, a similarly complex story. These verses are part of a narrative about Abraham and Sarah in the Philistine city of Gerar.

Briefly, in Genesis 20:1–16, Abraham passes Sarah off as his unmarried sister, with the consequence that she is taken into the harem of the king, Abimelech, and remains there for a while. At some point, the king plans to be intimate with her, but God stops him, appearing to him in a dream and explaining that she is Abraham's wife. Abimelech returns her to Abraham. Even though nothing about the infertility of Abimelech and his family during Sarah's sojourn in the palace is mentioned earlier in the story, Genesis 20:17 relates that Abraham then prays on behalf of the king and his household and that Gerarite women subsequently give birth.

The assumption in the story that their infertility was contingent on Sarah's removal to the palace is revealed to readers only in Genesis 20:18, *after* the end of the story: "Indeed, YHWH stopped every womb of the house of Abimelech on account of the matter of Sarah, wife of Abraham." The onset of the infertility, initially unnoticed and unreported, must have occurred between the events reported in Genesis 20:2, where Abimelech "took Sarah [into his harem]," and Genesis 20:3, where God came to Abimelech in a dream and said to him: "Behold, you are dead on account of the woman that you took, since she is husbanded by a husband." Events narrated from Genesis 20:3, Abimelech's dream, through Genesis 20:17a, Abraham praying, took place within a single day: Abimelech tells his servants about the dream, scolds Abraham for deceiving him and precipitating the calamity, returns Sarah to Abraham, bestows gifts on both of them, and Abraham prays. According to the story, Sarah must have been in the household of Abimelech for some time before he thought to have relations with her, a period sufficiently long for widespread infertility to become noticeable.

Moreover, the report of Sarah's pregnancy and giving birth reported in Genesis 21:1–2—"*and YHWH had taken account of Sarah* as he had said and she conceived and bore," which exhibits the pattern of the *anterior construction*—must refer to events that occurred sequentially between Genesis 20:17a, where Abraham prays on behalf of Abimelech, and Genesis 20:17b, in fact, to events *before* the report in 20:17b that God had healed Abimelech's wife and his maidservants and *before* they conceived and gave birth. This is so because Genesis 18:14 narrates that Sarah was to have borne a son within a year *after* God visited Abraham's encampment en route to survey Sodom, and the visitation occurred *before* Abraham came to the city of Gerar and *before* Sarah was taken into the harem. Both the logic of the narrative and sensitivity to the anterior construction support Rashi's analysis.

8. The author of *The Book of Jubilees* (second century BCE) understood also that the man and the woman had sexual intercourse immediately after she was presented

to him, even before Adam came to the Garden: "The Lord, our God, imposed a sound slumber on him and he fell asleep. Then he took one bone from among his bones for a woman. That rib was the origin of the woman, from among his bones. He built up the flesh in its place and he built the woman. Then he awakened Adam from his sleep. When he awoke, he got up on the sixth day and he brought him to her. He knew her . . ." (*Jubilees* 3:5–6). Only after Adam was ritually purified was he placed in the Garden. Eve joined him there later, only after completing her period of purification (*Jubilees* 3:8–12). See J. T. A. G. M. van Ruiten, "The Creation of Man and Woman in Early Jewish Literature," in G. P. Luttikhuizen, ed., *The Creation of Man and Woman: Interpretations of the Biblical Narratives in Jewish and Christian Traditions*, Leiden: Brill, 2000, pp. 43–48. Ruiten discusses diverse interpretations in the Apocrypha and Pseudepigrapha about the time and place of the couple's first sexual relations and about the different evaluations of the act as neutral, as sin, or as the consequence of sin (pp. 48–62). See also the materials listed and discussed by D. P. Wright, in "Holiness, Sex and Death in the Garden of Eden," *Biblica* 77 (1996): 312–22. Wright concludes, after teasing out inferences from logical extrapolations of narrative details in the Garden story, that sexual intercourse occurred in the Garden.

9. D. Rothstein, "'And Jacob Came (In)to': Spousal Relationships and the Use of a Recurring Syntagm in Genesis and Jubilees," *Henoch* 29 (2007): 91–96; and see Zevit, "Syntagms in Biblical Hebrew," pp. 396–99. The other expressions collected and discussed by Rothstein are *b-w-'+be*, "to come in" (Josh 23:12), or *b-w-'+ 'al*, "to come on" (Deut 25:2), *'-l-h+ 'al*, "to ascend on" (Gen 31:10, 12 [used of goats]), or *h-l-k+ 'el*, "to go/walk to" (Amos 2:7 [the object of the preposition is a prostitute]).

10. The anterior construction is used again with the mention of Qayin in the second part of Genesis 4:2. There it indicates that even before the younger brother, Hebel, became a shepherd, Qayin had been a worker of the soil, like his father. The younger son engaged in an economic activity not dependent on heavy agricultural labor.

11. For examples of the *ky+t* (+ verb) construction, see Genesis 24:41; 30:16; Deuteronomy 24:15.

12. The verb occurs also in Genesis 14:19; Deuteronomy 32:6; Psalm 78:54. *Q-n-h* is not the verb used for "creating" in Genesis 1:1, 27; 2:4. That is *bārā'*, from the root *b-r-'*. The difference between *q-n-h* and *b-r-'*, if any, has yet to be established.

13. I. Pardes compares Hawwa's naming Qayin with Adam's calling her Isha, "woman." She views it as less an expression of pride than a statement intended to counter Adam's "displacement of the generative powers of the female body." See Pardes, *Countertraditions in the Bible*, pp. 47–48.

14. See R. S. Hess, *Studies in the Personal Names of Genesis 1–11*, Kevalaer: Butzon und Bercker; Neukirchen-Vluyn: Neukirchener Verlag, 1993, pp. 24–27.

15. M. Garsiel, *Biblical Names: A Literary Study of Midrashic Derivations and Puns*, Ramat Gan: Bar Ilan University Press, 1991, pp. 78–97, 203–8.

16. R. Albertz and R. Schmitt, *Family and Household Religion in Ancient Israel and the Levant*, Winona Lake, IN: Eisenbrauns, 2012, p. 247.

Chapter 19. Not a Leg to Stand On

1. Luther, *Lectures on Genesis 1–5*, p. 189.

2. Semantically akin to verbal forms of '-r-r, "to declare *'ārūwr;* to imprecate," is *q-l-l* in the Piel conjugation meaning "to make light, insignificant, paltry." It is employed when the context involves invoking ill on people. The correlative opposite of both these words is the Piel conjugation of *b-r-k*, meaning "to declare that X is *bārūwk,*" that is, in a passive state of having been empowered, strengthened, and/or increased. For the semantic field of words having to do with cursing, imprecation, and malediction, see H. C. Brichto, *The Problem of Curse in the Hebrew Bible* (= SBL Monograph Series XIII), Philadelphia: Society of Biblical Literature, 1963.

3. The meaning "to hedge, bind" is more apparent with Akkadian *arāru* than with the Hebrew, but since these are the only two languages in which the root '-r-r is productive, Speiser's point is reasonable. E. A. Speiser, "An Angelic Curse: Exodus 14:20," *Journal of the American Oriental Society* 80 (1960): 198; Speiser, *Genesis,* p. 24. In general, see Brichto, *Problem of Curse,* pp. 83–87, 113–15. Although there are more recent discussions, primarily in dictionaries, most rely on Brichto, for good reason, but do not advance our lexical understanding beyond his fundamental study.

When conjugated as a transitive verb, the root '-r-r may allude to some self-fulfilling power to bring about the diminished state, as in the case of execratory waters imbibed by a woman suspected of adultery by a jealous husband (Num 5:18–27) and the case of Balaam, a professional execrator hired to curse Israel by King Balak (Num 22:6). In these cases, however, the literary context clarifies that the power of diminution was neither in the waters nor in the words of Balaam. That this notion concerning words derived from '-r-r was not the result of singular Israelite authors reworking texts that told of magic, but reflects ancient Israelite lore in general, insofar as this is known to us, is borne out by additional attestations in different genres of biblical literature.

4. Jeremiah 17:5–6 appears at first to indicate both the activity through which one could become designated as *'ārūwr* and what would happen afterward, but close consideration of the structure of these verses and their images indicates that this is not the case. He who trusts in man and in his own strength and who turns away from YHWH is *'ārūwr;* that is, the act itself determines the state of the person who engages in it (verse 5). Once he is *'ārūwr, wehāyāh ke'ar'ār bā'arābāh,* "he will be like a juniper shrub in the wilderness"; that is, he will be lonely, isolated, and desolate (verse 6). Jeremiah does not say that the man is going to turn into a juniper, just as he does not say that the person who is *bārūwk* will turn into an abundantly watered tree (Jer 17:7–8). The language is figurative, a simile appealing to the psychological sense of well-being that Jeremiah understands to exist when one is within the covenantal sodality

but absent when one leaves it. Jeremiah uses *hāyāh + ke*, the verb of being, followed by the preposition *ke-*, meaning "to be like," not *hāyāh + le*, "to become."

5. Similar catastrophes listed in Leviticus 26:16–43 are conditioned threats.

6. Between the introduction and actual listing of the bad things that YHWH will do or bring about, again called *qelālōwt* in Deuteronomy 28:45, is a proleptic description of the circumstances and situations in which the nation will become diminished after the *qelālōwt* are activated. (Unfortunately, translations do not usually distinguish between words derived from '-*r-r* and those derived from *q-l-l*.) The diminishments are conveyed through a series of *'ārūwr* passages in Deuteronomy 28:16–19. In the translation I supply the word *are* in the first and last pairs of statements for the sake of clarity in English. No verb of being occurs or is necessary in the Hebrew:

> Diminished [are] you in the city;
> and diminished [are] you in the field;
> diminished, your basket and kneading trough;
> diminished, the fruit of your womb and the fruit of your
> soil, the issue of your cattle and the young of your flocks;
> diminished [are] you in your coming in and
> diminished [are] you in your going out. (Deut 28:16–19)

The section appears dynamic only because it is juxtaposed to verses 20–68, which contain active, transitive verbs.

7. Passages such as Genesis 12:3, Genesis 27:29, and Numbers 24:9 shed little light on the semantics of '-*r-r*. They are similar to the schoolyard formula intended to protect children from insults: "I'm the rubber; you're the glue. Everything bounces and sticks to you. Only compliments come through."

8. The only recent detailed study of the semantic field of curse in the Bible, a review of more than twenty verbs and nouns, is J. K. Aitken, *The Semantics of Blessing and Cursing in Ancient Hebrew* (= Ancient Near Eastern Studies Supplement 23), Louvain: Peeters, 2007. Aitken reaches no clear conclusion about the semantics of '-*r-r* (pp. 76–84) but concludes that *b-r-k* is about blessing, praising, and favoring (pp. 112–17). My conclusions differ from his in part because I assign greater significance than he does to the observation that '-*r-r* and *b-r-k* are correlatives.

9. For a more extensive discussion of performative utterances, see Aitken, *Semantics of Blessing and Cursing*, p. 13. Both verbs are used in this example, the story of Balak's solicitation, where Balaam makes a negative magical pronouncement against Israel using a verb from the root '-*r-r*: "Now, go please. Declare this nation diminished for my benefit [*'ārāh-līy*] because it is more powerful than I. Perhaps I will be able to smite him and I will chase him from the land. Indeed, I know that whom you declare strengthened [*tebārēk*] is strengthened [*meborāk*] and whom you declare diminished [*tā'ōr*] will become diminished [*yūw'ār*]" (Num 22:6). Balak hoped that the declaration of some *'ārūwr* formula would so weaken Israel that he could defeat it,

but he did not assume that the formula would vouchsafe victory. At best, it might provide him an edge.

10. Z. Zevit, "The First Halleluyah," in D. Miano and S. Malena, eds., *Milk and Honey: Essays on Ancient Israel and the Bible,* Winona Lake, IN: Eisenbrauns, 2007, p. 164.

11. The *yiqtol* verbs in the imperfect tense mark present-future time, or, stated differently, time not past. The time referent, present or future, is determined by context. See Zevit, *Anterior Construction,* pp. 49–57.

12. In some cases, when applied to humans, it refers to general movement without specification and is best translated as "went/bestirred himself," as in Genesis 35:22, "and Reuben went/bestirred himself and slept with Bilha, his father's concubine." See also Exodus 2:1, Deuteronomy 31:1, and Joshua 23:16, where forms of the verb *h-l-k* do not suggest any specific manner of movement, certainly not "walking."

13. An additional indication that the term referred generally to motion is its common employment as an infinitive absolute attached to other verbs as a sort of "helping verb." In such constructions, it bears the sense "continuous movement/continually moving," as in Genesis 8:3; 26:13; Joshua 6:9; Judges 4:24; Zechariah 8:21; Psalm 126:6.

14. Modern commentators are divided on whether the story intended to indicate that the serpent once had feet. See the material surveyed and summarized in A. D. Roitman, "'Crawl upon Your Belly' (Gen 3:14)—The Physical Aspect of the Serpent in Early Jewish Exegesis" (Hebrew), *Tarbiz* 64:2 (1995): 170–73. If the species of *nāḥāš* imagined in this story was an Isaianic *śārāp*, then at least some subspecies of these, whether real or imagined, were believed to have hands, feet, and wings (Isa 6:2–6; 14:29). Seraphim, symbolic of sacred sovereignty, were represented on inscribed Hebrew seals from the Iron Age II period in Israel (ca. 925–586 BCE) as unwinged, two-winged, and four-winged. Isaiah describes those in his vision as possessing six wings. Sometimes seraphim were described as completely serpentine, sometimes as partially human; see Joines, *Serpent Symbolism,* pp. 7–8, 49–51; Roitman, "'Crawl upon Your Belly,'" pp. 174–82; B. Sass, "The Pre-exilic Hebrew Seals: Iconism vs. Aniconism," in B. Sass and C. Uehlinger, eds., *Studies in the Iconography of Northwest Semitic Inscribed Seals* (= Orbis biblicus et orientalis 125), Fribourg, Switzerland: University Press, 1993, pp. 211–15. All figures in the Sass collection representing Israelite art are legless; therefore, those described by Isaiah as having feet, although he does not mention how many, may have been Egyptianized, for reasons not yet apparent to contemporary scholarship. For images of bipedal seraphim (Egyptian uraei), see the data in O. Keel, *Jahwe-Visionen und Siegelkunst* (= Stuttgarter Bibel-Studien 84/85), Stuttgart: Verlag Katholisches Bibelwerk, 1977, pp. 74–124.

15. A. W. Shorter, "The God Nehebkau," *Journal of Egyptian Archaeology* 21 (1935): 41–81; C. Herrmann, "Fünf phönizische Formen für ägyptische Fayencen," *Zeitschrift des Deutschen Palästina-Vereins* 105 (1989): 33–37. I thank Othmar Keel of the University of Fribourg for these references.

16. The verb is attested two additional times in the Bible: in Job 9:17. "With the storm *yešūwpēnīy* [he presses me], and he multiplies my wounds gratuitously"; and in Psalm 139:11, "And I say, darkness *yešūwpēnīy* [presses me], and night; light [is] around me." Psalm 139:11 is unclear. In Job 9:17, because of the parallelism with *peša'ay,* "wounds," the verb has been taken to mean "bruise, smite, wound." and the like, and that meaning transferred to the Genesis passages. In Hebrew, storms do not "hit" (as they do in English). They blow whirling winds (Jer 23:13) and powerful driving winds (Ezek 13:11–13) and cause large billows in the sea (Jon 1:4, 12). They are winds with attitude.

17. This helps clarify how Jacob could hold fast to Esau's "heel": he held him by the ankle (Gen 25:26). Although the story of Jacob's birth is well known, there are apparently no records of a baby exiting the womb with an outstretched arm. See E. Viezel, "The Influence of Realia on Biblical Depictions of Childbirth," *Vetus Testamentum* 61 (2011): 687.

18. The relationship is characterized by "enmity" in the same way that the relationship of David and Jonathan is supposedly characterized by the presence of God. It is described in words similar to those of the Genesis passage: "YHWH will be between me and you and between my seed and your seed forever" (1 Sam 20:42).

19. This description of the activity may be clear only to those who recall chasing and catching snakes and lizards in their youth.

20. Malul, *Studies in Mesopotamian Legal Symbolism,* pp. 118, 388 n. 22, 252–68, 432–39; and M. Malul, "'*Āqēb* 'Heel' and '*Āqab* 'to Supplant,' and the Concept of Succession in the Jacob-Esau Narratives," *Vetus Testamentum* 46 (1966): 197–98, 203.

21. See my initial hypothesis about the source of the serpent's motivation to do harm in Chapter 15.

22. Daniel C. Dennett of Tufts University, personal communication, March 2001; and see D. C. Dennett, *Consciousness Explained,* Boston: Little, Brown, 1991, pp. 385–86.

23. My interpretation of verses 13–19 is similar to that of B. Jacob, *Das erste Buch der Tora: Genesis,* Berlin: Schocken, 1934, pp. 111–22, but was developed independently, before I read his extensive exegesis. I am pleased to acknowledge the priority of his work.

24. "If you happen upon a bird's nest . . . in any tree or on the ground with fledglings or eggs and the mother roosting on the fledglings or on the eggs . . ." (Deut 22:6).

25. Examples of *zera'* referring to a single son are Genesis 15:3; 17:19; 19:32, 34; 21:12; 26:3, 4; 28:4; examples of it referring to a collective are Genesis 7:3, 13:16(?); 28:14(?); 46:6, 7; 48:4, 19; Exodus 28:43; Leviticus 18:21. In some cases the singular sense of "son" or the collective sense "progeny" or "sons" is supported by the presence of appropriate verbal or pronominal forms. Examples of the former are Genesis 4:25; 15:18; 16:10; 21:13; 22:17; Numbers 14:24. Some of these could be dismissed as cases where the verbs and/or pronouns are made to agree with the morphology of the noun, but

examples of the plural sense with appropriate verbs and pronouns place the burden of proof on those who dismiss them: Genesis 15:13; 17:7; Exodus 30:21.

26. The serpent is represented as a woman or snake-woman in a number of Renaissance paintings—for example, Lucas Cranach the Elder's *Paradise,* Raphael's *Fall from Grace,* and Michelangelo's *Fall* in the Sistine Chapel—because of a tradition that developed in church exegesis: see D. Sölle, J. H. Kirchberger, and H. Haag, *Great Women of the Bible in Art and Literature,* Grand Rapids, MI: Eerdmans, 1994, pp. 18–25. This representation may have arisen through the combination of the serpent with Lilith. In late medieval lore deriving from both Jewish Hellenistic magic and early medieval midrash, as well as from traditions in Byzantine Christianity, Lilith was considered Adam's first wife, who, once rejected, plotted against Eve. See Jo Milgrom, "Giving Eve's Daughters Their Due," *Bible Review* 12:1 (February 1996): 34–36.

27. T. I. Stores and R. L. Usinger, *General Zoology,* New York: McGraw-Hill, 1957, pp. 526–27; W. K. Purves, G. H. Orians, and H. C. Heller, *Life: The Science of Biology,* Salt Lake City, UT: Sinauer Associates, 1992, pp. 597–98. I thank S. Blair Hedges of Pennsylvania State University for updating me on this information (e-mail, February 25, 2008).

28. N. Vidal and S. Blair Hedges, "Molecular Evidence for a Terrestrial Origin for Snakes," *Proceedings of the Royal Society B: Biological Sciences* (Supplement) 271 (2004): S226–29, http://www.pubmedcentral.nih.gov/articlerender.fcgi?artid=1810015 (viewed February 22, 2012).

Chapter 20. No Bundle of Joy

1. L. C. Callister et al., "The Pain of Childbirth: Perceptions of Culturally Diverse Women," *Pain Management Nursing* 4:4 (2003): 145, 147–48.

2. The list in *Aboth d'Rabbi Nathan* was brought to my attention by Janet K. Smith when she was a doctoral student at the Union Institute and University (April 2007). The list is also found in *b. Erubin* 100b. In a chapter entitled "Eve's Curses," Judith R. Baskin discusses the rabbinic exegesis of Genesis 3:16 that provided the basis for the extended list of curses. See Baskin, *Midrashic Women,* pp. 74–76.

3. S. Parker, *The Human Body Book,* New York: DK Publishing, 2007, pp. 208–13.

4. The pains discussed in this chapter should not be confused with the three types of pain described in contemporary medical literature—somatic, visceral, and neuropathic—although there might be a correspondence.

5. English *writhe,* "to twist or contort the body (in pain)," which once referred to tying and fettering, illustrates a similar semantic development. See, for example, English *wreath,* "a ring of woven and interlaced grass, vines, flowers, or branches."

6. My analysis of these terms is based on data collected under the relevant roots in Kaddari, *Dictionary of Biblical Hebrew.*

7. A. Kalmanofsky, "Israel's Baby: The Horror of Childbirth in the Biblical Prophets," *Biblical Interpretation* 16 (2008): 68–69.

8. Carol Meyers is perhaps the first modern commentator to reject the idea that these verses refer to "pain," an idea introduced by the Greek translation of the Pentateuch. She prefers to render Hebrew *'iṣṣābōwn* as "toil"—"labor" in this context— arguing back from verse 17, where she takes it to mean "physical labor." This translation is problematic because another word, *'eṣeb*, derived from the same root, *'-ṣ-b*, also occurs in verse 16, where it cannot refer to toil but only to some sort of physical discomfort, as I propose later in the chapter. See Meyers, *Discovering Eve*, pp. 99–109. My discussion begins with her essential observations.

9. Words from *'-ṣ-b* are also used to refer to sadness, wistfulness, and mental fatigue. In Genesis 6:6, God regrets that he made people: *wayyit'aṣṣēb 'el libbōw*, "he tired himself to his heart"—that is, he tired his mind, he felt let down, disappointed, distraught, wistful, sad. See Genesis 34:7; Proverbs 10:10; 15:13, where that state of mind is contrasted with a happy mind; and 1 Chronicles 4:9–10, verses that allude to Genesis 3:16.

10. Callister et al., "Pain of Childbirth," pp. 146, 148.

11. A personal anecdote illustrates the power of words to conceptualize pain. During a winter camping trip to the Anza-Borrego wilderness in southern California, my daughter, then five years old, emerged from a tent, tripped, and fell into a mean thorn bush. She got to her feet hurt and confused. Then she noticed the thorns sticking out of her palms and through her overalls near her knees. Tears welled up in her eyes and from the turn of her lips, I knew that she was about to engage in some serious crying. Approaching her, I noticed that her face and eyes were okay, and so, coming to a stop before her, I kneeled down, put my hands on her shoulders, and said in as unworried a voice as I could muster, "Well, that's camping." She thought about it for a second, repeated in a blubbering whimper, "That's camping," and rushed into my arms for a big hug. The storm was averted. After the thorns were removed, she went off, limping a bit, to play. The phrase "that's camping" changed the experience of physical pain from something to cry about to something to bear. It came in handy on many other camping trips.

12. A. J. Bledstein, "Was Eve Cursed? (Or Did a Woman Write Genesis?)," *Bible Review* 9:1 (1993): 44–45.

13. In Genesis 4:7, the preposition linked to the noun is *'el*, indicating direction toward and often translated as "to"; in Song of Songs 7:11, the preposition is *'al*, rendered in English according to context as "on, near" or, with certain verbs expressing aggression or hostility, as "against." The difference suggests that the two phrases which use different prepositions should not be considered synonymous.

14. W. Vogels, "The Power Struggle between Man and Woman (Gen 3:16b)," *Biblica* 77 (1996): 204–6. Hans-Cristoph Aurin also interprets the verse in terms of sexual politics and male power. See H-C Aurin, "Your Urge Shall Be for Your Husband? A New Translation of Genesis 3:16b and a New Interpretation of Genesis 4:7," *Lectio Difficilior* 1 (2008): 1–18, http://www.lectio.unibe.ch/08_1/aurin.htm (viewed February 23, 2012).

15. Other discussions of *tešūwqāh* point out difficulties with interpretations based on sexual desire. See E. Qimron, "Biblical Philology and the Dead Sea Scrolls" (Hebrew), *Tarbiz* 58 (1989): 312; J. N. Lohr, "Sexual Desire? Eve, Genesis 3:16, and *tšwqh*," *Journal of Biblical Literature* 130 (2011): 231–46.

16. Zevit, *Religions of Ancient Israel*, pp. 18–22, 612–15.

17. These laws may be assigned to the tenth century BCE on the basis of their presuppositions about social organization and population distribution. See J. L'Hour, "Une législation criminelle dan le Deuteronome," *Biblica* 44 (1963): 1–28.

18. The case of Dinah in Genesis 34:1–31 serves as literary precedent, whether or not she was forcefully raped, a point left unclear in the story. Her father, Jacob, and most of her brothers chose not to act, but two brothers took it upon themselves to avenge the real or perceived wrong to their sister and thereby to themselves (verses 25, 30). An oral version of this story may have been part of Israelite lore in the tenth century BCE.

19. As a matter of legal fiction, the male children of Zelophahad's daughters and their husbands were then considered heirs of Zelophahad, their grandfather, so that the original patrimony was not lost to the tribe, and the lineage was carried on, providing a type of continuity similar to that addressed by the Levirate marriage law of Deuteronomy 25:5. See Numbers 36:2–12.

20. These accounts, reflecting how various norms worked in society, point to limitations in ancient Israel's legal system compared to legal systems under which we live. See P. Barmash, "The Narrative Quandary: Cases of Law in Literature," *Vetus Testamentum* 54:1 (2004): 8–14.

21. Although the translation of *'innāh* in Exodus 21:13 remains unsettled, the legal and theological issues raised by the verse are interesting. The major difficulty with this verse is that the word *'innāh*, understood to mean "forced" (2 Kings 5:7; Ps 90:10; Prov 12:24), indicates that God somehow set up the situation because he wanted a particular person dead. This interpretation implies that accidental deaths are occasioned by divine will, making perpetrators unwilling and unknown executioners of divine will. This understanding sheds light on *mōt tāmūwt* punishments for certain offenses against God but does not clarify why the killer in such cases is held to even a minor degree of culpability. See D. Daube, "Direct and Indirect Causation in Biblical Law," *Vetus Testamentum* 11 (1961): 225–56.

22. The narrative of Abraham's purchase of the cave from Ephron in Genesis 23 provides another example in which awareness of the general cultural and specifically legal background both of the tellers of the tale and of the characters represented within their milieu aid in understanding how and what the narrative meant in antiquity. See R. Westbrook, *Property and the Family in Biblical Law* (= Journal for the Study of the Old Testament Supplement Series 113), Sheffield, England: JSOT Press, 1991, pp. 24–35.

23. The principle adumbrated throughout the chapter—that unless specifically criminalized, all acts are permissible—is stated formally in section 6 of the "Preliminary

Provisions" of the *California Penal Code*: "No act or omission, commenced after twelve o'clock noon of the day on which this Code takes effect as a law, is criminal or punishable, except as prescribed or authorized by this Code, or by some of the statutes which it specifies as continuing in force."

The significance of gender and number on which much of the legal analysis in this and the preceding chapters depends is also addressed among the "Preliminary Provisions" in section 7: "Words used in this code in the present tense include the future as well as the present; words used in the masculine gender include the feminine and neuter; the singular number includes the plural, and the plural the singular" (http://www.leginfo.ca.gov/cgi-bin/displaycode?section=pen&group=00001-01000&file=2-24 [viewed March 11, 2013]).

Chapter 21. Toil and Trouble

1. For typical examples of *š-m-ʿ* + *be* + *qōwl/qōl* see Deuteronomy 8:20; 13:19; 16:5; 1 Samuel 8:9, 22; 15:24; 19:6; and for an example of *š-m-ʿ* + *le* + *qōwl/qōl* see Genesis 16:2; Exodus 15:26; 18:24; Judges 2:20; 1 Samuel 2:25; 15:1. See also Zevit, "Syntagms in Biblical Hebrew," pp. 399–400.

2. For an assessment of the role of women in Israelite daily life during the Iron Age, see Meyers, *Discovering Eve*, pp. 142–64.

3. Frisch, "Biblical Attitude toward Human Toil," p. 105.

4. The term *baʿabūwr* is usually rendered "for the sake of" (see Gen 8:21; 12:13, 16; 18:26, 29) or "in order to" or "so that" (Exod 9:16; 20:20; 1 Sam 1:6). This is simply a matter of conventional English usage in different literary contexts.

5. Isaiah 5:1–6a indicates some of what was involved in Judahite viticulture—which is not quite the same as gardening—and the frustrations that an agriculturalist might experience when, after doing everything right, his work yielded nothing. The activities described are breaking open the ground, removing large stones, planting the vines, building a watchtower, and making a pressing floor and insculpting a wine vat on an appropriate surface.

6. Genesis 5:29b interprets Genesis 3:17 as if God's statement resulted in a worsening of the agriculturalist's position. Despite vocabulary linking Genesis 5:29b and 3:17, the motif of man being inadequate to the task is actually found in Genesis 4:11–12, with the diminution/weakening/lessening of Qayin. There God declares that Qayin is *ʾārūwr min hāʾadāmāh*, "[even] more diminished than the ground . . . that took the blood of your brother from your hand"—that is, his prowess is insufficient to do agricultural work. God continues to tell him that "when you work [*taʿabōd*] the land, it will not increase giving its strength for you." The *yiqtol* verbs in Genesis 4:12 indicate a future situation different from the one he knew before he killed his brother. What will be different? Qayin will eventually discover that his work cannot overcome the natural limit on the yield capacity of his farmed plots and will experience it as a personal failure.

Speiser's and Brichto's understanding of *'arūwr* applies to this verse: Qayin is bound, restricted from enjoying the earth; whatever he does will be of no avail. See Speiser, *Genesis*, 20–30; Brichto, *Problem of Curse*, pp. 83–87.

Although Genesis 4:12 is usually rendered, "When you work the earth, it will not continue to give its strength to you," the phrase *lō' tōwsep tēt-kōḥaḥ lāk* may also be translated as "you will not [be able to] increase the giving of her [the earth's] strength for you." All your work will not increase productivity for your benefit.

7. This interpretation accords with the realistic appreciation of the necessity of human labor. In biblical literature, even God's activities are described using terms that describe physical labor, both in the Garden story (Gen 2:7–9, 15, 19, 21–22) and elsewhere (Amos 9:11; Ps 127:1–2). See Frisch, "Biblical Attitude toward Human Toil," pp. 106–17.

8. Rashi interprets these two laws as applying only to employees working in the vineyard or the field, apparently associating them with the laws in Deuteronomy 24:15–16. Logic is on Rashi's side because if a vineyard was located along a well-trodden path, a vintner certainly lost a certain amount of produce to nibbling passersby. Additionally, the status of unharvested produce as private property is clearly implied in the laws of Exodus 22:4–5 concerning the liability of individuals responsible for damaging such property and thereby diminishing the owner's income. If, however, Deuteronomic laws are considered part of a composition expressing an underlying worldview of what ought to be, their intent is to restrict the owner's control. Just as they allow others to snack on produce before harvest, they allow the poor to glean harvested but uncollected produce left in the field along with forgotten and unharvested produce. But no matter how interpreted, these laws contain nothing that could have made Israelite readers of the Iron Age consider their Edenic forebears violators of related norms or guilty under law. I thank Yonatan Zevit for bringing these passages to my attention.

9. Contemporary sensibilities cannot guide us historically. What may constitute a crime in one society may not be a censurable act in another. For example, no crimes in Israel are known to have been punishable by incarceration, even though prisons were known: Genesis 39:20–23; Jeremiah 37:15.

10. This midrash reflects a minority opinion in rabbinic thinking about the Garden story. I thank Yehiel Friedlander of the Hebrew University, who drew my attention to this midrash. See Ginzberg, *Legends of the Jews*, vol. 1, p. 82; vol. 5 n. 97.

Chapter 22. Out of the Garden

1. I. M. Kikawada points out that Hawwa's three-element appellation, *'ēm kol ḥay*, which he translates by "Mother of all living," parallels that of the Mesopotamian goddess Mami, *bēlet kala ilī*, "Mistress of all the gods," in Atrahasis I:246–48. In this myth, Mami was given her sobriquet after she created self-reproducing humankind. See I. M. Kikiwada, "Two Notes on Eve," *Journal of Biblical Literature* 91 (1972): 34.

The plot equivalent in the Garden story would have come after Hawwa produced her second child, doubling the human population. In the Atrahasis myth, Mami created seven pairs of humans, male and female, who were somehow born with umbilical cords that needed to be cut.

2. In addition to indicating the relevance of the Phoenician parallel name, S. C. Layton demonstrates how the Greek Septuagint transliteration of the name delimits the range of possible etymologies. See S. C. Layton, "Remarks on the Canaanite Origin of Eve," *Catholic Biblical Quarterly* 59 (1997): 24, 28.

3. Hebrew *ḥāy* is also related to Arabic *ḥiwā*, "a collection of tents," a word derived from Arabic *ḥ-w-y*, which is cognate to the Hebrew noun *ḥawwāh*. This noun, which is both a homograph and a homophone of the woman's new name, refers also to a farmstead settled by an extended family. It occurs in the name of a region referred to as *ḥawwōt yā'īr*, "the farmsteads of Yair," in Numbers 32:41 and Judges 10:4. This complicated situation in which consonantal /w/ and /y/ seem to appear and disappear is explained by describing them as "weak" consonants that sometimes flip back and forth between related languages and within the same language. Many data support this explanation.

4. See F. Brown, S. R. Driver, and C. A. Briggs, *A Hebrew and English Lexicon of the Old Testament* (corrected edition), Oxford: Clarendon Press, 1953 (originally published in 1907; hereafter BDB, for the initials of its authors); and L. Köhler and W. Baumgartner, *Hebräisches und Aramäisches Lexikon zum Alten Testament* (third edition), Leiden: Brill, 1967. In Old South Arabic, a language known only from inscriptions, *ḥwy* also refers to a clan, perhaps a clan of serfs. Cf. J. C. Biella, *Dictionary of Old South Arabic, Sabean Dialect,* Chico, CA: Harvard Semitic Museum, 1982, pp. 168–69. As the discussion and references in BDB indicate, the etymology of the word had been worked out by the end of the nineteenth century, but many exegetes have not applied this research to the Genesis passage.

5. The expression *'mr + l* where the preposition introduces the person addressed is attested in Genesis 3:13; 4:15; 1 Samuel 20:2; 2 Samuel 2:21.

6. BDB, s.v. *ḥwh* I. Between words derived from the roots *ḥ-y-y, ḥ-y-w,* and *ḥ-w-y* there is confusion and a crossover of such meanings as "to be, to live, to be animate, to turn, to twist and turn, to circle, to gather together, to collect." Thus Hawwa's name may be explained and interpreted in a number of different ways legitimately. My preference for connecting it to kin terminology is based on the story's employment of kinship terms throughout and the implications of Adam's statement for the continuation of the story. Admittedly, any Israelite hearing the name could have associated it with both meanings, "life" and "kin," simultaneously.

7. The parallels referred to later in this chapter conform to the sensible caveats expressed by S. J. Lieberman in "Are Biblical Parallels Euclidean?" *Maarav* 8 (1992): 90–94. They derive from texts concerned with similar matters and coming from the

same chronological horizon and from a civilization whose cultural contacts with Israel preceded its political influence after the ninth century.

8. W. G. Lambert and A. R. Millard, *Atra-Ḥasīs: The Babylonian Story of the Flood*, Oxford: Clarendon Press, 1969, tablet I, lines 294–360, pp. 65–67; tablet II–III, pp. 73–97; and the introduction, pp. 1–25.

9. A. D. Kilmer, "The Mesopotamian Concept of Overpopulation and Its Solution as Reflected in the Mythology," *Orientalia* 41 (1972): 171–75. It is not accidental that the Mesopotamian flood tradition is concerned with urban dwellers—people living in a circumscribed territory. V. A. Hurowitz republished an Old Babylonian text hymning sex either as essential for the city or as basic to urban life. See Hurowitz, "Old Babylonian Bawdy Ballad," p. 548, and literature cited there.

10. A. D. Kilmer cites a Greek parallel to the motif of overpopulation. The goddess Earth (Gaia) felt overburdened by an excess of humans so she requested that Zeus lighten her load. He sent the Theban wars and later set the stage for the Trojan war so that death would empty the world. See Kilmer, "Mesopotamian Concept of Overpopulation," p. 176.

11. I. M. Kikawada and A. Quinn, *Before Abraham Was*, Nashville, TN: Abingdon Press, 1985, pp. 46–48. Kikawada and Quinn present many other parallels from the ancient Near East and the classical world, reflecting the same concern and similar patterning.

12. The translation of Genesis 6:3 is problematic in that the meaning of *yādōwn*, rendered here conventionally as "abide," has not been established lexicographically, in part because the meaning of the verse in context is not clear. It clearly has to do with the conjoining of the *benēy 'elōhīym,* some type of divine beings, with the available daughters mentioned in Genesis 6:2, but philology has yet to clarify the verse. See G. J. Wenham, *Genesis 1–15* (Word Biblical Commentary), Waco, TX: Word Books, 1985, pp. 135–47. God's reaction in verse 3 warrants the inference that an original story to which the snippet Genesis 6:1–3 alludes may possibly have told of the *benēy 'elōhīym* attempting to achieve longevity for their progeny. Nothing in the extant text indicates that the editor of this pericope perceived anything wrong with the matrimonial arrangements per se or with the attempt at eugenics. Moreover, close reading of verse 4 indicates that contrary to the widespread interpretation of the Nephilim-Giborim heroes as the progeny of the unions, they are of the same generation as the "daughters." See H. N. Wallace, "The Toledot of Adam," in J. A. Emerton, ed., *Studies in the Pentateuch* (= Vetus Testamentum Supplement 41), Leiden: Brill, 1990, pp. 31–32.

13. Culturally, it would have been inconceivable within the Yahwistic circles that transmitted these stories that sexual man could become divine. T. Frymer-Kensky emphasizes that YHWH was not sexed. Although he bestowed procreative powers and fertility, he did not explicitly grant potency. See Frymer-Kensky, *In the Wake of the Goddess*, pp. 189–91.

14. Kilmer, "Mesopotamian Counterparts," p. 43.

15. M. Buber, "The Tree of Knowledge," in *On the Bible: Eighteen Studies*, New York: Schocken, 1968, pp. 20–21.

16. Ibid., p. 21.

17. Malul, *Studies in Mesopotamian Legal Symbolism*, pp. 122–38.

18. *KTU* 1.17.VI.33–38. See M. Astour, "The Nether World and Its Denizens at Ugarit," in B. Alster, ed., *Death in Mesopotamia, Papers Read at the XXVIe Rencontre assyriologique internationale*, Copenhagen: Akademisk Forlag, 1980, p. 234; B. Margalit, "Death and Dying in the Ugaritic Epics," in Alster, *Death in Mesopotamia*, pp. 252–53.

19. S. Dalley, *Myths from Mesopotamia*, Oxford: Oxford University Press, 1989, p. 150. W. G. Lambert has restored Atra-Hassis tablet III, column VI: 147–50: "[you], birth goddess, creatress of destinies, [assign death] to the peoples." See W. G. Lambert, "The Theology of Death," in Alster, *Death in Mesopotamia*, pp. 57–58. According to this reading, humankind was formed to be reproductive and mortal. The Mesopotamian flood story, then, is not about the introduction of death into the world but about premature death, similar to what is implied by the expression *mōwt tāmūwt*. I thank Jacob Klein of Bar Ilan University for referring me to Lambert's study.

20. See Dalley, *Myths from Mesopotamia*, pp. 182–88, and see p. 187. Kilmer mentions that Adapa was the son of Ea. See Kilmer, "Mesopotamian Counterparts," pp. 40–41.

21. Mettinger, *Eden Narrative*, pp. 104–9.

22. Gilgamesh, tablets IX–XI: 278–83, in Dalley, *Myths from Mesopotamia*, pp. 95–120.

23. Dalley, *Myths from Mesopotamia*, p. 119.

24. A. S. Kapelrud, "You Shall Surely Not Die," in A. Lemaire and B. Otzen, eds., *History and Tradition of Early Israel: Studies Presented to Eduard Nielsen* (= Vetus Testamentum Supplement 50), Leiden: Brill, 1993, pp. 53–54, 61.

25. N. Vulpa, "Irony and the Unity of the Gilgamesh Epic," *Journal of Near Eastern Studies* 53 (1994): 275–83.

26. T. Jakobsen, "Death in Mesopotamia," in Alster, *Death in Mesopotamia*, pp. 19–24.

Chapter 24. A Literal Translation of a Literary Text

1. M. Weiss, *The Bible from Within: The Method of Total Interpretation*, Jerusalem: Magnes Press, 1984, pp. 1–73.

2. No biblical datum can be interpreted as suggesting that natural, timely death was ever viewed as evil or as an event that people could or wished to avoid. Moreover, there is no reason to assume that this conception was uniquely Israelite. People throughout the ancient Near East had traditional knowledge that the self continued in some subterranean netherworld or spirit-filled otherworld, although they did not

know how or why this occurred. Inasmuch as continuation after death was an unquestioned given for them, the anxiety and angst about death that characterizes parts of contemporary societies ought not be retrojected as psychological universals. See S. M. Paul, "Emigration from the Netherworld in the Ancient Near East," in K. Van Lerberghe and A. Schoors, eds., *Immigration and Emigration within the Ancient Near East: Festschrift E. Lipinski* (= Orientalia Lovaniensia Analecta 65), Leuven: Uitgevreij Peeters en Departement Oriëntalistiek, 1995, pp. 221–24 and bibliography cited there.

Chapter 25. Allusions to the Garden Story in the Hebrew Bible

1. My translation amends *ky 'dm* to *k'dm*.

2. Garsiel, *Biblical Names*, pp. 138–39.

3. As is common in Job, this verse is open to other renderings that might remove it from this list. Verses in Job 31:33–34, 38–40, allude to events in the life of the first family, but verses 33 and 38 conflate Adam with Qayin since Adam did not "hide" a transgression in the earth.

4. The vision of the Valley of Dry Bones reported in Ezekiel 37:1–10 describing the reversal of human decay and decomposition does not allude to the formation of the human in the Garden story. A series of allusions to a Tree of Life (and/or Knowledge)— Ezekiel 47:12; Psalms 1:3; 92:13–15; Proverbs 3:17–18; 11:30; 13:12–13—either represents a complex development of themes in the Garden story centuries after it was composed or, more likely, adverts to a complex of mythemes drawn from stories unknown to us. Ezekiel 28:11–19, reporting a bejeweled mountainous Eden inhabited by the king of Tyre, protected there by a cherub, refers to another, quite different story about an Eden somewhere in contemporary Lebanon.

5. In Israel, the attitude toward motherhood was very positive, and both men and women wanted to have children: Genesis 30:1; 1 Samuel 1:1–8; Jeremiah 20:15; Job 3:3; Psalm 127:3. See K. van der Toorn, *From Her Cradle to Her Grave: The Role of Religion in the Life of the Israelite and the Babylonian Woman*, Sheffield, England: JSOT Press, 1994, pp. 77–92.

6. The meaning of Proverbs 13:12 that contains the same expression is not clear.

7. The image of a verdant tree symbolizing temporal power is used by Ezekiel as a metaphor for Assyria. He refers to the tree as greater than the cedars "in the garden of God" and to its branches as stronger than those of cypresses. "No tree in the garden of God was as beautiful as it"; "all the trees of Eden envied it" (Ezek 31:3–9). In the second century BCE the author of Daniel 4 borrowed Ezekiel's imagery and wove it into the dream of Nebuchadnezzar, where the tree symbolized the Babylonian king himself (Dan 4:7–18). In both texts, the image is not a Tree of Knowing or Life. Ezekiel makes explicit that his tree was quite extraordinary, unlike others in the garden. In both Ezekiel and Daniel, the height and magnificence of the tree is a sign of false self-aggrandizement and power. Ezekiel's Assyrian tree is cut down and left to deteriorate

(Ezek 31:12–14). Daniel's Nebuchadnezzar tree is cut down, but a stump is left, a promise that a repentant Nebuchadnezzar will regain his kingdom (Dan 4:20). The restoration element of the stump is borrowed from Isaiah 11:1–2. I thank Yair Zakovitch of the Hebrew University for reminding me of these two trees in the course of a lecture on March 31, 2008.

8. A. Brenner and F. Van Dijk-Hemmes, *On Gendering Texts: Female and Male Voices in the Hebrew Bible*, Leiden: Brill, 1993, pp. 48–57, 117–30.

9. R. Atwan and L. Wieder, *Chapter into Verse: A Selection of Poetry in English Inspired by the Bible from Genesis through Revelation*, New York: Oxford University Press, 2000, p. 15; also available at http://www.celtoslavica.de/sophia/Traherne_Eden .html (viewed March 29, 2008).

10. In 1903, arguing on grounds similar to those adopted in this study but with a more philosophical orientation, Cambridge theologian F. R. Tennant concluded that so far as the Old Testament is concerned, "there is no evidence that any connexion between human sinfulness and Adam's transgression had as yet occurred at all to the Hebrew mind." See Tennant, *Sources*, p. 104.

Chapter 26. Contra the Common Interpretation

1. Frymer-Kensky, "Ideology of Gender," p. 185.

2. G. Lerner, *The Creation of Patriarchy*, New York: Oxford University Press, 1986, pp. 212–15. The claim, initiated by the late Marija Gimbutas and advocated by Jeannine Davis-Kimball, that matriarchal societies are discernible in archaeological evidence from the Neolithic period in Europe has few followers today because it remains unsubstantiated. L. Osborne shows that Gimbutas's assertions were most influential and popular among those least qualified to evaluate them on the basis of the evidence that she presented: cultural theorists in the humanities. The assertions received a fair hearing but did not achieve acceptance among qualified archaeologists or among text-based historians of culture. See L. Osborne, "The Woman Warriors," *Lingua Franca* (December–January 1998): 51–53.

Ideas about a prehistoric history of matriarchy predate Gimbutas by almost a century. Her work was important because she claimed to provide the archaeological data supporting the claim. The matriarchal hypothesis was first advanced by a Swiss jurist, Jacob Bachofen (1815–87), who based his claims on an analysis of the social world presupposed in Egyptian and Greek myths. He proposed that the original society revealed by the myths was what he termed a "Gynaikokratie" (*gyné*, "women" + *kratos*, "rule") governed by *Mutterrecht*, laws recognizing the elite, anchoring status of women. All kinship and heredity rights in this society were based on matrilineal descent. This system, according to Bachofen, was eventually overtaken by a more mature, complex, male-oriented system that found full expression in Rome.

Bachofen's ideas enjoyed wide circulation and consideration in the mid-nineteenth century. They were accepted by Marxists and had a mixed reception among students of history but were largely rejected by evidence-based scholars of ancient religion. See S. Georgoudi, "Creating a Myth of Matriarchy," in Pauline S. Pantel, ed., *A History of Women in the West,* vol. 1: *From Ancient Goddesses to Christian Saints,* Cambridge, MA: Belknap Press, 1992, pp. 449–57; M. D. Press, "(Pytho)Gaia in Myth and Legend: The Goddess of the Ekron Inscription Revisited," *Bulletin of the American Schools of Oriental Research* 365 (2012): 9–17.

3. See Brenner's discussion of how the maleness of Israelite society is reflected also in the language of the Bible: A. Brenner, "Review of David E. S. Stein, *The Contemporary Torah: A Gender-Sensitive Adaptation of the JPS Translation,*" *Mo'ed: Annual for Jewish Studies* 18 (2008): 57–61.

4. Increasingly, feminist theologians and students of biblical literature recognize this, as did feminist historians earlier. For example, T. Frymer-Kensky emphasizes forcefully that since patriarchal institutions and the ideologies supporting them preceded the Bible in its cultural milieu, they can reasonably be expected to find expression within the Bible. See T. Frymer-Kensky, *Reading the Women of the Bible: A New Interpretation of Their Stories,* New York: Schocken, 2002, pp. xiv–ix. She elaborates by pointing out that the Bible contains only one negative statement about women: "The only misogynist statement in the Bible comes very late in Biblical development, in the book of Ecclesiastes, and shows the introduction of the classical Greek denigration of women into Israel" (p. xvi).

5. Frymer-Kensky, "Ideology of Gender," p. 187.

6. Meyers, *Discovering Eve,* pp. 145–54; and C. Meyers, "Material Remains and Social Relations: Women's Culture in Agrarian Households of the Iron Age," in W. G. Dever and S. Gitin, eds., *Symbiosis, Symbolism, and the Power of the Past: Canaan, Ancient Israel, and Their Neighbors from the Late Bronze Age through Roman Palaestina,* Winona Lake, IN: Eisenbrauns, 2003, pp. 425–44; W. G. Dever, *The Lives of Ordinary People in Ancient Israel: Where Archaeology and the Bible Intersect,* Grand Rapids, MI: Eerdmans, 2012, pp. 159–89.

7. C. Meyers, "Of Drums and Damsels: Women's Performance in Ancient Israel," *Biblical Archaeologist* 54 (1991): 23–25.

8. A study of women's customary and legal rights in Ugarit and Israel compared with their rights in Mesopotamia and Egypt reveals that whereas Egypt sometimes stood apart from what was acceptable elsewhere, there was broad commonality except perhaps in cultic matters. Mesopotamian women seem to have been more involved on the official side of cults. See Marsman, *Women in Ugarit and Israel,* pp. 701–38.

9. H. Blumenberg, *Work on Myth,* Cambridge, MA: MIT Press, 1985, p. 177. A. Momigliano has pointed out that biblical writers used chronology from creation on, making no distinction between a mythological and a historical age. See A. Momigliano, "Time in Ancient Historiography," *History and Theory* 8 (1966) (= *History and the Concept of Time*): 18–20. This is evidence that they considered creation and the subsequent events in Genesis 1–11 part of a historical age.

Chapter 27. Beyond the Tower of Babel

1. H. Jacobson, *A Commentary on Pseudo-Philo's "Liber Antiquatatum Biblicarum" with Latin Text and English Translation*, Leiden: Brill, 1996, p. 91 (for the translation) and pp. 199–210 (for the background of the book).

2. In a sophisticated and well-informed book, G. A. Anderson traces how this came about. He illustrates how scripture influenced theology, how theology shaped the understanding of scripture, and how oral interpretations were read back into the text and then expressed in the plastic arts and literature. See G. A. Anderson, *The Genesis of Perfection: Adam and Eve in Jewish and Christian Imagination*, Louisville, KY: Westminster John Knox, 2001.

Bibliography

Aitken, J. K. *The Semantics of Blessing and Cursing in Ancient Hebrew* (= Ancient Near Eastern Studies Supplement 23). Louvain: Peeters, 2007.

Albertz, R., and R. Schmitt. *Family and Household Religion in Ancient Israel and the Levant*. Winona Lake, IN: Eisenbrauns, 2012.

Alshech, E. "Out of Sight and Therefore Out of Mind: Early Sunni Islamic Modesty Regulations and the Creation of Spheres of Privacy." *Journal of Near Eastern Studies* 66 (2007): 267–90.

Alster, B., ed. *Death in Mesopotamia: Papers Read at the XXVIe Rencontre assyriologique internationale*. Copenhagen: Akademisk Forlag, 1980.

Alter, R. *Genesis*. New York: W. W. Norton, 1996.

Anderson, G. A. *The Genesis of Perfection: Adam and Eve in Jewish and Christian Imagination*. Louisville, KY: Westminster John Knox, 2001.

Arey, L. B. *Developmental Anatomy*. Philadelphia: W. B. Saunders, 1954.

The Assyrian Dictionary of the Oriental Institute of the University of Chicago. 21 vols. Edited by Martha T. Roth. Chicago: Oriental Institute of the University of Chicago, 1956–. http://oi.uchicago.edu/research/pubs/catalog/cad/.

Astour, M. "The Nether World and Its Denizens at Ugarit." In *Death in Mesopotamia: Papers Read at the XXVIe Rencontre assyriologique internationale*, edited by B. Alster, 227–38. Copenhagen: Akademisk Forlag, 1980.

Atwan, R., and L. Wieder. *Chapter into Verse: A Selection of Poetry in English Inspired by the Bible from Genesis through Revelation.* New York: Oxford University Press, 2000.

Augustine. *The Literal Meaning of Genesis*, vol. 2, translated and annotated by J. H. Taylor. New York: Newman Press, 1982.

Aurin, H.-C. "Your Urge Shall Be for Your Husband? A New Translation of Genesis 3:16b and a New Interpretation of Genesis 4:7." *Lectio Difficilior* 1 (2008): 1–18. http://www.lectio.unibe.ch/08_1/aurin.htm (accessed February 23, 2012).

Bar-Asher, M. "Mishnaic Hebrew: An Introductory Survey." *Hebrew Studies* 40 (1999): 115–51.

Barkay, G. *Ketef Hinnom: A Treasure Facing Jerusalem's Walls.* Jerusalem: Israel Museum, 1986.

———. "Tombs and Entombment in Judah during the Biblical Period" (Hebrew). In *qbrym wmnhgy qbwrh b'rṣ yśr'l b't h'tyqh* (*Graves and Burial Customs in the Land of Israel in Antiquity*), edited by I. Singer, 96–164. Jerusalem: Yad Yitzhaq Ben Tsvi, 1994.

Barmash, P. "The Narrative Quandary: Cases of Law in Literature." *Vetus Testamentum* 54:1 (2004): 1–16.

Barr, J. *The Garden of Eden and the Hope of Immortality.* Minneapolis, MN: Fortress, 1993.

Bartor, A. "The Juridical Dialogue: A Literary-Judicial Pattern." *Vetus Testamentum* 53 (2003): 445–64.

Baskin, J. R. *Midrashic Women: Formations of the Feminine in Rabbinic Literature.* Hanover, NH: University Press of New England, 2002.

Beek, M. A. *Atlas of Mesopotamia: A Survey of the History and Civilization of Mesopotamia from the Stone Age to the Fall of Babylon.* New York: Nelson, 1962.

Bell, L. A. *Visions of Women.* Clifton, NJ: Humana Press, 1983.

Bellis, A. O. *Helpmates, Harlots, Heroes: Women's Stories in the Hebrew Bible.* Louisville, KY: Westminster John Knox, 1994.

Ben-Hayyim, Z. "'zr kngdw: A Proposal" (Hebrew). *Leshonenu* 61:1–2 (1998): 45–50.

Ben Iehuda, E. *Thesaurus Totium Hebraitus* (Hebrew). Vol. 14. Tel Aviv: LaAm, 1952.

Berlinerblau, J. *The Secular Bible: Why Nonbelievers Must Take Religion Seriously.* New York: Cambridge University Press, 2005.

Biella, J. C. *Dictionary of Old South Arabic, Sabean Dialect.* Chico, CA: Harvard Semitic Museum, 1982.

Bledstein, A. J. "Was Eve Cursed? (Or Did a Woman Write Genesis?)" *Bible Review* 9:1 (1993): 42–45.

Bloch-Smith, E. *Judahite Burial Practices and Beliefs about the Dead* (=Journal for the Study of the Old Testament Supplement Series 123). Sheffield, England: Sheffield Academic Press, 1992.

Blumenberg, H. *Work on Myth.* Cambridge, MA: MIT Press, 1985.

Boer, R. T. "Twenty-Five Years of Marxist Biblical Criticism." *Currents in Biblical Research* 5:3 (2007): 298–321.

Borowski, O. *Daily Life in Biblical Times.* Atlanta, GA: Society of Biblical Literature, 2003.

———. "Eat, Drink and Be Merry: The Mediterranean Diet." *Near Eastern Archaeology* 67:2 (2004): 96–107.

Bouteneff, P. C. *Beginnings: Ancient Christian Readings of the Biblical Creation Narratives.* Grand Rapids, MI: Baker Books, 2008.

Boyarin, D. *Carnal Israel: Reading Sex in Talmudic Culture.* Berkeley: University of California Press, 1993.

Brenner, A. *The Israelite Woman: Social Role and Literary Type in Biblical Narrative.* Sheffield, England: JSOT Press, 1985.

———. "Review of David E. S. Stein, *The Contemporary Torah: A Gender-Sensitive Adaptation of the JPS Translation.*" *Moʻed: Annual for Jewish Studies* 18 (2008): 57–61.

Brenner, A., and F. Van Dijk-Hemmes. *On Gendering Texts: Female and Male Voices in the Hebrew Bible.* Leiden: Brill, 1993.

Breuer, M. "The Study of Bible and the Primacy of the Fear of Heaven: Compatibility or Contradiction?" In *Modern Scholarship in the Study of Torah: Contributions and Limitations,* edited by S. Carmy, 159–80. Northvale, NJ: Jason Aronson, 1996.

Brichto, H. C. *The Names of God: Poetic Readings in Biblical Beginnings.* Oxford: Oxford University Press, 1998.

———. *The Problem of Curse in the Hebrew Bible* (=SBL Monograph Series XIII). Philadelphia: Society of Biblical Literature, 1963.

Bronner, L. L. *From Eve to Esther: Rabbinic Reconstructions of Biblical Women.* Louisville, KY: Westminster John Knox, 1994.

Brown, F., S. R. Driver, and C. A. Briggs. *A Hebrew and English Lexicon of the Old Testament* (corrected edition). Oxford: Clarendon Press, 1953.

Bruins, H. J. *Desert Environment Agriculture in the Central Negev and Kadesh Barnea during Historical Times*. Nijkirk, The Netherlands: Midbar Foundation, 1986.

Buber, M. "The Tree of Knowledge." In *On the Bible: Eighteen Studies*, 14–21. New York: Schocken, 1968.

Byatt, A. S. *Possession*. New York: Random House, 1990.

Callister, L. C., I. Khalaf, S. Semenic, R. Kartchner, and K. Velvilainen-Julkunin. "The Pain of Childbirth: Perceptions of Culturally Diverse Women." *Pain Management Nursing* 4:4 (2003): 145–54.

Calvin, J. *Commentary on Genesis*, translated and edited by John King. Vol. 1, part 6 (Latin, 1554; English, 1578). This Calvin Translation Society Edition of 1847 is cited from http://www.iclnet.org/pub/resources/text/m.sion /cvgn1–06.htm.

Carmody, D. L. *Biblical Woman: Contemporary Reflections on Scriptural Texts*. New York: Crossroad, 1988.

Carr, D. "The Politics of Textual Subversion: A Diachronic Perspective on the Garden of Eden Story." *Journal of Biblical Literature* 112 (1993): 577–95.

Cassuto, U. *A Commentary on the Book of Genesis*. Part I. Jerusalem: Magnes Press, 1991. (Hebrew original, 1944.)

Childs, B. S. *Biblical Theology of the Old and New Testaments*. Minneapolis, MN: Fortress, 1993.

Clarke, A. *The Holy Bible: Notes and Practical Observations*. London: Fisher, Son and Co., 1847.

Coleman, L. *An Historical Text Book and Atlas of Biblical Geography*. Philadelphia: J. B. Lippincott, 1862.

Colson, F. H., and G. H. Whitaker. *Philo*. Vol. 1. (Loeb Classical Library.) London: William Heinemann; New York: G. P. Putnam's Sons, 1939.

Cooper, A. "The Plain Sense of Exod 23:5." *Hebrew Union College Annual* 59 (1988): 1–22.

Cornelius, I. "The Garden in the Iconography of the Ancient Near East: A Study of Related Material from Egypt." *Journal for Semitics* 1 (1989): 204–28.

———. "Some Pages from the Reception History of Genesis 3: The Visual Arts." *Journal of Northwest Semitic Languages* 23 [1997]: 221–34.

Cross, E. B. "Traces of the Matronymic Family in the Hebrew Social Organization." *Biblical World* 36 (1910): 407–14.

Dalley, S. "Ancient Mesopotamian Gardens and the Identification of the Hanging Gardens." *Garden History* 21 (1993): 1–13.

———. *Myths from Mesopotamia*. Oxford: Oxford University Press, 1989.

Daube, D. "Direct and Indirect Causation in Biblical Law." *Vetus Testamentum* 11 (1961): 246–69.

Delcor, M. "Two Special Meanings of the Word *yd* in the Hebrew Bible." *Journal of Semitic Studies* 12 (1967): 230–40.

Delitzch, F. *A New Commentary on Genesis*. Vol. 1. Edinburgh: T & T Clark, 1888.

Dennett, D. C. *Consciousness Explained*. Boston: Little, Brown, 1991.

Dever, W. G. *The Lives of Ordinary People in Ancient Israel: Where Archaeology and the Bible Intersect*. Grand Rapids, MI: Eerdmans, 2012.

Dickson, K. "Enki and the Embodied World." *Journal of the American Oriental Society* 125 (2005): 499–515.

Dietrich, M., O. Loretz, and J. Sanmartin. *Die keilalphabetische Texte aus Ugarit*. Neukirchen-Vlyun: Neukirchener Verlag, 1976.

Driver, S. R. "Grammatical Notes: On Genesis II, 9b." *Hebraica* 2 (1885–86): 33.

Duran, Shimon Ben Zemah. *Sefer Hatashbetz*. part 2 (Hebrew). Lemberg: U. W. Salat, 1891.

Dusinberre, E. R. M. *Aspects of Empire in Achaemenid Sardis*. Cambridge: Cambridge University Press, 2003.

Ellis, T. A. "Is Eve the 'Woman' in Sirach 25:24?" *Catholic Biblical Quarterly* 73 (2011): 323–42.

Ellisson, C. G., and J. P. Bartkowski. "Conservative Protestantism and the Division of Household Labor among Married Couples." *Journal of Family Issues* 23 (2002): 950–85.

Engnell, I. "'Knowledge' and 'Life' in the Creation Story." In *Wisdom in Israel and in the Ancient Near East* (= Vetus Testamentum Supplement 3), edited by M. Noth and D. W. Thomas, 103–19. Leiden: Brill, 1955.

Erman, A. *Life in Ancient Egypt*. London: MacMillan, 1894.

Even-Shoshan, A. *A New Concordance of the Bible*. Jerusalem: Kiryat Sepher, 1980.

Fassberg, S. E. "Which Semitic Languages Did Jesus and Other Contemporary Jews Speak?" *Catholic Biblical Quarterly* 74 (2012): 263–80.

Feder, Y. *Blood Expiation in Hittite and Biblical Ritual: Origins, Context, and Meaning*, Atlanta, GA: Society of Biblical Literature, 2011.

Finstuen, A. S. *Original Sin and Everyday Protestants: The Theology of Reinhold Niebuhr, Billy Graham, and Paul Tillich in an Age of Anxiety*. Chapel Hill: University of North Carolina Press, 2009.

Fox, E. *In the Beginning: A New English Rendition of the Book of Genesis.* New York: Schocken, 1983.

Fox, M. V. "Words for Wisdom: *tbwnh* and *bynh*, *'rmh* and *mzmh*, *'sh* and *twšyh*." *Zeitschrift für Althebraistik* 6 (1993): 149–69.

Freedman, H., and M. Simon. *Midrash Rabbah: Genesis.* Vol. 1. London: Soncino Press, 1939.

Freedman, R. D. "Woman, a Power Equal to Man." *Biblical Archaeology Review* 9:1 (1983): 56–58.

Friedman, R. E. *The Bible with Sources Revealed.* San Francisco: HarperSanFrancisco, 2003.

Frisch, A. "The Biblical Attitude toward Human Toil." In *Jewish Biblical Theology: Perspectives and Case Studies,* edited by I. Kalimi, 101–18. Winona Lake, IN: Eisenbrauns, 2012.

Fronzaroli, P. "Componential Analysis." *Zeitschrift für Althebraistik* 6 (1993): 79–91.

Frymer-Kensky, T. "The Ideology of Gender in the Bible and the Ancient Near East." In *DUMU-E2-DUB-BA-A: Studies in Honor of Ake W. Sjöberg,* edited by H. Behrens, D. Loding, and M. T. Roth, 185–92. Philadelphia: Samuel Noah Kramer Fund, 1989.

———. *In the Wake of the Goddess: Women, Culture, and the Biblical Transformation of Pagan Myth.* New York: Free Press, 1992.

———. *Reading the Women of the Bible: A New Interpretation of Their Stories.* New York: Schocken, 2002.

Garsiel, M. *Biblical Names: A Literary Study of Midrashic Derivations and Puns.* Ramat Gan: Bar Ilan University Press, 1991.

Gaster, T. H. *Myth, Legend and Custom in the Old Testament.* New York: Harper and Row, 1969.

George, A. R. *The Babylonian Gilgamesh Epic: Introduction, Critical Edition, and Cuneiform Texts.* Vol. 1. Oxford: Oxford University Press, 2003.

Georgoudi, S. "Creating a Myth of Matriarchy." In *A History of Women in the West,* vol. 1: *From Ancient Goddesses to Christian Saints,* edited by Pauline S. Pantel, 449–63. Cambridge, MA: Belknap Press, 1992.

Gesenius, W. *Gesenius' Hebrew Grammar as Edited and Enlarged by the Late E. Kautzch* (second English edition). London: Oxford University Press, 1910.

Gevirtz, S. "Of Patriarchs and Puns: Joseph at the Fountain, Jacob at the Ford." *Hebrew Union College Annual* 46 (1975): 33–54.

Gilbert, S. F., and Z. Zevit. "Congenital Human Baculum Deficiency: The Generative Bone of Genesis 2:21–23." *American Journal of Medical Genetics* 101:3 (July 2001): 284–85.

Giller, P. "The Common Religion of Safed." *Conservative Judaism* 55:2 (2003): 24–37.

———. *The Enlightened Will Shine: Symbolization and Theurgy in the Later Strata of the Zohar.* Albany: State University of New York Press, 1993.

Gilmore, G. "An Iron Age Pictorial Inscription from Jerusalem Illustrating Yahweh and Asherah." *Palestine Exploration Quarterly* 141:2 (2009): 87–103.

Ginzberg, L. *The Legends of the Jews.* 7 vols. Philadelphia: Jewish Publication Society, 1909.

Glassner, J.-J. "À propos des Jardins mésopotamiens." In *Jardins d'Orient* (= Res Orientales, vol. 3), edited by R. Gyselen, 9–17. Paris: Le Groupe pour l'Étude de la Civilisation du Moyen-Orient, 1991.

Goedicke, H. "Adam's Rib." In *Biblical and Related Studies Presented to Samuel Iwry,* edited by A. Kort and S. Morschauser, 73–76. Winona Lake, IN: Eisenbrauns, 1985.

Gordis, R. "The Knowledge of Good and Evil in the Old Testament and the Qumran Scrolls." *Journal of Biblical Literature* 76 (1957): 123–38.

Gordon, C. H. "Erēbu Marriage." In *Studies on the Civilization and Culture of Nuzi and the Hurrians,* edited by M. A. Morrison and D. I. Owen, 155–60. Winona Lake, IN: Eisenbrauns, 1981.

Greenfield, J. C. "A Touch of Eden." In *Orientalia J. Duchesne-Guillemin emerito oblata,* edited by P. Lecoq, 219–24. Leiden: Brill, 1984.

Greenfield, J. C., and A. Shaffer. "Notes on the Akkadian-Aramaic Bilingual Statue from Tell Fekherye." *Iraq* 43 (1988): 109–16.

Grigson, C. "Plough and Pasture in the Early Economy of the Southern Levant." In *The Archaeology of Society in the Holy Land,* edited by T. E. Levy, 245–68. London: Leicester University Press, 1995.

Gruber, M. *The Motherhood of God and Other Studies.* Atlanta, GA: Scholars Press, 1992.

Gütterbock, H. G., and H. A. Hoffner. *The Hittite Dictionary.* Vol. P, fascicle 3. Chicago: Oriental Institute, University of Chicago, 1997.

Hamilton, G. J. *The Origins of the West Semitic Alphabet in Egyptian Scripts.* Washington, DC: Catholic Biblical Society, 2006.

Harrison, J. E. *Themis: A Study of the Social Origins of Greek Religion.* London: Merlin Press, 1977. First published in 1912.

Hartley, J. E. *The Semantics of Ancient Hebrew Colour Lexemes.* Louvain: Peeters, 2010.

Hecht, A. "Naming the Animals." In *The Transparent Man.* New York: Knopf, 1990.

Herrmann, C. "Fünf phönizische Formen für ägyptische Fayencen." *Zeitschrift des Deutschen Palästina-Vereins* 105 (1989): 27–41.

Heschel, A. J. *Heavenly Torah as Refracted through the Generations.* London: Continuum International, 2006.

Hess, R. S. *Israelite Religions: An Archaeological and Biblical Survey.* Grand Rapids, MI: Baker Academic, 2007.

———. *Studies in the Personal Names of Genesis 1–11.* Kevalaer: Butzon und Bercker; Neukirchen-Vluyn: Neukirchener Verlag, 1993.

Hoch, J. E. *Semitic Words in Egyptian Texts of the New Kingdom and Third Intermediate Period.* Princeton, NJ: Princeton University Press, 1994.

Hoffner, H. A. "From Head to Toe in Hittite: The Language of the Human Body." In *"Go to the Land I Will Show You": Studies in Honor of Dwight W. Young,* edited by J. E. Coleson and V. H. Matthews, 247–59. Winona Lake, IN: Eisenbrauns, 1996.

Horowitz, W., T. Oshima, and S. Sanders. *Cuneiform in Canaan: Cuneiform Sources from the Land of Israel in Ancient Times.* Jerusalem: Israel Exploration Society and the Hebrew University, 2006.

Hospers, J. H. "Polysemy and Homonymy." *Zeitschrift für Althebraistik* 6 (1993): 114–23.

Hunt, N. B. *Historical Atlas of Mesopotamia.* New York: Checkmark Books, 2004.

Hurowitz, V. A. "The Expression *ûqsāmîm beyādām* (Numbers 22:7) in Light of Divinatory Practices from Mari." *Hebrew Studies* 33 (1992): 5–15.

———. "An Old Babylonian Bawdy Ballad." In *Solving Riddles and Untying Knots: Biblical, Epigraphic, and Semitic Studies in Honor of Jonas C. Greenfield,* edited by Z. Zevit, S. Gitin, and M. Sokoloff, 543–58. Winona Lake, IN: Eisenbrauns, 1995.

———. "'Proto-Canonization' of the Torah: A Self-Portrait of the Pentateuch in Light of Mesopotamian Writings." In *Study and Knowledge in Jewish Thought,* edited by H. Kreisel, 31–48. Beer Sheva: Ben Gurion University of the Negev Press, 2006.

Hwesen, R. H. *Armenia: A Historical Atlas.* Chicago: University of Chicago Press, 2001.

Jackson, B. S. *Wisdom-Laws: A Study of the Mishpatim of Exodus 21:1–22:16.* Oxford: Oxford University Press, 2006.

Jacob, B. *Das erste Buch der Tora: Genesis.* Berlin: Schocken, 1934.

Jacobs, N. J. *Naming-Day in Eden: The Creation and Recreation of Language* (revised edition). London: Collier-Macmillan, 1969.

Jacobson, H. *A Commentary on Pseudo-Philo's "Liber Antiquatatum Biblicarum" with Latin Text and English Translation.* Leiden: Brill, 1996.

Jakobsen, T. "Death in Ancient Mesopotamia." In *Death in Mesopotamia: Papers Read at the XXVIe Rencontre assyriologique internationale,* edited by B. Alster, 19–24. Copenhagen: Akademisk Forlag, 1980.

Johnson, J. W. "The Creation." In *God's Trombones: Seven Negro Sermons in Verse,* 15–17. New York: Penguin Classics, 2008. (First published in 1927.)

Johnson, M. D. "Life of Adam and Eve." In *The Old Testament Pseudepigrapha,* vol. 2, edited by J. H. Charlesworth, 249–95. Garden City, NY: Doubleday, 1985.

Joines, K. R. *Serpent Symbolism in the Old Testament.* Haddenfield, NJ: Haddenfield House, 1974.

Kaddari, M. Z. *A Dictionary of Biblical Hebrew* (Hebrew). Ramat Gan: Bar Ilan University Press, 2006.

Kalmanofsky, A. "Israel's Baby: The Horror of Childbirth in the Biblical Prophets." *Biblical Interpretation* 16 (2008): 60–82.

Kaltner, J., S. L. McKenzie, and J. Kilpatrick. *The Uncensored Bible: The Bawdy and Naughty Bits of the Good Book.* New York: HarperOne, 2008.

Kant, I. *On History.* Edited by L. W. Beck. Indianapolis: Bobbs-Merrill, 1963.

Kapelrud, A. S. "You Shall Surely Not Die." In *History and Tradition of Early Israel: Studies Presented to Eduard Nielsen* (= Vetus Testamentum Supplement 50), edited by A. Lemaire and B. Otzen, 50–61. Leiden: Brill, 1993.

Kasher, M. M. *Torah Shelemah: The Complete Torah Talmudic-Midrashic Encyclopedia of the Pentateuch* (Hebrew). Vol. 19. New York: American Biblical Encyclopedia Society, 1992.

Kee, H. C. "Testaments of the Twelve Patriarchs." In *The Old Testament Pseudepigrapha: Apocalyptic Literature and Testaments,* edited by J. H. Charlesworth, 775–828. Garden City, NY: Doubleday, 1983.

Keel, O. *Jahwe-Visionen und Siegelkunst* (= Stuttgarter Bibel-Studien 84/85). Stuttgart: Verlag Katholisches Bibelwerk, 1977.

———. *The Symbolism of the Biblical World: Ancient Near Eastern Iconography and the Book of Psalms.* Winona Lake, IN: Eisenbrauns, 1997.

Kendall, C. *What Really Happened in the Garden of Eden? And Rebuttal to: Eve, Did She or Didn't She?* New York: Vantage Press, 2007.

Kennedy, J. *Studies in Hebrew Synonyms.* Oxford: Williams and Norgate, 1898.

Kikawada, I. M. "Two Notes on Eve." *Journal of Biblical Literature* 91 (1972): 33–37.

Kikawada, I. M., and A. Quinn. *Before Abraham Was.* Nashville, TN: Abingdon Press, 1985.

Kilmer, A. D. "The Mesopotamian Concept of Overpopulation and Its Solution as Reflected in the Mythology." *Orientalia* 41 (1972): 160–77.

———. "The Mesopotamian Counterparts of the Biblical Nepilim." In *Perspectives on Language and Texts: Essays and Poems in Honor of Francis I. Andersen's Sixtieth Birthday, July 28, 1985,* edited by E. W. Conrad and E. G. Newing, 39–43. Winona Lake, IN: Eisenbrauns, 1987.

———. "Speculations on Umul, the First Baby." In *Kramer Anniversary Volume: Cuneiform Studies in Honor of Samuel Noah Kramer,* edited by B. Eichler, 265–71. Neukirchen-Vluyn: Neukirchener Verlag, 1967.

Kimelman, R. "The Seduction of Eve and Feminist Readings of the Garden of Eden." *Women in Judaism: A Multidisciplinary Journal* 1:2 (1998). http://www.utoronto.ca/wjudaism/journal/vol1n2/eve.html (viewed November 3, 2009).

———. "The Seduction of Eve and the Exegetical Politics of Gender." *Biblical Interpretation* 4 (1996): 1–39.

Kitchen, K. A. *On the Reliability of the Old Testament.* Grand Rapids, MI: Eerdmans, 2003.

Köhler, L., and W. Baumgartner. *Hebräisches und Aramäisches Lexicon zum Alten Testament* (third edition). Leiden: Brill, 1967.

———. *The Hebrew and Aramaic Lexicon of the Old Testament* (revised edition). Leiden: Brill, 1995.

Korpel, M. C. A. *A Rift in the Clouds: Ugaritic and Hebrew Descriptions of the Divine.* Münster: Ugarit Verlag, 1990.

Kramer, S. N. "Enki and Ninhursag: A Paradise Myth." In *Ancient Near Eastern Myths Relating to the Old Testament* (second and revised edition), edited by J. P. Pritchard, 37–41. Princeton, NJ: Princeton University Press, 1955.

———. *History Begins at Sumer* (third revised edition). Philadelphia: University of Pennsylvania Press, 1981.

Kugel, J. L. *How to Read the Bible: A Guide to Scripture Then and Now.* New York: Free Press, 2007.

———. *Traditions of the Bible: A Guide to the Bible as It Was at the Start of the Common Era.* Cambridge, MA: Harvard University Press, 1998.

Kushner, H. S. *How Good Do We Have to Be? A New Understanding of Guilt and Forgiveness.* Boston: Little, Brown, 1996.

Kutscher, E. Y. *A History of the Hebrew Language.* Jerusalem: Magnes Press; Leiden: Brill, 1982.

Lambden, S. N. "From Fig Leaves to Fingernails: Some Notes on the Garments of Adam and Eve in the Hebrew Bible and Select Early Post Biblical Jewish Writing." In *A Walk in the Garden: Biblical, Iconographic, and Literary Images of Eden* (= Journal for the Study of the Old Testament Supplement Series 136), edited by P. Morris and D. Sawyer, 74–94. Sheffield, England: JSOT Press, 1992.

Lambert, W. G. "The Theology of Death." In *Death in Mesopotamia: Papers Read at the XXVIe Rencontre assyriologique internationale,* edited by B. Alster, 53–66. Copenhagen: Akademisk Forlag, 1980.

Lambert, W. G., and A. R. Millard. *Atra-Ḥasīs: The Babylonian Story of the Flood.* Oxford: Clarendon Press, 1969.

LaSor, W. S., D. A. Hubbard, and F. W. Bush. *Old Testament Survey: The Message, Form, and Background of the Old Testament.* Grand Rapids, MI: Eerdmans, 1982.

Layton, S. C. "Remarks on the Canaanite Origin of Eve." *Catholic Biblical Quarterly* 59 (1997): 22–32.

Lerner, G. *The Creation of Patriarchy.* New York: Oxford University Press, 1986.

Leslau, W. *Comparative Dictionary of Geʿez.* Wiesbaden: Otto Harrassowitz, 1987.

Levinson, B. M. *"The Right Chorale": Studies in Biblical Law and Interpretation.* Tübingen: Mohr Siebeck, 2008.

Levison, J. R. *Portraits of Adam in Early Judaism from Sirach to 2 Baruch.* Sheffield, England: Sheffield Academic Press, 1988.

Leyton, B. *The Gnostic Scriptures: A New Translation with Annotations and Introduction.* Garden City, NY: Doubleday, 1987.

L'Hour, J. "Une législation criminelle dan le Deuteronome." *Biblica* 44 (1963): 1–28.

Lieberman, S. J. "Are Biblical Parallels Euclidean?" *Maarav* 8 (1992): 81–94.

Littauer, F., and F. Littauer. *After Every Wedding Comes a Marriage.* Eugene, OR: Harvest House, 1981.

Lohr, J. N. "Sexual Desire? Eve, Genesis 3:16, and tšwqh." *Journal of Biblical Literature* 130 (2011): 227–46.

Longman, T., III. *How to Read Genesis.* Downers Grove, IL: InterVarsity Press, 2003.

Longstaff, T. R. W. *Evidence of Conflation in Mark? A Study in the Synoptic Problem.* Missoula, MT: Scholars Press, 1977.

Lowes, J. L. "The Noblest Monument in English Prose." In *Essays in Appreciation*, 3–31. Boston: Houghton Mifflin, 1936.

Luther, M. *Lectures on Genesis 1–5.* Vol. 1 of *Luther's Works*, edited by Jaroslav J. Pelikan. St. Louis, MO: Concordia Publishing House, 1958.

Macalister, R. A. S. *The Excavations of Gezer.* Vol. 3. London: John Murray, 1912.

MacDonald, N. *What Did the Ancient Israelites Eat? Diet in Biblical Times.* Grand Rapids, MI: Eerdmans, 2008.

Maldamé, J-M. "Adam, Ève et le serpent: Péché du monde et péché l'Adam." *Cahiers Disputatio* I (2008): 15–39.

Malul, M. "'Āqēb 'Heel' and 'Āqab 'to Supplant,' and the Concept of Succession in the Jacob-Esau Narratives." *Vetus Testamentum* 46 (1966): 190–212.

———. *Studies in Mesopotamian Legal Symbolism* (= Alter Orient und Altes Testament 221). Neukirchen-Vluyn: Neukirchen Verlag; Kevelaer: Butzon und Bercker, 1988.

Margalit, B. "Death and Dying in the Ugaritic Epics." In *Death in Mesopotamia: Papers Read at the XXVIe Rencontre assyriologique internationale*, edited by B. Alster, 243–54. Copenhagen: Akademisk Forlag, 1980.

Marsman, H. J. *Women in Ugarit and Israel: Their Social and Religious Position in the Context of the Ancient Near East.* Leiden: Brill, 2003.

McEntire, M. H. *The Blood of Abel: The Violent Plot in the Hebrew Bible.* Macon, GA: Mercer University Press, 1999.

Merril, C. W. H. "Gold." In *The Mineral Resources of the World*, vol. 2, edited by W. Van Royen and O. Bowles, 125–29. New York: Prentice Hall, 1952.

Mettinger, T. N. D. *The Eden Narrative: A Literary and Religio-historical Study of Genesis 2–3.* Winona Lake, IN: Eisenbrauns, 2007.

Meyers, C. *Discovering Eve: Ancient Israelite Women in Context.* New York: Oxford University Press, 1988.

———. "Material Remains and Social Relations: Women's Culture in Agrarian Households of the Iron Age." In *Symbiosis, Symbolism, and the Power of the Past: Canaan, Ancient Israel, and Their Neighbors from the Late Bronze Age through Roman Palaestina*, edited by W. G. Dever and S. Gitin, 425–44. Winona Lake, IN: Eisenbrauns, 2003.

———. "Of Drums and Damsels: Women's Performance in Ancient Israel." *Biblical Archaeologist* 54 (1991): 16–27.

Milgrom, Jacob. "Sex and Wisdom: What the Garden of Eden Story Is Saying." *Bible Review* 10:6 (1994): 21, 52.

———. *Studies in Levitical Terminology*. Berkeley: University of California Press, 1970.

Milgrom, Jo. "Giving Eve's Daughters Their Due." *Bible Review* 12:1 (February 1996): 34–36, 48.

Millard, A. R. "The Etymology of Eden." *Vetus Testamentum* 34 (1984): 103–5.

Miller-Naudé, C., and Z. Zevit, eds. *Diachrony in Biblical Hebrew*. Winona Lake, IN: Eisenbrauns, 2012.

Milne, P. J. "Feminist Interpretation of the Bible: Then and Now." *Bible Review* 8:5 (1992): 38–43, 52–53.

Moberly, R. W. "The Mark of Cain—Revealed at Last?" *Harvard Theological Review* 100 (2007): 11–22.

Momigliano, A. "Time in Ancient Historiography." *History and Theory* 8 (1966) (= *History and the Concept of Time*): 1–23.

Moore, G. F. "Tatian's Diatessaron and the Analysis of the Pentateuch." *Journal of Biblical Literature* 9 (1890): 201–15.

Moore, K. L. *Clinically Oriented Anatomy* (third edition). Baltimore, MD: Williams and Wilkins, 1992.

Morris, P. "Exiled from Eden: Jewish Interpretation of Genesis." In *A Walk in the Garden: Biblical, Iconographical, and Literary Images of Eden* (= Journal for the Study of the Old Testament Supplement Series 136), edited by P. Morris and D. Sawyer, 117–66. Sheffield, England: JSOT Press, 1992.

Naeh, S. "'zr kngdw, kngd mšḥytym: Forgotten Meanings and a Lost Proverb" (Hebrew). *Leshonenu* 59 (1996): 99–117.

Nesbitt, M. "Plants and People in Ancient Anatolia." *Biblical Archaeology* 58 (1995): 68–81.

Onians, R. B. *The Origins of European Thought*. Cambridge: Cambridge University Press, 1988.

Osborne, L. "The Women Warriors." *Lingua Franca* (December–January 1998): 50–57. http://linguafranca.mirror.theinfo.org/9712/nosborne.html (viewed November 10, 2009).

Ottoson, M. "Eden and the Land of Promise." In *Congress Volume: Jerusalem, 1986* (= Vetus Testamentum Supplement 40), edited by J. A. Emerton, 177–88. Brill: Leiden, 1988.

Pagels, E. H. *Adam and Eve and the Serpent in Gen 1–3* (= Occasional Papers of the Institute for Antiquity and Christianity, no. 12). Claremont, CA: Institute for Antiquity and Christianity, 1988.

———. *Adam, Eve, and the Serpent.* New York: Vantage, 1989.

Pardes, I. *Countertraditions in the Bible: A Feminist Approach.* Cambridge, MA: Harvard University Press, 1992.

Parker, S. *The Human Body Book.* New York: DK Publishing, 2007.

Paul, S. M. "Emigration from the Netherworld in the Ancient Near East." In *Immigration and Emigration within the Ancient Near East: Festschrift E. Lipinski* (= Orientalia Lovaniensia Analecta 65), edited by K. Van Lerberghe and A. Schoors, 221–27. Leuven: Uitgevreij Peeters and Departement Oriëntalistiek, 1995.

———. "The 'Plural of Ecstasy' in Mesopotamian and Biblical Love Poetry." In *Solving Riddles and Untying Knots: Biblical, Epigraphic, and Semitic Studies in Honor of Jonas C. Greenfield*, edited by Z. Zevit, S. Gitin, and M. Sokoloff, 585–97. Winona Lake, IN: Eisenbrauns, 1995.

———. "Untimely Death in the Semitic Languages." In *Divrei Shalom: Collected Studies of Shalom M. Paul on the Bible and the Ancient Near East, 1967–2005*, 223–38. Leiden: Brill, 2005.

Phipps, W. E. *Genesis and Gender: Biblical Myths of Sexuality and Their Cultural Impact.* New York: Praeger, 1989.

Polak, F. H. "Development and Periodization in Biblical Prose Narrative (First Part)" (Hebrew). *Beit Mikra* 152 (1997): 30–52.

———. "Sociolinguistics: A Key to the Typology and Social Background of Biblical Hebrew." *Hebrew Studies* 47 (2006): 115–62.

———. "Style Is More Than the Person: Sociolinguistics, Literary Culture, and the Distinction between Written and Oral Narrative." In *Biblical Hebrew: Studies in Chronology and Typology*, edited by I. Young, 38–103. London: T and T Clark, 2003.

Pongratz-Leisten, B. "Divine Agency and the Astralization of the Gods in Ancient Mesopotamia." In *Reconsidering the Concept of Revolutionary Monotheism*, edited by B. Pongratz-Leisten, 137–87. Winona Lake, IN: Eisenbrauns, 2011.

Pontifical Biblical Commission. "The Jewish People and Their Sacred Scriptures in the Christian Bible." Issued by the Pontifical Biblical Commis-

sion in 2001. http://www.vatican.va/roman_curia/congregations/cfaith/pcb
_documents/rc_con_cfaith_doc_20020212_popolo-ebraico_en.html; http://
www.vatican.va/roman_curia/congregations/cfaith/pcb_docume%09nts/rc
_con_cfaith_doc_20020212_popolo-ebraico_en.html (viewed September 25,
2009).

Pope, M. *Song of Songs*. Garden City, NY: Doubleday, 1977.

Press, M. D. "(Pytho)Gaia in Myth and Legend: The Goddess of the Ekron
Inscription Revisited." *Bulletin of the American Schools of Oriental Research* 365 (2012): 1–25.

Purves, W. K., G. H. Orians, and H. C. Heller. *Life: The Science of Biology*. Salt
Lake City, UT: Sinauer Associates, 1992.

Qimron, E. "Biblical Philology and the Dead Sea Scrolls" (Hebrew). *Tarbiz* 58
(1989): 297–315.

Radday, Y. T. "The Four Rivers of Paradise." *Hebrew Studies* 23 (1982): 23–32.

Ramsey, G. W. "Is Name-Giving an Act of Domination in Genesis 2:23 and
Elsewhere?" *Catholic Biblical Quarterly* 50 (1988): 24–35.

Reifenberg, A. *The Soils of Palestine: Studies in Soil Formation and Land Utilization in the Mediterranean*. London: Thomas Murby, 1947.

Reisenberger, A. T. "The Creation of Adam as Hermaphrodite and Its Implications for Feminist Theology." *Judaism* 42:4 (1993): 447–452.

Rofé, A. *Introduction to the Literature of the Hebrew Bible*. Jerusalem:
Simor, 2009.

Roitman, A. D. "'Crawl upon Your Belly' (Gen 3:14)—The Physical Aspect of
the Serpent in Early Jewish Exegesis" (Hebrew). *Tarbiz* 64:2 (1995): 157–82.

Rosellini, H. *Monomenti dell' Egitto e della Nubia*. Vol. 2: *Monomenti Civili*.
Pisa: Presso N. Capurro, 1834.

Rosen, B. "Subsistence Economy in Iron Age I." In *From Nomadism to Monarchy: Archaeological and Historical Aspects of Early Israel*, edited by
I. Finkelstein and N. Naaman, 339–51. Jerusalem: Yad Izhaq Ben Zvi and
the Israel Exploration Society; Washington, DC: Biblical Archaeological
Society, 1994.

Rosenberg, J. R. "The Garden Story Forward and Backward." *Prooftexts* 1
(1989): 1–27.

Rotenberg, M. *Christianity and Psychiatry: The Theology behind the Psychology* (Hebrew). Tel Aviv: Ministry of Defense, 1994.

———. *Damnation and Deviance: The Protestant Ethic and the Spirit of Failure*. New Brunswick, NJ: Transaction Publishers, 2003. (First published in
1978.)

Rothstein, D. "'And Jacob Came (In)to': Spousal Relationships and the Use of a Recurring Syntagm in Genesis and Jubilees." *Henoch* 29 (2007): 91–103.

Ruiten, J. T. A. G. M. van. "The Creation of Man and Woman in Early Jewish Literature." In *The Creation of Man and Woman: Interpretations of the Biblical Narratives in Jewish and Christian Traditions*, edited by G. P. Luttikhuizen, 34–62. Leiden: Brill, 2000.

Ryan, C. W. *Guide to Known Mineral Deposits of Turkey*. Ankara: Office of International Economic Cooperation, Ministry of Foreign Affairs, 1960.

Sarma, D. P., and T. G. Weilbaecher. "Human *os penis*." *Urology* 35 (1990): 349–50.

Sarna, N. *On the Book of Psalms: Exploring the Prayers of Ancient Israel*. New York: Schocken, 1993.

Sass, B. "The Pre-exilic Hebrew Seals: Iconism vs. Aniconism." In *Studies in the Iconography of Northwest Semitic Inscribed Seals* (= Orbis biblicus et orientalis 125), edited by B. Sass and C. Uehlinger, 194–256. Fribourg, Switzerland: University Press, 1993.

Sauer, J. A. "The River Runs Dry." *Biblical Archaeology Review* 22:4 (1996): 52–57, 64.

Scheibeitz, H., and H. Wilkins. *Atlas Radiographic Anatomy of the Dog and Cat* (third edition). Philadelphia: W. B. Saunders, 1978.

Schmid, K. "Loss of Immortality? Hermeneutical Aspects of Gen 2–3 and Its Early Reception." In *Beyond Eden: The Biblical Story of Paradise (Gen 2–3) and Its Reception History*, edited by K. Schmid and C. Riedweg, 58–76. Tübingen: Mohr Siebeck, 2008.

Schulweis, H. M. *For Those Who Can't Believe: Overcoming the Obstacles to Faith*. New York: Harper Perennial, 1994.

Scolnic, B. E. *If the Egyptians Drowned in the Red Sea Where Are Pharaoh's Chariots? Exploring the Historical Dimensions of the Bible*. Lanham, MD: University Press of America, 2005.

Sekine, S. *Transcendency and Symbols in the Old Testament* (= Beihefte zu Zeitschrift für die altestamentliche Wissenschaft 275). Berlin: Walter de Gruyter, 1999.

Shepherd, M. B. "The Compound Subject in Biblical Hebrew." *Hebrew Studies* 52 (2011): 107–20.

Shevack, M. *Adam and Eve: Marriage Secrets from the Garden of Eden*. New York: Paulist Press, 2003.

Shorter, A. W. "The God Nehebkau." *Journal of Egyptian Archaeology* 21 (1935): 41–81.

Singer, A. *The Soils of Israel*. Berlin: Springer, 2007.

Singer, I. "The Hittites and the Bible Revisited." In *Archaeological and Historical Studies in Honor of Amichai Mazar on the Occasion of His Sixtieth Birthday*, edited by A. M. Meier and P. de Miroschedji, 273–56. Winona Lake, IN: Eisenbrauns, 2006.

Sisson, S., and J. D. Grossman. *The Anatomy of Domestic Animals*. Philadelphia: W. B. Saunders, 1953.

Sitchin, Z. "Rivers of Eden? The Four Rivers Identified." *Biblical Archaeological Review* 22:6 (1996): 15–16.

Sivan, D., and Z. Cochavi-Rainey. *West Semitic Vocabulary in Egyptian Script of the 14th to the 10th Centuries BCE* (= *Beer Sheva* 6 [1992]). Beer Sheva: Ben Gurion University of the Negev Press, 1992.

Ska, J. L. "Genesis 2–3: Some Fundamental Questions." In *Beyond Eden: The Biblical Story of Paradise (Gen 2–3) and Its Reception History*, edited by K. Schmid and C. Riedweg, 1–27. Tübingen: Mohr Siebeck, 2008.

Skinner, J. *A Critical and Exegetical Commentary on Genesis*. New York: Charles Scribner's Sons, 1910.

Smith, M. S. "Why Was 'Old Poetry' Used in Hebrew Narrative? Historical and Cultural Considerations about Judges 5." In *Puzzling Out the Past: Studies in Northwest Semitic Languages and Literatures in Honor of Bruce Zuckerman*, edited by M. J. Lundberg, S. Fine, and W. Pitard, 197–212. Leiden: Brill, 2012.

Smith, W. Robertson. *Kinship and Marriage in Early Arabia*. Cambridge: Cambridge University Press, 1885.

Sölle, D., J. H. Kirchberger, and H. Haag. *Great Women of the Bible in Art and Literature*. Grand Rapids, MI: Eerdmans, 1994.

Speiser, E. A. "An Angelic Curse: Exodus 14:20." *Journal of the American Oriental Society* 80 (1960): 198–200.

———. *Genesis*. Garden City, NY: Doubleday, 1964.

Stager, L. "Jerusalem and the Garden of Eden." *Eretz Israel* 26 (1999): 183–94.

Stark, R. *What Americans Really Believe: New Findings from the Baylor Survey of Religion*. Waco, TX: Baylor University Press, 2008.

Starodoub-Scharr, K. "The Royal Garden in the Great Royal Palace of Ugarit: To the Interpretation of the Sacral Aspect of the Royalty in the Ancient Palestine and Syria." In *Proceedings of the Twelfth World Congress of Jewish Studies, Jerusalem, July 29–August 5, 1997: The Bible and Its World*, edited by R. Margolin, 253–68. Jerusalem: World Union of Jewish Studies, 1999.

Steiner, R. C. *Stockman from Tekoa, Sycomores from Sheba: A Study of Amos' Occupations*. Washington, DC: Catholic Biblical Association of America, 2003.

Steinsaltz, A. *Torah Commentary in Responsa Literature from the Eighth through the Sixteenth Century* (Hebrew). Jerusalem: Keter, 1978.

Stordalen, T. *Echoes of Eden: Genesis 2–3 and Symbolism of the Eden Garden in Biblical Hebrew Literature*. Leuven: Peeters, 2000.

———. "Heaven on Earth or Not? Jerusalem as Eden in Biblical Literature." In *Beyond Eden: The Biblical Story of Paradise (Gen 2–3) and Its Reception History*, edited by K. Schmid and C. Riedweg, 28–57. Tübingen: Mohr Siebeck, 2008.

Stores, T. I., and R. L. Usinger. *General Zoology*. New York: McGraw-Hill, 1957.

Stratton, B. J. *Out of Eden: Reading, Rhetoric, and Ideology in Gen 2–3* (= Journal for the Study of the Old Testament Supplement Series 208). Sheffield, England: Sheffield Academic Press, 1995.

Sturtevant, E. H. *A Hittite Glossary* (second edition). Philadelphia: Linguistic Society of America and University of Pennsylvania, 1936.

Sundt, J. L., and F. T. Cullen. "The Correctional Ideology of Prison Chaplains: A National Survey." *Journal of Criminal Justice* 30 (2002): 369–85.

Tennant, F. R. *The Sources of the Doctrines of the Fall and Original Sin*. New York: Schocken, 1968. (First published in 1903.)

Tertullian, Quintus Septimus Florens. "The Apparel of Women." In *Visions of Women*, edited by L. A. Bell, 78–81. Clifton, NJ: Humana Press, 1983.

Thomason, A. K. "Representations of the North Syrian Landscape in Neo-Assyrian Art." *Bulletin of the American Schools for Oriental Research* 323 (2001): 63–96.

Tigay, J. H. "Conflation as a Redactional Technique." In Tigay, *Empirical Models for Biblical Criticism*, 53–95.

———. "The Evolution of the Pentateuchal Narratives in the Light of the Evolution of the Gilgamesh Epic." In Tigay, *Empirical Models for Biblical Criticism*, 21–52.

———. *"lō' nas lēḥōh* 'He Had Not Become Wrinkled' (Deut 34:7)." In *Solving Riddles and Untying Knots: Biblical, Epigraphic, and Semitic Studies in Honor of Jonas C. Greenfield*, edited by Z. Zevit, S. Gitin, and M. Sokoloff, 345–50. Winona Lake, IN: Eisenbrauns, 1995.

Tigay, J. H., ed. *Empirical Models for Biblical Criticism*. Philadelphia: University of Pennsylvania Press, 1985.

Tischler, J. *Hethitisches etymologisches Glossar.* Fascicle 2. Innsbruck: Institut für Sprachwissenschaft der Universität Innsbruck, 1978.

Tolbert, M. A. "Protestant Feminists and the Bible: On the Horns of a Dilemma." In *The Pleasure of Her Text: Feminist Readings of Bible and Historical Texts,* edited by A. Bach, 5–23. Philadelphia: Trinity International Press, 1990.

Tompkins, J. P. "An Introduction to Reader-Response Criticism." In *Reader-Response Criticism: From Formalism to Post-Structuralism,* edited by J. P. Tompkins, ix–xxvi. Baltimore, MD: Johns Hopkins University Press, 1980.

Toorn, K. van der. *From Her Cradle to Her Grave: The Role of Religion in the Life of the Israelite and the Babylonian Woman.* Sheffield, England: JSOT Press, 1994.

Towner, W. S. "Interpretations and Reinterpretations of the Fall." In *Modern Biblical Scholarship: Its Impact on Theology and Proclamation,* edited by F. A. Eigo, 53–85. Villanova, PA: Villanova University, 1984.

Trible, P. "Depatriarchalizing in Biblical Interpretation." *Journal of the American Academy of Religion* 41 (1973): 30–48.

———. *God and the Rhetoric of Sexuality.* Philadelphia: Fortress, 1978.

———. "If the Bible Is So Patriarchal, How Come I Love It?" *Bible Review* 8:5 (1992): 45–47, 55.

Turner, L. A. *Announcements of Plot in Genesis.* Sheffield, England: JSOT Press, 1990.

Vaux, R. de. *Ancient Israel: Its Life and Institutions.* New York: McGraw-Hill, 1961.

Vidal, N., and S. Blair Hedges. "Molecular Evidence for a Terrestrial Origin for Snakes." *Proceedings of the Royal Society: London Biological Sciences* (Supplement) 271 (2004): S226–29. http://www.ncbi.nlm.nih.gov/pmc/articles/PMC1810015/.

Viezel, E. "The Influence of Realia on Biblical Descriptions of Childbirth." *Vetus Testamentum* 61 (2011): 685–89.

Vincent, R. P. H. "Un calendrier agricole israélite." *Revue Biblique,* N.S., 6 (1909): 243–69.

Vogels, W. "The Power Struggle between Man and Woman (Gen 3:16b)." *Biblica* 77 (1996): 197–209.

Vulpa, N. "Irony and the Unity of the Gilgamesh Epic." *Journal of Near Eastern Studies* 53 (1994): 275–83.

Wallace, H. N. *The Eden Narrative* (=Harvard Semitic Monographs 32). Atlanta, GA: Scholars Press, 1985.

———. "The Toledot of Adam." In *Studies in the Pentateuch* (= Vetus Testamentum Supplement 41), edited by J. A. Emerton, 17–33. Leiden: Brill, 1990.

Ward, W. H. *The Seal Cylinders of Western Asia.* Washington, DC: Carnegie Institution of Washington, 1910.

Weiss, M. *The Bible from Within: The Method of Total Interpretation.* Jerusalem: Magnes Press, 1984.

Wenham, G. J. *Genesis 1–15* (Word Biblical Commentary). Waco, TX: Word Books, 1985.

Werkentin, F., M. Hofferbert, and M. Baurmann. "Criminology as Police Science or: 'How Old Is the New Criminology?'" *Crime and Social Justice* 2 (1974): 24–41.

Westbrook, R. "A Matter of Life and Death." *Journal of the Ancient Near Eastern Society* 25 (1997): 61–70.

———. *Property and the Family in Biblical Law* (= Journal for the Study of the Old Testament Supplement Series 113). Sheffield, England: JSOT Press, 1991.

Westermann, C. *Genesis 1–11: A Commentary.* Minneapolis, MN: Augsburg Publishing House, 1984.

Whybray, R. N. *The Intellectual Tradition in the Old Testament* (= Beihefte zu Zeitschrift für die altestamentliche Wissenschaft 135). Berlin: Walter de Gruyter, 1974.

Wieseltier, L. *Kaddish.* New York: Knopf, 1998.

Wilkinson, J. G. A *Popular Account of the Ancient Egyptians.* New York: Harper and Brothers, 1854.

Wiseman, D. J. "Mesopotamian Gardens." *Anatolian Studies* 33 (1983): 137–44.

Wright, D. P. "Holiness, Sex and Death in the Garden of Eden." *Biblica* 77 (1996): 305–29.

Yarhouse, M. A., and J. N. Sells. *Family Therapies: A Comprehensive Christian Appraisal.* Downers Grove, IL: InterVarsityPress Academic, 2008.

Yee, G. A. *Poor Banished Children of Eve: Women as Evil in the Hebrew Bible.* Philadelphia: Fortress, 2003.

Young, I., R. Rezetko, and M. Ehrensvärd. *Linguistic Dating of Biblical Texts.* Vol. 2, *A Survey of Scholarship, a New Synthesis and a Comprehensive Bibliography.* London: Equinox, 2008.

Zevit, Z. *The Anterior Construction in Classical Hebrew.* Atlanta, GA: Scholars Press, 1998.

―――. "The First Halleluyah." In *Milk and Honey: Essays on Ancient Israel and the Bible*, edited by D. Miano and S. Malena, 157–64. Winona Lake, IN: Eisenbrauns, 2007.

―――. "The Gerizim-Samarian Community In and Between Texts and Times: An Experimental Study." In *The Quest for Context and Meaning: Studies in Biblical Intertextuality in Honor of James A. Sanders*, edited by C. A. Evans and Sh. Talmon, 547–72. Leiden: Brill, 1997.

―――. *Matres Lectionis in Ancient Hebrew Epigraphs*. Cambridge, MA: American Schools of Oriental Research, 1980.

―――. "Not-So-Random Thoughts Concerning Linguistic Dating and Diachrony in Biblical Hebrew." In *Diachrony in Biblical Hebrew*, edited by C. Miller-Naudé and Z. Zevit, 455–89. Winona Lake, IN: Eisenbrauns, 2012.

―――. *The Religions of Ancient Israel: A Synthesis of Parallactic Approaches*. London: Continuum, 2001.

―――. "Syntagms in Biblical Hebrew: Four Short Studies." In *En pāsē grammatikē kai sophiā: Saggi di linguistica ebraica in onore di Alviero Niccacci, ofm*, edited by G. Geiger and M. Pazzini, 393–403. Jerusalem: Franciscan Printing Press, 2011.

―――. "The Two-Bodied People, Their Cosmos, and the Origin of the Soul." In *Maven in Blue Jeans: A Festschrift in Honor of Zev Garber*, edited by S. L. Jacobs, 465–75. West Lafayette, IN: Purdue University Press, 2009.

Index